Toward a National Power Policy

Toward a National Power Policy

The New Deal and the Electric Utility Industry, 1933-1941

PHILIP J. FUNIGIELLO

University of Pittsburgh Press

Library of Congress Catalog Card Number 72-92695

ISBN 0-8229-3263-6

Copyright © 1973, University of Pittsburgh Press

All rights reserved

Media Directions Inc., London

Manufactured in the United States of America

Chapter 9 is an expanded version of "Kilowatts for Defense: The New Deal and the Coming of the Second World War," *Journal of American History*, 56 (Dec. 1969), 604-19, reprinted by permission of the *Journal of American History*.

TO MY PARENTS

Contents

Acknowledgments

In the course of researching and writing this book I have necessarily become indebted to many people and institutions whose encouragement and information have enabled me to accomplish my task. Their words and thoughtful comments have been most helpful and greatly appreciated, and I take this opportunity to record my thanks.

I wish first to acknowledge my debt to the New York University Graduate School of Arts and Science, especially to Professor Bayrd Still and the faculty in the history department. I am grateful particularly to Professor Vincent P. Carosso, whose interest, critical judgment, and encouragement are in the finest traditions of scholarship. Professors Gerald D. Nash of the University of New Mexico and Thomas P. Govan of the University of Oregon read an earlier version of the chapters on holding-company legislation and provided useful criticisms; Elmo Richardson of Washington State University and Wesley Dick of Albion College shared their knowledge of the Bonneville Power Administration with me. Finally, I wish to thank Professor Richard Maxwell Brown and my colleagues at the College of William and Mary who encouraged me to complete this undertaking.

Portions of the research for this study were supported by the New York University Graduate School of Arts and Sciences, the Samuel S. Fels Fund, the Committee on Faculty Research of the College of William and Mary, and the National Endowment for the Humanities. Their generous assistance at a number of critical stages enabled me to devote my full attention to this project.

Many libraries have eased the work of research. I particularly want to acknowledge the assistance of the staff of the Franklin D. Roosevelt Library, Hyde Park, New York, and, in Washington, D. C., the staffs of the National Archives, the Manuscript Division of the Library of Congress, and the Federal Power Commission. The personnel of the University of Washington Library generously guided me through its considerable collection of manuscripts pertaining to public power in the Pacific Northwest. The resources of the New York Public Library, the Earl Gregg Swemm Library of the College of William and Mary, and the New York University libraries were also made available to

ix

me. Mrs. Harold L. Ickes kindly granted me permission to use the Harold L. Ickes Papers in the Library of Congress, and Mr. Leonard Eesley permitted me to use the records in the possession of the Federal Power Commission. I also want to thank two contemporaries of the Roosevelt era who so generously took the time to answer my questions: the Honorable Burton K. Wheeler and Mr. Benjamin V. Cohen.

Beyond the academic field, the confidence and cooperation of my family have been an inestimable source of strength.

Introduction

"To whatever strange ports we are wafted on the warm breeze of the New Deal, we shall not see the lotus land of laissez-faire again. That is probably the major historical fact of our generation."[1] Thus did William Orton assess the results, in 1935, of three years of Rooseveltian economics. The era of Franklin D. Roosevelt and the New Deal has, ever since, commanded scholarly and popular attention for what it did and failed to do to reshape American institutions and values. Innovation, imaginative experimentation, cynicism, energy, success, and failure were its distinguishing characteristics. Until "Dr. Win-the-War" replaced "Dr. New Deal," few economic, social, or political institutions escaped the attention of the New Dealers. The Roosevelt administration had made it impossible, as Orton and many others recognized, for the American people to return to the idea of a mythical golden age.

It is a commonplace that each age writes its own history, for man perceives the past in the foreshortened perspective of his own experience. Thus contemporary scholars, many of whom were active participants in the events they described, debated the question of whether the New Deal was a logical climax to social and economic patterns in transition over many years or a sharp break with the past. This debate persisted among the first post-New Deal generation of scholars, who added the intriguing thought that there may have been not one but two or more New Deals. Their arguments evolved from the belief that Theodore Roosevelt's New Nationalism inspired the early New Deal, whereas President Wilson's New Freedom doctrines became the fulcrum for the later Rooseveltian policies. More recently, radical historians have cast aside these distinctions as inconsequential and have argued that the New Deal was a meaningless and ineffectual effort to shore up an economic system that should have been allowed to perish.

The questions that each generation of scholars asks are fundamental

1. William Orton, "Culture and Laissez-Faire," *Atlantic Monthly,* 155 (June 1935), 46.

to an understanding of the historical process. They may be repeated and scrutinized because they broaden our knowledge of a particular historical phenomenon. The story of the New Deal's determination to foster a measure of public accountability in the electric-utility industry and to evolve a national power policy for distributing the fruits of electricity to all Americans, regardless of wealth, status, or location, is a more limited topic. However, I believe that an analysis of one major theme may give a new dimension to our perspective of the New Deal—a period when so much of modern America was in the process of taking form.

Historians, by and large, have left the controversial subject of power policy to lawyers, economists, and political scientists. This book represents a modest attempt to place into historical perspective the New Deal's power program. It relates the early background of specific legislative items and events to the theme of a national power policy. It attempts to demonstrate that, at nearly every stage of that policy's formulation, comprehensive planning theory vied with a more pragmatic, almost *ad hoc,* approach to power policy. And lastly, it suggests that the Roosevelt administration, over the protests of many loyal New Dealers, emphasized resource planning less and less in decision-making after 1935.

My choice of the areas of research to be explored was governed by the legislation and actions which *contemporary* government officials and private-utility executives considered as the primary elements of an integrated power policy. These components include holding-company legislation, rural electrification, the creation of the Tennessee Valley Authority and the Bonneville Power Administration, the activities of the Federal Power Commission, and the decision to establish a National Defense Power Committee. To explain further the inability of the New Deal to evolve a comprehensive national power policy, in the sense that planners used the term, this study focuses upon the complexities of top-level policy-making and the vast network of interpersonal relationships that had to be worked out in each case, all of which led to conflict and compromise.[2]

More precisely, the analysis is extended to ideological differences among New Dealers, bureaucraticly inspired differences over strategy and methodology, the impact of personality and status conflicts upon policy implementation, and the organizational dysfunctions endemic to large bureaucratic institutions. This schema, when viewed against

2. Charles E. Jacob has done some preliminary work along these lines. See his *Leadership in the New Deal* (Englewood Cliffs, N.J., 1967).

the early history of the electric-power companies, has the merit of disclosing new information concerning the fragile, often stormy, relationship of the federal government to the private-utility industry and the public-power movement.

A word of caution should be introduced at this point. The electric-power field is so broad that this book does not pretend to be exhaustive. We need to know, for example, much more about the workings of both the public-power movement and the private utilities' political activities, the integration of the power network, the impact of rate-making upon socioeconomic growth, and the increasingly significant relationship between power development and ecology. Also, not being a trained economist, I am less concerned with the objective economic circumstances of the utility industry in the 1920s and 1930s; I leave that area of controversy to the economists and accountants. My focus is on the perception of the utility industry's condition by the political leadership of the New Deal and how the New Dealers reacted politically and through legislation. This preliminary foray into a highly complex subject emphasizes the politics surrounding the movement toward a national power policy; hopefully, it will stimulate other historians to engage their energies in these and similar topics.

The holding company[3] as an instrument of American capitalism attained a permanent foothold in the electric-power business in 1905. In that year the General Electric Company organized the Electric Bond and Share holding company in response to specific financial and technical difficulties. In the ensuing decade Bond and Share's impressive record of selling securities and mobilizing the resources of many investors under a central management did not pass unnoticed. Indeed, it offered the manufacturers of electrical equipment, engineering and construction firms, and investment bankers the opportunity

---

3. The 1935 holding-company legislation defined a holding company as:

(A) any company which directly or indirectly owns, controls, or holds with power to vote, 10 per centum or more of the outstanding securities of a public utility company or of a company which is a holding company by virtue of this clause ... and, (B) any person which the Commission determines, after notice and opportunity for hearing, directly or indirectly to exercise ... such controlling influence over the management or policies of any public utility or holding company as to make it necessary or appropriate in the public interest or for the protection of investors or consumers that such person be subjected to the obligations, duties, and liabilities imposed in this title upon holding companies. (Public Law No. 333, 74th Cong., reprinted in Gilman G. Udell, comp., *Laws Relating to Securities Commission Exchanges and Holding Companies* [Washington, D.C., 1964], 60)

to free the industry from the constraints that had inhibited it from realizing its true growth potential.[4]

World War I marked a turning point in the history of the electric-power industry, since it created unprecedented demands for large quantities of cheap energy. In the immediate postwar period, the industry established itself on a professional footing and embarked upon an extended career of rapid growth.[5] Aggressive utility officials transformed once isolated plants into larger and more efficient units. They consolidated managerial decisions under a single roof and interconnected the various load centers by means of transmission lines. A single or, at most, a few modern plants serviced large geographic areas. Perhaps the most dramatic aspect of their operations was the creation of regional superpower networks by linking together hitherto independent, smaller systems. Superpower, or Giant Power as the integrated systems were commonly called, afforded the industry two advantages fundamental to the generation of reliably cheap current. The first was to guarantee the generating capacity required to satisfy the demand for electricity in any twenty-four-hour period; the second was to hold to a minimum the quantity of reserve power needed to insure continuous service.[6]

With its ease of access to the money markets and its ability to draw from a central reserve of managerial and engineering talent, the holding company played the crucial role in underwriting utility growth and consolidation. The principle of geographic diversification of investments minimized financial risks, maximized profits, and, in general, strengthened whole systems. As a result, the private utilities could

---

4. These problems included: the highly speculative nature of the industry in its infancy, debt limitations upon the operating company and other restrictions upon the purchase of electrical equipment, and problems of plant construction and management. For a fuller analysis see Norman S. Buchanan, "The Origin and Development of the Public Utility Holding Company," *The Journal of Political Economy,* 44 (Feb. 1936), 42-43; and James C. Bonbright and Gardiner C. Means, *The Holding Company* (New York, 1932), chs. 1, 5-7.

5. Statistics dramatically attest to the industry's growth, particularly in the urban areas of the nation. In 1929, for example, electric-power companies sold 76 billion kilowatt hours of electricity to 24,249,000 customers as compared with 31 billion kilowatts in 1920 and only 10 billion in 1910. Capitalization totaled over $11 billion, as power sales increased nearly 700 percent between 1910 and 1920. Nearly $3 billion was invested in 1927, the peak year for funding in the decade. See Frank L. Blanchard, "Customer Ownership of Public Utilities," *The Fifth District Banker,* 2 (July 1930), 13-14; John S. Porter, ed., *Moody's Manual of Investments: Public Utility Securities* (New York, 1930), 17; and Martin G. Glaeser, *Public Utilities in American Capitalism* (New York, 1957), 377.

6. U.S. Congress, Senate, *Electric Power Industry, Supply of Electrical Equipment and Competitive Conditions,* doc. no. 46, 70th Cong., 1st sess. (Washington, D.C., 1928), 176-78.

offer more and better service to an increasingly urbanized population in the 1920s. It did so at a constantly falling rate, even though high fixed and variable costs plagued the industry.

Shortly after the depression of 1920-21, a new breed of entrepreneur entered the industry. The pioneers of the prewar period had been, and still were, interested primarily in the production of cheap and abundant electricity. They wanted to make money, of course, but the pecuniary motive was balanced by the desire to render efficient service. The newcomers, really promoters and speculators, often came from nonutility backgrounds. They entered the field with the primary objective of making as much money as quickly as they could.[7] Howard C. Hopson of Associated Gas and Electric and W. B. Foshay—archetypal figures of this new breed—fed upon the public's indifference and ignorance to manipulate holding-company control of operating properties. They followed no discernible pattern in their quest, but so feverish was their pace that they scarcely had time to rationalize the jerry-built structures.

Although these men never represented more than a small fraction of the number of holding- and operating-company officials, their manipulations ultimately tarred the entire utility industry with the brush of irresponsibility. While they enhanced their personal fortunes, they also did violence both to the service concept of a public utility and to the regulatory principle (based upon a continuous administrative relationship with the business to be regulated) that had been the cornerstone of governmental policy in the public-utility field before World War I. In the process they exposed the industry to the strictures of the law and gave renewed vigor to the critics of their quasi-sovereign powers.

The origins of the critics of the power companies can be traced to two traditions. One, rooted in the antimonopoly and antitrust agitation of the Grangers and Progressives, recognized that neither the courts nor the state commissions had been effective. They perceived that, in the ongoing corporate revolution, management was not only being separated from ownership (thus undermining the principle of

---

7. Between 1924 and 1930, most of the new holding-company securities that were floated were not for the construction or improvement of operating properties but were for the purchase of outstanding voting securities of operating companies and the pyramiding of the companies over which they wielded control. See Louis Loss, *Securities Regulation*, 2 vols. (Boston, 1961), I, 133; U.S. Congress, *Electric Power Industry, Supply of Electrical Equipment*, 178; the *New York Times*, Mar. 22, July 1, 1932; July 13, 28, Aug. 14-24, 1935; and Twentieth Century Fund, *Electric Power and Government Policy* (New York, 1948), 42-46.

accountability) but was itself falling into the hands of small, self-perpetuating control groups.[8] They argued that a new, strengthened relationship between government and business had to be worked out. The other tradition had evolved from the federal government's ownership and operation of hydroelectric projects in World War I. These critics saw in the wartime experience a precedent for government-produced cheap electricity and government-coordinated development of the nation's rivers and streams. Although often at odds over goals and tactics, the proponents of the public tradition closed ranks in the 1920s and directed their criticisms against the private utilities.

The ensuing chapters describe the efforts of the New Deal to build upon the criticism of big business that utility opponents had set in motion in the late 1920s. They show the reactions of the Roosevelt administration to the antimonopoly and planning traditions and examine how the ideological tension between the two was manifested in the policies adopted. And lastly, this study examines the resiliency of the privately owned electrical industry, showing how it attempted to use its economic and political resources to hold the government and critics at arm's length.

8. See particularly Adolph Berle and Gardiner C. Means, *The Modern Corporation and Private Property* (New York, 1932), 76 ff.

Abbreviations

AFUI	American Federation of Utility Investors
BPA	Bonneville Power Administration
CNPP	Committee on National Power Policy
CREA	Committee on the Relation of Electricity to Agriculture
CVA	Columbia Valley Authority
EHFA	Electric Home and Farm Authority
FPC	Federal Power Commission
FTC	Federal Trade Commission
NARUC	National Association of Railway and Utility Commissioners
NDPC	National Defense Power Committee
NELA	National Electric Light Association
NPPC	National Power Policy Committee
NPPDC	National Power Policy and Defense Committee
NRA	National Recovery Administration
OPM	Office of Production Management
PUD	Public Utility District
PWA	Public Works Administration
REA	Rural Electrification Administration
RFC	Reconstruction Finance Corporation
SEC	Securities and Exchange Commission
TVA	Tennessee Valley Authority
WIB	War Industries Board

Toward a National Power Policy

CHAPTER I

Politics, Power, and the Federal Trade Commission

On the occasion of the Muscle Shoals power controversy in 1924, Republican Congressman Theodore Burton of Ohio remarked: "What policy of economy or conservation of public rights or interests can we insist upon if we throw this away?"[1] Surrendering the Shoals to private-utility development, he continued, held out possibilities for corruption that made Teapot Dome look like a bagatelle and Doheny and Sinclair innocent lambs. Burton, in his colorful manner, was arguing for federal development of the site in order to bring the fruits of cheap power to the largest number of people. His reference to the oil-lease scandal of 1923-24 served to remind listeners that conservation, especially the power question, was still an unresolved issue. The controversy between public-power versus private-power development was the one cause to which liberal Democrats and insurgent Republicans still rallied.[2]

Tracing their antecedents to prewar progressivism, these reformers had since shed the naiveté that one need only expose injustice and a righteous public would demand retribution. Prosperity-induced apathy had replaced public involvement. In their frustration, reformers looked to the countervailing power of the government to keep errant corporations in line and to guarantee the ordinary citizen equal access to the nation's resources, particularly to cheap, abundant electrical energy.

The task of persuading the government to intervene, however, was not easy because the institutions of government were hostile to the use of federal power for regulatory or eleemosynary purposes. Republican presidents vetoed legislation that interfered with the free play

---

1. U.S. Congress, *Congressional Record*, 68th Cong., 1st sess., 65 (Mar. 5, 1924), 3640.
2. "Washington Notes," *New Republic*, 46 (Mar. 31, 1926), 169-70.

3

of the market or otherwise tampered with the system.[3] This was true particularly in the case of the electric-utility industry where Congress, the presidency, and the courts saw legislation as an attempt to usurp state jurisdiction and replace it with federal control as a prelude to complete public ownership. State regulation, meanwhile, was haphazard and, in many instances, nonexistent, thereby increasing the critics' feelings of frustration.

In January 1925, Senator George W. Norris of Nebraska, a maverick Republican, arose from his desk on the Senate floor and, in a voice heavy with feeling, announced to his colleagues that "practically everything in the electrical world is controlled either directly or indirectly by a Gigantic Power Trust."[4] He also declared that he would introduce a resolution authorizing the Senate to investigate the dimensions of the conspiracy in advance of appropriate legislation. Norris's dedication to the advancement of public power was no secret, but his demand for an investigation revived all the animosity that Senator Thomas Walsh's inquiry into the Teapot Dome oil scandals had stirred.[5]

Norris's speech, and the already existing agitation for public development of the Tennessee River basin, raised fundamental questions about the nation's electric-power industry and the role of the federal government in formulating power policy. Unlike some of his contemporaries—such as David E. Lilienthal and Milo R. Maltbie, the dynamic reformer of the New York Public Service Commission in 1930, who believed in state *and* federal regulation and who advocated a limited number of publicly owned municipal systems—Norris really preferred complete government ownership of the industry. In the grim atmosphere of a hostile Senate chamber, he could scarcely be aware that his speech was the beginning of a long, tortuous reexamination of the modes by which the private-power industry traditionally conducted its business.[6]

3. For an analysis of business and reform in the 1920s see John D. Hicks, *Republican Ascendancy, 1921-1933* (New York, 1960), 50, 125-26, 199; Clarke A. Chambers, *Seedtime of Reform* (Minneapolis, 1963), 24-25, passim; James W. Prothero, *The Dollar Decade* (Baton Rouge, La., 1954); William E. Leuchtenburg, *The Perils of Prosperity, 1914-1932* (Chicago, 1958); Martin Glaeser, *Public Utilities in American Capitalism* (New York, 1957), 206 ff., 377 ff; and Henry F. May, "Shifting Perspectives on the 1920's," *Mississippi Valley Historical Review,* 42 (Dec. 1956), 405-27.
4. *Congressional Record,* 68th Cong., 2d sess., 66 (Jan. 2, 1925), 1101-07. Also ibid. (Feb. 9, 1925), 3382 ff. For Norris's public career see George W. Norris, *Fighting Liberal: The Autobiography of George W. Norris* (New York, 1945), chs. 11-24.
5. See Burl Noggle, "The Origins of the Teapot Dome Investigation," *Mississippi Valley Historical Review,* 44 (Sept. 1957), 237-66.
6. George W. Norris, "Boring from Within," *The Nation,* 121 (Sept. 16, 1935), 297-99; Norris to Donald Richberg, Oct. 14, 1931, George W. Norris Papers, tray 26, box 4, Library of Congress (hereafter cited as Norris Papers).

The issue of whether a Power Trust existed occupied congressional attention for the remainder of the session, as first Norris and then other reformers accused the utility magnates of subverting democratic institutions. Martin J. Insull, president of the Middle West Utilities Corporation, the third largest holding-company system in the United States, rushed to defend the industry against the charge of conspiracy to suborn the public welfare. Addressing a national radio audience as the guest of Halsey, Stuart & Company, the investment-banking house responsible for underwriting Middle West's growth, he declared vehemently that the public should consider the trust "a myth until the politicians, professors, and editors who talk about it so glibly condescend to give us more definite information about it."[7] Insull's speech reflected the general attitude of the industry and received wide circulation among conservative elements in the business community.

While the more liberal members of the profession viewed with a jaundiced eye the substitution of centralized governmental regulation for local control, articulate conservatives passionately denounced paternalism and socialistic interference. Merle Thorpe of *Nation's Business,* an advocate of self-policing by industry, tried to steer a middle course. He wrote that the most serious problem confronting the nation was "to reconcile the regulation of control by our Government of our public utilities, with the advantages which we properly associate with private ownership, individual initiative, and the profit motive."[8] The majority of people undoubtedly preferred Thorpe's solution to Norris's, since public-power enthusiasts were relatively few in number in the twenties.[9] Even among proponents of federal regulation there were some who were quickly losing confidence in the ability of capitalism to correct its abuses. Although Morris Llewellyn Cooke, director of Pennsylvania's Giant Power Survey, was not among the latter, he, too, confessed that his "confidence in regulation as a public device is certainly not getting any stronger."[10] The future head of the Rural Electrification Administration (REA), anticipating the pragmatism of the New Deal, then added: "On the other hand I believe that we have got to do everything in our power to shore up a system which in the end is sure to go."[11]

7. See Carl D. Thompson, *Confessions of the Power Trust* (New York, 1932), xviii.
8. Merle Thrope, "As the Business World Wags," *Nation's Business,* 18 (Sept. 1930), 14.
9. See, for example, Morris L. Cooke, "The Long Look Ahead," *The Survey,* 51 (Mar. 1, 1924), 600-04, 651.
10. Morris L. Cooke to George W. Norris, Feb. 4, 1925, Judson King Papers, box 60, Library of Congress (hereafter cited as King Papers).
11. Ibid.

Meanwhile, in both houses of Congress, Progressives, on February 9, 1925, narrowly persuaded a majority of their colleagues to vote for Joint Resolution 329, directing the Federal Trade Commission (FTC) to investigate the extent to which oligopoly existed in the electric-power industry.[12] Norris, the author of the document, feared that the centralized power of big business would upset the competitive system of private enterprise. In speech after speech he reiterated that the real issue was whether or not rapid consolidation of ownership and control was creating oligopolies in violation of the Sherman Antitrust Act and thereby menacing free enterprise and the public welfare. He was convinced that it was.[13]

Two years later, the FTC reported its findings to the Senate. It declared that there was no conclusive evidence of a national monopoly over power generation and its distribution. The closest it came to unearthing evidence of a "Power Trust" was its observation that there existed a *tendency* for holding-company systems, such as the North American Company and Middle West Utilities, to enhance their control over operating properties within certain geographic areas. Actually, the very reference to a Power Trust, although effective as reform rhetoric, was misleading in both its understanding of public-utility economics and the policies that had evolved from them. And given the special conditions under which the electric utilities functioned—that is, they required enormous amounts of capital, had very high fixed costs, and yielded a relatively low return on total investment—if a Power Trust had been identified and dismantled, and small independent units restored, the net effect would have been regressive. Excessive competition, inefficiency, and higher rates would have been the result.[14]

Nonetheless, Senate critics were benumbed by the FTC's findings and by the Justice Department's ruling that the original appropriations

12. The General Electric Company, because of its control of the Electric Bond and Share Company, was the particular target of the resolution, which also designated for study the question of whether the utilities were expending money to influence popular attitudes against public ownership. U.S. Congress, *Joint Resolution No. 329*, 68th Cong., 2d sess. (Washington, D.C., 1925).

13. Norris originally had tacked his amendment to a resolution authorizing an investigation of the tobacco trust. The amendment would have included an inquiry into the activities of the public-utility industry. See *Congressional Record*, 68th Cong., 2d sess., 66 (Feb. 7, 1925), 3219; ibid. (Feb. 9, 1925), 3283-89 ff.

14. The report had investigated the structure of the industry prior to December 30, 1924, and indicated what percentage each holding-company system generated and sold of the national output of electrical energy. U.S. Congress, Senate, *Electric Power Industry, Control of Power Companies*, doc. no. 213, 69th Cong., 2d sess. (Washington, D.C., 1927), 50-51; and Thomas K. McCraw, *TVA and the Power Fight, 1933-1939* (Philadelphia, 1971), 4-9.

excluded any inquiry into the propaganda or lobbying activities of the private utilities. They denounced the report as a whitewash and accused the commission of subservience to the interests it had been established to regulate.[15] Thoroughly angered and disheartened, Norris, Thomas J. Walsh of Montana, Clarence Dill of Washington, Robert M. La Follette, Jr., of Wisconsin, and Burton K. Wheeler of Montana pressed for an independent congressional inquiry—one similar to Walsh's probing investigation of the Teapot Dome scandal.[16]

Their demand, however, contravened the desires of the Coolidge administration and also disturbed many of their colleagues, business leaders, and the public. Having been burned badly in the oil scandal, the political parties were not especially anxious to have another investigation. The public, on the other hand, feared that another blow to the reputation of business leaders, coming so soon after the first one, might well upset the fragile prosperity it was enjoying.[17] Nevertheless, there were independent voices demanding an impartial investigation of utility practices. From academic circles and the pages of the liberal *New Republic,* criticism of the financial manipulations of holding companies grew more incessant.[18] Professor William Z. Ripley, who had established a national reputation during the Wilson administration as the foremost authority on corporations, trusts, and railroads, took up the cudgels against the concentration of power and wealth—"the con-

15. The FTC did not examine the confidential records of holding companies but drew its conclusions from questionnaires mailed to the parent company. Nor did it analyze the reasons why independent companies became affiliated with larger systems and what impact this had upon their financial structure. It did, however, think that the pyramiding of companies was serious enough to call for legislative "consideration." See "Politics Discovers a Power Trust," *Literary Digest,* 93 (Apr. 2, 1927), 12.

16. Walsh was the popular choice of public-power enthusiasts to conduct the inquiry because of his handling of the Teapot Dome scandal.

17. Judson King, "The Genesis of TVA," ch. 16, pp. 13-14, typewritten MS in King Papers.

18. See, for example, George Putnam, "Concentrated Power or Divided Risk," *Independent,* 121 (Aug. 11, 1928), 126-27; and "Cost of Concentration," ibid., 121 (Aug. 18, 1928), 159-60. One author was amazed at the bull market in normally conservative utility securities; another predicted that overcapitalization would impair the credit of individual companies and threaten the structure of the entire industry. Stuart Chase of Dartmouth, the author of books attacking corporate waste, observed that public-service commissions were powerless to regulate the securities of interstate holding companies. And, in *Public Utility Commission of Rhode Island* v. *Attleboro Steam and Electric Company,* U.S. 83 (1927), holding companies were excluded from the definition of a public utility. See H. S. Raushenbush, "Concentration of Control," *New Republic,* 47 (May 26, 1926), 28-30; Stuart Chase, "Upward and Onward," ibid., 45 (Dec. 2, 1925), 35-36; Irston R. Barnes, *Cases on Public Utility Regulation* (New York, 1938), 87-89; and Hugh L. Elsbree, *Interstate Transmission of Electric Power: A Study in the Conflict of State and Federal Jurisdictions* (Cambridge, Mass., 1931), 73-75.

trol of control"—in the electric-utility industry. "I believe that the trouble has to do with the growing dissociation of ownership of property from the responsibility for the manner in which it shall be put to use," he observed.[19] Ripley was convinced, by late 1926, that President Coolidge should recommend to Congress "a searching inquiry by real experts, stripped of all political bias and affording a field day for comers; an open contest in which the truth, regardless of self-interest, shall prevail."[20]

Privately, Ripley had the ear of neo-Populist western congressmen who applauded his criticisms of Wall Street and the large eastern corporations. They responded particularly well to his prescriptions for eradicating holding-company abuses. He told Senator Walsh, in a letter analyzing the public stake in the solvency of the electric-utility industry, that "there ought to be Federal supervision by the Federal Trade Commission, if we had one that was worth the name, or else by the Federal Power Commission in the Department of the Interior."[21] The details of federal regulation had already been outlined in his article, "From Main Street to Wall Street," which posed the idea of counterbalancing the centralized power of the federal government against the concentrated power of the megacorporation. Walsh, meanwhile, indicated that he was strongly inclined to pursue an investigation of the power industry along lines that Ripley had suggested.[22]

The impetus for a new investigation actually came from other, unexpected, sources. The bull market in securities collapsed briefly between January and March 1926, causing industrials, rails, oils, and motors to suffer heavily. The securities of electric-utility holding companies were especially hard hit, prompting one critic to warn that extravagant speculation endangered the credit of every holding company. It was time that promoters "realized their responsibility to the public," he declared.[23] A few enlightened operating-company execu-

19. Ripley offered as possible solutions: (1) having the Interstate Commerce Commission extend its jurisdiction over the electric-power industry, and (2) having Congress revitalize the FPC by permitting it to establish a federal licensing and incorporation system to regulate interstate holding-company transactions. See William Z. Ripley, "From Main Street to Wall Street," *Atlantic Monthly*, 137 (Jan. 1926), 106, and his *Main Street and Wall Street* (Boston, 1927).

20. Ripley, "More Light!—And Power Too," *Atlantic Monthly*, 138 (Nov. 1926), 687.

21. Ripley to Thomas J. Walsh, Jan. 19, 1926. Thomas J. Walsh Papers, box 270, Library of Congress.

22. Ibid.

23. North American, for example, dropped from a high of 67 to a low of 42; United

tives, meanwhile, began to deplore openly the financial legerdemain of the holding company. Samuel Ferguson, president of the Hartford Electric Company, knew of "no more reprehensible abuse than for speculators to buy up companies for higher prices, put them into a holding company, and then by trading on the credulity of the investing public ... to unload the holding companies' securities at advanced prices."[24]

Although his critique was taken seriously in responsible quarters, not even Ferguson's remarks were enough to undermine public resistance to federal regulation. Nevertheless, six days after the FTC had filed its report, on February 28, 1927, Senator Walsh delivered a major speech in support of his resolution for a new Senate investigation. He pointedly ignored the FTC's findings, asserting that the federal government had never enforced properly the Sherman Antitrust Act.[25] The resolution did not come as a surprise to the private utilities, for it was common knowledge that Progressive senators had little confidence in the FTC, its personnel, or its rulings. Old-line utility executives, who had built up their systems when competition was keen and meaningful regulation nonexistent, prepared to meet the challenge to their freedom of operation. As was true of other business leaders of the day, they saw the specter of socialism in the efforts of the federal government to define the parameters of their activities.[26]

Under most circumstances, these executives could also rely upon the support of investment bankers in their opposition to federal interference. Even utility executives of the caliber of Ferguson and Insull, who had adopted fundamentally sound fiscal practices and had deplored the malpractices of a minority, could be relied upon to resist a new federal investigation. Joseph P. Tumulty, an attorney for Middle West, who advised his clients to cooperate in the event that the Walsh resolution succeeded, was a voice in the wilderness. He had written, in 1927, that the Montana Democrat would relentlessly but fairly pursue his investigation, and from it might come constructive legislation. Unfortunately, the industry did not heed Tumulty's good counsel and

---

Gas Improvement from 144½ to 84. Middle West Utilities declined 26 points and American Light and Traction 64 points. See Charles A. Gulick, "Holding Companies in Power," *New Republic,* 47 (May 26, 1926), 25-28.

24. Quoted in U.S. Congress, Senate, *Supply of Electrical Equipment and Competitive Conditions,* doc. no. 46, 70th Cong., 1st sess. (Washington, D.C., 1928), 217-18.

25. *Congressional Record,* 69th Cong., 2d sess., 68 (Feb. 28, 1927), 4991 ff.

26. Davis G. Cullom, "The Transformation of the Federal Trade Commission, 1914-1929," *Mississippi Valley Historical Review,* 49 (Dec. 1962), 451.

forfeited, thereby, the opportunity to put its own house in order.[27]

In the Senate, meanwhile, conservatives whose political fortunes were linked to the private utilities resorted to parliamentary maneuvering to ward off the investigation. Republican Senator Charles Deneen of Illinois, for example, anticipated the resolution by introducing a bill whose ostensible purpose was to prevent fraud in the sale of securities.[28] Industry officials rallied to the Deneen bill in the expectation that it would deflect the Walsh resolution. Tumulty, however, felt that this was a serious miscalculation; he wrote to Judge George Cooke that Walsh would quickly perceive its purpose and, "instead of helping the situation, it will doubtless aggravate and embarrass it."[29] Although his fears were premature just then, Tumulty was right to be concerned. The timing of the resolution was not propitious because the White House and various business organizations opposed it. The resolution and the Deneen bill were quietly pigeonholed in committee.[30]

The abortive resolution, nonetheless, had been a warning and portent of further difficulty for utility holding companies. But industry officials, instead of taking the opportunity to police themselves, reacted with a publicity campaign designed to discourage public-power and federal intervention for the future. In June 1927, five months after the death of the resolution, the National Electric Light Association (NELA), the utility industry's trade association, organized the Joint Committee of National Utility Associations. This body represented on a national scale the trade associations of electric, gas, and electric-railway utilities and was the instrument for executing the propaganda campaign.[31] George B. Cortelyou, formerly Theodore Roosevelt's secretary of the

27. Joseph P. Tumulty to George A. Cooke, Feb. 15, 1927, National Archives, Record Group 46, "Senate Special Committee to Investigate Lobbying Activities," Case Files, box 98 (hereafter cited as "Senate Lobby Investigation"). Tumulty was a good example of a Wilsonian liberal who, in the 1920s, identified with the more progressive elements of the business community. He deplored holding-company abuses as unsound and, in the end, counterproductive. See John M. Blum, *Joe Tumulty and the Wilson Era* (Boston, 1951), 266, and passim.

28. The true purpose of the Deneen bill (S. 5769) was to kill support for the Walsh resolution by purporting to correct the abuses which Walsh had singled out for criticism. Deneen, incidentally, was among the recipients of Insull's largess, for the utility magnate made it a practice to contribute to all candidates at election time. *Congressional Record,* 69th Cong., 2d sess., 68 (Feb. 18, 1927), 4108; and Forrest McDonald, *Insull* (Chicago, 1962), 256.

29. Tumulty to Cooke, Feb. 21, 1927, "Senate Lobby Investigation," Case Files, box 98.

30. George W. Norris to William Ritchie, Sept. 6, 1935, Norris Papers, tray 72, box 4.

31. King, "The Genesis of TVA," ch. 16, p. 15.

treasury, agreed to serve as chairman.[32] He announced, shortly after taking office, that the committee would use its treasury of $400,000 to refute the misrepresentations of irresponsible radicals in Congress.[33]

Almost immediately thereafter, the committee launched a whirlwind campaign to persuade informed opinion that the industry was a responsible one and was contributing to the national economic and social welfare. Over the radio, in the press and the schools, and from the pulpit its agents indoctrinated the public to the positive benefits of a privately owned and operated electric-power industry. The consumer, as Norris and others commented bitterly, shouldered the expense of this propaganda in the form of higher electric-light bills.[34] Ultimately, however, it was neither a backlash from the propaganda nor the agitation of disgruntled congressmen that precipitated the searching inquiry into utility malpractices. It was the confluence of several separate incidents converging in a presidential election year and climaxed by a nationwide depression.

Senator Walsh, late in December 1927, took advantage of a more receptive atmosphere to introduce a new resolution similar to the one that had failed to move the Sixty-ninth Congress. The thrust of this resolution went directly to the pyramiding practices of utility holding companies by attempting to restrain them from issuing new securities at inflated values. Walsh believed that this practice particularly endangered the industry's stability and thereby the national economy. At the last minute, Senator Norris persuaded him to include in the resolution a clause authorizing an inquiry into the propaganda activities of the power companies.[35] The revised resolution clearly repudiated the earlier findings of the FTC and was a prelude to vigorous federal regulation.

32. In spite of his close association with the reform-minded Theodore Roosevelt, Cortelyou maintained close ties to the conservative, business-dominated eastern wing of the Republican party. He was president of the New York Consolidated Gas Company after 1909, and president of the NELA in the 1920s. Thus he lent respectability to the committee and gave the private-power companies a facade behind which they could conduct lobbying and other propagandistic activities. See *Dictionary of American Biography*, s.v. "George B. Cortelyou," supp. II.

33. The committee's objectives were implemented with the assistance of twelve regional "Committees of Public Information," the United States Chamber of Commerce, the Investment Bankers' Association, the National Association of Manufacturers, the Farm Bureau Federation, the National Association of Railway and Utility Commissioners, and insurance companies. See George W. Norris, "Power Trust in the Public Schools," *The Nation,* 127 (Sept. 18, 1929), 296-97.

34. The propaganda activities are described in Joseph Barnes, *Willkie* (New York, 1952), 53; Stephen Raushenbush, *The Power Fight* (Indianapolis, Ind., 1937), 126-33; and Arthur M. Schlesinger, Jr., *The Crisis of the Old Order* (Boston, 1957), 120-21.

35. *Congressional Record,* 70th Cong., 1st sess., 69 (Dec. 17, 1927), 788.

Walsh's resolution received an unforeseen assist from the Republican senatorial election scandals, in 1926, in Pennsylvania and Illinois. Shortly after the election of William S. Vare in the Keystone State, the press disclosed that the private utilities had made heavy financial contributions to his campaign in order to defeat the primary bid of the Progressive candidate, who had the endorsement of the public-power-minded governor, Gifford Pinchot. At approximately the same time in Chicago, the press there revealed that Samuel Insull had made a generous contribution to the election of Frank L. Smith, former chairman of the Illinois Commerce Commission.[36] In both instances reformers and public-power enthusiasts, angry over the defeat of their own candidates, chose to interpret the contributions as further evidence that the Power Trust was sabotaging the democratic process and seducing public officials.

The elections had become the object of public controversy by 1927, causing the Senate to refuse to seat Smith and Vare.[37] The matter did not end there because Democratic Senator James Reed of Missouri seized upon the Smith-Insull connection to advance his own presidential ambitions. He quickly announced his determination to expose the "malevolent influence" of Samuel Insull and the Power Trust. Reed's action was also intended to provide him with a campaign issue separate from that of his presidential rivals, Governor Alfred E. Smith of New York and William E. Borah of Idaho. What it actually accomplished was to give the Walsh resolution a new lease on life.[38]

The second factor that accounted for the favorable senatorial reception accorded the resolution derived from the evolutionary nature of utility financing. Minor bond houses were attracted to utility financing, after 1924, in the expectation of making a quick killing on the market. They ignored the fact that utility financing was no longer the open race it had been prior to World War I. Latecomers found themselves in the awkward position of having to create new holding companies to purchase operating properties and float securities or of establishing

36. Smith, as chairman of the Interstate Commerce Commission, had come under attack from reformers for allegedly being a tool of the Insulls. His critics included a number of individuals who figured prominently in the New Deal, including Harold L. Ickes, Donald Richberg, Paul O. Douglas, and Charles E. Merriam. McDonald argues that Insull's campaign contributions have been highly exaggerated. See McDonald, *Insull*, 256 ff.; "What the Senate Says to Pennsylvania," *The Nation*, 123 (July 21, 1926), 50-51; and "Smith and Vare Barred Out," *Literary Digest*, 95 (Dec. 24, 1927), 10-11.

37. Thomas J. Walsh, "Can a Senator-Elect Be Denied His Seat?" *Congressional Digest*, 6 (Nov. 1927), 303-06; and McDonald, *Insull*, 252-56.

38. See " 'Jim' Reed's Opening Blast," *Literary Digest*, 95 (Oct. 29, 1927), 10-11.

investment trusts. The latter sold their securities to the public, using the proceeds to acquire control of established holding-company systems. The situation, fraught with instability, guaranteed rivalry and competition among banking houses.[39]

J. P. Morgan & Company, eager to turn a profit but also repelled by the disorder and waste it encountered, entered the electric-power and gas utility field in 1927. The United Corporation, a superholding company enjoying a capitalization twenty times that of United States Steel, was the instrument of Morgan's will for capturing bond accounts. Within a relatively brief period, most of the major holding-company systems, with the notable exception of Middle West Utilities, came under its domination.[40] Samuel Insull had, very shrewdly, circumvented the influence of the New York investment-banking houses by going directly to Lombard Street or to Halsey, Stuart & Company in Chicago for financial assistance. His independent spirit irritated the New York bankers, many of whom were eager to see him broken.[41] Their opportunity came in 1928 when Martin Insull acquired a major holding-company system in the eastern United States, thereby precipitating a vicious conflict with the Morgan banking and utility interest. The depression, following on the heels of the destruction of Middle West, whetted the reformers' appetites for federal control of holding-company practices.[42]

Thus, the conjunction of several external developments within the space of a brief period of time assisted the passage of Walsh's resolution through the Senate. These included the creation of the Morgan super-holding company, the United Corporation; its rivalry with the Insull utility empire; the controversial senatorial elections; Norris's condemnation of the NELA and its creation, the Joint Committee of National Utility Associations; and speculation in holding-company securities. The onset of the depression late in 1929 kept the federal inquiry going. Indeed, the rise and fall of the reputations of several vigorous utility executives, especially Samuel Insull, would parallel

39. Norman S. Buchanan, "The Origin and Development of the Public Utility Holding Company," *The Journal of Political Economy*, 44 (Feb. 1936), 44 ff.

40. The only other holding-company systems free of the United Corporation were the Byllesby group (Standard Gas and Electric) dominated by the investment banking house of Ladenburg, Thalman & Co., and the Doherty group (Cities Service). See McDonald, *Insull*, 249; and Vincent P. Carosso, *Investment Banking in America: A History* (Cambridge, Mass., 1970), 259, passim.

41. Ibid.

42. Martin Insull, Samuel's brother, was president of Middle West at this time. Cf. McDonald, *Insull*, 250-52.

the rise and fall of the private utilities' reputation for public service.[43]

As introduced on December 17, 1927, S. Res. 83 provided that the Senate appoint a five-man committee to inquire into the conduct and operations of utility holding companies in the electric-light and power industry.[44] Upon a successful motion of Senator George H. Moses of New Hampshire, a foe of the resolution, the Senate referred the document to the Committee on Interstate and Foreign Commerce whose chairman, Republican James E. Watson of Indiana, was known to be hostile to it.[45] The committee conducted public hearings on it between January 16 and January 26, 1928. Apart from Senator Walsh, nearly all the major witnesses testified against the resolution.

Walsh's testimony followed three main lines and was intended to override the objections of industry spokesmen. He defined the resolution's purpose narrowly, noting that the investigation was intended to evaluate the soundness of holding-company securities and the control which parent companies exercised over operating properties;[46] he attempted to establish the fact that the Senate's investigatory powers extended not only to the transmission and distribution of energy across state lines but also to the interstate sale of holding- and operating-utility securities; and, lastly, Walsh attempted to anticipate and deflect parliamentary strategems to cripple the inquiry.[47] Concluding his remarks, he expressed the hope that public disclosure would motivate the industry's leaders to implement reforms in advance of congressional legislation. "Of course," he added, "my hopes may not be realized."[48]

Hard on Walsh's heels there appeared a host of unfriendly witnesses whose intent was to bury the resolution beneath an avalanche of critical testimony. Cortelyou and former Senator Irvine L. Lenroot of Wisconsin came armed with briefs, prepared by experts in utility law, to set forth the NELA's objections to the resolution.[49] Representatives

43. McCraw, *TVA and the Power Fight,* 12. Some observers, incorrectly I think, attributed Walsh's zeal in attacking the utilities to presidential ambitions. Cf. Oswald G. Villard, "Presidential Possibilities," *The Nation,* 126 (May 9, 1928), 533-35.
44. "First Blood in the Power War," *New Republic,* 54 (Feb. 9, 1928), 56.
45. *Congressional Record,* 70th Cong., 1st sess., 69 (Dec. 19, 1927), 817. Critics of the resolution hoped it would be buried in committee.
46. U.S. Congress, Senate, Committee on Interstate and Foreign Commerce, Hearings on S. Res. 83, *Investigation of Public Utility Corporations,* 70th Cong., 1st sess. (Washington, D.C., 1928), 5-13 (hereafter cited as *Investigation of Utility Corporations*).
47. Ibid.
48. Walsh was referring to the practice of amending the original motion by substituting language so broad as to include every conceivable subject. Thus, he specifically excluded the telephone and telegraph utilities. See ibid., 16.
49. Cortelyou's testimony is in ibid., 95-96, 103-07, and Lenroot's in ibid., 58-63. Both men argued that Walsh should have presented specific evidence of wrongdoing

of the National Association of Railway and Utility Commissioners (NARUC), the state public-service commissions, the Investment Bankers Association, and investors' organizations eagerly endorsed their testimony. The case against S. Res. 83 rested primarily upon the industry's fear of federal interference in its operations under the guise of regulation. Cortelyou, for example, argued that regulation was properly a function of state government because the utility business was essentially local.[50] Henry R. Hayes, president of the Investment Bankers Association, asserted that the inquiry would demonstrate that there was no need for federal action, while James A. Emery of the National Association of Manufacturers condemned the resolution as a violation of the First and Fourteenth Amendments.[51] Dean John Madden of the New York University School of Commerce attempted to demonstrate that the holding company was basic to the American corporate structure and not unique to the electric-power field. But it remained for Frederick C. Ecker of the Metropolitan Life Insurance Company, and chairman of the Committee of Owners of Railroad and Public Utilities Securities, to sum up the sentiments of all concerned. It was "important that the confidence in these securities should not be disturbed," he declared.[52]

The committee's hearings disclosed many facts about the operation of the electric-power business, but the most significant was that utility executives, investment bankers, and Wall Street lawyers had formed a community of interest in opposition to federal intervention. They feared, particularly, competition from government-produced electric power and, therefore, had their lobbyists working hard to alter pending legislation for the federally sponsored Muscle Shoals, Boulder Dam, and Mississippi valley flood-control projects.[53] Journalist Mark Sullivan, who was one of the few newspaper columnists to actively interest himself in the proceedings, had a firm grasp of the real stakes. Observing

---

to the committee. Ironically, Lenroot had been a staunch La Follette Progressive prior to World War I and had served as chairman of the Teapot Dome investigation. After leaving the Senate, he became an apologist for the utility industry. He received $20,000 for testifying against the resolution.

50. This was a bid for the support of the NARUC, which feared it might lose its influence with the state commissions if federal regulation became a reality. See Edward Smykay, "The National Association of Railway and Utility Commissioners as the Originators and Promoters of Public Policy for Public Utilities" (Ph.D. diss., University of Wisconsin, 1956).

51. For the testimonies of Hayes, Emery, and Lewis Gettle see *Investigation of Utility Corporations*, 24-32, 35-36, 177-86.

52. For the testimonies of Madden (which the utilities underwrote) and Ecker see ibid., 52-53, 145-51.

53. See the *New York World* editorial, Jan. 24, 1928, reprinted in ibid., 246.

that neither Smith's nor Insull's name had been mentioned in the course of the hearings, he noted that the reformers hoped to link the election scandals to holding-company abuses and to use the resolution as the springboard for extensive federal intervention in the power industry.[54] Sullivan concluded that they would hold the investigation, no matter what recommendation the committee presented to the Senate.[55]

Meanwhile, conservative members of the Commerce Committee attempted to restrict the investigation solely to the interstate transactions of power companies, including the source of their capital assets, their securities, service charges and management fees, and interlocking directorships.[56] They circumvented the intent of the original resolution, which was to determine the extent to which the utilities had used their funds to influence the electorate against public ownership, by excluding from the inquiry utility contributions to elections below the national level.[57] Democratic Senator Henry B. Hawes of Missouri commented acidly that this was just the beginning; he predicted that the committee would emasculate other sections of the resolution before reporting it to the Senate.[58] Walsh, however, was aware that the committee feared the resolution would usurp the jurisdiction of the state commissions and tried to reassure it on this point. Having already exposed the gray area between state and federal jurisdiction, he was confident that an inquiry into the securities offerings of interstate holding companies would get at the major grievances.[59]

A week later, on February 2, 1928, the committee reported the amended resolution to the Senate, with the recommendation that the president of the Senate, Charles Gates Dawes, should appoint a five-man investigating committee. Dawes, incidentally, had extensive ties to the banking and utility community of Chicago. Nor did the conserva-

54. Mark Sullivan, "Senate to Study Financing of Public Utilities," *New York Herald Tribune*, Jan. 26, 1928.

55. Ibid.

56. The resolution initially drew no distinction between holding and operating companies whose business was primarily intrastate and those engaged in the interstate distribution of power. The percentage of energy transmitted across state boundaries in 1928 was 9 percent but was growing rapidly. The utilities relied upon this figure to support their contention that the power business was essentially local and not subject to federal jurisdiction.

57. U.S. Congress, Senate, Committee on Interstate and Foreign Commerce, *Investigation of Public Utility Corporations*, Senate report no. 225, 70th Cong., 1st sess. (Washington, D.C., 1928), 1-2.

58. Ibid.; the *New York Times*, Jan. 25, 1928.

59. Walsh's attitude toward the sale of holding-company securities in interstate commerce may be found in the *Congressional Record*, 70th Cong., 1st sess., 69 (Feb. 13, 1928), 2892.

tive opposition end with the report; it continued on the floor of the Senate during three days of bitter, vitriolic debate.[60] The focal point of the controversy was the amendment, offered by Senator Walter George of Georgia, to transfer the conduct of the inquiry from the Senate to the FTC.[61] This tactic provoked outrage from Progressive senators, who feared that a second FTC investigation would simply repeat the whitewash of the first.[62]

Democratic party ranks broke down repeatedly during the debate.[63] Walsh declared that FTC Commissioner William E. Humphrey worshiped at the temple of big business. The larger the corporation the more sacrosanct it was to him. Democrat William Cabell Bruce of Maryland, a foe of the Teapot Dome inquiry, retorted that Walsh was afflicted with presidential fever. "The Senator from Montana ... has succumbed to the propensity for investigation ... ," he declared. "He is like a tiger who tastes human blood and then becomes a maneater for the rest of his life."[64]

Prior to the final vote, Walsh sought an adjournment that would give him time to muster support for the resolution minus the George amendment. Three times the opposition defeated him on roll-call votes for adjournment. It soon became obvious to friends and foes alike that, the longer debate persisted, the stronger the proponents of the FTC inquiry were becoming.[65] Senator Hugo Black of Alabama, therefore, moved to open the investigation to the public.[66] At last, on the evening of February 15, 1928, the Senate passed S. Res. 83 with the George and Black amendments intact.[67] The vote was forty-six to

60. The *New York Times,* Feb. 2 and 16, 1928.

61. See *Congressional Record,* 70th Cong., 1st sess., 69 (Feb. 13, 1928), 2891, for the George amendment. For the critical remarks of Walsh and Norris see ibid., 2895 ff.

62. Senate liberals had ample grounds for objecting to the FTC. President Coolidge, in 1925, appointed William E. Humphrey—his campaign manager and confidant of the lumber interests of the Pacific Northwest—chairman. Humphrey had previously accused the FTC of being "an instrument of oppression and disturbance" to big business. During his chairmanship he instituted a new set of procedures for the FTC to follow, including closed hearings, settlement of cases by "stipulation" rather than prosecution, and the end to sweeping economic studies. See Cullom, "Transformation of the FTC," 445-49; "Portrait" [Humphrey], *Review of Reviews,* 71 (June 1925), 70; and Pendleton Herring, "The Federal Trade Commissioners," *George Washington Law Review,* 8 (Jan.-Feb. 1940), 356.

63. *New York Herald Tribune,* Feb. 16 and 17, 1928.

64. *Congressional Record,* 70th Cong., 1st sess., 69 (Feb. 13, 1928), 2892 ff.; (Feb. 14, 1928), 2953-54. See also Thompson, *Confessions of the Power Trust,* 5; and Alfred Lief, *Democracy's Norris* (New York, 1939), 307.

65. *Congressional Record,* 70th Cong., 1st sess., 69 (Feb. 15, 1928), 3029-35.

66. Ibid., 3024-25, 3035.

67. In its final form, S. Res. 83 directed the FTC to investigate the financing of interstate electric and gas companies, and to provide the Senate with a monthly progress

thirty-one for the resolution. The strenuous opposition of Democrats to the originally conceived Senate inquiry had carried the day. The *New York Herald Tribune* exulted over the key role of the Southern Democracy in substituting the FTC for a Walsh-inspired investigation: "There has been a decided change in the temper of the Senate since 1924, when the Insurgent-Democrat combination was at the height of its power. ... But Southern Senators are becoming much more conservative in matters affecting business and industry. The spirit of La Follette no longer rules."[68]

The FTC investigation might well have glossed over holding-company malpractices had not the circumstances in which the agency conducted the inquiry undergone significant change. The Black amendment, which modified the FTC rule of a closed investigation, proved of enormous significance upon closer observation, for it guaranteed that the reformers could closely monitor the agency's hearings. Even Senator Millard Tydings of Maryland, a Democrat who later consistently voted against New Deal legislation, put the commission on notice that, if it failed to make "a complete, searching, fair and non-political probe," he would introduce legislation to abolish it.[69] Joe Tumulty, ever persistent, again warned the power companies not to resort to obstructive tactics, "as a result of which there is bound to come an investigation by the Senate itself which may prove very harassing and injurious in its effect."[70]

The decisive factors, however, were a fortuitous change in the commission's personnel prior to the start of the inquiry and the stock market collapse of October 1929. The selection of Robert E. Healy, a Vermont Republican, as solicitor general of the agency was a misfortune for utility executives. Healy brought to the position a basically conservative temper with a strong sense of justice and dedication to the public interest. "If these utility fellows are found guilty," he told Judson King, director of the public-power-oriented National Popular

---

report and, upon completion of the inquiry, with a summary report. It also empowered the FTC to examine the question of whether the utility industry had attempted to influence elections. See ibid., 3027-28.

68. *New York Herald Tribune*, Feb. 17, 1928.

69. The *New York Times*, Feb. 18, 1928; and George W. Norris, "The Ultimate Goal of Public Utility Regulation," *Public Utilities Fortnightly*, 5 (Mar. 6, 1930), 266. On Tydings's anti-New Deal voting record post-1933, see James T. Patterson, *Congressional Conservatism and the New Deal* (Lexington, Ky., 1967), 25, 72 n.

70. Tumulty to Bernard J. Mullaney, Feb. 27, 1928, "Senate Lobby Investigation," Case Files, box 98. See also Gifford Pinchot to William E. Humphrey, Feb. 22, 1928, and Humphrey's acerbic reply, Feb. 28, 1928, William E. Humphrey Papers, box 1, Library of Congress.

Government League, "they will be condemned out of their own mouths and official records." King, at that moment, knew that the probe was "in competent hands and there would be no whitewash."[71]

The stock market crash, in the interim, had wiped out millions of dollars in paper investment and plunged the nation into depression. The captains of industry and finance, as the Pecora committee investigating stock-exchange operations disclosed, had feet of clay. The public, outraged, attributed the disaster indiscriminately to Insull, the Wigginses, the Mitchells, and the Morgans—the archetypal Wall Street promoters.[72] In this atmosphere of hostility congressional critics of the power industry launched a new drive to apply federal statutes to the interstate transactions of utility holding companies.[73] On January 6, 1930, for example, Republican Senator James Couzens of Michigan introduced legislation the objectives of which were to strengthen the Water Power Act of 1920, and to reorganize the Federal Power Commission (FPC), extending its jurisdiction to utility holding companies. "In short," Couzens observed, "I have attempted to reach the two great dangers of interstate power transmission—the interstate operating utilities and the interstate holding or 'affiliate' company. I have attempted to do it in a way that will avoid the usual objection to the centralization of power in the Federal Government."[74]

State public-service commissioners put fierce pressure upon Congress to emasculate the holding-company title. Their primary fear was that the proposal to establish "joint boards" of state and federal representatives within the FPC could mean the destruction of state jurisdiction over utility rates and charges.[75] But there were other objections to the holding-company title as well. The bill went far beyond President Hoover's dictum that federal regulation was justified only where state

71. King, "The Genesis of TVA," ch. 19, pp. 5-7.
72. McDonald's study of Samuel Insull is a lucid apologia for the utility magnate's actions. He concludes that the public incorrectly identified Insull with Wall Street promoters in bringing on the stock market collapse and the depression. But see also John K. Galbraith, *The Great Crash 1929* (Boston, 1955), 4, 84, 120, 161; "Insull Crisis Dramatizes Plight of Investment Holding Groups," *Business Week*, 137 (Apr. 20, 1932), 18-19; John T. Flynn, "What Happened to Insull?" *New Republic*, 70 (May 28, 1932); and N. R. Danielian, "From Insull to Injury: Study in Financial Jugglery," *Atlantic Monthly*, 151 (Apr. 1933), 497-508.
73. Gifford Pinchot, "The Long Struggle for Effective Federal Water Power Legislation," *George Washington Law Review*, 14 (Dec. 1945), 9-20; and Dozier A. DeVane, "Highlights of the Legislative History of the Federal Power Act of 1935 and the Natural Gas Act of 1938," ibid., 33.
74. James Couzens, "Why the Couzens Bill Will Not Undermine the Power of the State Commissions," *Public Utilities Fortnightly*, 6 (Aug. 7, 1930), 140.
75. See, for example, Harold E. West, "The Menace of the Couzens Bill," ibid., 6 (Nov. 13, 1930), 587.

and local jurisdiction was demonstrably inadequate. Apart from other deficiencies (there was some doubt that the legislation adequately regulated the securities of interstate holding companies), the holding-company title failed because Couzens neglected to cultivate those congressional leaders whose support was essential.[76]

Despite its limitations, the Couzens bill was important in the subsequent evolution of federal holding-company policy. It signified that between 1920 and 1930 neither the private-utility industry nor the reformers were wholly successful in imposing their views upon the other, but the bill also marked the resurgence of the Federal Power Commission as a dynamic agency. In urging Congress to include the business of interstate power companies within the jurisdiction of the Water Power Act, the FPC helped sustain the principle of federal regulation in the depression.[77]

Beyond this, the Couzens bill had the effect of precipitating a new debate over the adequacy of state regulation.[78] H. Lester Hooker of the NARUC noted that recent state elections had "swept into public office men who ranked among the most outspoken critics of state regulation, including several of the more radical group who have aligned themselves frankly with the advocates of government ownership and operation on the strength of their assertion that state regulation had fallen down."[79] Congress, in the interim, had adopted a posture of

---

76. W. H. Blood, Jr., "The Present Status of Public Utility Regulation in the United States of America," *Stone & Webster Journal*, 45 (Dec. 1929), 740-49; William Z. Ripley, "Public Utility Insecurities," *Forum*, 88 (Aug. 1932), 66-72; and Judson King, "Letter to Members of the League," *National Popular Government League Bulletin*, 94 (Feb. 1932), 6. Later, when the New Deal was considering similar legislation, Morris L. Cooke wrote: "Almost no one has any enthusiasm for the type of Federal regulation of holding companies contemplated by the Couzens bill, perhaps the author least of all" (see Cooke to Ickes, Apr. 6, 1934, National Archives, Record Group 48, National Power Policy Committee Records, General Classified File 103, box 7 [hereafter cited as NPPC Records, GCF]).

77. "Power Commission Asks Holding Company Control," *Electrical World*, 103 (Feb. 3, 1934), 200.

78. Francis X. Welch, "Another Year of Grilling for the Public Utility Companies," *Public Utilities Fortnightly*, 8 (Aug. 6, 1931), 169-70; *Eleventh Annual Report of the Federal Power Commission* (Washington, D.C., 1931), 10-11; and *Holding Company Control of Licenses of the Federal Power Commission* (Washington, D.C., 1932), vii, 1. Ray Lyman Wilbur, Hoover's secretary of the interior, had testified that the securities of interstate licensees should be subject to FPC jurisdiction, but nothing further came of it. See U.S. Congress, House, Committee on Interstate and Foreign Commerce, Hearings on H.R. 11408, *A Bill to Reorganize the Federal Power Commission* ... , 71st Cong., 2d sess. (Washington, D.C., 1930), 74-76.

79. H. Lester Hooker, "The Raid of the Radicals on State Regulation," *Public Utilities Fortnightly*, 6 (Dec. 25, 1930), 772-78.

watchful waiting—reluctant to act until more facts and public sentiment had crystallized.[80]

As the depression worsened and the FTC disclosed shocking evidence of holding-company mismanagement, critics of the industry reopened the debate over the traditional modes by which the industry had conducted its business. They also sought to appeal to a broader spectrum of the public, and were partially successful in doing so. Three schools of thought emerged from the critics' deliberations.[81] The proponents of strictly state or federal regulation were at the opposite ends of the spectrum; the advocates of a mixture of more effective state and federal control, who probably constituted the largest number, stood in the center. (The number of supporters of outright nationalization was negligible.) Although each faction had its own pet solution for the holding-company problem, they all drew from a common intellectual source, Justice Louis D. Brandeis. The author of *Other Peoples' Money* condemned the holding company as "the antithesis of democracy" and urged its abolition as the *sine qua non* for restoring the average citizen to control of his money and business. In 1931, Brandeis wrote to Gifford Pinchot a memorandum in which he outlined some of his thoughts. Perhaps the most revealing aspect of the document was the violent emotional repulsion which economic concentration had induced in this gentle man. "To present the case against the Holding Company in a few words is necessarily to state it dogmatically and ... leaves out the emotional considerations, which, perhaps in the last consideration[,] are the more important reasons for opposition ... ," Brandeis stated. Ultimately, he opted for federal regulation as the only practical solution.[82]

The "federalists," however, were in the least tenable position be-

80. Adam H. Ulm, "The Proposal of Federal Aid to States in Holding Company Regulation," ibid., 11 (Mar. 2, 1933), 276-82; and Ben H. Lewis, "The Bogie of Federal Regulation," ibid., 12 (Aug. 31, 1933), 259.

81. See, for example, "Lauds Holding Company Aims," *Barron's,* 10 (Sept. 15, 1930), 27; Ernest T. Clough, "Holding Company Bonds Have Investment Merit," ibid., 11 (Aug. 19, 1931), 8; C. W. Thompson, "The Contest Over the Right to Regulate the Utility Holding Company," *Public Utilities Fortnightly,* 8 (Sept. 17, 1931), 340-48; "Does the Electrical Industry Want Holding Company Control?" ibid., 10 (Aug. 18, 1932), 215-17; and John E. Zimmerman, "U.G.I. Policy," *Evening Bulletin* (Philadelphia), Jan. 2, 1931, clipping in Gifford Pinchot Papers, box 2031, Library of Congress (hereafter cited as Pinchot Papers).

82. Louis D. Brandeis, "The Case Against the Holding Company," Nov. 23 [?] 1931, memorandum in Pinchot Papers, box 2029. Brandeis thought that Congress would want to legislate a federal incorporation or licensing system to regulate what he viewed as parasitical corporations controlling the interstate transmission and distribution of energy.

tween 1929 and 1933 because of the hostility of the Hoover administration to direct federal action.[83] Nonetheless, they were catalysts of
the debate when, in 1929, Norris and Pinchot declared that a Power
Trust had seized control of the nation's power supply and proceeded
to name General Electric, the Mellons, the Morgans, H. M. Byllesby,
Doherty's Cities Service group, and Insull's Middle West Utilities
as the prime culprits.[84] Afterward, western congressmen, including
Homer T. Bone and Clarence Dill of Washington and James P. Pope
of Idaho, who represented states where public power was a burning
issue, took up the cudgels. They cooperated with public-power organizations, such as the National Popular Government League and Carl
D. Thompson's Public Ownership League, to pressure the industry
to adopt its rate structure from the original value of utility properties
rather than their actual value. Their ultimate goal was to attain lower
rates for their constituents within the context of a national power policy
and, incidentally, to dislodge the political influence of the private utilities in their states. Thus they advocated federal legislation to strengthen
the Water Power Act to give the FPC jurisdiction over holding-
company operations and to ruthlessly expose holding-company
abuses.[85]

The federalists did not succeed in imposing their views upon the
moderates until after they had persuaded them that state regulation
was a failure and piecemeal reforms would not suffice. The refusal
of enlightened state commissioners, such as David E. Lilienthal[86] of
Wisconsin, to surrender a portion of their jurisdiction to a federal

83. In 1932, for example, Senator Robert B. Howell of Nebraska proposed an amendment to the Revenue Act to provide for a 3 percent tax on energy generated from
privately owned utility plants. With administration consent, conservatives shifted the
levy to the consumer, over liberal protests. And, in 1933, Norris could find little support
for legislation to eliminate the holding company via taxation. See Norris to Henry
Feldhus, June 7, 1932, and John P. Robertson to E. F. Stepp, Aug. 13, 1932, Norris
Papers, tray 81, box 8; and Henry D. Boenning to Norris, Aug. 13, 1932, ibid., tray
66, box 5.

84. "The Power Monopoly—Its Make-up and Its Menace," *New York Times,* Feb.
4, 1929. Berle and Means demonstrated in 1932 that, of the $81 billion held by the
two hundred largest nonbanking corporations as of January 1, 1930, electric and gas
utility corporations accounted for nearly $19 billion. It should be noted, however, that
the authors never use the epithet *Power Trust* in their book. See Adolph Berle and
Gardiner C. Means, *The Modern Corporation and Private Property* (New York, 1932),
ch. 3, table I.

85. See, for example, the correspondence between King and Norris in King Papers.
King also maintained a correspondence with other public-power-minded officials in executive and legislative positions.

86. Lilienthal declared, on several occasions between 1932 and 1934, that the state
legislatures should empower the commissions with authority to regulate every transaction

agency and the efforts of the governors of Oregon, Wisconsin, Iowa, Illinois, and Texas to persuade their legislatures to clothe the state commissions with more stringent powers made the task more difficult.[87] Meanwhile, Pinchot's call for vigorous federal action, in 1931, merely sowed dissention among the members of the Progressive Conference, meeting in Washington, D.C.[88] The federalists won a partial victory, in April 1932, when Professor James C. Bonbright of Columbia University, secretary of the New York Power Authority, persuaded a round table conference on utility regulation to endorse the principle of broader state and federal cooperation.[89] Professor Ripley of Harvard, who was among those present, concurred and, before adjourning, the conferees ratified two proposals: first, that the federal government incorporate interstate holding companies for the purpose of regulating their securities, and secondly, that there be established "national and state power planning either by existing commissions or by special boards, so that future developments may be economically sound and in accord with the needs of the people."[90]

Gradually but predictably, the liberal advocates of state regulation came to despair that the legislatures would, indeed, strengthen the public-service commissions, or that the NARUC would modify its support of the status quo. The association was a captive of the utility interests and fought to preserve the jurisdiction of the states from federal encroachment.[91] It regularly rejected, from 1930 onward, the pleas of Lilienthal, John H. Bickley of Wisconsin, Milo Maltbie of

---

between a holding company and its affiliate. See the *New York Times*, Oct. 12, 1932; David E. Lilienthal, "Four Point Program for Legislation," *Electrical World*, 101 (Apr. 1, 1933), 423; and Lilienthal, "Birchrods? Legislative Suggestions for Regulating the Public Utility Industry and Its Alter Ego, the Holding Company," *State Government*, 5 (Feb. 1934), 39.

87. Joseph P. Chamberlain, "Regulation of Public Utility Holding Companies," *American Bar Association Journal*, 17 (June 1931), 368.

88. "What the Progressive Conference Committee Proposes to Do About the Utilities," *Public Utilities Fortnightly*, 8 (Nov. 26, 1931), 676-83. See also Pinchot's speech of June 2, 1931, in the Pinchot Papers, box 2031, and his typed memorandum, "Holding Companies," n.d., in ibid., box 2029.

89. Bonbright rejected the notion that an evil Power Trust had conspired to use the holding company to defraud the public. He perceived that the abuses were largely historical, that is, the product of rapid expansion and changes that had occurred within the industry over a relatively short period of time. See James C. Bonbright and Gardiner Means, *The Holding Company* (New York, 1932), 222; and the *New York Times*, Apr. 9 and 10, 1932.

90. Ibid.

91. The conservatism of the NARUC on the matter of federal interference has been ably described in Smykay, "The NARUC as Originators and Promoters of Public Policy for the Public Utilities."

New York, Mayland Morse of New Hampshire, and Clyde L. Seavey of California for an affirmative stand in support of effective state regulation.[92] John Shaugnessy of Nevada, chairman of the conservative Committee on Intercorporate Relations, succinctly stated the association's policy in 1931: "Our review of the subject matter fails to disclose the necessity for drastic changes in legislation with respect to holding companies."[93] Rebuffed, Lilienthal considered withdrawing from the association "with a ringing statement" but, upon further reflection, he decided to remain and continue the fight for stiffer state regulation.[94]

The initial breach in its obdurate stance occurred in 1933, and then it was only partial. Commissioner Shaugnessy permitted the committee to debate propositions clearly implying that state regulation had failed. He would not permit, however, a vote on the issues, and reaffirmed that regulation was not the responsibility of the federal government. "It is the state's duty to protect its people in such cases," he declared.[95] Shaugnessy's words, unfortunately, rang hollow because, in 1932, Insull's Middle West Utilities had collapsed, as did the Foshay companies, Central Public Service, and others. And Owen D. Young of General Electric had given damaging testimony, in February 1933,

92. One reporter, in 1930, described these men, prematurely and erroneously I think, as "liberal-radicals whose trend is toward the federalization of industry and the tenets of government operation and ownership" (David Lay, "The Association of Commissioners Grows a Left Wing," *Public Utilities Fortnightly*, 8 [Nov. 12, 1931], 579, 585). But see also "The Annual Convention of the N.A.R.U.C.," ibid., 10 (Dec. 8, 1932), 706-09; NARUC *Proceedings*, 44th Annual Convention [Washington, D.C., 1932], 52-63, 88-97; and David Lilienthal, *The Journals of David E. Lilienthal*, 5 vols. (New York, 1964-71, I, 19.

93. Legal authorities, economists, and a number of utility commissioners were less confident that state regulation had been effective. They noted that the Court in *Smyth v. Ames*, 169 U.S. 466 (1899), and in the 1927 *Attleboro* decision had cast doubt on whether a holding company was a public utility and had placed the interstate transmission and sale of energy beyond the reach of public-service commissions. They also observed that the absence of arm's-length bargaining between the parent company and its affiliate made regulation of banking transactions difficult; that accounting practices were neither uniform nor public; that only one-half of the state commissions were empowered to regulate security issues; that service contracts were, in the main, unregulated; and that only four states even admitted the relationship between depreciation and dividends. On these points see David Lilienthal, "The Regulation of Public Utility Holding Companies," *Columbia Law Review*, 29 (Apr. 1929), 404-40; and "Recent Developments in the Law of Public Utility Holding Companies," ibid., 31 (Feb. 1931), 189-207. For further evidence consult, "Extending Control Over Public Utility-Affiliate Financial Transactions," *Harvard Law Review*, 46 (Jan. 1933), 508-15; and David Lilienthal, "Regulation of Public Utilities During the Depression," ibid., 46 (Mar. 1933), 745-75.

94. Lilienthal, *Journals*, I, 20.

95. NARUC *Proceedings*, 45th Annual Convention (Washington, D.C., 1933), 257-58. See also "What the State Commissioners Are Thinking About," *Public Utilities Fortnightly*, 14 (Dec. 6, 1934), 736-43.

to the Senate Banking Committee that Insull himself had been unable to comprehend the crazy patchwork of pyramided companies that was Middle West.[96] The *Philadelphia Record* noted that Insull's collapse focused public attention upon holding-company abuses in a way the FTC could not. The *Public Utilities Fortnightly* declared: "A new movement toward complete, workable Federal control of holding companies, toward more stringent control of operating companies, protecting not only private ownership but also the investor and the consumer, is upon us."[97] Liberals within the NARUC perceived that the federal-securities legislation of 1933-34 was a preliminary to federal holding-company regulation. They resigned themselves to it, particularly after the conservative majority indicated it would do no more than exhort the states to vigilance.[98]

Meanwhile, as critics debated the merits of state versus federal regulation, Preston K. Arkwright of the Georgia Power Company urged his colleagues to refute the canard about the existence of a Power Trust. He asked that they educate the public to the true facts in order to discourage talk of public ownership and federal regulation.[99] As a matter of self-preservation therefore, and because of a genuine concern for the industry's future growth, holding-company executives, the heads of operating utilities, and investment bankers put aside their differences temporarily in order to rebut the critics' accusations. Their response began with a defense of the power industry specifically, but it quickly broadened into a general apologia for private enterprise. The editors of the *National Electric Light Association Bulletin*, for example, pointed out that the FTC had failed to substantiate the exis-

96. U.S. Congress, Senate, Hearings pursuant to S. Res. 84, *Stock Exchange Practices*, 6 pts., 72nd Cong., 2d sess. (Washington, D.C., 1932-33), pt. 5, 1516-19 ff; Ewin L. Davis, "The Influence of the Federal Trade Commission's Investigations of Federal Regulation of Interstate Electric and Gas Utilities," *George Washington Law Review*, 14 (Dec. 1945), 21-29; and James M. Landis, "The Legislative History of the Securities Act of 1933," ibid., 28 (Oct. 1959), 29-39.

97. Quoted in Francis X. Welch, "The Effect of the Insull Collapse on State Regulation," *Public Utilities Fortnightly*, 10 (Nov. 10, 1932), 578.

98. On the New Deal's securities legislation and the states' "blue-sky" laws see Louis Loss, *Securities Regulation*, 2d ed., 2 vols. (Boston, 1961), I, 19, passim. Colonel William T. Chantland of the FTC had written to Norris: "I am glad to notice that you still have in mind holding company legislation. I know you will recall that none of the specific things as to holding companies ... were finally included in the Securities Act. So that practically speaking, there has been no holding company legislation" (Chantland to Norris, Dec. 5, 1933, Norris Papers, tray 80, box 7).

99. Preston K. Arkwright, "What About Holding Companies?" *The Fifth District Banker*, 2 (July 1930), 8-9.

tence of a monolithic Power Trust.[100] Samuel Ferguson, Wendell Willkie of Commonwealth and Southern, and C. F. Blanchard, the editor of *Standard Statistics,* observed that the FTC had employed different definitions and accounting procedures that greatly exaggerated the prevalence of "write-ups" and other abuses.[101] John P. Coughlan of Pacific Gas and Electric caustically concluded that corporate morals in the twenties had been no worse than individual morals.[102]

Beyond this, utility leaders accused politicians and reformers of being insensitive to the industry's financial problems, and of succumbing to the frantic demands of a minority for public power. William Prendergast, a retired New York public-service commissioner; Thomas N. McCarter of the Public Service Corporation of New Jersey; and William J. Donovan, a prominent Wall Street lawyer representing the Morgan utility interests, accused the industry's detractors of ignoring the detrimental impact which their continuous demand for rate reductions had upon the industry's economic structure and its ability, in the future, to serve the public.[103] Matthew S. Sloan, president of the NELA, meanwhile, defended the reorganizations and consolidations which had generated holding-company systems like Middle West and Stone and Webster. He declared that the separation of ownership from management was not a phenomenon unique to the utility industry but was the ineluctable concomitant of a mature capitalistic economy and the rush of technology.[104]

100. "Senator Norris Answered," *National Electric Light Association Bulletin,* 18 (Feb. 1931), 227. See also Bernard J. Mullaney, "Camouflage and Smokescreens," *The Fifth District Banker,* 2 (July 1930), 13-14; and F. R. Phillips, "Thoughts of an Operating Executive," *Electrical World,* 102 (Oct. 7, 1933), 460-64.

101. "Senator Norris Answered," 227; "Close Supervision of Utilities Urged Before Investment Bankers," *Electrical World,* 101 (June 3, 1933), 708-09; and W. C. Gilman, "Financial Practices of Few Endanger Utilities' Credit," ibid., 99 (Jan. 16, 1932), 134-36.

102. John P. Coughlan, "Public Utilities and the Public," *National Electric Light Association Bulletin,* 19 (Dec. 1932), 712.

103. Statistics indicated that, in fact, there had been an almost uninterrupted reduction in household rates, from 8.3¢ per day per kilowatt hour in 1914 to 5.3¢ in 1934, in heavily populated areas. Service in rural areas still was expensive, relatively speaking. See Edwin Gruhl, "The Electric Dollar," *National Electric Light Association Bulletin,* 17 (July 1930), 431-35; William A. Prendergast, "Has State Regulation Protected the Public's Interest?" ibid., 426-28; "Sees New Public Attitude," *Electrical World,* 103 (Mar. 10, 1934), 378; Editorial, *Public Service* [Corporation of New Jersey] *News,* 12 (Jan. 1, 1935), 4; and William J. Donovan, "Is the Interest of the Public Inconsistent with the Interest of the Utilities?" *Stone & Webster Journal,* 46 (June 1930), 721.

104. John P. Coughlan of Pacific Gas and Electric succinctly summarized this viewpoint, in 1932, when he declared: "American business has become so large and so complicated, requiring so much capital and so much talent, that it cannot be carried on by a few owners using their own limited funds, but must of necessity be administered by great corporate organizations, staffed by men hired because of their special skill

The industry's united front crumbled, however, after the debate shifted to the more exacting issue of how to proceed in eradicating the most flagrant abuses. Howard Hopson of Associated Gas and Electric, representing the most reactionary elements, refused to admit the urgency of any reform, and demanded retention of the status quo. Others, more circumspect, desired self-reform and "frankness in that which, to most people, is the twilight zone of holding companies and their dealings."[105] The majority opted for a combination of self-policing and improved state regulation to avoid what Francis E. Frothingham of the Investment Bankers Association described as "the remote, bureaucratic, deadening touch" of the federal government.[106] Precisely how far state regulation should go was uncertain. Philip H. Gadsden, vice-president of United Gas Improvement, took what he thought was a radical position when he told the Missouri Association of Public Utilities that the states should approve all management and service fees.[107] One anonymous operating executive, however, wrote that local operating companies should be managed freely and without "outside [i.e., holding company] interference."[108] Floyd L. Carlisle, head of the Niagara-Hudson Power Corporation, and Alex Dow of Detroit Edison also wanted the state commissions to require holding companies to deal with their affiliates on the basis of equality. They were firsthand

---

or experience" (John P. Coughlan, "Public Utilities and the Public," 712). See also Matthew S. Sloan, "Consolidations in the Electric Utility Industry," *National Electric Light Association Bulletin,* 16 (Oct. 1929), 629-31; Henry R. Hayes, "Public Confidence in the Power Industry," ibid., 18 (Feb. 1931), 77-80; and W. A. Jones, "A National Viewpoint of Utility Problems," *Electrical World,* 96 (Oct. 18, 1930), 731-32.

105. Albert Nalle, "Let the Public in on the Industry's 'Secrets'," ibid., 100 (Sept. 24, 1932), 396-97. Commonwealth and Southern, under Willkie's vigorous leadership, and a few other systems had begun to simplify their corporate structures even before the 1935 legislation. See Ranald A. Finlayson, "The Public Utility Holding Company Under Federal Regulation," *The Journal of Business of the University of Chicago,* 16, supp. (July 1946), 4.

106. "Report of the Public Service Securities Committee," *Investment Banking,* 5 (Nov. 14, 1934), 41-47. For a similar opinion see American Bar Association, *Report ... 56th Annual Meeting* [Baltimore, 1933], 660-74; *Report ... 57th Annual Meeting* [Baltimore, 1934], 565-87; Everett W. Vilett, "Investment Merit of the Electric Utility Industry," *National Electric Light Association Bulletin,* 16 (Sept. 1929), 588; and William Prendergast, "The 'Ordeal by Water' of the Holding Company," *Public Utilities Fortnightly,* 11 (May 11, 1933), 595.

107. "P. H. Gadsden Takes Advanced Stand on Public Utility Regulation," *Electrical World,* 99 (May 7, 1932), 794. Three years later, Gadsden was in the vanguard of those opposing federal legislation. A strong endorsement of state regulation also came from the Byllesby Engineering and Management Corporation. William J. Hagenah, "Public Utility Regulation and Its Accomplishments," *National Electric Light Association Proceedings,* 86 (1929), 85.

108. "Let Correction Come from Within the Industry," *Electrical World,* 98 (Aug. 1, 1931), 189.

victims of the practice of bilking the subsidiaries for the benefit of the parent company.[109] Ferguson pointed out, by way of agreement, that it was the operating companies' bonds that had remained sound in the depression.[110]

Granted that the Power Trust was a fabrication conjured up by neo-Populist western legislators, whose constituents smarted under the colonial domination of eastern corporations, one wonders if the charges of holding-company malfeasance were simply a residue of pre-World War I trust-busting, as Martin Insull believed.[111] The evidence from government and private-utility sources indicates that the critics had a solid foundation for their grievances. Statements taken from utility executives, trade-association journals, and the FTC's inquiry documented the disadvantages of holding-company control accurately, if not dispassionately. More so than the hurried final summary report of 1935, which was heavily larded with hostile language, the commission's interim reports were reasonably complete and objective statements of some nineteen abuses requiring remedial action. The substance of the reports had indicated that the sharp practices of interstate holding companies were beyond the scope of state regulation and often had resulted in a deterioration of service at the operating level that directly affected the consumer.[112]

The investigation had almost completely shattered the private utilities' reputations for public service. To Lilienthal, Norris, and the reformers it was a godsend. Rather unwisely, responsible utility executives never accepted the findings of the commission, or even responded to criticism from within the fraternity. To outsiders it seemed that the industry was incapable of putting its own house in order. It was

109. Floyd L. Carlisle, "The Control of Public Utility Corporations," *National Electric Light Association Bulletin,* 17 (Nov. 1930), 681; and *Wall Street Journal,* Sept. 30, 1925.

110. Samuel Ferguson, "How to Remove Popular Misunderstandings of Utilities," *Electrical World,* 102 (Dec. 2, 1933), 731; see also the *New York Times,* May 18, 1934.

111. Both the utilities and their critics attributed a greater degree of unity to their opponents than, in fact, often existed. See Martin J. Insull, "Holding Companies and Their Relation to Regulation," *National Electric Light Association Bulletin,* 17 (July 1930), 420; the *New York Times,* June 25, 1931.

112. H. M. Cameron, "The Holding Company at the Crossroads," *Electrical World,* 99 (Feb. 20, 1932), 354-55. For a discussion of the "write-up" controversy, see Douglas H. Bellemore, "The Public Utility Holding Company" (Ph.D. diss., New York University, 1938), 317 ff.; and Merwin H. Waterman, who also questioned the economic and territorial advantages of diversification, in *Financial Policies of Public Utility Holding Companies* (Ann Arbor, 1936), 2 ff.

not surprising then that apologists and critics, instead of conducting a dialogue, often talked past each other.

Meanwhile, the likelihood of federal intervention on a new and unprecedented scale was enhanced in 1933-34 as the new Democratic administration under Franklin D. Roosevelt took office. Many of the utilities' most ardent critics had assumed governmental positions from which they could influence the New Deal's power policy. Secretary of the Interior Harold L. Ickes, for example, and Donald Richberg, a member of the original "Brain Trust," had been bitter foes of Insull in Chicago; Morris L. Cooke, a Bull Moose Progressive and confidant of Pinchot, was active in utility reform in Pennsylvania before and after World War I; Harry Slattery, future administrator of the REA, figured prominently in the Teapot Dome investigation; and Leland Olds had served under Governor Roosevelt as a member of the New York State Power Authority.[113] But it was Morris Cooke, in his capacity as chairman of the Mississippi Valley Committee in the Department of the Interior, who made one of the first moves, under New Deal auspices, to effect federal regulation of utility holding companies. He wrote to Judson King, in 1934, that he was seeking suggestions for utilizing the resources of the Mississippi valley in a national power policy that would promote the widest distribution of electricity at the lowest economically feasible rates. He considered federal holding-company legislation indispensable to a successful policy.[114]

Cooke elucidated his ideas, in April 1934, in a letter to Secretary Ickes.[115] He declared that electric-power generation was as fundamental to the fulfillment of New Deal promises as soil conservation or extending financial credits. Yet, there was "no adequate national power policy coordinating isolated new moves," and without this it was small wonder that certain policies seemed opportunistic, if not illogical, giving rise to criticism. "One glance at a map showing franchise territories or holding company operating areas reveals an uncoordinated maze responding but feebly to State controls and not at all to Federal control, except through the very limited authority of the FPC over hydrogenerating current," he observed. "And yet it is clear that we should now be at least paving the way for the more complete

113. For Ickes's early career as a reformer in Illinois see Harold L. Ickes, *The Autobiography of a Curmudgeon* (New York, 1943), esp. chs. 8-10; and Rexford G. Tugwell, "The Sources of New Deal Reformism," *Ethics*, 64 (July 1954), 249-76.

114. Morris L. Cooke to Judson King, Feb. 16, 1934, King Papers, box 8.

115. Cooke to Ickes, Apr. 6, 1934, NPPC Records, GCF 103, box 7.

electrification of the country and its coordination." Cooke indicated, and Ickes agreed, that the president might wish to establish a committee to analyze power policy and discuss its implications for the future growth of the nation.

The president's past words and actions, which had exhibited liberal infusions of the New Nationalism's receptivity to federal regulation and the antibigness ethos of the Sherman Antitrust Act, strengthened the belief that he would establish a national-power-policy committee.[116] Addressing an audience of 8,000 wildly cheering partisans of public power in Portland, Oregon, in 1932, Roosevelt had accused the industry of mishandling the interests of consumers and investors. He offered an eight-point plan for regulating financial and other transactions of holding and operating companies.[117] Its salient features included:

1. Publicity as to all capital issues of stocks, bonds, and other securities, liabilities and indebtedness, capital investment, and frequent information as to gross and net earnings

2. Publicity on ownership of stocks and bonds and other securities, including the stock and other interests of all officers and directors

3. Publicity with respect to all intercompany contracts and services and interchange of power

4. Regulation and control of holding companies by the Federal Power Commission and the same publicity with regard to such holding companies as provided for the operating companies

5. Cooperation of the Federal Power Commission with the public-utilities commissions of the several states, obtaining information and data pertaining to the regulation and control of such public utilities

6. Regulation and control of stocks and bonds and other securities on the principle of prudent investment only

---

116. In 1931, Roosevelt wrote of the utilities: "They have not been content with a fair return upon investment. They have sown the wind; they may reap the whirlwind." Franklin D. Roosevelt, "How Will New York's Progressive Proposals Affect the Investor?" *Public Utilities Fortnightly,* 7 (June 25, 1931), 810-12. See also the following for insights into Roosevelt's views on the power issue: Roosevelt, "The Real Meaning of the Power Problem," *Forum,* 82 (Dec. 1929), 327-32; Samuel I. Rosenman, "Governor Roosevelt's Power Program," *Nation,* 129 (Sept. 18, 1929), 302-03; and "Governor's Theories About Power," *Review of Reviews,* 88 (Dec. 1931), 32. For the influence of the New Nationalism and New Freedom philosophies on the New Deal, see Daniel G. Fusfeld, *The Economic Thought of Franklin D. Roosevelt and the Origins of the New Deal* (New York, 1956), 251-58; and Richard S. Kirkendall, "The Great Depression: Another Watershed in American History," in *Change and Continuity in Twentieth Century America,* ed. John Braeman et al. (Columbus, Ohio, 1964), 147.

117. Samuel I. Rosenman, comp., *Public Papers and Addresses of Franklin D. Roosevelt,* 13 vols. (New York, 1938-50), I, 734-40.

7. Abolishing by law the reproduction-cost theory for rate-making and establishing in place of it the actual money, prudent-investment principle as the basis for rate-making

8. Legislation making it a crime to publish or circulate false or deceptive matter relating to public utilities.

The presidential aspirant also had listed a ninth point that was of particular significance to citizens of the Pacific Northwest because it encouraged the public-power movement in that area. Frequently ignored, this point demanded retention of the title to all water-power sites by the people, and endorsed government ownership and operation of utilities, when necessary to obtain good service and fair rates. Further along in his speech Roosevelt clarified his meaning: he opposed government ownership and operation of all utilities and reaffirmed that their development should remain, with certain exceptions, a function of private initiative and capital. The fact that a community could opt for public power, he observed, "will, in most cases, guarantee good service and low rates to its population."[118]

The Portland speech was, by all accounts, the most forthright and lucid statement of policy to emanate from either presidential candidate. It encompassed the subjects most interesting to Roosevelt—corporate finance, government in business, public regulation, conservation, and the rural life. It was a milestone in the evolution of a national power policy because, viewed through the dark glass of the depression and widespread unemployment, it promised Americans no less than a "new deal" in the sphere of public-utility regulation.

The speech, however, also hinted at Roosevelt's essentially pragmatic approach to power policy. He understood perfectly well that the power to transmit electricity was crucial, because if the public developer lacked the authority to construct transmission lines, he also lacked the means for getting the energy to market. Similarly, Roosevelt encouraged the public-power movement because he needed it to build up grass-roots support for federal action.[119] He was not offering a radical blueprint for transforming the basic structure of the utility industry, or for substituting socialism for private enterprise. His resort to federal action was intended to preserve the industry from the more radical demands of others for nationalization by rendering the holding company accountable to a public agency.

118. Ibid.
119. McCraw, *TVA and the Power Fight*, 33.

CHAPTER II

The Genesis of Holding-Company Legislation

The federal government gave cogent expression to the philosophy of a managed economy when, during World War I, President Woodrow Wilson established the War Industries Board (WIB). Wilson's assistant secretary of the navy, Franklin D. Roosevelt, relied heavily on this experience in the depression-haunted thirties to meet early domestic crises.[1] The coordinated program of unemployment relief and public works, for example, continued the planning principle, and even extended it to the realm of power policy. Thus, when federal officials drafted legislation to regulate the fiduciary and operating practices of interstate holding companies, their intention was to set it in the context of a national power policy.

Government planning for a national power policy was neither innovative nor radical in the 1930s, for people had been talking about it at least since the end of the war.[2] The decision to build a federally owned and operated nitrate and power project at Muscle Shoals, Alabama, in 1916, was merely a visible and dramatic step in this direction. It culminated in the Tennessee Valley Authority (TVA) legislation of May 1933. The passage of this act indirectly facilitated the efforts of public-power enthusiasts and New Deal officials to enact holding-company legislation in 1935.[3]

The convergence of specific interests in the early depression years made feasible enactment of the TVA legislation. These included a

1. See Gerald D. Nash, "Experiments in Industrial Mobilization: WIB and NRA," *Mid-America,* 45 (July 1963), 157-74; and "The New Deal and the National Power Problem," *Congressional Digest,* 13 (Oct. 1934), 233-35.

2. See the illuminating report of Colonel Charles Keller, *The Power Situation During the War* (Washington, D.C., 1921).

3. The literature on the TVA is voluminous, and I have made no effort to treat it in detail but have attempted simply to relate its origins and early history to other

desire to develop the Tennessee River for navigation, flood control, and hydroelectric energy; the employment of the government-owned nitrate plants at Muscle Shoals and Sheffield, Alabama, for manufacturing fertilizer and munitions; and public interest in regional planning and resource development.[4] Before 1916, Congress considered and rejected every bill for the private development of the site. The first reason was political: the applications of the privately owned power companies coincided with the maturation of the Progressive reform movement, a by-product of which was the conservation of natural resources for public use. The second factor was economic: the cost of private development of the site was prohibitive, and, unfortunately, few utility men had the vision to foresee the growth of long-distance power transmission or the development of the electrochemical industry.[5]

The outbreak of war in Europe in the summer of 1914, however, stirred new interest in the Shoals project because of its potential for electrochemical nitrate synthesis. Congress enacted, on June 3, 1916, the National Defense Act, which empowered the government to harness the river's energy for nitrate and fertilizer production.[6] At the

---

aspects of the New Deal's power program. For representative studies see Charles H. Pritchett, *The Tennessee Valley Authority: A Study in Public Administration* (Chapel Hill, N.C., 1943); David E. Lilienthal, *TVA: Democracy on the March* (New York, 1944); Roscoe C. Martin, *TVA: The First Twenty Years; a Staff Report* (Tuscaloosa, Ala., 1956); Gordon R. Clapp, *The TVA: An Approach to the Development of a Region* (Chicago, 1955); Philip Selznick, *TVA and the Grass Roots: A Study in the Sociology of Formal Organization* (New York, 1949); and Wilmon H. Droze, *High Dams and Slack Waters: TVA Rebuilds a River* (Baton Rouge, La., 1965). There are also biographies in progress of each of the original three members of the TVA's board of directors. Professor Robert A. Lively of Princeton University is writing on Lilienthal's career; Roy A. Talbot of Vanderbilt University is doing a doctoral dissertation on Arthur Morgan; and Elizabeth L. MacMahan of the University of North Carolina is planning a dissertation on the career of Harcourt A. Morgan.

4. For the development of interest in the Muscle Shoals site in the latter nineteenth and early twentieth centuries, see Judson King, "A Brief Chronology of Muscle Shoals Legislation," n.d., in Judson King Papers, box 80, Library of Congress (hereafter cited as King Papers); Sarah E. Winger, "The Genesis of TVA" (Ph.D. diss., University of Wisconsin, 1959), chs. 1-3; and Samuel P. Hays, *Conservation and the Gospel of Efficiency* (Cambridge, Mass., 1959), esp. ch. 13.

5. Norman E. Wengert, "Antecedents of TVA: The Legislative History of Muscle Shoals," *Agricultural History*, 26 (Oct. 1952), 141-42. Samuel Insull of Middle West Utilities and Grover Neff of the Wisconsin Power and Light Company were exceptions. They were experimenting with rural electrification long before it became fashionable.

6. The government needed an independent and reliable source of nitrates for munitions to complement its plants in West Virginia and Tennessee. Southern congressmen, particularly "Cotton Ed" Smith, saw the possibilities of using the nitrates for cheap fertilizer to aid southern agriculture. Smith, of South Carolina, authored section 124 of the National Defense Act, which provided for the public ownership and operation of the nitrate

war's end, Wilson Dam, astride the Tennessee River, was well advanced in construction, although by no means finished. During the next decade, the question of whether to surrender the incompleted project to private entrepreneurs or to have the government complete it disrupted nearly every session of Congress.[7] Senator Norris, for example, wanted a federal agency, preferably the FPC, to coordinate the development of all power sites within the watershed into a regional grid, until such time as Congress authorized construction of a national public-power system comparable to England's. Unfortunately, he could not persuade the Republican administrations of the 1920s to pursue a policy that seemed socialistic to them.[8]

Meanwhile, Henry Ford, the automobile manufacturer, offered to purchase the unfinished project in 1921 for private development. Sensing that acquisition by Ford would eliminate the possibility of a multipurpose, public development of the Tennessee watershed, Norris spearheaded the successful fight to block the sale.[9] And, because of his approach to water-power development, his fundamental humanitarianism, and his belief in progress, Norris soon entered into a loose association with professional planners whose scope had broadened from city to metropolitan and regional planning, from mere civic adornment to social and economic purposes.[10] The reason was obvious;

---

facilities. See U.S. Congress, *Congressional Record*, 64th Cong., 1st sess., 53 (Mar. 10, 1916), 3882; (Mar. 30, 1916), 5137; (June 3, 1916), 9231, passim.; and *United States Statutes at Large*, 64th Cong., 1st sess., 39, pt. I, ch. 134, sec. 124, 1916.

7. *Congressional Record*, 66th Cong., 3rd sess., 60 (Mar. 3, 1921), 4430; and Alfred Lief, *Democracy's Norris* (New York, 1939), 252.

8. The *New York Times*, Jan. 17, 1924; and Preston J. Hubbard, *Origins of the TVA* (Nashville, 1961), 114-23.

9. George W. Norris, *Fighting Liberal: The Autobiography of George W. Norris* (New York, 1945), 249-59; John D. Hicks, *Republican Ascendancy, 1921-1933* (New York, 1960), 62-63. The fundamental reason why no one obtained the Shoals in the 1920s, apart from Norris's dogged opposition, was that none of the offers from private interests satisfied Congress. Also, southern farm leaders voted against legislation that failed to guarantee cheap fertilizer. Private-power interests fought the chemical industry for control of the site, while, together with their Wall Street affiliates, both attacked Ford's offer. See Wengert, "Antecedents of TVA," 145 ff.

10. Most planners in this period were disciples of the Scottish biologist Patrick Geddes, who lectured in the United States in 1923. In his widely influential book, *Cities in Evolution,* Geddes propounded the doctrine of a regional unity of "place, work, and folk in environment, function, and organism." The members of the Regional Planning Association of America, among whom were Lewis Mumford, Clarence Stein, Benton MacKaye, and Frederick L. Ackerman, synthesized his ideas to promote public control over urban form and land use. From this the next step was to apply Geddes's ideas to regional-resource planning in the Tennessee valley. For an elaboration of this point see Patrick Geddes, *Cities in Evolution* (London, 1915), 198 ff.; Johnny B. Smallwood, "George W. Norris and the Concept of a Planned Region" (Ph.D. diss., University

regional planners of the quality of Benton MacKaye perceived in the development of cheap electricity a talisman for revitalizing rural America. Joseph K. Hart, for example, wrote in 1924 that "giant power, under public control, with power distributed to all on equal terms, offers economic freedom to humanity, the hope of communities within which intellectual freedom can be realized and the culture of the spirit will be possible."[11]

The first significant progress in the drive to develop the Tennessee River under public auspices occurred in 1928, when Congress authorized the construction of Boulder Dam on the lower Colorado River. True, the decision to proceed was sandwiched between two presidential vetoes of TVA bills, but it did initiate a distinctly more favorable political climate for federal-resource development.[12] Shortly thereafter, the Army Corps of Engineers strongly endorsed the concept of coordinated water usage of the Tennessee River. In 1930 the chief engineer of the Reclamation Service under Theodore Roosevelt, Frederick H. Newell, writing a new preface to Charles Van Hise's *Conservation of Natural Resources,* observed that the remedy for water-usage disputes lay in "wise and comprehensive state-and-nation-wide planning with full consideration of all possible future needs such as have been undertaken in city planning." Frederic A. Delano, chairman of the National Resources Production Department of the highly influential Chamber of Commerce, reported that "proper coordination of the development and operation of the major sites in this watershed is essential to the full use of the waterpower possibilities at Muscle Shoals."[13]

The intervention of the depression and the presidential election of Franklin D. Roosevelt, in 1932, soon gave Norris and regional planners

---

of North Carolina, 1963), 197-200 ff.; and Roy Lubove, *Community Planning in the 1920's: The Contribution of the Regional Planning Association of America* (Pittsburgh, 1963), ch. 6.

11. Joseph K. Hart, "Power and Culture," *The Survey,* 51 (Mar. 1, 1924), 627-28; see also for the impact of planning Frederic A. Delano, "Regional Planning Next!" *National Municipal Review,* 13 (Mar. 1924), 144-45; and Henry Vincent Hubbard, "Planning the City and the Region—Then and Now," *The American City,* 43 (Sept. 1930), 99-100.

12. Coolidge, by pocket veto, defeated Norris's TVA bill in 1928; the following year, Hoover vetoed similar legislation in a message that was a ringing defense of private enterprise. See Norris, *Autobiography,* 267 ff.

13. See Hubbard, *Origins of TVA,* 275-76; Smallwood, "Norris and the Concept of a Planned Region," 325; and U.S. Chamber of Commerce, *Muscle Shoals, a Groundwork of Fact: Special Report of the National Water Power Policies Committee* (Washington, D.C., 1930), 15, 25-26. Delano's committee also called for "proper coordination and comprehensive planning for flood control, navigation, and power development in the Tennessee Valley."

a unique opportunity to test their ideas. During the campaign, Roosevelt had signaled his acceptance of the tactics of regional planning to create a more favorable environment conducive to human development.[14] And at Portland he championed public-power projects both to facilitate the broadest consumption of power and to serve as yardsticks for electric rates. Optimistic that he would champion public power, Norris, Hiram Johnson, Burton Wheeler, and the National Progressive League stumped the country for his election. The president-elect formally pledged himself to Norris's proposal for multipurpose development of the Tennessee valley on January 21, 1933, before an audience in Montgomery, Alabama.[15] Judson King afterward observed that this decision established precedents, far more important than any previous action, for the regulation and utilization of water resources and regional planning.[16]

In some respects, however, Roosevelt's approach to the problems of the Tennessee valley rested upon more generalized principles of planning, whereas Norris's attitudes had reflected more narrowly a concern for power and water-resource development.[17] In his message requesting TVA legislation, the president stated on April 10, 1933: "It is clear that the Muscle Shoals development is but a small part of the potential public usefulness of the entire Tennessee River. Such use, if envisioned in its entirety, transcends mere power development." Therefore, he asked the Congress to establish a corporation cloaked with the power of government, but possessed of the flexibility and initiative of private enterprise to undertake "the broadest duty of planning for the proper uses, conservation and development of the natural resources of the Tennessee River drainage basin and its adjacent terri-

14. Franklin D. Roosevelt, "Growing Up by Planning," *The Survey*, 68 (Feb. 1, 1932), 483 ff. Roosevelt specifically endorsed the concept of regional planning in a 1931 conference attended by Lewis Mumford of the Regional Planning Association of America. See Charles S. Ascher, ed., "University of Virginia Regional Roundtable," *City Planning*, 7 (Oct. 1931), 262.

15. The speech is reprinted in Edgar B. Nixon, comp., *Franklin D. Roosevelt and Conservation*, 2 vols. (Washington, D.C., 1957), I, 133. A few months earlier, Roosevelt discussed, at a Warm Springs press conference, a plan for a gigantic experiment—a planned economy in the area—to relieve unemployment, restore forests, halt flood damage, bring cheap power to the farm, decentralize industry, and move families from submarginal lands to reclaimed river bottoms. He clearly believed that the Tennessee River was a national rather than a local problem and should be approached in national terms. See Samuel I. Rosenman, comp., *Public Papers and Addresses of Franklin D. Roosevelt*, 13 vols. (New York, 1938-50), III, 466.

16. Judson King, *The Conservation Fight* (Washington, D.C., 1959), ch. 22.

17. Norris's own ideas underwent change between 1916 and 1933. He attended a Public Super-Power Conference in January 1924 under the auspices of public-ownership groups that wanted the federal government to operate the Shoals as part of a national

tory for the general social and economic welfare of the nation."[18]

The president appointed Dr. Arthur E. Morgan, president of Antioch College, first director of the TVA board and gave him a free hand to select his colleagues. Morgan brought to the project a righteous, moralistic sense of high mission and an unequivocal conviction that man could remake his environment in a rational mould.[19] He insisted that the TVA was "not primarily a dam-building program, a fertilizer job or power transmission job" but a vast blueprint for "a designed and planned social and economic order." If the United States succeeded in transforming the Tennessee watershed, Roosevelt declared, "we can march on, step by step, in a like development of other great natural territorial units within our borders." For the private utilities such a prospect was disconcerting to say the least, and gave more than transient significance to the success or failure of the TVA.[20]

In retrospect, the TVA program turned out to be planning in a moderate, limited, and piecemeal fashion. It did not evolve into the national experiment (or even the "yardstick") that Morgan and the public-power enthusiasts had hoped; nor did it interfere with the fundamental character of an economy based upon private enterprise and corporate profit. Neither did it culminate in any fundamental redistribu-

---

public-power system. From this experience he began to see the possibilities inherent in having a government agency coordinate the development of all potential power units within a single watershed. The example of Ontario's state-operated power system convinced him that it was possible to construct a regional power grid as a first step in the creation of a national power grid. From this early emphasis upon power production, Norris moved gradually toward regional planning without ever embracing the rigidly doctrinaire principles espoused by Socialists, Marxists, or even professional planners. It is clear, however, that Roosevelt, in 1931, was more receptive to comprehensive resource planning, whereas Norris's primary interest was, and remained, power production. See Smallwood, "Norris and the Concept of a Planned Region," 200 ff.; and the *New York Times,* Jan. 17, 1924. For an illuminating analysis of Ontario's public-power system, whose success strongly influenced American public-power enthusiasts, see Sir Adam Beck, "Ontario's Experience," *The Survey,* 51 (Mar. 1, 1924), 585-90, 650-51.

18. *Congressional Record,* 73rd Cong., 1st sess., 77 (Apr. 10, 1933), 1423. For a discussion of the early emphasis upon regional planning see Bruce Netschert, "Electric Power and Economic Development," in *The Economic Impact of TVA,* ed. John R. Moore (Knoxville, Tenn., 1967), 7; and Howard Mehinick and Lawrence L. Durisch, "Tennessee Valley Authority: Planning in Operation," *Town Planning Review,* 24 (July 1953), 116-45.

19. Morgan, who described the region as "a [great] laboratory," selected David E. Lilienthal and Dr. Harcourt A. Morgan, president of the University of Tennessee, to make up the original TVA board. See Arthur E. Morgan, "Planning in the Tennessee Valley," *Current History,* 38 (Sept. 1933), 665-66.

20. Arthur E. Morgan, "Bench-Marks in the Tennessee Valley," *Survey Graphic,* 23 (Jan. 1924), 43; and *Congressional Record,* 73rd Cong., 1st sess., 77, pt. 2 (Apr. 10, 1933), 1423.

tion of wealth in the nation, as radical planners advocated. It did elevate the economic and social standards of the inhabitants of the Tennessee valley—no mean feat. But even this success, undeniably important as it was, needs qualification; for the absence of adequate financial resources, congressional hostility, and the indifference of one of TVA's first directors, David E. Lilienthal, to comprehensive planning set parameters to the experiment. As early as 1935, the TVA was concentrating upon only two aspects of the national power program: the increased production and transmission of electricity from public- and private-generating facilities and the lowering of rates to promote greater consumption. The failure to move beyond these two points was the crux of the feud between Lilienthal and Morgan.[21]

But who could know this in 1933? Roosevelt, prior to the conclusion of his TVA message, declared that "this power development of war days leads logically to national planning." He employed the metaphor of war and depression again the following year when, upon the recommendation of federal officials, he established the National Power Policy Committee (NPPC).[22] Henry T. Hunt, general counsel of the Public Works Administration (PWA), authored the presidential letter creating the committee. The document, which Roosevelt signed on July 29, 1934, reflected the New Nationalism and TVA commitment to planning, but also the determination of the Interior Department to retain paramount influence in formulating a national power policy.[23] The committee, whose composition included the eight federal agencies most concerned with power matters, was intended to serve not merely as a fact-finding body, but rather as "one for the development and unification of national power policy." Its function was to develop legislation

---

21. Thomas K. McCraw's fine study, "Morgan v. Lilienthal: The Feud Within TVA" (Master's thesis, University of Wisconsin, 1967) demonstrates this point clearly. See also, David E. Lilienthal, *TVA: Democracy on the March* (New York, 1944), 206-13.

22. Rosenman, *Public Papers of FDR*, 2, 122-23; and Harold L. Ickes, *The Secret Diary of Harold L. Ickes: The First Thousand Days*, 3 vols. (New York, 1953-54), 1, 174-75. See also William E. Leuchtenburg, "The New Deal and the Analogue of War," in *Change and Continuity in Twentieth Century America*, ed. John Braeman et al. (Columbus, Ohio, 1964), 81-144.

23. See Henry T. Hunt's draft letter to Ickes, May [?] 1934, and Ickes to Roosevelt, June 29, 1934, National Archives, Record Group 48, Records of the National Power Policy Committee, General Classified File 103, box 1 (hereafter cited as NPPC Records, GCF). The PWA, established in June 1933 under Title II of the National Industrial Recovery Act, was a hothouse for the policies of collective action and national planning. Ickes, Delano, and Charles E. Merriam, its leading figures, had been foes of Insull. See "Purposes and Policies of Public Works Administration," *Monthly Labor Review*, 37 (Oct. 1933), 797-800, and Barry D. Karl, *Executive Reorganization and Reform in the New Deal* (Cambridge, Mass., 1963).

for the closer cooperation "of the several factors in our electrical power supply—both public and private—whereby national policy in power matters may be unified and electricity be made more broadly available at cheaper rates to industry, to domestic, and particularly to agricultural consumers."[24] If the planning of a national power policy became the central task of the committee, federal holding-company legislation emerged as the keystone of that policy.

Unhappily, the committee did not prove commensurate to its broader mandate. The president, as was his habit, never clearly defined the scope or limit of its authority vis-à-vis lesser governmental bureaus drafting their own power legislation; nor did he demonstrate a sustained public or private interest in the committee's work, after Congress enacted the federal holding-company bill in 1935. The reason for the committee's weakness lies in the fact that it was only an advisory body; it had no independent existence in statutory law or constituency, but was subject to dissolution at the will of the chief executive. Its effectiveness flowed and ebbed with Roosevelt's own interest.[25]

The idea of a centralized power-planning body, with the opportunities it might afford to relieve the unemployment crisis, undoubtedly appealed to the president's sense of the dramatic. But it also fired the politically explosive problem of where to draw the line between federal and state jurisdiction. The *Birmingham* (Alabama) *News* recognized this as soon as the administration disclosed to the press the committee's existence. Somewhat surprisingly, however, the *News* editorial of July 17 interpreted the announcement as reaffirmation of state regulation. Other papers were less sanguine. The trade journal, *Electric Light and Power,* reflected the attitude of a strong segment of the utility industry; it approached the news with an equal mixture of ignorance, contempt, and caution. For example, one of its reporters, Harper Leach, sneered that New Deal committees sprang up "like toadstools after a rain" and noted that the NPPC contained "the usual patter of amateurs, endowed social workers and political bureaucrats in discussing power." Its composition in a modern industrial society was "equivalent to applying a committee of tallow candlemakers and mule-breeders to work out a policy to provide light and power for the United

---

24. Henry T. Hunt to Ickes, May [?] 1934, NPPC Records, GCF 103, box 1. Hunt originally proposed a committee of fifteen comprised of people from a broader range of occupations, but McNinch persuaded Ickes to reduce it to a body of eight federal officers whose agencies were immediately concerned with power policy.

25. It might be noted also that the president expected the NPPC to meet only infrequently.

States," he concluded. Beneath this braggadocio, Leach noted that the industry was nervously awaiting the government's next move.[26]

Meanwhile, the initial gathering of NPPC members occurred on July 18, 1934, in the office of Secretary Ickes. The agenda focused upon organizational matters, particularly the question of which subcommittees to establish for the purpose of drafting legislation, and also upon recent activities in the holding-company field. Ickes, as chairman, led the discussion and, midway through the conference, the members arrived at a decision. Dr. Elwood Mead of the Bureau of Reclamation would handle the politically delicate problem of state and federal relations; David Lilienthal of the TVA would take on the task of effecting an adequate supply of power, from public and private sources, to meet the nation's future demands; Thomas W. Norcross, Assistant Forester, and Morris L. Cooke of the Mississippi Valley Committee would tackle the rural-electrification program; while General Edward M. Markham, head of the Army Engineers and the most cautious member of the committee, investigated hydroelectric power, flood control, and power supply as related to national-defense requirements. Frank McNinch, an FPC commissioner, would continue his agency's studies of the electric-rate structure and the feasibility of constructing a national power grid. The committee appointed Judge Robert Healy, who had gone from the FTC to the Securities and Exchange Commission (SEC), to shoulder the burden of holding-company malpractices.[27]

The conferees devoted the remainder of the meeting to a discussion of the holding-company problem. Basil Manly, the FPC vice-chairman attending in lieu of McNinch, announced that the FPC had not advanced very far in its inquiry, "except in preliminary work." Unaware that the commission was contemplating holding-company legislation, Healy asked, somewhat incredulously, whether it was working "on the same subject as the Trade Commission is." Manly acknowledged that it was and, recalling the substance of a previous conference with

26. "Raising an Issue of Fundamental Importance," *Birmingham News*, July 17, 1934, reprinted in Francis X. Welch, "Can State Commissions Regulate Federal Utilities?" *Public Utilities Fortnightly*, 14 (Aug. 16, 1934), 224; and Harper Leech, "Except Men Who Know About Power Development," *Electric Light and Power*, 12 (Aug. 1934), n.p., clipping in Morris L. Cooke Papers, box 275, Franklin D. Roosevelt Library (hereafter cited as Cooke Papers).

27. Samuel Ferguson, an FTC commissioner, had persuaded Ickes to include Healy on the committee, because of the latter's familiarity with the holding-company problem and to give representation to the SEC. "Minutes of a Meeting of the National Power Policy Committee," July 18, 1934; Hunt to Ickes, June 14, 1934; Ickes to members of the NPPC, July 18, 1934, in NPPC Records, GCF 103, boxes 10, 1, 8.

Roosevelt, declared: "I think what the President had in mind was that both agencies should work independently with the idea that after we moved along a certain distance we could get together and iron the thing out."[28] Ickes, in defense of the president, interjected that this procedure would spare the committee the necessity of undertaking an extended investigation. "We could take the findings of these two boards," he stated. Healy, clearly disconcerted by what he considered to be inefficient utilization of government agencies, was about to criticize this procedure, when Ickes again interrupted. He stated flatly that the committee would take their findings and use them as the basis of its work.[29]

If anything of importance came out of this conference, it was the fact that the administration was, for the first time, seriously contemplating holding-company regulation as part of a broader power policy. Roosevelt appreciated the possibilities, more than the pitfalls, in encouraging three independent bodies to work on identical legislation. He expected them, at some undefined point, to coordinate and integrate their recommendations. The strategem was typically Rooseveltian and was employed frequently in drafting controversial legislation. When it succeeded, as it did in this particular instance, it was highly effective; although even in the drafting stage of the holding-company bill, it caused some confusion. To the outsider, however, the practice confirmed his suspicion that anarchy was rife in the New Deal's bureaucracy.[30]

28. The FPC's legal staff was approaching the holding-company problem, in 1934, from three fronts: Hugh L. Elsbree attempted to establish the fact that there were interstate, regional, and national aspects of holding-company activity which put the companies within the range of the Interstate Commerce Commission's power; Ambrose Doskow tried to show how Congress might share its commerce power for the purpose of regulation with joint boards composed of FPC and state authorities; and J. F. Lawson argued that holding companies, because they functioned as investment companies, might be brought within the purview of the national banking laws. See Hugh L. Elsbree, "Tentative Proposals for Federal Control," Oct. 19, 1934; Ambrose Doskow, "Outline of Subjects to Be Covered in Considering Holding Company Regulation," Oct. 17, 1934; J. F. Lawson, "Federal Control Over Holding Companies in the Electric Utility Industry," Oct. 16, 1934, in Federal Power Commission Records, General File, 21-31-1, part I (hereafter cited as FPC Records, GF). The records are in the possession of the commission in Washington, D.C.

29. "Minutes of a Meeting of the National Power Policy Committee," July 18, 1934, NPPC Records, GCF 103, box 10.

30. In a confidential letter to the editor of *Today* magazine in October 1934, Judson King alluded to a recent dinner conversation with FPC Commissioner McNinch. Their discussion "developed the fact, which I know to be true, that there is a good deal of confusion even in the minds of the Administration men to say nothing of the country over the relation of the various agencies and surveys the President has set up in pursuance of his power policy." King concluded that, if the president would only clarify his policy,

The committee, meanwhile, convened once again in August to hammer out the remaining procedural matters. McNinch and Healy feared that its legislative proposals would carry little weight, if each subcommittee recruited outside personnel. They reasoned that the president was more inclined to accept the unanimous advice of his own men. Cooke, therefore, moved that each subcommittee should consist of the chairman plus one or more members of the whole committee who would be authorized to consult with outside experts. The net effect of his motion, as it developed later, was to bind the members of the NPPC to support the recommendations of the subcommittee.[31]

Since procedural matters were under discussion, Healy requested the committee to authorize the services of Benjamin V. Cohen as his legal counsel. He did not know whether he was available but observed: "I have great respect for the ability of Ben Cohen drafting bills that will stand the test." Morris Cooke, in the interim, had already laid before Cohen "some literature that may intrigue him," and had asked Felix Frankfurter of Harvard and Judge Julian Mack to persuade him to accept the assignment. Flushed with excitement, Healy interjected: "Don't let Cohen get away from you. There may be other plans for him, I know, but I think he will be more intrigued by this than anything." Although Cohen was assigned to the PWA, Ickes stated that he would detach him temporarily to the committee, for he was anxious to produce a holding-company bill in time for the January session of Congress.[32]

A Harvard law graduate, Cohen had imbibed the Brandeisian-New Freedom philosophy from Professor Frankfurter.[33] The *Weltanschauung* of this ideology, in many respects, ran counter to the national-planning tradition because it proposed to atomize large economic agglomerates in order to restore competition.[34] Brandeis had written, in 1913, that those who managed other peoples' money were trustees acting for others, and Cohen included this caveat in the securities legislation of 1933-34. He employed the same legal aphorism again

"it would dissipate the charge going round that there is confusion, duplication of effort and financial waste" (King to W. P. Beazall, Oct. 10, 1934, King Papers, box 9).

31. "Minutes of a Meeting of the National Power Policy Committee," Aug. 29, 1934, NPPC Records, GCF 103, box 10.

32. Ibid.

33. For Cohen's background see "Portrait," *Review of Reviews,* 92 (May 1935), 15; "Necks In: Irishman and Jew Keep Quiet Behind Today's Rooseveltian Brain Trust," *Literary Digest,* 123 (May 22, 1937), 7-8; and "Twins: New Deal's Legislative Architects," *Newsweek,* 6 (July 13, 1935), 24-25.

34. See James J. Hannah, "Urban Reaction to the Great Depression" (Ph.D. diss., University of California, 1956), esp. 229-57.

in drafting the holding-company bill. Thus, in a real sense, the Public Utility Holding Company Act of 1935 rounded out the earlier financial legislation.[35]

The initial step in drafting a federal holding-company bill was to pinpoint precisely the gaps in existing law. Early in September 1934, Dr. Mead canvassed the state commissions for recommendations. He was eager to allay their fears of federal encroachment, and noted that the president had drawn the committee's attention specifically to the need for active cooperation with the states. The NPPC intended "not only to recognize and respect very fully the rights and prerogatives of the States but to cooperate with them." Before closing, Mead asked the commissioners for suggestions "as to how the Federal authority may cooperate with your state not only in bringing about more effective regulation but supplementing your own authority in ways in which you think will be helpful." The responses, unfortunately, were discouraging. Of thirty-six states responding to his questionnaire, twenty-seven reluctantly agreed to cooperate but offered no firm suggestions. Arkansas, Delaware, Georgia, Louisiana, Montana, New Jersey, North Carolina, Rhode Island, Tennessee, Texas, Virginia, and West Virginia—where holding-company control was strongest—did not bother to reply.[36]

Cohen, meanwhile, had joined the committee and was actively seeking a preliminary impression of the type of regulation the industry believed desirable. He conferred with H. V. Cooke, an official who played down the need for federal regulation. Cooke acknowledged that the companies would welcome "any *suggestions* for a simplification of the corporate structure which allows the retention of at least one holding company as a form of combination," but viewed dimly any direct order. If the federal government had to interfere, he preferred that it establish a counterpart agency to the Interstate Commerce Commission to regulate new security issues.[37] O. C. Merrill, a former

35. See Louis D. Brandeis, *Other People's Money and How the Bankers Use It* (New York, 1913). There is no evidence that Cohen actively promoted the integration of the nation's power facilities, although he wrote much of the legislation that would have provided the base for a national power grid.

36. The commissioners, judging from the reply of Riley E. Elgen of the District of Columbia, really wanted the federal government to function solely in a fact-finding capacity, using its authority to uncover illicit holding-company practices which would be reported to the state commissions for action. See Elwood Mead to Cooke, Sept. 11, 1934, Cooke Papers, box 275; Mead to State Utility Commissioners, Sept. 17, 1934, and "Summary of the Replies of the State Commissioners," Dec. 15, 1934, in NPPC Records, GCF 103, box 4.

37. Cohen noted Cooke's ambivalence toward federal action throughout the meeting.

FPC commissioner and head of the American section of the World Power Conference, was far more critical of the highly integrated and centralized holding company as exemplified by Electric Bond and Share. He considered it not only less responsive to technological innovation but also "the source of greater evils arising from inter-company financial transactions, and particularly service charge contracts." Merrill prescribed control of securities, uniform accounting practices, publicity for service charges, and separation of bankers from control of holding companies, "although it would not altogether take the holding companies out of the banking field." But, he concluded, the only truly effective reform would come as the result of "economic expansion and pressure afforded by governmental projects" such as the TVA.[38]

Cohen believed that if these early talks were indicative, he would evidently encounter a diversity of opinions, especially on the basic need for federal legislation. But even among the staunchest advocates of state regulation there seemed to be an ambivalence. They trumpeted, at first, the efficacy of state control but conceded, in the end, that federal action might be necessary in specific areas. Judge Healy, meanwhile, was eager to cast a wider net. He wrote to Cohen that the NPPC should invite the Edison Electric Institute to confer with his subcommittee. The latter apparently had misgivings because he showed the letter to Morris Cooke. Cooke was of the opinion that the committee should approach the Institute, but only after dissident members had an opportunity to speak with Cohen. He warned Healy not to expect too much from the institute because its advice was likely to be of 1890 vintage. "I need not tell you that individual opinions in this industry are held at a discount, especially when they are tendered to government—state or Federal," he added. "The effort has been made to have the industry speak as with one voice."[39] Upon further reflection, he informed Cohen that the subcommittee should not discuss the problem with the Edison Institute for the present, but to confine its canvass to a selected group of the best minds in the business.[40]

Cooke's argument was persuasive, because shortly thereafter Cohen asked him to draw up a list of utility executives, bankers, business

---

"Memorandum of a Conference Between H. V. Cooke and B. V. Cohen," Sept. 20, 1934, in NPPC Records, GCF 103, box 13.

38. "Memorandum of a Conference Between O. C. Merrill and B. V. Cohen," Sept. 27, 1934, in ibid. Merrill had been dissatisfied with the FPC's ineffectiveness under President Hoover and had resigned in 1930.

39. Cooke to Healy, Sept. 27, 1934, in NPPC Records, Cohen Office File, box 10.

40. See Cohen's letter to Healy, Sept. 27, 1934, in NPPC Records, GCF 103, box 17.

leaders, and academicians with whom the subcommittee might consult. By the first of October, Cooke listed the names of Willkie, Ferguson, James Lee Loomis, Harold Stanley, and Adolph A. Berle, Jr., among others. These men had, in one manner or another, exhibited "their interest in such matters as regulation for the benefit of the investor in public utility securities, the establishing of lower rates as a means for increasing consumption and lower costs of electricity and similar steps."[41] The subcommittee's next step was to draft a letter to these men inviting them to confer with Cohen or Healy on the holding-company problem. They were encouraged especially to offer suggestions for legislation.[42]

Throughout the fall of 1934 Cohen commuted back and forth between Washington, D. C., and New York City culling utility executives' opinions. The pattern of the meetings was set in the first conference, on October 5, 1934, with C. F. Groesbeck, the chairman of the board of Electric Bond and Share. Cohen intended to initiate a freewheeling discussion of the industry's problems, the merits of the holding-company form, as well as the fiscal and managerial hardships it worked on operating companies and the public. He wished, above all, to break "the deadlock of distrust that threatened the healthy growth of the utility industry."[43] The meeting, unfortunately, was not productive, he wrote afterward, because Groesbeck "tended on the whole merely to discuss problems that I presented and kept his own suggestions, if he had any, pretty much to himself." During the course of the interview, however, Cohen detected the ambivalence toward federal regulation that he had seen in H. V. Cooke and, to a lesser degree, in Merrill. Groesbeck had agreed, initially, that the federal government should require uniform accounting practices, but then demurred, rather vigorously, on the grounds that the government would thereby attain "an entering wedge by [its] control of accounts."[44]

This emotional and highly ambivalent antipathy toward federal intervention manifested itself in discussions with other utility officials. Alex

41. Ibid. Loomis was president of the Connecticut Mutual Life Insurance Company; Stanley, a senior partner in the banking firm of Morgan, Stanley & Co.; and Berle, professor of law at Columbia University.
42. See, for example, Morris Cooke to Harold Stanley, Oct. 3, 1934, Cooke Papers, box 275.
43. "Memorandum of a Conference with C. F. Groesbeck," Oct. 5, 1934, NPPC Records, GCF 103, box 13.
44. Ibid. Louis H. Egan of Union Electric Light and Power Company of St. Louis remarked, later that afternoon, that Groesbeck "did not like the idea of revolutionizing the practices of the industry" (see "Memorandum of a Conference with Louis H. Egan," Oct. 5, 1934, in ibid.).

Dow of Detroit Edison advocated a federal policy of laissez faire, declaring that holding companies would become self-regulatory in the natural course of the economic cycle. If they did not, then "existing state laws concerning operating companies would, if properly administered, effectively take care of the situation." Samuel Ferguson, Louis Egan, president of Union Electric Light and Power of St. Louis, and James Lee Loomis, the head of Connecticut Mutual Life Insurance, agreed. They condemned holding-company abuses and defended the soundness of operating companies and their bonds, but each man feared also that federal interference would circumscribe private enterprise and discourage future expansion.[45] After taking this strong stance in behalf of state regulation, they outlined the practices of holding companies which required regulation. These included enforcing uniform accounting practices, putting managerial and service contracts on a cost basis, regulating new security issues, and effecting greater economies. James F. Fogarty of the North American Company declared that the holding companies should be made to pursue the policies of the better companies, "such as North American, which was to acquire properties only at prices upon which the properties quite readily could yield a fair return, properties which formed an economically strong unit in themselves or which rounded out properties already owned."[46]

However, obliquely, utility officials conceded that the reforms they desired could be accomplished only on a national basis and then through federal regulation. For the holding company had assumed the dimensions first of a regional and then of a national problem. State-commission regulation was demonstrably inadequate to cope with interstate holding companies. Fogarty, for example, ten days after his initial meeting with Cohen, stated that a federal agency should "qualify" the securities of these companies.[47] Ferguson and Loomis wanted the Roosevelt administration to "clarify" for the public the difference between unsound holding-company securities and the safe bonds of operating companies. Egan and others wanted uniform accounting practices, but conceded that there was no way, short of a federal requirement, to obtain it.[48] Demanding the benefits of a federal regulation, they could not

---

45. Operating-company executives were particularly bitter at the attempts of holding companies such as Niagara-Hudson and Commonwealth and Southern to force them into larger systems or to deprive them of local management. See "Memorandum of a Conference with Alex Dow, Judge Healy, and B. V. Cohen," Oct. 12, 1934, and "Memorandum of a Conference with James Lee Loomis," Oct. 9, 1934, in ibid.

46. "Memorandum of a Conference with James F. Fogarty," Oct. 8, 1934, in ibid.

47. "Memorandum of a Conference with James F. Fogarty," Oct. 18, 1934, in ibid.

48. Groesbeck had suggested that the New York Stock Exchange should enforce

bring themselves psychologically to accept governmental intervention.

Wendell Willkie of Commonwealth and Southern went as far in the direction of accommodating federal regulation as was politically feasible. He indicated, during a conversation with Cohen, that he could live with a system of federal incorporation of holding companies, SEC regulation of their securities, and the restriction of new issues to common stocks. But he warned against making reforms by legislative fiat because any abrupt action would injure innocent investors and curtail future growth.[49] Willkie, quite frankly, was worried about the future prospects of the private-utility industry in the United States, and hoped that these concessions would ward off more drastic federal action.[50] There was also a certain pragmatism in his willingness to accommodate the NPPC, for Commonwealth and Southern had already taken steps to mitigate the problems he identified.[51] Nonetheless, the question which gnawed in the minds of Cohen, Healy, and Oswald Ryan, general counsel of the FPC, was the extent to which Willkie represented the industry's thinking. They were not wholly satisfied that he did.[52]

---

uniform accounting practices but, in view of the recent investigation into stock market manipulations, Cohen declared that this was not "acceptable practically or politically." See "Memorandum of a Conference with C. F. Groesbeck," Oct. 5, 1934, in ibid. (for the stock exchange investigation see Ferdinand Pecora, *Wall Street Under Oath* [New York, 1939]).

49. Willkie also suggested that the federal government abolish intermediate holding companies; eliminate the gamut of preferred stocks, bonds, and warrants; put contracts on a cost basis; segregate electric and gas holdings; and confine holding-company investment to an investment trust. "Memorandum of a Conference with Wendell L. Willkie," Oct. 19, 1934, in ibid.

50. Soon after he learned that the administration was contemplating legislation, Willkie contacted the FPC to discuss a *modus vivendi* whereby the industry could cooperate with the government. Their past relations were unimportant, he declared, but the "uncertainty as to what might happen in the future was their greatest problem." Willkie indicated that, if the industry's leaders had a clearer understanding of the government's policy, "they were prepared to cooperate if at all possible" (see McNinch to Roosevelt, Jan. 23, 1935, Franklin D. Roosevelt Papers, Office File 235. Franklin D. Roosevelt Library [hereafter cited as Roosevelt Papers, OF]). H. Hobart Porter of American Water Works and Electric Company and Joseph P. Tumulty expressed nearly identical sentiments and urged their colleagues to cooperate. See Porter to Tumulty, Oct. 30, 1934; Tumulty to Porter, Nov. 21, 1934, in National Archives, Record Group 46, "Senate Special Committee to Investigate Lobbying Activities," Case Files, box 98.

51. John Sherman Porter, editor of *Moody's Manual of Investments: Public Utility Securities* (New York, 1930) noted that Commonwealth and Southern was already taking steps to put service contracts on a cost basis.

52. Samuel Murphy, vice-president of Electric Bond and Share, for example, took a strong position in favor of leaving the existing centralized holding-company system intact although, in Cohen's words, he could make "no economic justification for doing so." See "Memorandum of a Conference with Samuel Murphy," Nov. 9, 1934, NPPC Records, GCF 103, box 17.

While utility officials grappled with the desirability of having federal regulation, the investment bankers adamantly fought any such interference.[53] Irving W. Bonbright, the retired head of Bonbright & Company, launched into a bitter tirade against the New Deal, condemning it for placing too much emphasis upon reform and not enough upon recovery. He declared that the government's attack upon the industry was politically motivated, and warned Cohen that it would undermine investors' confidence. Bonbright simply ignored Cohen's observation that the political left and public-power enthusiasts would intensify their attacks upon the utilities, if the administration did not offer legislation. Harold Stanley of J. P. Morgan & Company, by contrast, spoke more softly but to the same point. He argued, initially, that state commissions should regulate management and service contracts but then declared that the industry should abolish such contracts altogether. Cohen, astonished at his sudden reversal, probed for an explanation. Whereupon Stanley announced that he preferred to have the companies forgo the profits than "to have regulation going into all the minutiae of the costs of such contracts." Cohen concluded from this exchange that Stanley regarded regulation "as a necessary evil at best."[54]

Academicians and professional students of the holding company, at the same time, advised the subcommittee to proceed with federal legislation. Professor Martin G. Glaeser of the University of Wisconsin, a utilities expert, observed that "in this legislation, involving coordination between state and federal regulation, you are up against one of the frontiers of regulation."[55] The government might have to experiment in order to avoid the state-federal conflicts plaguing the TVA,

---

53. The FTC had observed that there was "great pressure on holding company managements to give [more] attention to the desires and alignments of investment bankers in the formation and operation of holding company groups ... than to the interests of widely scattered stockholders who are the equitable owners of the company so managed" (United States Senate, *Summary Report of the FTC ... on Economic, Financial and Corporate Phases of Holding and Operating Companies of Electric and Gas Utilities* [Washington, D.C., 1935], part 72-A, 75 ff.). On the problem of service contracts see ibid., 599-692.

54. See "Memorandum of a Conference with Irving Bonbright," Oct. 8, 1934, and also with Harold Stanley, Oct. 8, 1934, in NPPC Records, GCF 103, box 13. Bonbright was the cousin of James C. Bonbright, coauthor of *The Holding Company* and a proponent of federal regulation.

55. Martin G. Glaeser to Robert Healy, Oct. 24, 1934, and Nov. 3, 1934; Healy to Glaeser, Nov. 13, 1934, in NPPC Records, GCF 103, box 17. See also the correspondence between Cohen and Frederick Gruenberg and Milo Maltbie of the Pennsylvania and New York commissions; James C. Bonbright and William Z. Mosher; Gardiner C. Means of the Department of Agriculture; SEC Commissioner George C. Matthews; William E. Mosher, staff director of the FPC's rate and power survey; and William T. Chantland of the FTC.

but he was confident that the FPC was equal to the task.[56] The most startling suggestion, perhaps, came from Adolph A. Berle, Jr., the Columbia law professor and New Deal consultant, who submitted to Judge Healy a lengthy memorandum. After tracing the institutional evolution of the holding company in American capitalism, Berle wrote that the objective should be "to eliminate all holding companies as rapidly as possible without doing too great damage to the business structure." The industry would fight tooth and nail against this, but he insisted that the government must set a time limit beyond which the holding company must be dissolved. Berle suggested that the process begin with the bottom-rung company and work up gradually to the super-holding company. The FPC, employing an incorporation procedure, might then restrict an operating company to an integrated system.[57]

Berle's recommendations were premised upon the earlier analogous experience of the railroad industry. That experience afforded him the opportunity to propose an amendment to section 77-b of the federal bankruptcy law to cover the utility-holding-company situation. Under it, the FPC would serve as receiver or trustee and also would approve reorganization plans. He also advocated forming a "catch-all" liquidation trust for "rag bag" companies that were unable to integrate into any system. The FPC, presumably, would allow the trust to exchange its stock with the holding company in order to protect its operating affiliates from "being thrown to the wind." The alternatives were severe rate regulation, "until the holding company goes through the bankruptcy and the general smash which characterized the railroad field," or nationalization. "I do not think any such plan would be politically possible at this time," Berle concluded of the latter, "though I myself would prefer to see government-ownership of power, centered in the hands of a group of separate regional concerns analogous to the Tennessee Valley Authority, with the Power Commission sitting ultimately as a kind of Control Board."[58]

56. See David E. Lilienthal, *The Journals of David E. Lilienthal*, 5 vols. (New York, 1964-71), 1, 711-15.

57. Berle wrote: "The objective ought to be to allow a consolidation of the operating companies accompanied by a dissolution of the holding companies so that ultimately the security holders in the holding companies would receive securities in the operating companies" (Adolph A. Berle, Jr., to Robert Healy, Nov. 30, 1934, NPPC Records, Cohen Office File, box 10).

58. Ibid. A week later, Berle wrote a more subdued letter to Cohen. "It depends on how wide an attack you want to make on a very strong front," he stated. He thought that the FPC should make every effort to retain the benefits of integration, even as it was abolishing the holding company. "A simple method of providing for the elimination

Shortly before Thanksgiving, Cohen reviewed the subcommittee's progress in a lengthy letter to Judge Healy, and disclosed the rough outlines of a draft bill for his inspection. "The subject matter, as you know, is extremely difficult and complicated," he wrote, "and for that reason it has seemed to me that a discussion of concrete provisions is likely to be more helpful in the clarification of ideas at this stage than a mere statement of principles without reference to their incorporation in a tangible legislative proposal." His draft took up where the FTC's investigation left off: "It recognizes, not simply that the holding company form has been abused, but that there are certain difficulties springing from the absence of arms-length bargaining among controlled and affiliated interests, and that these difficulties by their very nature, require some regulation if the holding company form is to be allowed to stand." Cohen did not contemplate total elimination of the holding company, but its strict regulation; for the industry was "a very real actuality today," having large amounts of capital invested in it that could not be readily untied. In these circumstances, he wrote, "*the bill does not outlaw the holding company but regulates and restricts the use of the holding company form* and provides a mechanism through which, over a period of time, existing holding company structures may be simplified, and their field limited to a sphere where their economic advantages may be demonstrable."[59]

Cohen then outlined the essential features of his draft bill, including the rationale underlying each provision. They had evolved either as the specific suggestions of industry leaders and experts (as in the requirement that holding companies execute service contracts at cost) or were the product of many years of debate and argument (as in the provision for uniform accounting practices).[60] The basic assumptions, however, were that the federal agency responsible for enforcing the law would have sufficient authority to punish evasions and also

---

would be a progressive increase of taxation upwards in case you do not feel like brutally cutting off the existence of the holding company," he concluded (Berle to Cohen, Dec. 8, 1934, in ibid., box 17).

59. Cohen to Judge Healy, Nov. 23, 1934, in ibid., box 10 (emphasis mine).

60. Ibid. The bill required federal registration of interstate holding companies, as well as registration of any holding company that had made a public offering of its securities in interstate commerce in the past seven years. "The bill consequently is very clearly akin in its jurisdictional aspects to the Securities Act of 1933 and the Securities Exchange Act of 1934," Cohen observed. He did not consider the latter provision an ex post facto penalty because the holding companies had "set forces in motion by use of interstate commerce which have continuing effects which can be controlled by no one state." The companies also were required to file more comprehensive statements of their financial affairs, to submit new issues to commission review, to receive the prior approval of

the requisite time to render adjustments in holding-company practices. As to the latter, Cohen provided the systems with an incentive to adjust their structures to the long-range interest of their security holders. He inserted in the bill an amendment to the Revenue Act that would encourage the voluntary simplification of corporate structures. He also met squarely the controversial issue of state-federal relations. "I have no doubt as to the power of the federal government to meet the most important problems connected with holding company regulation," he wrote. "The attempt to meet the problems is not an attempt to interfere with the rights of the states to control the operations of utilities within their confines." The bill, however, afforded an opportunity to meet "the problems arising from the national marketing of securities and from the active relations, by way of service contracts and other arrangements, maintained by the holding companies with their subsidiaries in different states through the channels of interstate commerce." Conceived in this light, federal regulation "need not absorb state regulation," Cohen concluded, but was a "necessary step in making state regulation effective."[61]

Early in December, Thomas G. Corcoran and SEC Commissioner James M. Landis, who had cooperated with Cohen in drafting the securities legislation of 1933-34, entered the picture. Cohen asked them to participate in writing the final version of the NPPC bill. The president, meanwhile, was devoting considerable time and energy to several courses of action that the administration might pursue. On Friday, November 16, 1934, he, along with Senator Norris, Ickes, Lilienthal, and a score of newspaper reporters, had boarded a train for an inspection tour of the TVA projects. They arrived on Sunday morning in Tupelo, Mississippi, the first municipality serviced with TVA power. Speaking before a large audience in a natural amphitheater, Roosevelt served notice that the federal government, in keeping with the New Deal's commitment to a national policy of cheap power and rural electri-

---

the commission before acquiring the capital assets of another company, to limit rigidly the ownership of property and securities not directly related to the utility business, to follow uniform accounting practices, to perform service contracts on a cost or mutual basis, and to desist from the practice of upstream loans. The question of which federal agency should exercise jurisdiction was wisely left open to forestall interagency rivalry while the bill was in the formative stage. The FTC, FPC, and SEC each could have claimed the right to administer the law. However, Cohen approached the bill chiefly as a fiduciary problem rather than a power question, and it seems likely that he intended from the outset to give primary jurisdiction to the SEC.

61. Ibid.

fication, intended to build "little TVA" projects in other sections of the country.[62]

The president's announcement struck the industry like a lightning bolt. Its leaders vehemently arose in opposition. The Edison Electric Institute declared that it would challenge the constitutionality of each project, while Robert Winsmore, a close observer of utility matters, noted that the president's attack upon private enterprise afforded "further impetus to the widespread agitation that is affecting the status of public utility companies of all kinds." He predicted that the utilities would strike back in "aggressive self-defense." A week later, after the companies had the opportunity to reexamine the Tupelo speech, Winsmore reported that they expected the NPPC to recommend FTC licensing of interstate holding companies which would "sharply curb the companies, and perhaps force drastic changes in their structures." He guessed that the legislation would affect adversely ten million investors and about fourteen billion dollars in securities. But he cautioned his readers that, "while uneasiness over such investments is not unnatural, hysteria is obviously dangerous."[63]

Thus, the administration's intention to propose federal holding-company legislation to the Seventy-fourth Congress—probably through a licensing or incorporation system—had become common knowledge.[64] Roosevelt, however, never seriously entertained either procedure. Instead, he informed a gathering of his top power-policy advisers, late in November, that he preferred to use the taxing power of Congress to eliminate holding companies entirely.[65] On the occasion of this Warm Springs meeting, the president also declared that "a holding company which exists for the control of operating companies was against the public interest and, since it couldn't be regulated, should be abolished." He then instructed those present to draft the necessary legislation. Rexford G. Tugwell, the chief architect of plan-

62. Lilienthal, *Journals*, 1, 40-41; and Ickes, *Secret Diary*, 1, 224-27.

63. See Robert Winsmore's "Public Utility Concerns May Become Aggressive in Self-Defense," *Literary Digest*, 118 (Dec. 1, 1934), 36; "Public Utility Firms Plan Court Tests of Power Issue," ibid., 118 (Dec. 15, 1934), 45; and "Proposals to Curb Power Holding Companies," ibid., 118 (Dec. 8, 1934), 36.

64. Attorney General Homer Cummings did, in fact, chair a committee which considered the federal-incorporation approach but nothing came of its deliberations. See Ickes to Cummings, Dec. 7, 1934, and Cummings to Ickes, Dec. 12, 1934, National Archives, Record Group 48, Department of the Interior Records, General Administrative File, box 510.

65. It was this misreading of the administration's intention that accounted, in large measure, for the industry's revulsion against the Wheeler-Rayburn bill. See, for example, the *Kiplinger Washington Letter*, Dec. 27, 1934.

ning among the braintrusters, who subscribed to the Populist dictum that there was no such thing as a private monopoly, and David Lilienthal, who no longer put much stock in regulation, endorsed Roosevelt's decision. Commissioner McNinch, of the FPC, alone had reservations, for he knew that neither the commission nor the NPPC was contemplating abolition. According to Lilienthal, McNinch "tried to get it perfectly clear that what the President wanted was not some form of regulation of holding companies." He fell silent after Roosevelt affirmed his intention to eliminate the holding company.[66]

On the return trip to Washington, McNinch weighed the events of the previous evening. He was clearly in a quandary and immediately apprised Cohen of the president's decision. Both men agreed that the solution still lay in the congressional power to regulate the interstate sale of holding-company securities. But whereas Cohen decided to push forward along this line, McNinch ordered the FPC staff to examine the legal implications of eliminating holding companies via taxation.[67] He also conferred with Robert H. Jackson and Herman Oliphant, Treasury Department officials whom Secretary Henry Morgenthau, Jr., had assigned to draft a bill embodying the president's directive.[68] McNinch disclosed to them his concern that this new element would disrupt their calculations for the revenue bill in preparation. Specifically, how could the Treasury reconcile abolishing the holding company with its need for more revenues to fund the growing public-works program? Oliphant conceded that this was a problem, and that he

66. The details of the meeting are reported in Lilienthal, *Journals,* I, 45. Those in attendance included Cooke, McNinch, Manly, and Rexford Tugwell. Curiously, neither Cohen, Healy, nor Ickes appears to have been present.

67. J. F. Lawson worked up a memorandum, dated Dec. 4, 1934, premised on the Court's sanction in *Patton* v. *Brady* (184 U.S. 608), 1901, for Congress to use its taxing authority to legislate a business out of existence. "On the whole," Lawson concluded, "the elimination of the exemption from taxes and the abolishing of the consolidated return by any group of corporations would seem the most effective method of eliminating the holding company." Ambrose Doskow, in a second memo, suggested that Congress might impose a tax on the dividends of holding companies as another alternative. See J. F. Lawson to Oswald Ryan, Dec. 4, 1934; Ambrose Doskow to Ryan, Dec. 4, 1934, FPC Records, GF, 21-3d-1, part I.

68. Both men were at work on a new revenue bill, the central feature of which was a graduated corporate income tax and a tax on intercorporate dividends. The bill was rooted in the Brandeisian hostility toward big business and reflected the atomistic approach to business fashionable in certain government circles. Jackson, for example, raised the holding-company issue, in August 1935, in testimony before the Senate Finance Committee. He summed up his position thus: "We do not wish to discourage the growth of small concerns. It is the existence of healthy and profitable small concerns that gives our economy the elasticity and flexibility in production and prices that are so valuable" (quoted in Eugene C. Gerhart, *America's Advocate: Robert H. Jackson* [Indianapolis, Ind., 1958], 71).

and Jackson would have to resolve it before coming to grips with holding-company dissolution.[69]

Roosevelt, meanwhile, continued to pursue the taxation approach upon his return from Georgia. He forwarded to McNinch and Morgenthau evidences of holding-company mismanagement received from SEC Commissioner Joseph P. Kennedy, and broached the subject to the members of the National Emergency Council.[70] The council met on December 11, 1934, and, in the course of its deliberations, the president commented upon the FTC's investigation. He also laid down two basic policies for his advisers to follow: first, he announced that he could live with holding companies which performed managerial functions, "providing they are paid for the service of management only; and provided they do not hold stock in any of the companies which they manage"; and secondly, he did not want investment trusts to have a voice in the management of any of the companies in which they held securities. "Those two rules could be carried out in national policy and it would solve half of the financial troubles we have been in the last 25 years," Roosevelt concluded. With no more concern for the intricacies of the problem, the president committed his administration to eliminating all but a few holding-company systems.[71]

Nine days later, the members of the NPPC reassembled.[72] McNinch was obviously ill at ease, for he asked immediately whether Roosevelt had apprised Ickes of his intentions. Upon receiving a negative re-

69. See McNinch to Roosevelt, Dec. 28, 1934, Roosevelt Papers, OF 235; John M. Blum, ed., *From the Morgenthau Diaries, Years of Crisis, 1928-1938* (Boston, 1959), 305.

70. See, for example, Roosevelt to Morgenthau, Dec. 20, 1934, Roosevelt Papers, OF 235.

71. When McNinch reminded the president that the NPPC was drafting legislation, Roosevelt seemed genuinely surprised and appeared to have forgotten about the committee. Although he did not make an issue of it, he did state: "I don't think we need a special committee on that. We have got far enough on it so that the Federal Trade Commission and the Power Commission, the Treasury Department, and the Attorney-General's Office will be able to clear up the whole thing." The NPPC continued to draft the legislation, but, needless to say, the president's comment did not enhance its reputation and only underscored the fact that proliferation of federal agencies and committees often resulted in confusion. Donald Richberg, the president's adviser, recognized this and urged a definite understanding whereby government agencies would clear their legislative projects with the White House in advance of going to Congress. See "Proceedings of the National Emergency Council," Dec. 11, 1934, microfilm in Franklin D. Roosevelt Library.

72. On December 18, 1934, Ickes wrote a memorandum to clarify his own thinking and the committee's procedure. He reaffirmed his intention to have a bill ready for January 1, 1935, but rejected as unfeasible a decision to hold more frequent conferences of the full committee. See Ickes's uncirculated memorandum, Dec. 18, 1934, NPPC Records, GCF 103, box 10.

sponse, he proceeded to summarize the situation as he understood it. McNinch believed that the president wanted to keep open all his options, and, for this reason, he had encouraged several agencies to draft holding-company legislation. He had not accepted as binding the recommendations of any one group as yet, although the Treasury's scheme to tax the companies out of existence appealed to Roosevelt's dramatic instincts. The immediate task was to persuade him that strict regulation would accomplish the reforms he wanted and still preserve the managerial and financial advantages of holding-company control. "I do not think he does want written reports from this committee on policy matters," McNinch concluded, "but would rather have an informal presentation to him from the chairman or sub-chairman to avoid the possibility of the framing of a policy and the approval of this Committee, which might not completely coincide with his views."[73]

In light of this information, Ickes turned to Judge Healy and inquired whether his subcommittee had completed its report. The latter replied that the draft bill for the regulation of holding companies was still undergoing revision, but "I think we are up to date in a general way." Healy wanted McNinch and Cooke to reexamine it before distributing copies to the committee for approval. McNinch, at this point, interjected that the president would manifest "displeasure if any of us, unwittingly or otherwise, were to circulate any of this information beyond that group." He suggested sending Roosevelt an advance copy of the text for comment, but Ickes and Cohen, fearing that it might leak to the press, firmly opposed doing so. Cohen observed that by limiting the bill at the present time to NPPC members, "you have the benefit of the committee's criticism without it in any way having the committee approve the bill, so that if any changes are desired later, it would not appear to be going contrary to the committee's wishes." Besides, he wanted the unanimous support of the committee before confronting the president. Cohen knew that a strong endorsement in favor of regulation would have to weigh heavily in the president's calculations when he finally decided upon the policy of the administration.[74]

Having agreed to follow this procedure, the committee adjourned, leaving Cohen to work on the revisions. Joel D. Wolfsohn, the committee's secretary, circulated the revised draft among the members

---

73. McNinch elaborated further that Roosevelt wanted only progress reports and additional evidence of holding-company abuses rather than formal recommendations from the committee. See "Minutes of a Meeting of the National Power Policy Committee," Dec. 20, 1934, in ibid.
74. Ibid.

immediately after the new year. He warned them, in advance of the first January meeting, to criticize it, but to keep the contents strictly confidential.[75] Cohen, meanwhile, wrote a memorandum for Ickes's use, in which he analyzed the philosophy behind the bill. The document reaffirmed in all essentials the Brandeisian distrust of big business, and argued that federal regulation was a necessary prelude to restoring the integrity of local, that is, state-commission, jurisdiction. Cohen noted that the bill did not fragment economic conglomerates simply because they were large, but only where great size resulted in inefficiency, the restriction of competition, or the wielding of unbridled economic and political power.[76] He anticipated that the utilities would launch a legal attack against it. To minimize the threat, he had written the bill so that separate provisions might be tested in the courts without having the constitutionality of the whole challenged.

The first reactions came early in January 1935. Dr. Mead indicated that his staff attorney had examined the bill and "advises me that he has no suggestions to offer." Lilienthal commented that the draft seemed "admirably suited to the purpose desired to be effected," although he questioned the desirability of regulating holding-company securities. "My reason for this doubt is that it may tend to dignify these so-called securities," he wrote to Healy. Lilienthal also conceded

75. See, for example, Joel D. Wolfsohn to Cooke, Jan. 2, 1935, Cooke Papers, box 275. The draft of Dec. 19, 1934, underwent subsequent revisions but without changing the basic format of the original. The first three sections established the title of the bill, the abuses requiring correction, and the basis of federal jurisdiction. Section four made it unlawful for holding companies, unless registered, to use the mails or interstate commerce to market securities. Sections five, six, and seven dealt with the registration of companies and the issuance of securities. "These revisions look toward a more accurate reflection in the amount of holding company securities of the prudent investment in underlying companies, and to the ultimate simplification of security structure and underlying properties." Section eight restricted the business of a holding company to owning the securities of operating companies alone; section nine further limited the investment possibilities of a company whereas section ten permitted a holding company to acquire the securities and properties of other systems, but only where the commission deemed this to be in the public interest. This meant that there would be no more economically or geographically scattered systems. Section eleven originally provided for the simplification and reorganization of systems, and rested on the premise that holding companies would continue to survive but under strict regulation. At the insistence of the president, this section later was rewritten to include the mandatory dissolution of holding companies after January 1, 1940. Sections twelve through fifteen regulated the abuses most often cited in FTC reports, whereas sections sixteen through twenty-nine borrowed heavily from the administrative procedures of the Securities Exchange Act. The various draft bills may be found in NPPC Records, GCF 103, box 18.

76. Cohen to Ickes, Jan. 7, 1935, in ibid., box 17. Cohen wrote: "In too many instances, the holding company has not brought to the American people the advantage claimed for it, but has been an instrument through which undue economic power has been concentrated in the hands of a few powerful groups."

that his bitterness was probably intensified "by recent perusal of the results of your activities as Chief Counsel for the FTC."[77] General Markham provided the only other extensive commentary. He adopted a basically cautious and practical approach to the holding-company problem. The bill "seemed to cover the situation admirably," he wrote to Wolfsohn, but added that more flexibility and the liberalization of certain provisions would materially enhance its chances of surviving the criticism of Congress.[78] Markham's critique was important and worth considering because it disclosed precisely the kinds of obstacles the bill encountered in the legislative mill.

On all essentials though, committee members accepted the basic premise and provisions of the December draft. Wolfsohn confirmed this in reference to the draft bill of January 11, 1935. "The revised draft does not differ in substance from previous draft sent you on January 2," he wrote to Morris Cooke. Subsequent revisions focused upon refinement of language and the shifting and renumbering of sections.[79]

While the committee reworked the bill, President Roosevelt was delivering, on January 4, 1935, his State of the Union address to the Seventy-fourth Congress. In reading the prepared text, he misdelivered one sentence. The manuscript spoke of restoring sound conditions in the electric-power industry through "abolition of the evil features of holding companies." Before Congress, however, the president read it as the "abolition of the evil of holding companies." His listeners interpreted his statement to mean that he intended to abolish all holding companies, although he explained subsequently that he meant "the evils of holding companies," without implying that everything about them was evil. Nevertheless, there was a substantial amount of truth in this Freudian slip, for the presidential address inaugurated the administration's campaign to educate the public to the need for federal action.[80]

Thereafter, a continuous outpouring of critical statements emanated from federal sources. The FPC termed federal regulation a "necessity" for the protection of investors and consumers; the FTC hurriedly re-

---

77. Elwood Mead to Wolfsohn, Jan. 7, 1935; Lilienthal to Healy, Jan. 8, 1935, in ibid.

78. For a fuller exposition of Markham's criticisms see Edward M. Markham to Wolfsohn, Jan. 12, 1935, in ibid.

79. Wolfsohn to Ickes, Jan. 14, 1935, in ibid.; and Wolfsohn to Cooke, Jan. 14, 1935, Cooke Papers, box 275. This statement is based upon a comparison of the draft bills.

80. The *New York Times,* Jan. 5, 1935; and Arthur M. Schlesinger, Jr., *The Politics of Upheaval* (Boston, 1960), 305.

leased three chapters of its final report, which declared that compulsory federal licensing or incorporation, outright elimination, or taxation might provide "a reasonably effective solution to the holding company problem." David Lilienthal told the Economic Club of New York that the holding company was a financial parasite which the government should eliminate in accordance with its national power policy. Roosevelt, simultaneously, disclosed, during a press conference, the substance of an FPC study of operating-company bonds held by institutional investors. Their value was higher than at any time prior to the crash, he noted, and declared that this was proof that the industry was lying when it said that federal legislation would wipe out the savings of "widows and orphans."[81] The campaign peaked on January 13, when Sam Rayburn of Texas, chairman of the House Committee on Interstate and Foreign Commerce, demanded that his colleagues abolish all holding companies. In neo-Populist rhetoric, he alleged that the holding company was the conspiratorial instrument of Wall Street lawyers to enslave the country.[82]

The utilities had known for several months that federal legislation was in the works and, in a futile effort to forestall radical changes, Willkie, Fogarty, Ferguson, and Groesbeck met with FPC Commissioner McNinch. The conference, which occurred, ironically, on January 4, did not go well because McNinch made it clear that he was not speaking for the president or the administration but only for the commission. This did not prevent him from laying down minimum conditions that the utilities would have to fulfill in order to establish a basis for cooperation. The requirements coincided with the major

81. *Summary Report of the FTC*, part 72-A, 832, passim. Edgar McCulloch, an FTC commissioner, who died in 1933, had conducted the principal part of the investigation with diligence and an attitude of skeptical intelligence. Ewin L. Davis, a New Dealer, succeeded him as chairman and assumed responsibility for compiling the report. But because of the president's insistence that the FTC present its final report by January 1, 1935, in time to submit holding-company legislation to Congress, it was inevitable that the summary should consist of little more than a catalog of holding-company sins. Davis intended to extend the investigation and authored a resolution, in 1934, to that effect. Congressman John Rankin introduced H.J. Res. 333, but it never got out of committee. See William T. Chantland to George W. Norris, May 7, 1934, George W. Norris Papers, tray 80, box 7, Library of Congress; and Forrest McDonald, *Let There Be Light: The Electric Utility Industry in Wisconsin, 1881-1955* (Madison, 1957), 316. For the criticisms of Lilienthal and Roosevelt see the *New York Times*, Jan. 12, 13, 15, 26, 1935.

82. *Congressional Record*, 74th Cong., 1st sess., 79 (Jan. 13, 1935), 374 ff. The following day Rayburn modified his demand and asked the president to include in the administration's legislation a preamble declaring that holding companies were a "temporary necessary evil" which eventually would be eliminated in the public interest (*New York Times*, Jan. 15, 1935).

provisions of the NPPC bill: the simplification of corporate structures; the elimination of intermediate companies through an orderly process of liquidation; the reorganization of service companies on an independent, competitive basis; and securities regulation. As a conciliatory gesture, he agreed to pass along the administrative bureaucracy any proposals that the industry wished to make. The utility spokesmen, understandably, were distraught by what they considered his inflexible attitude, and protested that radical readjustments would destroy the value of utility securities. The chasm of misunderstanding and suspicion was unbridgeable, as McNinch noted afterward. "While all of them expressed a measure of optimism as to the ultimate results," he wrote to Roosevelt, "we do not feel at all certain they will finally meet the requirements and our attitude is one of 'watchful waiting' with some hope, but not too much confidence."[83]

McNinch's analysis was even more perceptive than he knew, for, in mid-January, negotiations between the industry and the administration collapsed altogether. Louis Howe, the president's confidant, described the circumstances that precipitated the severance of further talks. He informed Roosevelt on January 11, 1935, that Harvey C. Couch, president of the Arkansas Power and Light Company and a former Reconstruction Finance Corporation (RFC) official, was eager to arrange a face-to-face meeting between the president and utility officials. The latter sought a clarification of the administration's position (with respect to the holding-company controversy, rural-electrification programs, and public power) in an effort to dispel the animus that was poisoning their relations. Howe believed that Groesbeck was the prime mover behind the conference, but he advised the president to consent to the meeting and to obtain an agreement beforehand on certain "basic facts." The industry had to agree, first, that the federal government had jurisdiction in utility matters because of Congress's authority to regulate interstate commerce; secondly, the government, in accordance with the national power policy, had the responsibility of guaranteeing low electric rates consistent with a reasonable profit for the power companies; thirdly, the industry would adjust interest rates according to the safety of the investment (a departure from the prevailing practice); and fourthly, utility officials would have to accept the president's interpretation that operating-utility bonds, unlike holding-company securities, were stronger than ever before.[84]

83. The details are reported in McNinch to Roosevelt, Jan. 23, 1935, Roosevelt Papers, OF 235.
84. Louis M. Howe to Roosevelt, Jan. 11, 1935, in ibid., OF 284.

The response of utility officials evidently satisfied the president because he scheduled the meeting for mid-January.[85] David E. Lilienthal, who maintained the only comprehensive and extant account of the conference, noted that Roosevelt was in especially good form, waxing eloquently on the subject of holding-company mismanagement. Couch and Groesbeck attempted, without any success whatsoever, to defend the industry, whereas Willkie kept silent. As the president persisted in repeating the catalog of holding-company sins, Lilienthal observed that Willkie became highly agitated. Suddenly, he yanked his glasses from his breast pocket and, using them as a pointer, crouched forward and thrust them in Roosevelt's direction. "If you will give us a Federal incorporation law, we can get rid of holding companies," he shouted. Couch and Groesbeck recoiled, "as if Willkie had suddenly produced a gun and started shooting." Lilienthal noted that "from the moment he did this pointing job, the conference was on a completely different basis." The exchange grew increasingly bitter as the president jutted his chin and became less and less conciliatory. Willkie, in desperation, finally asked: "Do I understand then that any further efforts to avoid the breaking up of utility holding companies are futile?" Roosevelt shot back, "It is futile," and the meeting broke up.[86]

Shortly after this falling out, the members of the NPPC reconvened to consider Cohen's latest revisions. Almost immediately, their remarks turned to two matters which he raised. Cohen was concerned about the "politics of reform" now that the bill was in its final stages. General Markham feared that congressmen might view the bill as evidence of executive encroachment upon legislative prerogatives. Cohen shared his fear and proposed that the committee express its views in a general report. He preferred to have the NPPC bill originate in Congress because *"it is always helpful if Congress feels that the particular bill is their bill and not the bill of the executive. Everyone may know that the executive branch has been very active when it is presented, still there is the condition."*[87]

Cohen then asked the committee to accelerate its work on the report

85. Lilienthal does not specify the precise date, but it was probably sometime between January 16 and 18, 1935 (see Lilienthal, *Journals*, I, 46-47).

86. Ibid.

87. Cohen was not being cynical, for he recognized the strategic and psychological importance of having the chairmen of the House and Senate commerce committees sponsor the bill. See "Minutes of a Meeting of the National Power Policy Committee," Jan. 17, 1935, NPPC Records, GCF 103, box 10; also Cohen to Healy, Jan. 9, 14, 1935, in ibid.

to accompany the bill, "in order that our work should not be neglected or at least be available for consideration."[88] Beneath the rhetoric, it was clear that he was afraid the Treasury's tax-elimination scheme might undercut the NPPC's regulatory approach. Vice-Chairman Manly, of the FPC, speaking for McNinch who was ill, assured him and the committee that the general objectives of the bill accorded with FPC thinking. He added that, if there were any reservations, they would be "to some particular section of the bill, or some particular method of reaching an end rather than any major difference."[89] Although Cohen was reassured, this caveat later came back to haunt him. Before the meeting adjourned, the members voted to send the bill to the president by January 19, to give him the report soon thereafter, and to leave the final disposition of both up to him.[90]

Roosevelt, in the interim, grew increasingly eager to lay before Congress some firm legislative proposals. For, in the wake of his State of the Union address, congressional power enthusiasts, either from ideological conviction or because it was politically popular with their constituents, manifested a new spirit of urgency.[91] The ideologues, among whom Norris in the Senate and John Rankin of Mississippi in the House clearly stand out, demanded federal legislation as an intermediate step toward the goal of public ownership. Roosevelt never really shared this dream; instead, he advocated legislation that would

88. Ibid.

89. Title IV, holding-company regulation, in the FPC's draft bill, "Federal Public Utilities Act of 1935," never proceeded beyond the drafting stage. After the NPPC was established, holding-company regulation assumed secondary importance to the task of strengthening the Federal Water Power Act. Also, Commissioner Clyde L. Seavey's marginalia on the November 1934 draft makes it very clear that the FPC approach did not deal adequately with the problem of holding-company securities. The entire story may be pieced together in Federal Power Commission, *Sixteenth Annual Report of the Federal Power Commission* (Washington, D.C., 1936), 17-25; McNinch to Roosevelt, Aug. 20, 1934, King Papers, box 74; McNinch and Manly to Marvin McIntyre, Nov. 11, 1934, Roosevelt Papers, OF 284; and Ambrose Doskow to Oswald Ryan, Sept. 13, 1934, and Willard Gatchall to Ryan, Oct. 20, 1934, FPC Records, GF, 21-31-1, pt. I. A copy of the draft bills of November and December 1934, with Seavey's comments, may be found in ibid., 21-3d-2, pts. I and II.

90. See Ickes to Roosevelt, Jan. 18, 1935, NPPC Records, GCF 103, box 10.

91. Felix Frankfurter reported to Justice Brandeis that "F. D. is really hot on holding cos. and for drastic action" (quoted in William E. Leuchtenburg, *Franklin D. Roosevelt and the New Deal* [New York, 1963], 154). For similar sentiments see Frankfurter to Roosevelt, Jan. 24, 1935; Roosevelt to Frankfurter, Feb. 9, 1935, Roosevelt Papers, OF 293 and President's Personal File 140 (hereafter cited as PPF). In the interim, Rayburn had requested Dr. Walter M. Splawn, a Texan and economist for the Interstate Commerce Commission, to prepare a report and a bill for his committee.

reform and preserve the private-enterprise character of the power industry.[92] Therefore, in order to retain the initiative in legislation, the president summoned a White House conference of advisers to decide which policy to follow—whether to regulate the holding company as Cohen and the NPPC proposed, or to abolish it by means of the Treasury's intercorporate-tax scheme.[93]

The meeting commenced early on the afternoon of January 21 in the Oval Room of the White House. The president's opening remarks suggested that he leaned toward the more dramatic of the alternatives, the Treasury proposal to tax the companies out of business. He explained that he wished to eradicate them now, lest a future administration, more complaisant, permit them a free hand. Cohen and Corcoran argued that the NPPC bill promoted the strictest federal regulation short of destroying the holding company and its advantages. It also went beyond financial regulation to require the companies to simplify their capital structures and reorganize their systems to conform to logical economic and geographical patterns. Secretary Ickes strongly supported their argument, and, after a heated exchange among his advisers, the president finally gave his consent to a modified version of the NPPC bill.[94]

Roosevelt agreed to the elimination of all utility holding companies which controlled more than one geographically integrated system after January 1, 1938, but also demanded the compulsory dissolution of every holding company within five years. This was the later infamous "death-sentence" clause of section eleven of the Wheeler-Rayburn

92. Roosevelt's advice to Newton D. Baker, in 1934, revealed indirectly his attitude. Rumor had it that McCarter and the Edison Electric Institute wanted to hire Baker, President Wilson's former secretary of war, to advise the industry on how to fight the government on the TVA, holding-company regulation, and other power matters. Roosevelt commented: "One of my principal tasks is to prevent bankers and businessmen from committing suicide! You and I know as 'practical men' (as T. R. said) that if the utilities want to get into real trouble with the Congress and the public they will start a fight—and such a fight can only hurt them and their stockholders" (Roosevelt to Baker, Nov. 8, 1934, Roosevelt Papers, PPF 669).

93. Those present included Morgenthau, Jackson, Oliphant, Cummings, McNinch, Manly, Ewin Davis, Cohen, Corcoran, and Donald Richberg. January 22 or 23 was the most likely date of the conference. Schlesinger, in *Politics of Upheaval*, 305, places it "a few days after" the State of the Union address. Roosevelt, however, did not receive a copy of Cohen's bill before January 18. The *New York Times* of January 22 and 23 reported that the White House was holding conferences on holding-company legislation but did not report any decisions that may have been reached.

94. The writer has relied upon the accounts of Schlesinger, *Politics of Upheaval*, 305-06; Leuchtenburg, *FDR and the New Deal*, 154-55; and Louis Koenig, *The Invisible Presidency* (New York, 1960), 259.

bill.[95] He also insisted that Cohen and Corcoran rewrite the language of the first section to include a violent denunciation of the holding-company abuses condemned in the FTC report.[96] The president wanted a bill that breathed fire. The Treasury bill was shelved, although administration officials agreed they would not trade on the primary objective of eliminating the holding company.[97]

Although one unidentified high-administration official, a euphemism for the president himself, leaked to the press that legislation was advancing toward the ultimate elimination of the holding company, there was no public disclosure of the decisions reached in the conference. Secretary Morganthau would only comment in response to reporters' queries that the president was "sending us home to do more homework on the problem." The reason for the delay was actually the result of a more serious consideration; the FPC began to issue signals that the bill, as written, did not entirely satisfy its legal staff.[98] With the approval of the commissioners, Ambrose Doskow, Oswald Ryan, and other lawyers had decided to make a strong bid to preserve the integrity of the FPC's jurisdiction over all aspects of the interstate transmission of power, including the circulation of new holding-company securities. They also demanded that the NPPC tie the amendments to the Federal Water Power Act to holding-company legislation. Doskow and Ryan reasoned that the amendments, as a single parcel bearing the president's imprimatur, had a better chance of passing through Congress unscathed, particularly if opponents focused their criticism upon the holding-company title.[99]

95. Section ten of H.R. 5423 contained the so-called "death sentence." In S. 1725, it appeared in section eleven and was enacted finally as section 11-b of the Public Utility Holding Company Act of 1935.

96. Walter Lippmann described the administration's legislative program as "the spirit of American individualism in its original form" (Walter Lippmann, *Interpretations, 1933-1935* [New York, 1936], 383).

97. The idea that the "death sentence" was inserted originally for trading purposes was advanced first by Raymond Moley, *After Seven Years* (New York, 1939), 303, and perpetuated by Schlesinger and other historians. It is doubtful that Moley was in a position to know this inasmuch as he did not participate in any of the conferences. There is no evidence to support this interpretation in any of the material that I have consulted. Also, Cohen has affirmed that the president did not have in mind any such thought at the time (Cohen to Funigiello, letter, Sept. 26, 1965).

98. The *New York Times*, Jan. 22, 1935. Ambrose Doskow speculated, as early as December 1934, that the NPPC would approach the holding company chiefly as a financial problem, and he concluded that it would name the SEC to administer the law. See Doskow to Ryan, Dec. 30, 1934, FPC Records, GF, 21-31-2, part II.

99. Doskow stated the case for FPC jurisdiction on January 16, 1935. He noted that sections 6 and 7-d of Cohen's bill empowered the commission to decide whether

Healy and Cohen both interpreted the commission's objections as a bold ploy to wrest the administration of the holding-company law from the SEC.[100] Because time was drawing short, they placed the controversy squarely before the president, and asked him to render a judgment. Roosevelt, as was his wont, trimmed. After a heated interchange among his advisers, he decided to consolidate holding-company regulation and the amendments to the Water Power Act into a single piece of legislation. He instructed Attorney General Homer Cummings to head a task force to work out the details. Presumably, he wanted the SEC to exercise jurisdiction in matters pertaining to securities regulation but the FPC to have authority over other aspects of utility operations. Cummings appointed representatives from several executive agencies to rework the bill, but the actual task of rewriting fell upon Cohen's shoulders.[101]

Cohen quickly discovered that defining the areas of administrative jurisdiction was a more complex task than he had anticipated. Nonetheless, he observed in a letter to the attorney general, postmarked January 22, 1935, that he had recast portions of the bill to confer upon the FPC greater jurisdiction over operating-company activities, particularly service, sales, and construction contracts. He also explained that the term "commission" still referred to the SEC, but added that its authority to approve the acquisition of securities or capital assets of a holding company would be invalid, "unless and until there shall have been attained from the Federal Power Commission a certificate that such acquisition will serve the public interest by advancing economy and efficiency in the operation of a geographically and economically integrated public utility system."[102] Cummings regarded the changes as superficial, however, and he, Ryan, and Dozier DeVane,

---

a new security was adapted to the capital structure of a utility. He noted also that this would carry the commission into the planning aspect of the nation's utilities, and this was "a task for a body expert in utility matters, and not for one devoted to protecting the investor against the sale of fraudulent securities." Doskow concluded from this that "the act should be administered by the Federal Power Commission." See Doskow's unsigned memorandum to Ryan, Jan. 16, 1935, in ibid., part I; also, Benjamin V. Cohen to author, interview, Washington, D.C., May 12, 1965.

100. See, for example, the revealing letter of Manly to Healy, Jan. 18, 1935, FPC Records, GF, 21-31-1, part I.

101. The other members were Corcoran, Oliphant, Ryan, Splawn, and FTC Commissioner Davis.

102. Cohen to Cummings, Jan. 22, 1935, FPC Records, GF, 21-31-1, part I. In the process of revising, Cohen dropped the section providing for the regulation of investment trusts as being too complicated a problem and meriting a separate bill. Thus he laid the foundation for the Investment Company Act of 1940.

also of the FPC, insisted that Cohen's revisions did not conform to the president's instructions.[103]

A deadlock persisted for several days thereafter, because neither Cohen nor the Cummings-FPC faction were willing to abandon any more than was absolutely necessary of their original positions. Until Sam Rayburn of Texas, the chairman of the House commerce committee, and Senator Wheeler intervened, the impasse threatened to forestall any holding-company legislation in the Seventy-fourth Congress. Each man wanted to introduce the consolidated bill at the earliest opportunity, before its critics coalesced in opposition. Therefore, they insisted that Cummings submit the consolidated bill to them by Monday, January 28. They would iron out any conflicts that still remained during committee hearings. In order to move the factions off dead center Cohen and Corcoran met, on January 25, with Ryan and DeVane to resolve their differences. Together they agreed that wherever there were overlapping provisions in the bill Cohen would insert a clause in the holding-company title which authorized the SEC to exempt from its jurisdiction utility matters that were subject to Title II, the amendments to the Water Power Act. He also would rewrite section three of Title I, to establish the machinery for resolving conflicts arising from jurisdictional disputes.[104]

There is considerable evidence to indicate that, even after this compromise, the FPC and the FTC had serious reservations about the holding-company bill. Colonel William T. Chantland of the FTC wrote later that the NPPC bill was "apparently written to carry out what seems to be the Administration policy, namely to eliminate the holding company in about six years." If so, he wrote, "it would seem to me to be better policy to see the Treasury Department taxation bill and to await the results of that, particularly if there were added to that bill a direct prohibitive statute as recommended by the Federal Trade Commission." Chantland believed the result would be accomplished "with very much less expense and greatly less burden upon the industries."[105] But the president, Rayburn, and Wheeler were demanding a bill to take to Congress, and the Justice Department ruled that the NPPC bill withstood the test of constitutionality. Cummings, therefore, passed on the final revision to Roosevelt with the

103. See Dozier DeVane, "Genesis of the Public Utility Act of 1935," undated memorandum in ibid.

104. Ibid.

105. Chantland also thought that the bill placed the burden of proof upon the commission instead of the holding company where it belonged. Chantland to FPC Commissioners, Feb. 5, 1935, in ibid., 21-3d-2, part II.

notation that "Representative Sam Rayburn will introduce in the House the holding company control bill as now drawn and amended." On February 6, 1935, he and Senator Wheeler put the bill into the legislative hopper. The Wheeler-Rayburn bill (H.R. 5423 and S. 1725) was quickly referred to the appropriate House and Senate commerce committees for intensive hearings.[106]

Aside from the Scripps-Howard papers, press reaction was overwhelmingly negative. Urban and small-town newspaper editorials indicated that the bill had gone beyond any degree of regulation that was desirable and was positively destructive in its intent.[107] The Greenville, South Carolina, *News* asked: "Cannot abuses be eliminated without the destructive program contemplated by these bills?" They were "vicious and unfair" said the Erie, Pennsylvania, *Dispatch-Herald*. The *Press* of Grand Rapids, Michigan, predicted that their enactment would "decrease the purchasing power of millions" of Americans and cause Treasury receipts to decline. The *Boston Transcript* exhorted Congress and the president to "make sure whom and what they are smashing." It was not necessary "to kill" the holding company in order to curb its abuses, observed the *Philadelphia Record*.[108] The nearly unanimous hostility of the press to the dissolution features of the bill portended the bitter struggle that lay in the path of its enactment.

106. Cummings to Roosevelt, Feb. 6, 1935, Roosevelt Papers, OF 293.
107. See, for example, the Committee of Public Utility Executives' fly sheet of hostile editorials in "Opinions" File, Roosevelt Papers, OF 284.
108. Ibid.

CHAPTER III

Congressional Hearings

A week after introducing the holding-company bill into Congress, Representative Sam Rayburn commenced public hearings before the House Committee on Interstate and Foreign Commerce. Rayburn's optimism that the committee would endorse the bill quickly and without substantial modification was soon dashed when influential committee members spoke against the legislation. Utility officials, investment bankers, and leaders of the American Bar Association also recorded their opposition to federal legislation and, ultimately, induced the House to pass a substantially weaker bill. Not until April 15, 1935, did the committee finish taking testimony, and it did not file a report until June 22. The report on H.R. 5423 differed substantially from the Senate bill on the vital matters of corporate simplification and service contracts.[1]

By contrast, Senator Burton K. Wheeler opened and closed hearings on the counterpart bill, S. 1725, within two weeks.[2] His committee went into executive session on April 29 and reported back to the Senate an amended bill on May 24. Senate bills S. 2796 retained the provisions requiring the compulsory dissolution of holding companies and strict regulation of service contracts. For Roosevelt and the administration the contrast between the action of the House and of the Senate was their first clue that the Seventy-fourth Congress would be more difficult to manipulate than its predecessor.

Shortly after the committee hearings commenced, the utilities launched a campaign to defeat the bill.[3] Thomas N. McCarter of the Public Service Corporation of New Jersey dispatched a letter to stockholders warning them that their property was endangered; also, he urged them to unite with Dr. Hugh S. Magill's American Federation of Utility Investors (AFUI) to protest against the bill in its present

1. See the *Wall Street Journal*, Feb. 27, 1935.
2. There was slight difference between the original House bill (H.R. 5423) and the original Senate bill (S. 1725). See Henry A. Herman to Benjamin V. Cohen, Apr. 2, 1935, National Archives, Record Group 48, Records of the National Power Policy Committee, Cohen Office File, box 10 (hereafter cited as NPPC Records).
3. The propaganda against the bill is treated in greater detail in ch. 4.

form. Alex Dow of Detroit Edison complained that the legislation was so vaguely worded that it "seriously affects the values of all utility securities, those of operating as well as holding companies." Henry L. Doherty, fearing that Congress might enact it hurriedly, "without full realization of the disastrous effect upon the millions of investors in holding companies," told stockholders that the bill was "class legislation."[4] Despite these initial outbursts, holding- and operating-company executives were confident that Congress would not enact the Wheeler-Rayburn bill in its pristine form.[5]

The administration, meanwhile, was preparing a defense of the bill and eagerly accepted the invitation of Rayburn's committee to present witnesses in its behalf.[6] Morris L. Cooke told the Association of Bank Women, in mid-March, that "there is not a line in the Wheeler-Rayburn bill which destroys a value now inherent in any utility investment."[7] And FPC Commissioner McNinch prepared short form letters to respond to the avalanche of hostile mail that inundated the White House.[8]

As the controversy became more and more acrimonious, the president remained discreetly in the background. During the first month of committee hearings, Roosevelt maintained the fiction that the bill was simply a congressional measure,[9] and that, while the administration favored holding-company legislation, it was not endorsing the Wheeler-Rayburn bill. On February 15, he told White House reporters that his practice was not to comment on pending legislation, whereupon he talked off the record at considerable length about holding-company abuses. He maintained that the companies must return to their original

4. The *New York Times*, Feb. 21, 23, 24, 1935.
5. Cf. Hugh Magill to W. A. Jones, May 6, 1935, National Archives, Record Group 46, "Senate Special Committee to Investigate Lobbying Activities," Case File, box 101 (hereafter cited as "Senate Lobby Investigation"). S. R. Bertron of the Wall Street law firm, Bertron, Griscom & Co., wrote to Louis Howe that business confidence was at a low ebb. "The Administration sadly needs to restore business confidence throughout the country and to do it quickly," he observed, but "the assertion that the President is backing the Holding Company Bill has done infinite harm." And Louis McHenry, an appraiser in the Middle West Utilities "smash" wrote to Commerce Secretary Daniel C. Roper that the bill should not be enacted, "as it will be a great injustice to the security holders of these securities." Bertron to Howe, Feb. 28, 1935, Franklin D. Roosevelt Papers, Office File 293, Franklin D. Roosevelt Library (hereafter cited as Roosevelt Papers, OF); and Louis McHenry to Daniel C. Roper, Mar. 2, 1935, ibid., OF 3.
6. See Sam Rayburn to Ewin Davis, Feb. 7, 1935; Davis to Rayburn, Feb. 11, 1935, National Archives, Record Group 46, House Committee on Interstate and Foreign Commerce, folder on H.R. 5423, 74th Cong., 1st sess., 1935.
7. Morris L. Cooke, "The Meaning of Power in American Life," Morris L. Cooke Papers, box 275, Franklin D. Roosevelt Library.
8. Frank McNinch to Marvin McIntyre, Mar. 11, 1935, Roosevelt Papers, OF 235.
9. For example, see the Chicago *Journal of Commerce*, Mar. 8, 1935.

functions of management and investment if they expected to continue to exist.[10]

Continuing off the record, the president turned to the broader subject of business. A reporter asked whether he believed that "bigness of business is of itself undesirable." "I should say yes," Roosevelt replied, adding that sheer size per se was unhealthy. The danger inherent in bigness was that the top corporation executives could not be sufficiently acquainted with the detailed operation of their own businesses. But "the question of mere bigness," Roosevelt noted, was not as important as "the control of business." If a large number of interlocking companies were centered in the hands of a few individuals, control of the nation's industrial complex would gravitate toward them. "We are a great deal better off if we can disseminate both the control and the actual industrial setup as a whole," the president concluded.[11]

On March 12, when it appeared that the bill might founder in committee, Roosevelt openly endorsed the Wheeler-Rayburn bill as an administration measure. The circumstances surrounding the declaration of support cast light on the president's action. In the course of Judge Healy's testimony, Congressman Charles A. Wolverton, a New Jersey Republican and leader of the bipartisan coalition that was opposing the bill, elicited a remark that the bill might be superfluous.[12] Wolverton's questions were intended to demonstrate that regulation of the holding company was preferable to elimination and that the securities legislation of 1933-34 was adequate for this purpose. Two Democratic members of the House committee, George Huddleston of Alabama, a former Wilsonian Progressive, and Samuel B. Pettengill of Indiana, shared this belief.[13] Under close questioning, Healy stated that it was possible to prohibit holding-company abuses in the future without forcefully dismantling the systems. Corrective legislation, even the Securities Exchange Act, might suffice. To a number of observers this admission cast doubt on the necessity of the Wheeler-Rayburn bill.[14]

10. Roosevelt Press Conference Transcript no. 184, Feb. 15, 1935, Franklin D. Roosevelt Library. The president went so far as to deny that he had seen a copy of the Wheeler-Rayburn bill prior to its introduction in Congress.
11. Ibid.
12. "Biographical Sketches of Members of Subcommittee Dealing with Title I," Records of the Federal Power Commission, General File, 21-31-4, part I. The records are in the possession of the commission.
13. Republican Senators Daniel Hastings and Wallace White led the opposition in the Senate Commerce Committee.
14. U.S. Congress, House of Representatives, Hearings on H.R. 5423, Public Utility Holding Companies, 74th Cong., 1st sess. (Washington, 1935), 220-30 (hereafter cited as *Hearings on H.R. 5423*).

After the hearings resumed on March 1, Healy attempted to qualify his earlier testimony. The securities legislation was not adequate for regulating the holding company which should be eliminated, he testified. He revealed also that he intended to offer amendments to protect investors in holding-company securities. The primary amendment tolerated an indefinite postponement of compulsory dissolutions beyond the 1940 deadline, where enforcement would cause "substantial injury to investors or is not in the public interest." "I take the position," he told the committee, "that we should force eventual elimination of them, the arbitrary elimination of them, but with some discretion invested in the commission as stated here."[15]

The *New York Times* reported that Healy's amendments were "a partial victory for foes of the measure." They fell short of meeting the committee's objections; indeed, the nature and tone of the questions asked suggested to the *Times* correspondent that opposition was increasing. Actually, Judge Healy's retreat from the strongly worded dissolution provision did not surprise administration officials. Cohen and Ickes had been aware for some time that the judge was dissatisfied with the presidential decision to eliminate the holding company: he had consented to the demand for a strong bill because he expected the NPPC's report to give the government leeway in administering the law. On February 8, for example, Cohen informed Ickes that the report was incomplete "because Judge Healy is not quite prepared to recommend the abolition of the holding company." He thought that he could revise the language in a manner "that would not be patently inconsistent with the President's desire to eliminate the holding company." The same day, he sent a copy of the reworded report to Healy with the notation that it reconciled his objections with the principle embodied in the bill. Cohen thought that this was "a discrepancy which might disappear in any event with a more liberal interpretation of the Bill."[16]

Cohen's argument, that the SEC would adopt a commonsense approach in executing section eleven, prevailed upon Judge Healy who finally agreed to sign the NPPC report.[17] The major textual change in the draft, after the recommendation to eliminate the holding company,

15. Ibid., 282, 365-67.

16. The *New York Times*, Mar. 7, 1935; Cohen to Harold L. Ickes and Judge Healy, Feb. 8, 1935, NPPC Records, Cohen Office File, box 10.

17. Arthur Krock of the *Times* perceived that the administration was not advocating wild-eyed dissolutions or reorganizations for the sake of destroying the values of utility securities. Although a critic himself, he wrote that, when the industry and investors examined the legislation in the light of Joseph P. Kennedy's administration of SEC

was to insert the phrase, "where it serves no demonstrably useful and necessary purpose." Compulsory dissolution and reorganization, the document read, would be implemented without "undue dislocation of investment or the loss of operating economies which flow from economically and geographically integrated public utility systems."[18]

As the committee's questioning of government witnesses continued, Rayburn had difficulty controlling the course of the hearings. Pettengill indicated that he would propose a substitute plan for regulating the holding company. Both possibilities had occurred to Cohen who, in the interim, had drafted a presidential message to accompany the report. On March 6, Commerce Secretary Daniel Roper noted that the bill was, indeed, in difficulty. He wrote to Marvin McIntyre, the president's secretary, that the entire legislative program, especially the holding-company bill, was in the midst of a "storm area" and that the president should delay pushing ahead until the general business and legislative atmosphere cleared. He wrote that by December "measures which will be difficult, if not impossible, to have considered constructively at this time may be entirely feasible at the next session."[19]

Roper's opinion was that the forthcoming NPPC report would harden congressional opposition. He suggested that the president adopt a different approach. Let him hold a press conference, he wrote to McIntyre, and state unequivocally that "he is not following the plan of submitting bills to carry out the suggestions which he conveys to the Congress through various reports submitted, but [is] leaving the construction of the bills entirely to the Committees of the Congress." Also, he should meet with congressional leaders at an early date to pare down the legislative program and divide it into two classifications: "(1) those bills, or measures, which in the opinion of the President must be enacted

---

rules, of the new registration forms that had permitted Swift & Company to file its financial statement in only sixty pages, and of Judge Healy's testimony, the holding-company bill would be robbed of many of its "terrors" (*New York Times,* Mar. 8, 1935).

18. The preliminary and final drafts are located in NPPC Records, General Classified File (hereafter cited as GCF), box 8. Some members of the NPPC, including Lilienthal, had favored an early draft with stronger language but went along with the final version. Lilienthal, who was in Georgia on March 11, telephoned Cohen's office and requested that his name be signed to the report. He added that he would have been "even happier to have signed the Report with the stronger language which had been contained in the earlier draft" (Herman to Cohen, Mar. 11, 1935, in ibid.). See also U.S. Congress, House, *Report of the National Power Policy Committee on Utility Holding Companies,* House doc. 137, 74th Cong., 1st sess. (Washington, D.C., 1935).

19. See Pettengill's proposal as related by George H. Shaw to W. A. Jones and Henry L. Doherty, Mar. 15, 1935, "Senate Lobby Investigation," box 101; and Roper to McIntyre, Mar. 6, 1935, Roosevelt Papers, OF 3.

at this Session of Congress; and (2) those which could be passed over until the next Session." Roper evidently was unaware that the president had committed his support to Senator Wheeler and Congressman Rayburn for the bill with a stiff dissolution provision.[20]

Following Cohen's strategy, President Roosevelt transmitted the NPPC report on March 12 to the House Committee on Interstate and Foreign Commerce along with a strongly worded message. The message was a clear expression of the Brandeisian philosophy, declaring that the president had been watching "with great interest" the fight being waged against holding-company legislation and had seen much of the propaganda against the bill. He observed that similar tactics were used against the Securities Exchange Act, which everyone now considered to be constructive legislation. He predicted that the same would hold true for the Wheeler-Rayburn bill because it did not destroy legitimate investments in holding- and operating-company securities. It reestablished, rather, the arm's-length relationship between the holding company and its subsidiaries by confining the actions of the former to investment.[21]

The president maintained also that the worst evil of the holding company had been its tendency to promote a dangerous centralization of wealth and power in the electric industry. "Regulation has small chance of ultimate success against the kind of concentrated wealth and economic power which holding companies have shown the ability to acquire in the utility field." Companies without any discernible economic function had to go; the time was ripe for reversing the process whereby a few individuals controlled the decisions of free citizens. "I am against private socialism of concentrated private power as thoroughly as I am against governmental socialism." President Roosevelt proclaimed, "The one is equally as dangerous as the other; and destruction of private socialism is utterly essential to avoid governmental socialism."[22]

The message then proceeded to divorce the holding company from the mainstream of American law and business. It condemned the holding company as a "corporate invention which can give a few corporate insiders unwarranted and intolerable powers over other people's money." The cure was to eliminate the holding company and to restore local control to the operating companies. The diffusion of power and responsibility to local business, economically independent and standing

20. Ibid.
21. *Report of the NPPC*, 2316.
22. Ibid.

on its own feet—the Brandeisian formula—had been taken over by the president.[23]

President Roosevelt made only a fleeting reference to a primary function of the NPPC, the formulation of a national power policy for the American people. In his message, however, the president spoke vaguely about a "series of reports to coordinate Government policy on such power problems." Had he proclaimed to Congress and the nation that the Wheeler-Rayburn bill was the keystone of a national policy to plan for the current and future power needs of the American people, the president might have strengthened his case.

As it was, press reaction to the presidential message was about evenly divided. The Washington, D.C., *News,* for example, thought it "rang the bell on the utilities," while the Newark *Evening News* editorialized that it carried the "danger of burning down the house to get rid of the rats." The Jackson, Mississippi, *Daily News* claimed that the bill was being used as a vehicle for reelection. Arthur Krock of the *New York Times* acknowledged that it represented "personal conviction" as well as "essential politics" for Roosevelt. The cry of communism and dictatorship was just "stuff and nonsense," said Walter Lippmann. The bill was simply a "revival of old-fashioned, 100% American trust busting ... an attempt to recover some of that individualism and economic freedom which we hear so much about." Bertrand H. Snell, the leader of the dispirited Republican minority in the House, indignantly declared that the president had broken his promise not to comment on pending legislation.[24]

Neither the message nor the report silenced the industry's opposition, nor did they quell the revolt in the House committee. And after the government's witnesses testified, the industry's leaders presented their case against the bill. The broad outlines of the strategy employed by both sides at the hearings were immediately apparent. The government sought, by referring to the FTC's reports on the financial and operating histories of the major holding companies, to prepare a foundation upon which to defend specific sections in the House and Senate bills. Its witnesses reiterated the list of holding-company abuses and emphasized the advantages accruing from an integrated operating-utility system freed from the financial control of the holding company. The benefits of local service and local management were cited often, as was the conviction that the holding companies' stranglehold on the operating

---

23. Ibid.
24. Robert Winsmore, "The Threat to Utility Holding Companies," *Literary Digest,* 119 (Mar. 23, 1935), 40; and the *New York Times,* Mar. 14, 1935.

companies must be severed in favor of an arm's-length relationship.

The opponents of the Wheeler-Rayburn bill disputed the government's contention. Stressing the financial and managerial services that holding companies had afforded in the past, they cast doubt on the credibility of the FTC's findings. They admitted that a few companies had been guilty of the abuses cited, but stressed that these were a minority in the industry. Since the stock market collapse, these companies had taken steps to correct the worst practices and warned now that, if the bill passed and holding-company systems were dissolved, millions of dollars invested in securities would be destroyed. The prescription of the opposition was regulation and not elimination of the holding company. Throughout the hearings they presented a public image of reasonable men whose companies performed a public service for which the government was unjustly persecuting them. In the final analysis, the validity of the FTC's findings and the question of whether the industry had reformed itself since 1929 became the central issues fixing the atmosphere in which the House and Senate committees weighed the future of the holding company.

Because the same administration witnesses testified before both congressional committees their arguments may be presented together. Dr. Walter M. Splawn was the first expert to testify for the government. His testimony, centering on the nineteen abuses for which the FTC had condemned the holding company, became the point of reference to which all discussion returned.[25] The chief single advantage accruing from the proposed legislation was that it protected the legitimate interests of the investors in utility securities and of the public. The bill would constrain the managers of "other people's money" to exercise financial responsibility in performing their functions.

The only practical way to prohibit the recurrence of abuses was through stringent federal legislation. State public service commissions had demonstrated their inability to break the financial and managerial hold that economically useless holding companies had on operating utilities. The testimony of Colonel William T. Chantland of the FTC on this point was unequivocal. "When a system is in existence that performs no public service functions directly, and under which all of these abuses ... have been permitted to arise or persist and be carried on, the burden then shifts, so that unless the holding company

25. *Hearings on H.R. 5423,* 287 ff. See also Gordon C. Losee, "A History of the Public Utility Holding Company Act of 1935" (Master's thesis, University of Illinois, 1935). Losee's chronology is not always accurate, nor did he have access to the government's records.

sponsors can demonstrate to you conclusively that the continuance of the system is indispensable, they should go."[26]

The growing concentration of control in the power industry concerned most government witnesses. Dr. Splawn, for instance, declared that a few gigantic holding corporations, ruled by a handful of financiers and investment bankers, eventually would dominate the industry. Consumers, investors, and the public would be subjected to their caprices. Corcoran testified that this condition was tantamount to "private socialism." The country was obliged to rely upon the integrity of the men at the top of these pyramids. The trend toward concentrated control could be reversed by destroying the holding-company machinery that was unnecessary for "serving the public with electric and gas, and[,] if you can, [by eliminating] that machinery without taking the skin off the back of every investor in the country."[27]

The same witnesses also claimed that holding-company control was responsible for increasing the cost of gas and electric services to the consumer. Congressman Rayburn, during the hearings, attributed this to the holding companies' demand for excessive revenues from their subsidiaries in order to service their own securities. These securities had been floated with the expectation that the companies would take in more revenues than they actually did. Concentrated control also led to higher rates of service. "Such intensification of economic power beyond the point of proved economies not only is susceptible of grave abuse," he told the committee, "but is a form of private socialism inimical to the functioning of democratic institutions and the welfare of a free people."[28]

Again, the origin of the problem was the inability of the state commissions to regulate adequately holding companies that operated in interstate commerce. Chantland and Corcoran noted that their activities, especially the floating of securities, were beyond the jurisdiction of any single state. The former declared that state regulation was a failure because "all the regulation that a State can give, in that line, is very largely indirect." The Wheeler-Rayburn bill corrected this and

26. U.S. Congress, Senate, Hearings on S. 1725, Public Utility Holding Companies, 74th Cong., 1st sess. (Washington, D.C., 1935) (hereafter cited as *Hearings on S. 1725*). Benjamin V. Cohen and Thomas G. Corcoran, "Memorandum on Support of the Constitutionality of Public-Utility Holding Company Bill," in ibid., 807-20. For similar testimony see ibid., 75-90, 175-200; and *Hearings on H.R. 5423*, 55-120, 146-48, 260-65.
27. *Hearings on S. 1725*, 88-90, 202-04; *Hearings on H.R. 5423*, 178-83.
28. On this point see the Federal Power Commission, Rate Series Reports, nos. 1-3, issued in 1935, and the *New York Times*, Feb. 4, 1935. See also *Hearings on H.R. 5423*, 203 ff., 343-45.

other deficiencies by protecting the investor, the industry, and the public. It induced the industry to put its business on a sound financial footing after six years of mismanagement. The FPC had the authority to regulate the rates and services of interstate power companies, while the SEC, drawing upon information obtained from companies registered with it and having the power to scrutinize security issues and fees, discouraged poorly capitalized companies from functioning to the detriment of the utility industry. Beneath the umbrella of federal intervention the holders of utility securities would receive a fair return on their investment and the consumer would profit from better and cheaper service. In the end, a system of regional operating units would evolve, locally controlled by many small investors, to service geographically and economically contiguous territories.[29]

The most obvious fact to emerge from the congressional hearings was that the Roosevelt administration was determined to secure federal legislation to curb holding-company abuses. In spite of all opposition, some of which emanated within the government itself, the president had taken a firm stand in favor of eliminating the holding company. He made almost no effort to differentiate between holding companies that had performed their functions responsibly and those that had acted with little regard for the welfare of their security holders or the public. The testimony in behalf of section eleven seemed to bear out this interpretation.[30]

On the other hand, certain assumptions and charges that the administration's witnesses had made concerning economic concentration, financial malpractices, and higher rates for service were challenged by the industry's witnesses. The moment of truth was at hand for the utility executives who came to the hearings armed with charts, maps, and counterproposals. They were prepared also to discuss the financial history of each system and to demonstrate that the holding

29. Ibid., 115-22, 202-04. Senator Wheeler was strongly convinced that holding companies were responsible for the high rates that consumers paid. He claimed that the executives did not have any direct concern or stake in the communities their companies serviced, since their sole interest was the accumulation of greater profits. Where an operating company had a sound financial structure, he believed that it could perform the technological, managerial, and capital-acquiring functions itself (*Hearings on S. 1725,* 301-02, passim).

30. In the course of the hearings, none of the major groups that had agitated for regulation prior to and since the stock market crash appeared to testify for the administration's bill. In a few cases they apparently were deterred by the long, complex nature of the Wheeler-Rayburn bill; others, however, had gone over to a public-ownership position on the power question and would accept no less. See, for example, Judson King to Charles H. Porter, June 16, 1935, Judson King Papers, box 12, Library of Congress.

company had functioned well in the past and would continue to serve the industry and the public in meeting the nation's power needs.[31] As the correspondence between Joseph P. Tumulty and H. Hobart Porter revealed, the industry's leaders knew that federal legislation was in the offing and prepared their defense. In January 1935, for instance, Tumulty passed on Rayburn's suggestion to Porter that the industry disclose its views to his committee. Tumulty added that the committee would be more receptive to the views of an industry executive than to a battery of high-priced lawyers, "who are more inclined to argue the constitutional features of legislation than to discuss the real merits of the case." Warning Porter to lay his cards on the table and to propose constructive legislation, he declared that "it will be disastrous if the public utility companies do not recognize the critical situation which confronts them."[32]

By February, however, Tumulty was having second thoughts. The Supreme Court in the interim had handed down its decision in the so-called "hot oil" cases. Its invalidation of a New Deal law for the first time changed the complexion of things and Tumulty thought it imperative to challenge the holding-company bill precisely on constitutional grounds. "The constitutional phases grow more important with each passing day," he wrote, "and should be emphasized under the strongest professional leadership." In addition, utility men should bring themselves into a "closer association with the members of the subcommittee" concerned with holding-company legislation. Tumulty apparently wanted the industry to propose amendments for stricter regulation without eliminating the holding company, for he told Porter to assemble the executives "to confer with the subcommittee in an endeavor to work out a situation favorable to the companies as well as the Government."[33]

During the early spring of 1935, the chief executives of the major holding- and operating-company systems appeared to testify against the bill. Nonutility people, including Francis E. Frothingham of the Investment Bankers Association and Henry I. Harriman of the United States Chamber of Commerce, also appeared as witnesses. John E. Benton and H. Lester Hooker of the NARUC and Fred N. Oliver, the counsel for the National Association of Mutual Savings Banks,

31. "Executives Storm House Committee to Stop Bill," *Newsweek,* 5 (Apr. 13, 1935), 32-33; and Willkie, "Why the Rayburn Bill Must Be Stopped," *Forbes,* 35 (May 1, 1935), 11-12.
32. Tumulty to Porter, Jan. 29, 1935; Porter to Rayburn, Jan. 30, 1935, "Senate Lobby Investigation," box 98.
33. Tumulty to Porter, Feb. 20, 1935, in ibid.

added the weight of their organizations against the bill. Despite their differences over how best to handle the holding-company problem, they were in agreement that the Wheeler-Rayburn bill, which one Wall Street observer described as a feint "intended to draw opponents of the measure out of position and induce them to lower their guards," was not the solution.[34]

These witnesses argued that, since World War I, centralized management in the form of the holding company had enabled the industry to expand its plants and areas of service with a minimum of risk. John F. McFarlane, counsel for the Electric Bond and Share Company, testified that the principle of diversified investment had enabled the holding company to minimize the risk of total loss to the security holder. Although the evidence from a study conducted by Professor Merwin H. Waterman of the University of Michigan, who was sympathetic to the holding company, cast serious doubt on the validity of this principle in practice, nearly every one of the industry's witnesses endorsed it.[35]

Besides diversifying investments for greater protection, the holding company was a necessary instrument for raising capital for the operating companies. Wendell Willkie, among others, believed that this was the prime function of the holding company in a relatively young industry, one that needed fresh infusions of capital. Situated close to the money markets, the holding company was in a more advantageous position than the local operating companies to recruit capital. Willkie testified that access to the money markets, as well as the technological and managerial services that holding companies provided, accounted for the rapid growth of the electric utility industry in the United States.[36] He warned that the Wheeler-Rayburn bill would deprive the industry of these benefits by wiping out millions of dollars worth of holding-company securities, by dislocating the financial markets, and by disrupting the industry. This was the fear of banker Francis E. Frothingham, who felt that the bill was "picking out one industry and driving it into the ground." "It seems to me a mistaken policy," he told Congressman John Cooper, the ranking Republican on the committee.[37]

The fear that the bill would close the sources of capital in the rapidly expanding industry was used effectively to whip up support against

34. The *New York Times*, Apr. 14, 1935.
35. *Hearings on S. 1725*, 306-11, 526 ff., 778-83; cf. the study of Merwin H. Waterman, *Financial Policies of Public Utility Holding Companies* (Ann Arbor, 1936).
36. *Hearings on S. 1725*, 367, 550-54, 715-25.
37. *Hearings on H.R. 5423*, 1453. See also "Regulation Not Destruction Urged for Holding Companies," *Bankers Magazine*, 130 (Mar. 1935), 355-56.

it. James Lee Loomis of Connecticut Mutual Life Insurance Company analyzed the role of institutional investors in utility financing and warned the Senate committee that "the bill, if enacted into law, will close this outlet presently and perhaps prospectively to any further investment of private capital in the public utility industry." Fred N. Oliver, counsel for the National Association of Mutual Savings Banks, read into the record a statement that the bill "may impair the value of mutual savings banks' investments in mortgage bonds of operating electric light, power and gas companies." Dr. Hugh Magill of AFUI, meanwhile, had repeated similar warnings to the House committee.[38]

The utility executives claimed also that they were not opposing federal regulation per se, only this particular bill because it would destroy the industry. Willkie, in fact, testified that his colleagues welcomed "reasonable" federal legislation and presented to each committee a "substitute plan" outlining what he had in mind. The plan consisted of fourteen points, each taking the form of an amendment to the Securities Exchange Act. It consisted of such provisions as eliminating nonvoting stock, permitting the SEC to pass on a new stock issue, limiting the activities and financial interests of holding-company directors, and enforcing uniform accounting procedures. The supervision of the operating companies would continue to be left to the local communities and the state public service commissions. In return for promising to curb concentration in the future, Willkie expected the government to back down on the elimination or dismemberment of holding-company systems. A few of the fourteen proposals were included in the bill reported out of the House committee, but Willkie's "concessions" earned for him the enmity of the most reactionary members in and out of the industry. At the same time the Roosevelt administration, particularly Cohen, opposed the scheme. It relied too heavily on state regulation to satisfy New Dealers, and the president's inflexible stand had made it impossible for them to support further efforts to patch up a system they believed had failed.[39]

The administration's reassurances notwithstanding, utility spokesmen then testified that the Wheeler-Rayburn bill obliterated the line between federal and state jurisdiction. H. Lester Hooker, chairman of the Legislative Committee of the NARUC, testified that the association favored "strict and adequate regulation by the States to the

38. *Hearings on S. 1725*, 520-22; *Hearings on H.R. 5423*, 1752, 1782.
39. *Hearings on S. 1725*, 577, 597-614; and Joseph Barnes, *Willkie* (New York, 1952), 54-56, 86-87. Cf. Willkie, "The Rayburn Bill Substitute," *Electrical World*, 105 (Apr. 13, 1935), 989.

full extent of their power, and by the Federal Government only to the extent that the power of the States cannot control." He brushed aside the argument that the bill only supplemented state regulation. "However, notwithstanding these avowals," he concluded, "a close study and detailed analysis of the provisions of Title I and Title II, show that State regulation, and the powers reserved to the State are substantially emasculated and devastated."[40] Francis E. Frothingham went further and condemned the bill as the entering wedge of government ownership. "The excuse may be that it is in the public interest," he noted, but the argument was a "red herring." Nationalization of the industry, he declared, was the real purpose of the bill.[41]

The most bitterly criticized provision of the bill was section eleven, the "death sentence," which called for the simplification and compulsory dissolution of holding-company systems after 1940. It virtually guaranteed that the industry's leaders, whatever their attitudes toward government regulation or toward each other for that matter, would close ranks in opposition. Samuel Ferguson, one of the more liberal utility figures, could not perceive how eliminating the holding company would prevent a recurrence of abuses. "I would particularly point out," he told Senator Wheeler's committee, "that even if the breakup could be accomplished, still the purported objective of this bill—namely to prevent a repetition of abuses—would not have been achieved." "This is so obviously fundamental," he added, "that I fail to see how it has so wholly escaped the observation of the drafters of the bill." And T. Justin Moore, speaking for the Committee of Public Utility Executives, added: "Why kill the [holding] company before trying to regulate it?"[42]

John McFarlane, counsel for the much-criticized Electric Bond and Share Company, and representing the Committee of Public Utility Executives, capped the attack on the dissolution features of the bill. Even if the FTC's findings were substantially true, he argued, "this is the first time, so far as I know, that the Congress of the United States has under consideration a measure which proposed the elim-

---

40. *Hearings on S. 1725*, 747-48, 778-85; and *Hearings on H.R. 5423*, 727-29, 1604-08, 1659-77.

41. Ibid., 1452, 1464-65. Colonel Chantland of the FTC was not surprised that an investment banker should come to the defense of the industry. "The record in our report shows clearly how this came about," he wrote to Senator George W. Norris, "and I think the bill is needed quite as much for the banking angle as it is for the utility angle" (Colonel William T. Chantland to George W. Norris, Apr. 9, 1935, George W. Norris Papers, tray 80, box 7, Library of Congress [hereafter cited as Norris Papers]).

42. *Hearings on S. 1725*, 495, 577.

ination of useful units in the business world because of alleged or actual malpractices in various instances in that industry."[43] Most utility men, as a matter of conscience, shared the belief that section eleven had been inspired by the erroneous reports of the FTC. In December 1934, for example, Thomas N. McCarter, the president of the Edison Electric Institute, reminded President Roosevelt that the holding company was an indispensable vehicle for utility financing. Conceding that the power industry had experienced a period of "frenzied finance" and "wild speculation," he declared that this was past history. The holding company had resumed its proper role of financing and guiding the industry's expansion, and this was all the administration should consider. Most witnesses at the hearings adopted similar defenses.[44]

As a matter of fact, the administration had anticipated that the industry's heaviest attack would come against section eleven. And Roosevelt, Wheeler, and Rayburn adamantly opposed efforts to water down the bill or to accept substitute proposals to bolster state regulation. Corcoran, one of the architects of the bill, defended the compulsory dissolution provisions against the charge that legitimate investments would be destroyed while the SEC was reorganizing and simplifying holding companies along geographically and economically integrated lines. The SEC might implement section eleven through various schemes involving stock transfers, exchanges, disfranchisements, and property sales; it could execute reorganizations by bringing the systems before equity courts which could parcel the assets among stockholders.[45]

At the conclusion of the hearings the House and Senate committees retired into executive sessions to weigh the testimony and amendments to the bill. Meanwhile, interested parties speculated on the action that the full House and Senate might take. One observer declared that the administration's strategy was to have the Senate committee report out a drastic bill and the House a relatively mild one. "Thus, the real issue will be left for a conference committee," he wrote. And there, "Cochran [Corcoran?], acting as liaison for the President, will be able through Wheeler and Rayburn to get into the final conference report certain clauses of language which will appear to be innocent but which will carry much concealed authority." Another critic was less certain, but he warned Gadsden that the time was ripe "to take

43. Ibid.
44. Thomas N. McCarter, "A Memorial to the President of the United States," *Edison Electric Institute Bulletin*, 3 (Jan. 1935), 3-4; cf. *Hearings on S. 1725*, 293-95.
45. Ibid., 204-15.

a look at the situation ahead and to prepare for the developments that may occur when the bill is reported out of committee."[46]

In either event, the scene of the struggle shifted suddenly from the committee hearings to the floor of Congress.[47] Early in May 1935 the *New York Times* detected evidence that a movement was afoot "to take some of the teeth out of the measure." Conservatives were attempting to weaken the bill by proposing amendments in committee. An unofficial poll of the House committee disclosed that nine members opposed section eleven and only six favored it. Senator Daniel O. Hastings, Republican, of Delaware, a leading foe of the administration's policy, said the bill should be modified "so as to do some good and no harm." To destroy the holding companies, as this bill proposed, was simply outrageous. On May 27, the conservative opposition received encouragement from the Supreme Court which struck down the National Industrial Recovery Act. Justice Cardozo, one of the liberals, had condemned Congress's delegation of legislative authority to the head of the National Recovery Administration (NRA) as "delegation running riot."[48]

After it became clear that Rayburn's committee was in revolt, Senator Wheeler moved quickly to report his bill in order to avoid losing the initiative. On May 8, he and the Democratic majority on the committee thwarted Senator Hastings's effort to strike out the death sentence.

46. W. A. Jones to Henry L. Doherty, May 6, 1935; T. J. Ross to Philip Gadsden, May 7, 1935, "Senate Lobby Investigation," boxes 97, 98.

47. Whereas in the Seventy-third Congress the Senate had provided the opposition to the emergency legislation of the New Deal, the House was the center of opposition in the new Congress. Two factors that were vital in passing the crisis legislation of the Hundred Days were evidently no longer operative: the administration had disposed of the bulk of its patronage by 1935, and the feeling of crisis that had impelled the House to go along with the president's program had passed. This was not apparent to most observers when the Seventy-fourth Congress convened in 1935.

Also, in 1935 signs of economic recovery were on the horizon. House Democrats who were usually conservative in fiscal and business matters and who had swum with the tide during the crisis days were drifting back again into their old patterns of thought. In the new Congress they allied with conservative Republicans to oppose much of the legislation that emanated from the White House. These men formed the core of congressional opposition to the Wheeler-Rayburn Bill, the tax bill, the banking legislation, social-security programs, and the creation of the Works Progress Administration. See Raymond Moley, *After Seven Years* (New York, 1939), 302; James T. Patterson, *Congressional Conservatism and the New Deal* (Lexington, Ky., 1967), chs. 1, 2; Mark Sullivan, "A Political Analysis of the New Congress," *Congressional Digest,* 14 (Jan. 1935), 5, 31.

48. The *New York Times,* May 8, 1935; and *A.L.A. Schechter Poultry Corp. et al. v. United States,* 295 U.S. 553. The argument was put forth to prove that the bill gave to the SEC unconstitutional powers over the holding company.

The committee substituted another amendment postponing by two years the date when the SEC would effect compulsory dissolutions. With minor exceptions the SEC would not permit the present systems to continue beyond 1942.[49] The Senate bill, S. 1725, underwent other extensive revisions and was reported out to the Senate as S. 2796. Wheeler's tactics had not escaped criticism; Senators Hastings and William H. Dieterich, Democrat, of Illinois condemned the procedure, and noted that only eight of the twenty members had been present at the time of the vote. They also alleged that no more than seven knew the contents of the revised bill.[50]

On May 14, the committee filed the majority report with the clerk of the Senate. The report stated that the purpose of the bill was to atomize the unwieldy, concentrated political and financial power of holding companies and to affect savings for the consumers. Actually, it read more like an indictment than a report, thereby ensuring a virulent floor fight when the bill came before the Senate on May 29.[51] The debate, lasting two weeks, was intensely bitter, but, interspersed between epithets and predictions of impending disaster, the arguments were similar to the testimony that had been presented during the congressional hearings. Critics claimed that the bill violated constitutional safeguards by which Congress was prohibited from interfering with intrastate commerce.[52] Senator Hastings, his desk laden with law books as he spoke, told his colleagues that the bill unlawfully delegated congressional powers to an administrative agency, while denying the mails to legitimate businesses. Senator Wallace H. White, Republican, of Maine drew a parallel to the court's decision in the National Industrial

49. The *New York Times*, May 9, 1935.
50. Cf. *Senate Report 621*, Calendar no. 651, 74th Cong., 1st sess. (Washington, D.C., 1935), 1-293; Losee, "A History of the Public Utility Holding Company Act of 1935," ch. 3.
51. *Senate Report 621*, p. 11. The report declared:

The title requires that a holding company be permitted to hold only a single system of operating companies in order to break down dangerous and unnecessary nationwide financial interlockings in the essentially local operating utility business; to break down the concentration of the economic and political power now vested in the power trust; to reduce utility enterprises to a size and power which can successfully be regulated by local and Federal regulatory commissions; to rearrange the relationships between operating and holding companies on a functional basis so that intelligent regulation is possible; to confine the operations and the interest of each public utility system to a given region so that the system will have to work out a *modus vivendi* with the population of that region.

52. *Congressional Record*, 74th Cong., 1st sess., 79 (May 29, 1935), 8390-98.

Recovery Act case, and Dieterich affirmed that the bill was "obnoxious to the Constitution."[53]

The last argument was particularly telling because it placed the administration's spokesmen on the defensive. On June 4, Dieterich again raised the constitutional issue in a bid to sway uncommitted votes. "The Supreme Court," he declared, "held that an emergency was no justification for evading the Constitution." Unexpectedly, Senator Borah came to their defense; with calculated logic he told his colleagues: "The only question is whether holding companies dealing across state lines and selling securities and holding subsidiaries which send electricity across state lines are engaged in interstate business."[54]

Dieterich and Hastings then charged that S. 2796 was not the same bill that Wheeler had introduced in February, and implied that the Montana Democrat was attempting to hoodwink his colleagues. The committee had not been given an opportunity to read the revised bill; therefore the Senate should instruct the Judiciary Committee to examine it "in the light of the court decisions."[55] Wheeler retorted that the accusation was unjustified. "I've given a fair hearing on the bill," he said, "but I do not propose to stand idly by and let statements go unchallenged about treatment given the public utility companies." How could Dieterich know what was in the bill, he asked, "when he came to the committee meetings only for a few minutes each day and complained that members of his [Wheeler's] commission were present"?[56]

The thrust of Wheeler's defense went straight to the heart of his opponents' arguments. He stated that the bill applied only to interstate holding companies; the jurisdiction of the states over intrastate power companies remained intact. Nor was the bill an unconstitutional delegation of power to an administrative agency; it abolished all registered holding companies except in the few instances where first-degree companies were necessary to comply with state laws or to maintain efficient service in a contiguous foreign country. Wheeler received support from Senator George W. Norris, the archfoe of the power trust. Norris lectured his colleagues, on June 3, for nearly five hours, employing maps and charts to demonstrate that the consumer ultimately paid

53. Ibid., 8617, 8621-22 (June 4, 1935).
54. Ibid., 8617, 8441 (May 31, 1935).
55. The *New York Times,* May 30, 1935.
56. Ibid. The reference was to the presence of Cohen and Dozier DeVane of the FPC.

the piper for the utility holding companies' pyramided structures.[57] At this point the Business Advisory Council of the Department of Commerce, composed of influential Democratic businessmen such as W. Averell Harriman, injected a hitherto confidential report into the dispute. Although dated April 30, 1935, the document was not released until June 1, amid speculation that the administration had tried to suppress it because of its compromise position between the extremes of the Wheeler bill and no regulation.[58] The report argued that the government should gradually eliminate holding companies that were economically indefensible but permit strong companies to continue functioning, even to control five or more regional operating systems under strict supervision. It also incorporated a tax feature to induce companies to simplify their pyramided structures and a provision for the enfranchisement of all classes of stock.[59] After reading the report, Senator Wheeler maintained that "there was no possibility of such sweeping changes being written into the bill."[60]

Immediately thereafter, the Senate turned its attention to section eleven, the provision to simplify and eliminate holding-company systems by 1940. Senator Dieterich, on June 4, launched a stinging attack upon the compulsory dissolution provision. "The vicious part of this bill is Section 11, giving the Securities Commission, following its whim, without any fixed rules, the absolute power to destroy and fix the time in which the destruction shall be wrought. That is the death sentence," he claimed, and moved to substitute strict federal regulation.[61]

57. *Congressional Record,* 74th Cong., 1st sess. (June 3, 1935), 8492 ff. Norris preferred a more drastic bill in the direction of nationalizing the power companies.
58. J. H. Moseley to Chester H. McCall, May 18, 1935, National Archives, Department of Commerce, file 95261. The authors of the report, which was approved on May 2, 1935, included Gano Dunn, Winthrop Aldrich, and Dr. Karl T. Compton.
59. For the details leading up to the final report see Roper to Dunn, Dec. 9, 1935; Roper to Colonel Moses Greenwood, Jan. 15, 1935, in ibid.; also, Wetmore Hodges, "Notes on Public Utility Holding Company Bill," Mar. 20, 1935, Roosevelt Papers, OF 293; and Hodges to McIntyre, May 10, 1935, in ibid., OF 3-Q.
60. The *New York Times,* June 2, 1935.
61. Dieterich's opposition was part of a carefully mapped strategy to emasculate the most stringent features of the bill. On June 5 Hugh Magill of the AFUI disclosed how industry leaders intended to proceed. The Supreme Court's decision upsetting the National Industrial Recovery Act had boosted their morale; he noted also that opposition to the bill in Washington was so widespread that only the president's rigid attitude kept Congress from dropping it altogether. Magill wrote to Colonel George Montgomery that the AFUI had secured "the cooperation of a number of influential Senators in opposition to the bill and amendments have been introduced removing the so-called 'death sentence' which amendments will have to be voted on before the bill is passed" (see *Congressional Record,* 74th Cong., 1st sess. [June 4, 1935], 8618; and Magill to Montgomery, June 5, 1935, "Senate Lobby Investigation," box 101).

Notwithstanding these attacks, Wheeler was confident that the bill would pass with the substance of section eleven intact. But he was also wise enough to realize that some concessions would have to be made to the opposition. The controversial report of the Business Advisory Council, the National Industrial Recovery Act decision, Republican sniping, and the conviction that the bill was unconstitutional had caused many senators to waver. Democrats alone had proposed seventy amendments, thereby indicating considerable discontent within their ranks.[62] The persuasive oratory of Senator Fred Brown, Democrat, of New Hampshire alone had thwarted a motion to recommit the bill.[63]

During debate on Friday, June 7, Wheeler agreed to accept some amendments, his purpose being to allay the fears of key southerners that the bill might supplant state-commission jurisdiction over intrastate power companies. He also revealed that President Roosevelt had written to him saying that he wanted "this bill passed with Section 11 retained."[64] The strategy did not entirely succeed in silencing the opposition, and Wheeler was forced to delay a vote on the bill. Over the weekend he and Charles West, the president's liaison with Congress, met with Senator Kenneth McKellar, Democrat, of Tennessee to consider some eleventh-hour amendments.[65] Since he expected a close vote, Wheeler could not readily alienate a potential supporter. On the other hand, Senator Homer T. Bone believed that the McKellar amendments tore at the heart of the bill; Norris agreed, but he also felt that the original bill had not gone far enough. And, much to the chagrin of its proponents, Borah began to speculate publicly that section eleven might be unconstitutional, given the Court's attitude toward administrative agencies.[66]

62. For the amendments, many of which were of a clarifying nature, see the following pages in the *Congressional Record,* 7817, 8356, 8374, 8383, 8430, 8457, 8491-8532, 8614-36, 8671-91, 8705-11, 8750, 8772, 8837, 8841-44, 8845-58, 8927, 9040; and Losee, "A History of the Public Utility Holding Company Act of 1935," 112.

63. *Congressional Record,* 74th Cong., 1st sess. (June 5, 1935), 8705-11.

64. The *New York Times,* June 9, 1935.

65. The first amendment was drawn to protect the state public service commissions' jurisdiction over intrastate power companies; the second proposed to make the commissions' role as receivers in reorganization proceedings optional instead of mandatory. See Kenneth McKellar to Roosevelt, June 12, 1935, Roosevelt Papers, OF 293; *Congressional Record,* 74th Cong., 1st sess. (June 10, 1935), 8936-41.

66. Ibid. (June 10, 1935), 8946-48. A few senators, including Huey Long of Louisiana, opted for a more radical bill. Wheeler persuaded Long to stay away from the committee hearings, but the Kingfish was determined to have his say on the floor of the Senate. Resplendent in a white serge suit and pink shirt and necktie, he attacked the administration for failing to include the gas and telephone trusts under section eleven. Wheeler believed

Thus, the Montana Democrat was put in the difficult position of trying to balance contending interests. Dieterich, meanwhile, pressed his colleagues to accept a substitute section eleven, nullifying the compulsory dissolution feature, restricting the commission's jurisdiction, and substituting stricter federal regulation. Political observers predicted that a defeat of the Dieterich amendment would shift the fight to the House, where chances for striking out the death sentence were much better.[67] There was evidence to support this view, for the House committee already was in the process of revising key provisions of the Rayburn bill. The administration perceived the threat also, and assigned Corcoran to meet with House supporters to work out a strategy. At the invitation of Senator Robert M. La Follette, Jr., in mid-June, Corcoran met with the Wisconsin delegation in the House and with a similar group led by Maury Maverick, Democrat, of Texas to coordinate plans for a floor fight. The strategy was to amend the House bill by substituting sections eleven and thirteen (service contracts at cost) of the Senate bill.[68]

On Tuesday, June 11, both sides nervously sized up their own and the opposition's strength. Proponents of the bill were confident they had the votes to carry it, including the death sentence. After some preliminary debate, the Senate moved to vote on the Dieterich amendment; the roll call was forty-four to forty-four to strike the death sentence. For a few anxious moments Wheeler and Vice-President Garner feared the administration had suffered a defeat; then, Peter Norbeck, Republican, of South Dakota rose and cast his vote for the death sentence. The administration had triumphed by a single vote; Senator Norris admitted afterward that "the closeness of the vote ought to convince anyone that had the method proposed been a more severe one, it would undoubtedly have been lost."[69] Ironically, Dieterich's defeat may have been one of his own making. During the debate he had challenged Wheeler to prove that the president endorsed the death sentence, whereupon his rival whipped from his pocket a letter from the president, unequivocally endorsing the bill. The passage of the

---

that his criticisms actually were calculated to embarrass the president politically. For Long's remarks see ibid., 8933-35, 8941-43 (June 10, 1935), and Wheeler to author, personal interview, May 12, 1965.

67. *Congressional Record,* 74th Cong., 1st sess. (June 11, 1935), 9040-41.

68. On this point see *Statement by Thomas G. Corcoran in Reply to a Charge by Congressman Ralph Owen Brewster,* Roosevelt Papers, OF 1560.

69. *Congressional Record,* 74th Cong., 1st sess. (June 11, 1935), 9053; Norris to Max Aron, June 11, 1938, Norris Papers, tray 66, box 5.

entire bill by a fifty-six-to-thirty-two vote came almost as an anticlimax.[70]

In the House, however, the holding-company bill was in serious trouble. Huddleston and Pettengill had aligned with the Republican opposition to tie up the subcommittee's report until they could make drastic changes in the bill. Congressman John Rankin believed that Rayburn had lost control over his committee and, hence, suggested to President Roosevelt that the Senate's bill be sent directly to the House, bypassing the commerce committee. Unfortunately for the administration the maneuver failed after the Rules Committee refused to relax the regular procedure of the House.[71]

Meanwhile, the division within Rayburn's committee persisted. Critics of the measure initially were of two minds: some opposed the bill *in toto,* while others, recognizing the determination of the administration to take some action, wanted to substitute strict regulation for the death sentence.[72] The latter particularly argued that the federal government should simplify pyramided holding-company structures in lieu of eliminating them altogether. Eventually they reconciled their differences by combining two earlier proposals. The first was to report a bill that confined one holding company to each operating system, where the system covered a field wide enough to warrant having one; the second was to levy a series of taxes on intercorporate transactions and on the intermediate layers of holding companies. The critics argued that this procedure would accomplish the president's purpose of curbing abuses short of eliminating the instrument itself.

The House subcommittee did not report to the full committee until June 19, one week after the Senate had passed its bill. Its report, reflecting the views of the conservative members, stripped the bill of the compulsory dissolution provision and substituted discretionary power for the SEC.[73] A half hour after its release, the president denounced the report and reaffirmed his support of the death sentence. *New York Times* columnist Arthur Krock attributed Roosevelt's inflex-

---

70. Senator Borah was convinced that the bill was needed to halt the drift into public ownership that was sure to come if holding-company abuses were not curbed. Therefore he offered an amendment to dissolve every holding company except those in the first degree, which would be controlled by the SEC. See *Congressional Record,* 74th Cong., 1st sess. (June 11, 1935), 9042, 9050.

71. Rankin to Roosevelt, June 12, 1935, Roosevelt Papers, OF 293.

72. The *New York Times,* Apr. 17, 1935.

73. There were other differences also. The SEC, for example, was authorized to confine each holding company to one integrated system without reference to economic or geographic considerations as specified in S. 2796; its jurisdiction over securities subject to state regulation was dispensed with, as were the special judicial proceedings under

ible stand to political considerations; the president needed the support of the western Progressives in the forthcoming election. This group is "hot for the killing," Krock wrote, "and he must stand by them to the end."[74]

The subcommittee report ignited a revolt among the members of the full committee. From June 20 through June 22 Huddleston, Pettengill, and the Republicans were in rebellion against Rayburn's leadership; they voted to accept the substitute bill without the death sentence, rewrote and substantially weakened its declaration of policy, excluded a compromise 2 percent tax on dividends, and omitted entirely Title III which provided for the regulation of gas holding companies.[75] On June 22, the committee voted fifteen to seven to report the substitute bill to the House. Its action had severely impaired the president's prestige and Rayburn's effectiveness as manager of the House bill. As a consequence, the initiative fell to Wheeler and Corcoran to steer the death-sentence bill through the Congress.[76] A private poll of the House revealed the complexity of the task; it suggested that the administration lacked forty votes to win a floor fight. In addition, Corcoran's lobbying alienated a number of congressmen; Ralph Owen Brewster, Republican, of Maine, for example, charged that Corcoran had threat-

---

section eleven. The report also permitted the practice of upstream loans to continue and set aside the provision for placing service contracts on a mutual basis. Having reduced the original bill to a soft-toothed tabby, the authors of the report called for a 2 percent income tax levy on intercorporate dividends. See U.S. Congress, House, Report on 1318, *Committee Report on S. 2796*, Calendar no. 451, 74th Cong., 1st sess. (Washington, D.C., 1935), esp. 8-22; and the *New York Times*, June 20, 1935. The proposed discretionary authority for the SEC precipitated a conflict between SEC Commissioner Joseph P. Kennedy and Pettengill. The former argued that the House bill set no guidelines for the SEC except the nebulous concept of "the public interest." He recognized that the SEC rather than Congress would become the object of lobbyists' pressures. For this exchange see *Congressional Record*, 74th Cong., 1st sess. (July 9, 11, 16, 1935), 10838, 11050, 11248-49; and James M. Landis, *The Administrative Process* (New Haven, 1938), 55-56.

74. The *New York Times*, June 20, 1935. Cf. Roosevelt Press Conference Transcript no. 216, June 28, 1935, Roosevelt Papers; and Elmer Cornwell, Jr., *Presidential Leadership of Public Opinion* (Bloomington, Ind., 1965), 152 ff.

75. The exclusion of Title III was in part the result of effective lobbying by the gas interest but also because the hearings had virtually ignored the subject and Cohen believed that further study of gas holding companies was necessary. See *Committee Report on S. 2796*, 4-8; George H. Shaw to N. McGowan, Apr. 5, 1935, "Senate Lobby Investigation," box 101; and Cohen to author, personal interview, Washington, D.C., May 12, 1965.

76. Ibid. Hugh Magill noted that Wheeler was determined to enact the bill "in practically the form it was then before the Senate" (see Magill to Hugo Black, Aug. 2, 1935, "Senate Lobby Investigation," box 101).

ened to withhold funds for a power project at Passamaquoddy Bay, if he did not vote for the death sentence.[77]

Similarly, reports were circulated that Roosevelt had instructed Rayburn to oppose the report of his own committee. "Mr. Rayburn has a large personal following," one reporter noted, "and a move by him to substitute for the House measure the more punitive bill voted by the Senate would be expected to carry much weight on the floor."[78] Already there was grumbling over the committee's action. Maury Maverick, a fellow Texan, was furious; on June 20, he circulated to each member of Congress a letter denouncing the committee for tossing the president a crumb. "In other words, Congress lays down a policy and tells the Commission to decide for itself with reference to any particular company whether Congress' policy is wise or unwise. This is a sheer and cowardly abdication by Congress of its legislative function," he declared. Representative Rankin accused the committee of taking the teeth out of the bill, leaving behind "a mere empty shell."[79]

On June 27, the House formed itself into a Committee of the Whole to debate the substitute bill. After a Republican filibuster failed, Rayburn took the floor to urge passage of the Senate bill. Representative John Cooper, the ranking Republican member of the commerce committee, blunted the appeal. He denounced the death sentence, condemned "Wheelerism" (i.e., government ownership), and censured the administration for employing high-pressure tactics.[80] Meanwhile, rumors floated around Capitol Hill that proponents of the death sentence were trading votes, their favorite targets being the sponsors of the Frazier-Lemke Farm Mortgage Moratorium bill that was locked in the Rules Committee. One Wisconsin Progressive accused Democrats of deserting the president for "the bastard brat of the power trust"; on the other side of the aisle, Republicans taunted Democrats as "rubber stamps." The atmosphere was so charged and confused that Democratic leaders of the House refused to be responsible for the president's legislative program. In all the logrolling who could predict which way votes would go?[81]

As the debate grew more and more acrimonious, President Roosevelt attempted unsuccessfully to compose differences. He instructed his floor managers, Rayburn and Edward Eicher of Iowa, to offer two

77. For the details see the *Statement by Thomas G. Corcoran.*
78. The *New York Times,* June 21, 1935.
79. Circular letter of Maury Maverick, June 20, 1935; Rankin to Members of Congress, June 19, 1935, NPPC Records, GCF, box 17.
80. *Congressional Record,* 74th Cong., 1st sess. (June 27, 1935), 10301, 10327-29.
81. Ibid. (June 29, 1935), 10417; the *New York Times,* June 30, 1935.

motions: the first instructing the commerce committee to substitute the Senate's bill; the second calling for a separate record vote on section eleven. Representative John J. O'Connor of the Rules Committee, however, decreed that a record vote was out of order while the House was sitting as a committee.[82] The most he would permit was an unrecorded teller vote on the death sentence. On July 1, as members of the House passed between the two tellers, reporters from the Scripps-Howard paper, the Washington *Daily News,* strained from the press gallery to identify how each congressman had voted. When it was over, the tellers had counted 216 votes against section eleven and only 146 votes in favor.[83] The next day the House officially recorded the voting; the count this time stood at 258 to 147 against the death sentence. Power-conscious Democrats in the Pacific Northwest and the South voted overwhelmingly for section eleven, while eastern Democrats and conservative southerners deserted the president in droves. The key 258-to-147 vote revealed the existence—for the first time since the New Deal began—of a conservative coalition in the House. That body then passed the substitute bill 323 to 81.[84]

The reaction to the crucial teller vote was swift in coming. Arthur Krock labeled it "a political defeat of the first magnitude" for the president. Huddleston congratulated his colleagues for returning to their "constitutional prerogatives." The margin of defeat had been so great, House leaders declared, that neither a record vote nor the threat of reprisals would reverse it.[85] Rayburn conceded that the House was unmanageable and that the initiative had passed from his hands. On July 2, he declared that he would not ask that body to substitute the Senate bill. Exhausted, he warned his colleagues that, in all probability, this session would enact no holding-company legislation.[86] Representative Cooper disputed this, noting that the two houses were not far apart. The death sentence had carried in the Senate by one vote; he confidently expected that body to reverse itself and instruct its conferees to accept the House bill.[87] On July 13, the House in a record vote substituted its bill for the Senate bill. Walter Lippmann

---

82. Eicher also moved unsuccessfully to substitute section thirteen of S. 2796 for the House version in order to place service contracts on a mutual basis. See *Congressional Record,* 74th Cong., 1st sess. (July 1, 1935), 10509-12.

83. Ibid. (July 2, 1935), 10589-90, for a reprint of the teller vote from the Washington *Daily News.*

84. Cf. Patterson, *Congressional Conservatism and the New Deal,* 51-58.

85. The *New York Times,* July 2, 1935.

86. *Congressional Record,* 74th Cong., 1st sess. (July 2, 1935), 10635.

87. Ibid.

observed that the difference between the two bills was not substantial. "Under the Senate bill," he wrote, "the holding company must prove to the [Securities Exchange] commission and to the courts that it ought not to be dissolved eventually, and under the House bill the commission must prove to the court that the company ought eventually to be dissolved."[88]

While the House was weighing the fate of its bill, in the Senate critics revived their opposition, focusing this time upon the instructions that body should give to its conferees. Senator Dieterich, unable to persuade his colleagues to instruct the conferees to accept the House bill, suddenly withdrew his opposition to a motion to send the death-sentence bill to conference. Dieterich's capitulation was dictated by an agreement worked out the night before. At a meeting on July 9, Senator James F. Byrnes of South Carolina persuaded Wheeler to allow Dieterich to offer the motion to substitute the House bill for the death sentence. In return, Dieterich agreed to drop his opposition, if the Senate defeated his motion, and to permit a vote on sending the bill to conference. Then, if the conferees were unable to reconcile their differences, each side agreed to Byrnes's suggestion that the Senate should take another roll-call vote on the death sentence.[89]

Events proceeded according to plan; the Senate voted on July 10 to send S. 2796 to conference. Vice-President Garner selected the conferees and instructed them to stand firmly behind the death sentence. The choice of conferees assured the administration that its viewpoint would be well represented in the conference. Wheeler, Alben Barkley, Brown, and the Farmer-Laborite Henrik Shipstead had voted for the Senate bill; the Republican conferee, Senator White, against the bill. On July 13, Roosevelt wrote to Representative Edward Eicher, one of the House floor managers, that he was confident "we shall get something practical and in accordance with our principles as a result of the conference." Commissioner Manly, of the FPC, was less optimistic; he wrote to the president that, if the bill became deadlocked in conference, the provisions of Title I might be transferred to Title II in order to preserve holding-company regulation.[90]

The story of the conference committee was one of bitter arguing and recriminations. On July 24, for example, the meeting began peacefully enough but quickly degenerated into a bitter row. Wheeler re-

88. Quoted in *Literary Digest,* 119 (July 13, 1935), 4.
89. For Byrnes's role see the *New York Times,* July 11, 1935.
90. Roosevelt to Eicher, July 13, 1935, Roosevelt Papers, OF 293; and Manly to Roosevelt, July 5, 1935, Federal Power Commission Records, General File, 21-3d-1, part III.

quested the committee to permit Ben Cohen and Dozier DeVane of the FPC to participate as "expert advisers"; actually, he and Roosevelt feared that Huddleston might "pull the wool over Rayburn's eyes" and induce him to accept a weak bill.[91] The uproar that ensued temporarily overshadowed the fundamental differences on section eleven. Huddleston, red-faced and fuming, accused Wheeler of trying to lobby the conference. Members of the executive branch had no right to interfere in legislative business.[92] Wheeler retorted that Huddleston represented the views of the Power Trust; he also threatened to go into Ohio in 1936 to "help lick" Representative Cooper, another member of the House conference. Huddleston responded by describing Wheeler as a "four-flushing bluffer." The House, meanwhile, voted to instruct its conferees to insist upon the exclusion of Cohen and DeVane. Not until a week later did the House and Senate conferees compose their differences; on August 1 they agreed to permit the "expert advisers" to sit in the anteroom but not in the conference room itself.[93]

While the procedural dispute was unfolding, the protagonists tried to outflank each other on the death-sentence issue. On July 31, Huddleston motioned the House to discharge its conferees because they were unable to report a bill. Speaker Byrns ruled the motion out of order, whereupon Rayburn requested the House to instruct the conferees to accept the Senate bill. Rayburn had again misjudged the independent spirit of the House and the strength of the conservative opposition, for it voted 209 to 155 against the death-sentence bill. The Democrats had been almost evenly divided in their votes.[94]

Administration supporters were hopping mad at the turn of events. The *Wall Street Journal* reported that the New Dealers were "looking to blame someone for the revolt in the House against the death sentence." They were annoyed with Speaker Byrns for not lining up the votes, "and because they suspect that deep in his heart he isn't very sorry about it." Their disgust extended to his whip, Representative Boland of Pennsylvania, for voting against the death sentence, to Huddleston for trying to exclude Cohen from the conference, and to the Rules Committee chairman, O'Connor of New York.[95]

As the first week in August droned into the second and third weeks,

91. Wheeler and Cohen to author, personal interviews, Washington, D.C., May 12, 1965; and the *New York Times*, Aug. 24, 1935.
92. *Congressional Record,* 74th Cong., 1st sess. (Aug. 1, 1935), 12273.
93. Ibid.
94. Ibid. (July 31, 1935), 12238, for Huddleston's motion; ibid. (Aug. 1, 1935), 12271, for the vote on Rayburn's motion.
95. The *Wall Street Journal,* Aug. 5, 1935.

the conference deadlock persisted. Efforts to build a foundation for settling the dispute by clearing away the noncontroversial sections of the bill at first did not succeed. Congressmen Huddleston and Pettengill appealed to the president for concessions "to honest differences of opinion." On August 17, Pettengill wrote that there was so much in the two bills that should become law, "that even if Section 11 were blessed by all the saints of politics, it ought not to be permitted to strangle the rest of the bill in legislative childbirth."[96] He urged the president to instruct Wheeler to accept a lesser version of the Senate bill. Instead, Roosevelt avoided giving him a direct reply; Wheeler suspected that he was beginning to falter under the intense pressure. In a private conversation he told the president straight out that, if he had to take the bill back to the Senate, it would certainly die there. The bluntness of this observation apparently shook the president because he agreed to stand by the death-sentence bill and to risk the wrath of the conservative opposition within his own party.[97]

Only gradually and through the efforts of Felix Frankfurter was the conference deadlock finally resolved. A typewritten memorandum attached to a letter written by Frankfurter makes it possible to piece together the events leading to the compromise. The bill, he wrote, was tied up in conference on the issue of whether a holding company may control more than one integrated system of operating companies. "Huddleston (with 2 Republicans in his pocket) is irreconcilable and wants to water down even the House bill's recognition of one system as a norm." Rayburn was so anxious to have some bill reported that he was talking about a compromise enabling a holding company to control two operating systems of any size whatever. This was undesirable because "it leaves Willkie's Commonwealth and Southern and U.G.I., the two most powerful giant companies, completely intact."

By contrast, Frankfurter noted that the Senate conferees had formally offered a substantial concession, "not merely face-saving language." The concession enabled a holding company to control more than one operating system provided that the operating units were in the same locality, were small in size, and were incapable of separate economical operation. Huddleston had spurned the concession, thereby rendering an agreement impossible. Unless the Senate conferees capitulated to him or the House, "in a complete somersault," gave him new instruc-

96. Pettengill to Roosevelt, Aug. 17, 1935, Roosevelt Papers, OF 293.
97. Roosevelt to Pettengill, Aug. 23, 1935, in ibid.; and Wheeler to author, personal interview, Washington, D.C., May 12, 1965.

tions, or appointed new conferees, the impasse would persist. Frankfurter was not optimistic about the latter.

What courses of action were open to the president? To avoid capitulating to Huddleston the Senate conferees might be discharged and the bill allowed to die in conference. Or, Congress could be adjourned and the bill left in conference. The first option clearly was out, but "there is everything to gain and nothing to lose in keeping the bill in conference until January." In the interim, members of Congress, upon returning home to their districts, might find that their constituents supported the administration's bill. Besides, there was the strong possibility that "Associated Gas will fail before then and accelerate the growing sentiment in favor of the Senate bill." Also, "the personal antagonisms among House leaders which have been such a tremendous factor in the House stubbornness on the 'death sentence' and in Huddleston's position of control may be smoothed out before next January."

Frankfurter preferred to keep the bill in conference and the Congress in session until a satisfactory compromise was arranged. To still rumors in the congressional cloakrooms that he was willing to accept any kind of bill, Frankfurter advised Roosevelt to announce to the press that the House bill was clearly unacceptable. The Harvard law professor suggested the kind of statement that the president might give to the press; it was strongly worded, but left the door open for compromise:

> Now of course, I do not suggest ... that there can be only one form of words by which this policy can be translated into legislation. Since there is agreement between the Senate and the House in their professed objectives, I should think and I hope that ways may be found of carrying those objectives into effect which will commend themselves to all of us. But I shall certainly not be a party to any legislation which does not include specific and effective provisions for the elimination of the kind of corporate monstrosities which permit ten or eleven powerful groups to control practically all the operating utility companies in the United States.[98]

Meanwhile, on Sunday, August 18, the president held a strategy conference with selected House leaders and the Senate conferees. Chairman Doughton of the Ways and Means Committee assured those

98. The undated memorandum, attached to the Frankfurter letter, may be found in the Roosevelt Papers, President's Secretary's File, box 42.

present that he would delay the report on the tax bill in order to keep open the date of adjournment. Senator Alben Barkley, a southerner and less controversial figure than Wheeler, was chosen to introduce to the conference committee Frankfurter's compromise. On August 20, Wheeler disclosed its main outlines: it directed the SEC to permit a holding company to control more than one integrated utility system if the additional systems could not stand alone economically and were not so large or so scattered as to impair the advantages of localized management, efficient operation, or effective regulation. Also, the principle was established that the commission, beginning in 1938, would try to set up simplified integrated utility systems, and that no more than two holding companies would be allowed above their subsidiaries. Roosevelt was not wildly enthusiastic with the compromise but he agreed to go along, grumbling that "Felix sounds just like John W. Davis."[99]

After obtaining the president's consent, administration officials moved to persuade the opposition to relent. Vice-President Garner, a man of considerable influence in the Congress and skill as a parliamentarian, volunteered to handle opposition leaders in the House. On August 21, he presented a virtual ultimatum to Rules Committee chairman O'Connor, Representative Boland, the Democratic whip, and Speaker Byrns: either they lined up the votes for the Barkley compromise or the president would keep Congress in session until January.[100] Huddleston alone refused to be intimidated; he described the Barkley compromise as "a mere jumble of words." He proposed instead that the number of operating companies controlled by a holding company remain fluid, giving to the SEC discretionary authority in the matter. The Senate conferees rejected the counterproposal and the conference broke up.

After Barkley and Wheeler reported their failure to get an agreement, the administration decided to play its last card. Rayburn motioned the House to accept the holding-company bill, with the Barkley compromise on section eleven; for the benefit of recalcitrant Democrats

---

99. Roosevelt had made it clear during the conference that he would not shoulder the responsibility for abandoning the death sentence. And Huddleston, fearing that his continued opposition would split the party in Congress, proposed on August 20 that the SEC permit first- and second-degree holding companies to continue. See the *Wall Street Journal*, Aug. 20, 21, 1935; and Arthur M. Schlesinger, Jr., *The Politics of Upheaval* (Boston, 1960), 324.

John W. Davis, the Democratic presidential candidate in 1924, was considered to be a conservative. His Wall Street law firm represented such clients as AT&T.

100. The *New York Times*, Aug. 22, 1935. From the start of the legislative controversy O'Connor had favored a substantially weaker version of section eleven.

he also read into the record a letter from the president dated August 21. Actually, the letter had been drafted by Wheeler and Corcoran who withheld it from Rayburn until the last possible moment when it might be needed to screw up his determination against Huddleston. Now Rayburn was using it to demonstrate to foot-dragging members of his own party that the president was seeking to accommodate their reservations. "From my point of view," the letter bearing the presidential signature read, "it represents a greater recession from the Senate bill than I should like to see made. But I understand the urgent desire of many members of both Houses to have a bill worked out at this session, and to that end I hope the House will find this proposal of the Senate conferees acceptable."[101]

The strategy succeeded and on August 22 the bill, with the Barkley compromise, was jammed through the Congress. The vote in the House was 219 to 142. The *New York Times,* taking account of the lopsided vote of 203 Democrats for the compromise bill, observed that "many opponents ran to vote on orders of the Democratic high command and switched positions they had first taken."[102] On August 26, 1935, after clearing the compromise bill with the SEC and the FPC, the president affixed his signature.

101. See the White House memorandum dated Aug. 21, 1935, Roosevelt Papers, OF 293; and Wheeler to author, personal interview, Washington, D.C., May 12, 1965.
102. The *New York Times,* Aug. 23, 1935.

CHAPTER IV

The Opinion Makers

Title I of the Public Utility Holding Company Act of 1935 became law only after the administration refused to bow to fierce pressures to enact a substantially weaker bill. Roosevelt believed the legislation was necessary to rescue the industry from its own worst abuses and thereby preserve it. Whether he could have achieved the same results with less agitation or ill will is highly doubtful. On the other hand, there was probably less justification, other than political, for his continuing attacks on the private utilities, since he had no intention of nationalizing them as his most radical supporters demanded and since, as John Maynard Keynes wrote in 1938, the real criminals had long since moved out. Nonetheless, the rough handling of the legislation and the bitter lobbying campaign against it suggested the limits of what Congress and the public would accept.[1]

In their zeal to defeat what they genuinely perceived to be a dangerous law, the private utilities subjected the members of Congress and the public to one of the most carefully planned and executed lobbying campaigns in American history. Well-financed, the campaign was an early example in the use of communications media to manipulate public opinion. The lobbyists created an atmosphere in which sober-minded inquiry was difficult. The focus of their attack was directed against members of the House of Representatives whose brief tenure, or conviction, made them vulnerable to pressures to vote against the Senate's death-sentence bill. The lobbyists were less successful in persuading senators and ordinary citizens of the justice of their cause. The reasons were complex. While the utility propagandists denounced the administration, they also lacked confidence in the ability of an educated citizenry to make thoughtful judgments, which is the essence of democracy. They failed, too, because New Dealers resorted to similar tactics —but with a difference. The administration believed —and

---

1. John Maynard Keynes to Franklin D. Roosevelt, Feb. 1, 1938, Franklin D. Roosevelt Papers, President's Personal File 5325, Franklin D. Roosevelt Library (hereafter cited as Roosevelt Papers, PPF); and Thomas K. McCraw, *TVA and the Power Fight, 1933-1939* (Philadelphia, 1971), 157.

acted upon its conviction—that, once the public had the facts, it was capable of deciding the proper course of policy. The industry seemed incapable of grasping this elemental fact, at least until Willkie called attention to it in 1939. By then, however, the damage had been done.[2]

Beginning in February 1935, the date that the Wheeler-Rayburn bill was introduced, administration and utility lobbyists openly attempted to persuade congressmen of the righteousness of their respective causes. In July 1935, House members temporarily seized the initiative to vent openly the complaints that hitherto had been uttered covertly. Their resentment at being made targets from both pro- and anti-New Deal lobbyists had reached its limit and now they determined to strike back. Representative Ralph Owen Brewster accused the chief administration lobbyist, Thomas G. Corcoran, of threatening to sever PWA funds for a hydroelectric project on Passamaquoddy Bay, in Maine, if he cast a negative vote on section eleven. This indictment, which was not substantiated after investigation, did ignite a rebellion against all lobbyists, a revolt that had been simmering beneath the political surface for some time.[3]

On July 1, 1935, the House defeated a motion to substitute the Senate's bill for its own. A few days later, the powerful chairman of the Rules Committee, John J. O'Connor, and Congressman Pettengill maneuvered a resolution through the House calling for an inquiry into all the influence brought to bear on the bill regardless of the source. The House inquiry did not progress much beyond this point however. A lack of genuine commitment by some Democratic leaders for the Senate's bill, fear that the investigation would link key Democrats to the utilities, and the failure to vote adequate funds limited the scope of the House investigation. The Senate, in contrast, vigorously seized the initiative and pressed for a thorough inquiry. Senator Hugo L.

---

2. Willkie wrote: "So long as the public feels that it can get a more desirable service, everything considered, from privately owned utilities, it will continue to permit the operation of such companies. If the public believes otherwise, the fault is not with the public, but with the utilities, which either have not performed properly, have been disrespectful of the public, or, as in most cases, have neglected to cultivate the public mind" (Wendell L. Willkie, "The Strength That Comes from Adversity," *Electrical World*, 114 [June 3, 1939], 68-69). See also Richard Polenburg, "The National Committee to Uphold Constitutional Government, 1937-1941," *Journal of American History,* 52 (Dec. 1965), 582-98.

3. Charles Beard observed that the Brewster charge "simmered down to a question of veracity, in which the weight of evidence, if not conclusive, was on the side of the administration" (Charles A. Beard, "The New Deal's Rough Road," *Current History,* 42 [Sept. 1935], 630).

Black, with the consent of the administration, motioned for the creation of a special Senate committee to conduct the inquiry.[4]

Administration officials theorized that revelations of utility misconduct would lend powerful support for the stronger Senate bill when the congressional conference committee convened to reconcile the differences between the two bills. Cohen and Corcoran approached Wheeler to serve as chairman of the committee, but they were not successful. Despite his thorough knowledge of the bill and the utilities' financial practices and propaganda methods, Wheeler turned them down.[5] Tactically, he explained, his presence would be of dubious value because the public would look upon him as a persecutor of the industry. Also, he would be too busy guiding the Senate bill through the conference.

The task, therefore, was given to Senator Hugo Black. An archfoe of the private utilities, Black proved to be an outstanding choice from the administration's viewpoint. He possessed the crusading mentality that was needed to execute the committee's mandate. Further, he conceived of his function as that of exposing the utilities' propaganda which allegedly had blinded the public to the truth. Amid the sensational revelations that Black's committee unearthed in 1935 and 1936, the administration's own lobbying activity quickly paled and was quietly forgotten. Later, a writer noted that "the inquiry has cast a shroud of suspicion over the legitimacy of the public protest that welled up against the 'death sentence' for holding companies." Black's committee, observed Turner Catledge in the *New York Times,* has added "new proof to Mr. Roosevelt's accusations against these members of our commercial community."[6]

The Black committee's investigation revealed that the utilities had organized and financed a national campaign to incite investors and the general public against the Wheeler-Rayburn bill. In contrast to the formal and reasoned statements of utility executives before the House and Senate commerce committees the popular campaign was emotional, often apocryphal, playing on the fear that Roosevelt harbored dictatorial ambitions. Rational thought gave place quickly to irrational and blind feeling, as the industry feared that its very existence was at stake. This was not surprising, inasmuch as the utilities had all along been preaching that it was private enterprise, untrammeled

4. *Congressional Record,* 74th Cong., 1st sess., 79 (July 3, 8, 1935), 10689-92, 10806, 10811, 11003-05.
5. The *New York Times,* July 28, 1935.
6. Ibid.

by bureaucratic restrictions, that had been responsible for the electrification of America.

The dimensions of the industry's plan against the proposed legislation evolved gradually as the bill wended its way through the legislative process. In February, the Edison Electric Institute agreed to permit each company to argue its case against the bill separately. The institute officially remained aloof, taking no active role against the bills. Behind its facade as a statistical bureau, however, the institute's director, Bernard F. Weadock, pulled many of the strings guiding the campaign against the administration's holding-company policy.[7]

Actually, the institute spoke through a mouthpiece, the recently organized Committee of Public Utility Executives. Composed of executives whose companies also were members of the Edison Institute, the committee had engaged the New York and Philadelphia law firms of Simpson, Thacher & Bartlett and Sullivan & Cromwell to advise it as to what could be done legally to oppose the Wheeler-Rayburn bill. Its chairman, Philip Gadsden, was associated closely with Republican politics in Philadelphia.[8] After World War I, he had become the legislative fixture for United Gas Improvement in Washington. The institute, Weadock later admitted to investigators, supplied Gadsden's committee with funds, facts, and figures. "We agreed to furnish the ammunition," he confessed, "and let the Committee of Public Utility Executives do the fighting."[9]

The voice of the industry's opposition also was echoed through numerous front organizations. The AFUI closely parroted the charge that the bill would destroy the value of all utility securities. Although it professed to be an organization of ten million middle-class investors, founded to protect the interests of investors from financial abuses within the industry and from attacks upon it, Electric Bond and Share apparently was its chief architect. The New York *Journal of Commerce* in 1934 had described it as a "movement of stockholders inspired by utility companies and launched in Chicago in order to gain an appearance of independence of Wall Street."[10]

7. "Minutes of a Meeting of the Board of Trustees, Edison Electric Institute," Feb. 12 and April 11, 1935, National Archives, Record Group 46, "Senate Special Committee to Investigate Lobbying Activities," 75th Congress, Case Files, box 97 (hereafter only the file and box number will be cited).

8. "Report of Investigation on Philip Gadsden," n.d., General Files, box 1.

9. Quoted in George H. Brown to H. A. Blomquist, July 22, 1935, Case Files, box 97.

10. Quoted in William T. Chantland to Hugo Black, Aug. 2, 1935, General Files, box 2.

To finance the AFUI an ingenious plan was devised. The federation's directors affirmed that the organization had neither financial nor managerial ties with utility companies. At the same time it supplied its literature freely or at nominal cost "to all recognized organizations that are in a position to assist in reaching those interested in utility securities."[11] In practice, the utility companies—quite legally—were pushing the federation's literature at a price sufficiently above cost to pay its expenses. The material was sent to stockholders at the expense of the companies. The federation thereby received sufficient money to continue to propagate its cause.[12] "The beautiful part of it," an official admitted, "is that our finances are unassailable."[13] Even Black's committee had failed to compel it to disclose the source of its funds.

The federation apparently functioned as a one-man organization, despite the respectable names appearing on its letterhead. Some administration officials believed that the industry had recruited its president, Dr. Hugh S. Magill, because he had close ties with many religious groups and could swing their support against the administration's policies. "The fact that the organization was conceived by utility executives, promoted by them, financed by them, its membership secured by them, and its policies dictated by them," wrote Basil Manly, "is no doubt the reason that it is a 'safe' organization from their standpoint."[14]

The federation accused supporters of the Wheeler-Rayburn bill of being Communists, Socialists, and "spoilsmen in politics." Magill condemned them for advocating government ownership of utilities, and for subverting decent citizens "from the proven paths of true democracy, into the morasses of state Socialism and Communism, by the honeyed phrase 'socialized industry for the benefit of all'." Pleading for justice and a fair deal, Magill blamed the threat of government competition and exorbitant taxation for the losses that utility investors allegedly suffered.[15]

Both the federation and Gadsden's committee encouraged investors, bankers, and legal groups to testify against the bill or write protesting

11. Basil Manly to Black, Aug. 9, 1935, ibid.
12. Clarence Ridley to William E. Mosher, Apr. 6, 1935, Federal Power Commission Records, General File, 21-31-1, part II, located at the Federal Power Commission.
13. Walter (surname unknown) to George D. Key, Apr. 15, 1935, Case Files, box 91.
14. Manly to Black, Aug. 9, 1935, General Files, box 2.
15. Hugh S. Magill, *A Plea for Justice* (Chicago, 1935?), in Roosevelt Papers, Office File 293 (hereafter cited as OF).

letters to congressmen. In March, for example, a federation official set up a meeting between Magill and Catherine Curtis, the head of an organization called Women Investors in America, Inc.[16] In the lobby of Washington's Mayflower Hotel they planned a radio campaign against the bill and discussed the testimony Miss Curtis was to give to Rayburn's committee. Later, when the Black committee investigated the organization, Miss Curtis refused to disclose the source of her financing. Subpoenaed records revealed that the Women Investors of America, Inc., had been created principally to combat the holding-company bill. Utility money financed most of its activity, although the investment banking house of Blythe & Company had contributed $5,750 to it and Lammot Du Pont, who regularly supported conservative causes, gave $500.[17]

Gadsden's committee, meanwhile, encouraged the organization of protest committees in the states. He expected them to use their influence in political quarters against the bill. In April, the executive secretary of the Securities League of Massachusetts wrote Gadsden that his group was making it "rather unwise for politicians to use the utility industry for their scapegoat as they have done in the past." A few days later, he informed a member of the league that the investment banking houses throughout the states "are cooperating with us by spreading to their clientele the necessity of group action in a movement such as this."[18]

Investment and commercial bankers, as well as securities dealers, cooperated freely with the industry in its campaign of protest.[19] Three days after the bill was introduced, the investment firm of Adams, Mudge & Company indicated to Earle S. Thompson, the vice-president and treasurer of American Water Works and Electric Company, that it was prepared to cooperate "in any plan to secure the help of our clients who are security holders of yours as well as other holding companies."[20] A vice-president of J. P. Morgan & Company asked Thompson for a dozen copies of a letter he had written soliciting aid in order to place them "where they will be most effective in our cam-

16. Benjamin F. Castle to Clayton J. Howel, Mar. 14, 1935, Case Files, box 91.
17. For the list of contributors see the folder, "Women Investors in America, Inc.," Miscellaneous Files, box 106.
18. Edward Allen to Philip Gadsden, Apr. 10, 1935, Gadsden to Allen, Apr. 20, 1935, and Allen to A. C. Oliphant, June 5, 1935, Case Files, box 97.
19. T. J. Ross to Gadsden, Mar. 9, 1935, ibid.; and Charles L. Duke to Black Committee, n.d., Miscellaneous Files, box 105.
20. Andrew Adams to Earle S. Thompson, Feb. 9, 1935, W. L. Kleitz to Thompson, Feb. 27, 1935, ibid.

paign of opposition.'' The Bank of New York sent reprints of an editorial by the conservative journalist David Lawrence, entitled "The New Dictatorship," to its clients. "The substantial citizens of our country, however, must realize that the depression has created a demand for radical legislation on the part of many who do not foresee the evil consequences of the measures they advocate," wrote the bank's president, J. C. Traphagen. The bill would reduce the purchasing power of thousands of security owners, he warned, "a result opposite to the expressed aims of the New Deal."[21]

Blyth & Company, which was active in underwriting utility securities, demonstrated how effective investment-banking houses could be in mobilizing sentiment against the bill. Early in March, the firm sent a letter to more than three thousand investment bankers throughout the country warning them that the proposed legislation would "disastrously affect the value of ALL public utility securities, including those of operating companies and seriously retard business recovery." The letter was accompanied by a do-it-yourself kit describing the most effective techniques that securities salesmen should use to organize their clients' opposition. Wire Blythe & Company collect, the letter urged, and "advise whether you will cooperate."[22]

Throughout the committee hearings, opposition to the House and Senate bills was confined chiefly to groups that were most likely to be affected by the proposed legislation. The Edison Electric Institute, working through Gadsden's committee, turned to the most sophisticated techniques of advertising then available to persuade opinion makers that the administration's policy was unconstitutional, unnecessary, and dangerous for the industry and the nation. T. J. Ross, a partner in the public relations firm of Ivy Lee & Company, was given the task of handling the publicity campaign for the institute and its members. Ross, in effect, was the connection between Weadock and Gadsden.[23]

Ivy Ledbetter Lee had been a pioneering figure in the development of the public relations business. He perceived that the oligopolistic corporations, which were coming to dominate the American economy at the turn of the century, needed a better public image. He took upon himself the task of cosmeticizing their profile to give them a

21. J. C. Traphagen to clients, Feb. 28, 1935, ibid. See also similar letters from the Chase National Bank, Bennett & Palmer, and Harper & Turner, Inc., all in ibid.

22. Blythe & Company to Registered Investment Bankers, Mar. 7, 1935, Case Files, box 97.

23. See, for example, J. O. Bowen to H. A. Blomquist, July 17, 1935, ibid.

more personable and human appearance. In the course of a fascinating career, Lee handled the public relations for the Rockefellers, Guggenheims, Chryslers, and Bethlehem Steel. His techniques revitalized the entire field of opinion management.

Lee's working assumptions in the field of public relations counseling were relatively uncomplicated. "Publicity is one of the instruments in achieving any stated policy," he wrote. He believed that in the utility field "public relations were especially important because of the continual close relationship between the producer and the consumer." Identifying sponsorship and presenting the facts as known to the organization in whose behalf a statement was made formed the core of Lee's thinking. Application of his ideas was more sophisticated, however. For Lee employed the relatively new medium, radio, as well as press releases and interviews, speeches, magazine articles, and letters to eminent men (whose opinions would be likely to count with the general public) to sell his clients' messages.[24]

During the congressional hearings in February and March, Lee's firm concentrated its efforts on rallying the opposition of investors, bankers, and business groups. "The purpose of this memorandum," Ross informed Weadock and the members of the institute, "is to develop facts and the best method of presenting them to various groups of people in an effort to enlist their active support in the defeat of the present bill, or enactment of a bill to fairly regulate the industry." The facts, Ross stated, were that the proposed legislation was an unconstitutional invasion of individual and states' rights. The bill would establish rigid and restrictive control by a federal bureaucracy, would eliminate the holding company, would destroy the values of utility securities, and would lead to higher consumer rates for service. "These radical changes and losses to investors," Ross wrote, "will greatly retard national recovery, and be a distinct shock to incentive in furthering the development of the industry."[25]

Ross then proceeded to outline the most effective presentation of the facts to the group most likely to have an interest in seeing the bill defeated. They included a wide spectrum of the population, and presaged the more general appeal to the populace that would be made later. Citizens who feared the expansion of government power under the New Deal were to be told that "this legislation is only one step

---

24. Ivy Lee, "The Man Behind Steps Out: A Study in Public Relations," *Public Utilities Fortnightly*, 5 (Feb. 6, 1930), 141-50. See also *Dictionary of American Biography*, s.v. "Ivy Ledbetter Lee," supp. I.
25. Ross to Bernard F. Weadock, Feb. 23, 1935, Case Files, box 97.

in the Socialistic theories of the so-called Brain Trust who are dominant in the executive and legislative branches of the Government and who, if not stopped, . . . will soon change the form of Government."[26] Holding-company employees would face loss of jobs, while the employees of operating companies would be threatened with regimentation. Investors generally, and shareholders in the common stocks of holding companies in particular, were to be frightened by repeated threats that the "security market will be demoralized." Higher rates and inefficient service were predicted for consumers if the legislation passed.[27]

In sketching his plan for Weadock, Ross attempted to create among the various groups what might be described as a "conspiracy" neurosis.[28] Nonutility corporations would be persuaded that the New Deal was conspiring to destroy business and the free enterprise system. Insurance companies, for example, were to be told that their assets would be seized and used to fund the debt; banks would be included in the definition of a holding company in order to subject them to the law's "destructive measures." Retailers, distributors, and manufacturers might be classified as holding companies and their investors made vulnerable to the financial provisions of the bill. Subtle hints that the New Deal intended to throttle freedom of the press could be employed effectively to line up the support of publishers through their editorial columns. In sum, Ross's plan was a blueprint for a comprehensive attack on all New Deal policies, one that would appeal to such zealous defenders of "the American Way" as the Committee for the Nation and the American Liberty League.[29]

Ross moved swiftly to implement his plans. He had prepared for distribution among utility investors and businessmen a portfolio of pamphlet literature, broadsides, and press opinions condemning the Wheeler-Rayburn bill. This material included a pamphlet, "Memorandum Concerning the Economic Consequences of the Proposed Public Utility Act of 1935," detailing the potentially adverse impact of the bill upon operating companies, future utility financing, and the

26. For similar views see *Brief Analysis of Wheeler-Rayburn Bill* (Philadelphia, 1935), a pamphlet prepared by the United Gas Improvement Company, and F. M. Kerr to Preferred Stockholders of the Montana Power Company, Mar. 14, 1935, National Archives, Record Group 46, "Senate Hearings on S. 1725," Senate, 74A-E1, box 34 (hereafter cited as "Senate, S. 1725," 74A-E1).

27. Editorial, *Public Service* [Corporation of New Jersey] *News*, 13 (Mar. 15, 1935), 2.

28. Ibid. See also Philip Gadsden, "Who's Next?—An Open Letter to American Business Men," July 14, 1935, in "Senate, S. 1725," 74A-E1.

29. See Polenburg, "Committee to Uphold Constitutional Government," esp. 584.

market value of securities. Various editions capsuling newspaper editorials unfavorable to the administration's policy were mailed to members of Congress and to other prominent persons. David Lawrence's editorials, "The Right of Petition" and "The New Dictatorship," in which the conservative journalist attacked the expansion of government powers and defended the right to protest against such expansion, were reprinted and widely circulated.[30] Wendell Willkie's famous address before the United States Chamber of Commerce, "The New Year," in which he proclaimed that if the threat of government interference were removed the electric industry would do "more to lift this country out of the depression, take more men out of the bread lines and off relief rolls than any other industry . . . and do more than the Government itself can do with all its expenditures," was widely acclaimed and circulated.[31]

By mid-April the effectiveness of the industry's capacity to incite opposition to the bill among those directly interested in the future of such legislation had just about peaked. Featured articles appearing in such staid and respectable magazines as the *Review of Reviews* reflected the industry's viewpoint. Albert Shaw, Jr., editor of the *Review,* wrote Gadsden: "I feel sure that these will carry weight with our readers, and if there is any use that you can make of them in advance you are welcome to do so." The American Liberty League, the articulate voice of politically conservative legal opinion, denounced the holding-company bill as a step toward government ownership and operation of the utility industry. Later, its Lawyers Vigilance Committee declared that the bill was unconstitutional.[32]

An analysis, supplied to Ross by Ivy Lee, of one thousand newspaper editorials from February 10 through April 15, 1935, revealed that 62.6 percent were opposed to the Wheeler-Rayburn bill in its original form. Although the trend ran higher—to about 75 percent—between the first of March and the first of April, Ross still was not satisfied. He was aware that the law of diminishing returns would begin to operate if the same newspapers repeatedly printed critical editorials. Public opinion in the long run would grow weary and then suspicious. To avoid this situation Ross suggested that in the future more public statements should emanate from individual companies, individual shareholders,

30. Ross to Weadock, Mar. 16, 29, 1935, "Senate, S. 1725," 74A-E1.
31. Wendell Willkie, "The New Fear," *Vital Speeches,* 1 (May 20, 1935), 538-41.
32. Albert Shaw to Gadsden, Mar. 14, 1935, Case Files, box 101. See also "A Call to Action: The Rayburn-Wheeler Bill Must Be Defeated," American Federation of Utility Investors, *Bulletin,* 1 (Mar. 1935), Case Files, box 91; and George Wolfskill, *The Revolt of the Conservatives* (Boston, 1962), 137, 165.

and prominent people rather than from the press or the Committee of Public Utility Executives.[33]

After the Senate commerce committee reported the Wheeler bill to the full Senate in May, the second phase of the protest campaign was initiated. Emphasis was shifted in order to involve the general public more fully in the protest, and to cloak the interests of the industry in a mantle of respectability. Minutes of the meeting of the Board of Trustees of the Edison Electric Institute in May, and a pamphlet attached to the typed copy, revealed the members' deep dissatisfaction with the Senate bill. "In an apparent effort to allay the widespread public alarm," the pamphlet read, "the bill contains certain verbal changes. The new phraseology is merely an attempt to dress the wolf in sheep's clothing; its vicious nature is not changed."[34]

At this point in the campaign, Ross disclosed the details of a last desperate plan that had been prepared in anticipation of the Senate committee's strongly worded report. It unmistakably intended to kill the bill in an avalanche of protest from the man in the street who, presumably, was persuaded that the bill was a forerunner of other, more dictatorial, legislation. "I think it is one of the most powerful campaigns I have ever seen," Ross informed Gadsden.[35] His warning to use it only as a last resort was no longer necessary, for the Senate committee had voted to endorse the controversial section eleven.

The plan itself had been prepared in March with the assistance of the old and respected Philadelphia advertising firm of N. W. Ayer & Son, Inc. It was lucid in its grasp of the public's psychology and comprehensive in its attention to the minutiae which such a program entailed. Congressmen, the Ayer report observed, were fully aware that stockholders represented only a small segment of the public and that their influence was "qualified by the knowledge ... that they [stockholders] come from people whom they [congressmen] do not consider representative of the general public." For this reason it was "important that the source of these letters be extended to include the general public."

Until now, the report continued, the general public has remained largely passive because it had little information or understanding of the issues upon which to form an opinion. "It is our recommendation

33. Ross to Gadsden, Apr. 27, 1935, Case Files, box 101.
34. Edison Institute, "Minutes," May 16, 1935, and the pamphlet, *Federal Domination of Local Business: The True Purpose of the Public Utilities Bill,* 1 ff., Case Files, box 97.
35. Ross to Gadsden, Apr. 30, 1935, Case Files, box 101.

that your Committee immediately take effective steps to tell the public what this bill proposes and to interpret the bill in such a way that people can readily understand the many ways in which its passage will affect them." The total cost of such a campaign was estimated at $280,622.89. "As the first, quickest, and most direct action on your part," the report stated, "we recommend radio broadcasting." Fifteen-minute talks (preferably on CBS) on Sunday, Wednesday, and Friday evenings at 10:30 by a noted commentator such as H. V. Kaltenborn or John B. Kennedy, formerly associate editor of *Collier's*, were thought to be most effective. For maximum coverage at a minimum of expense the report included a shaded map of the United States. "Within this area," the caption read, "live 25,786,788 of the 29.9 million families in this country; 386 of the 435 members of the House of Representatives; plus 68 of the 96 Senators."

The radio commentator's task was fairly simple. He was to explain the bill's provisions in language that the layman could most readily understand, attack its injustices and dangers, and describe the remarkable growth of the electric industry. This growth, he was to emphasize, was made possible by the financial support given by the holding companies. This performed a double mission, the report noted. "These broadcasts will make clear to the public the reasons for disapproving the bill as now written, and they will also point out the justification for the continued existence of public utility holding companies."[36]

Coincident with the radio broadcasts a new campaign was recommended for the daily press. Actually there were to be two advertising campaigns; one sponsored by the Committee of Public Utility Executives; the other by operating companies of the parent holding companies whose executives were represented on Gadsden's committee. New York, Chicago, and Washington, D. C., were singled out as the targets of an intensive six-week campaign. "We have selected these three points," the report observed, "because of their financial and political importance and because, in the case of New York and Chicago, they represent such tremendous concentrations of population." Political considerations, as well as the necessity for involving citizens of all socioeconomic classes, made it "obligatory to use every major newspaper in each of these three cities."[37]

36. *Advertising Recommendations Prepared for Committee of Public Utility Executives* (Philadelphia, 1935), 1-10, in ibid. (hereafter cited as the Ayer report).
37. Ibid. The following amounts of money were among those allotted for newspaper advertisements: *New York Herald Tribune*, $3,553.20; *Wall Street Journal*, $2,646.00; *Washington Star*, $1,360.80.

The newspaper campaign was cleverly designed to insure that the industry's message filtered down into the local communities where it would reach the populace. Operating companies in the localities were requested to substitute holding-company messages attacking the Wheeler-Rayburn bill in place of their regular advertisements. "The uniformity of the message is important," the report declared. "If every operating company will run the same message that you are running, the newspaper publishers throughout the country will recognize this as a united effort of truly national character. Any newspaper ... will realize that it is receiving the local application of the national plan."[38] The local operating companies (and indirectly the consumer) were expected to foot the bill.

Other tactics also were suggested in order to defeat the proposed legislation. The report, for example, recommended a write-in campaign, in which the public would urge congressmen to vote against the bill. Another tactic, a whispering campaign to suggest that the president and the New Dealers were sick and insane, was not formally adopted in the Ayer report, although, unofficially, it became a vital part of the industry's campaign. Thomas N. McCarter of the Edison Electric Institute gave currency to rumors that the president was not well. In the early summer of 1935, the chairman of Electric Bond and Share apparently was approached by some utility officials who requested that it be incorporated into their campaign. By mid-July, *Time* magazine reported that Washington correspondents were being plagued by inquiries concerning the president's health.[39]

Immediate action was essential, the report insisted. "With the banking crisis of two years ago still fresh in memory, with the vicious securities legislation it entailed, that received aggressive popular support, we urge that you profit by this experience and exert every effort to reestablish the public regard and confidence that have been so ruthlessly destroyed during the past two years. The plan outlined in this memorandum has been designed to meet an immediate crisis."[40] Because it carefully plotted out the industry's opposition at each stage in the life of the bill, the Ayer report was eagerly seized upon by

38. Ibid. A student of the Detroit Edison Company has observed that "the Company's opposition to the law came from fears vaguely defined and quite general in their character. The opposition was to 'interference' and 'bureaucratic red tape' rather than to any specific provisions" (Raymond C. Miller, *Kilowatts at Work: A History of the Detroit Edison Company* [Detroit, 1957], 350).

39. Arthur M. Schlesinger, Jr., *The Politics of Upheaval* (Boston, 1960), 311, 314. See also "Whispering Campaign" folder in Roosevelt Papers, PPF 1.

40. Ayer report, 10.

utility executives, and it became their guiding light. It signaled the moment when the utilities should spearhead the opposition, the instant when they should pull back, and the time when the general public should be encouraged to take over. The report, in some respects, read like a piece of symphonic music with carefully staged crescendos and decrescendos.

The strategy to involve the general public in the protest was enormously effective. Letters inundated the White House and Congress imploring that section eleven, the death sentence, be modified or dropped altogether. The letters came from frightened citizens whom the utilities had persuaded that the bill would wipe out the savings that they had invested in holding-company securities. The utilities played on the fears of others that the New Deal's policy was a step along the road to nationalization and communism.[41] Other groups of citizens were persuaded to present stereotyped petitions and prayers to their congressmen. They were received from such places as the Kiwanis Club of Northumberland, Pennsylvania, and from Redlyn, Iowa. The one presented to Hamilton Fish, Jr., of New York's Twenty-sixth Congressional District was typical. "I will be seriously harmed if either of the public utility bills . . . becomes a law," it read. "The bills are unfair, unwise, and unnecessary."[42] Of the major groups directly interested in the legislation, the NARUC alone refused to take an official position on section eleven. Its members were hopelessly divided.[43]

Meanwhile, as the lobbyists swarmed over Capitol Hill and through the corridors of the Mayflower Hotel, President Roosevelt became more stubborn in his support of the death sentence. On June 28, he condemned the utility lobby in an angry press conference. It was, he declared, "the most powerful, dangerous lobby . . . that has ever been created by any organization in this country." Friends of the Wheeler-Rayburn bill applauded the president. One declared that he had not gone far enough, however, "because half the members of Congress should have been included because many are actually lobbying for the power companies."[44] Roosevelt's Dutchess County neighbor, Herbert Pell, endorsed the bill without reservation. A fairly large

41. For a sample of the correspondence see "Senate, S. 1725," 74A-E1, boxes 31-36.
42. See for example, National Archives, Record Group 46, "Petitions on Public Utility Act," House of Representatives, 74A-H6.8, boxes 14142-44.
43. Statement of Andrew R. McDonald quoted in "Commissioners' Attitudes on Wheeler-Rayburn Bill," *Public Utilities Fortnightly*, 16 (Nov. 7, 1935), 654.
44. Roosevelt Press Conference Transcript no. 216; and Orman Ewing to Marvin McIntyre, June 29, 1935, Roosevelt Papers, OF 284.

stockholder in General Electric and Electric Bond and Share, Pell complained earlier to Sam Rayburn that holding-company managements treated their shareholders "with even greater contempt than ... the general public."[45]

Although similar sentiments were voiced by small local organizations, none of the major groups that had agitated for holding-company regulation since 1925 took a strong stand in favor of the Wheeler-Rayburn bill. When the chips were down and the battle joined, they were conspicuously absent. A letter from Judson King, director of the National Popular Government League, to his friend, Professor Charles H. Porter of the Massachusetts Institute of Technology, casts some light on the reason. "As to the holding company bill," he wrote in June, "I have taken very little interest in it. It will not stop holding-company practices, any more than State Commissions have regulated them."[46] For King and the others direct public ownership and operation of the nation's utilities was the only acceptable solution. The president, however, never wholly sympathized with this viewpoint; he believed that tough federal regulation could accomplish the desired end. In the long run his analysis proved to be the more accurate.

Immediately after the president's statement, T. J. Ross, of Ivy Lee, warned Gadsden and the Committee of Public Utility Executives to counter the charges. "Believe substantial portion House membership may feel publication of press conference reports unchallenged by industry is likely to produce favorable attitude toward death sentence bill among their constituents," he cabled.[47] As the voting demonstrated later, there was some evidence to support Ross's fears. Congressmen and senators were reacting to the lobbying and the propaganda flood in unexpected ways. In fact, neither the administration nor the private-utility industry could predict with any degree of accuracy how the voting would go. Both sides made optimistic forecasts. Senator Matthew Neely, Democrat of West Virginia, for example, originally was a supporter of the controversial section eleven, but he was "persuaded" to vote against it. Harry S. Truman, a freshman senator from Missouri, resisted pressures from the utilities in his home state. After burning thirty thousand letters that had been piled on top of his desk, he voted for the bill. Congressman Donald C. Dobbins, Republican

45. Pell to Rayburn, May 25, and June 24, 1935, Herbert Pell Papers, box 12, Franklin D. Roosevelt Library.
46. Judson King to Charles H. Porter, June 16, 1935, Judson King Papers, box 12, Library of Congress.
47. Ross to Gadsden, June 29, 1935, Case Files, box 101.

of Illinois, voted against the bill in July. Later, however, he wrote to Magill that "the most nauseating thing" about his vote was that it met with the federation's approval. He then wrote to the Black committee wishing it "unbounded success" in exposing Magill.[48]

The reaction of Representative Richard Duncan, a Missouri Democrat, probably was most typical. "The character of the propaganda coming to us is enough to disgust anybody," he wrote. "We all have at least enough judgment to know that this sort of propaganda doesn't mean anything, and I expect ultimately we will have to throw the letters in the waste basket as it is impossible to answer them all, even to read them." Duncan voted against the death sentence.[49]

As the propaganda campaign raged, the House conducted, on July 1, a teller vote on the Wheeler-Rayburn bill. In a crucial test of sentiment the members voted to approve the legislation, but without the controversial section eleven. Foes of the measure were elated; McCarter of the Edison Electric Institute cabled congratulations to Gadsden for his splendid efforts. "There is a God in Israel after all," he wired.[50] And Hugh Magill exclaimed jubilantly that "for the first time in the history of our country, Congress has been definitely influenced by the letters and telegrams of millions of investors." Ross viewed the victory from a more realistic standpoint. "With the principal exception of Scripps-Howard papers," he observed, "newspapers appear to approve enthusiastically the action of the House in deleting the 'death sentence' provision."[51] Yet, he too was confident that the conference committee would resolve the differences in favor of a weak bill.

The conference committee, however, fell into a deadlock beginning with its first meeting. It was at that moment that the Roosevelt administration gave the signal to Senator Black's lobby-investigation committee, which until now had been going through the motions, to swing into high gear. Public exposure of the industry's lobbying and financial malpractice, the committee hoped, would arouse public indignation and lead to grass-roots pressure on the conferees to accept the stronger Senate bill.

The Black investigation, active from July 1935 to June 1936, unfolded an incredible story of lobbying, pressure politics, and intrigue. Its revelations were largely responsible for swinging public sentiment,

48. Harry S. Truman, *Memoirs*, 2 vols. (New York, 1955), I 151-52; and Donald C. Dobbins to Hugh S. Magill, Oct. 10, 1935, General Files, box 2.
49. Richard Duncan to W. D. Freer, Mar. 16, 1935, Case Files, box 92.
50. Thomas N. McCarter to Gadsden, July 1, 1935, Case Files, box 101.
51. Magill, "Investors Win a Great Victory," *Investor America*, 1 (July 1935), 1; and Ross to Weadock, July 6, 1935, Case Files, box 97.

which until now had opposed the administration, in favor of the death sentence. From February to the end of June, for example, Black's committee revealed that holding companies had made large contributions to the Committee of Public Utility Executives. Some of those who had contributed included: Electric Bond and Share, $22,065, Standard Gas and Electric, $14,010, Commonwealth and Southern, $13,140, North American, $13,125, United Gas Improvement, $10,755, Associated Gas and Electric, $7,890, Detroit Edison, $6,630, and American Water Works, $5,000. The total amount contributed by twenty of the leading holding and operating companies to this one organization alone was $152,065.[52] The committee left no doubt in the minds of its audience that the consumers were left to foot the bill in the form of higher rates.

The committee also demonstrated to the public what many individuals already knew or had privately suspected: that the utilities and their lobbyists had mailed thousands of telegrams to congressmen, signed with names picked out at random from city directories. One Western Union messenger admitted under oath that he was paid three cents for each signature he could muster. Gadsden disclosed that holding companies paid the expenses for bringing influential friends from all over the country to talk to congressmen. Under Black's prodding, he testified that the revenue to pay their expenses had come entirely from operating companies. Black drew the conclusion for the press that it was the public which in the end would pay. Congressman James Murray testified that he was cornered by one lobbyist who proceeded to "bewail the policies of the Administration . . . and incidentally brought up the Wheeler-Rayburn bill." Lurking beneath the surface of all this testimony were rumors that a number of congressmen had been bribed to vote against the bill.[53]

As the investigation droned on, Gadsden became a favorite target. He testified that his committee had paid about $300,000 to various legal firms to prepare briefs demonstrating that the bill was unconstitutional. John W. Davis, investigators reported, drew up a brief for Cities Service to distribute to its customers and shareholders. Until then, Cities Service had steadfastly denied any link with the Committee of Public Utility Executives.[54]

52. Wolfskill, *Revolt of the Conservatives,* 227-45; and Gadsden to James A. Hill, July 10, 1935, Case Files, box 101.
53. U.S. Congress, Senate, Hearings pursuant to S. Res. 165, and S. Res. 184, *Senate Special Committee to Investigate Lobbying Activities,* 74th Cong., 1st sess. (Washington, D.C., 1935), 61-64, 92, 23 (hereafter cited as "Black Committee Hearings").
54. "Report of Investigator George S. Burns," n.d., Case Files, box 92.

Gadsden's presence before the committee frequently provoked heated exchanges. At one point, when the committee was trying to establish whether the utilities were behind the flood of mail protesting against the bill, the following interchange occurred:

Senator Schwellenbach: I ask you whether you thought it proper to spend between a half million and a million dollars to influence legislation on one bill.

Gadsden: If it is legally spent, open and above-board, I think it is all right. You must bear in mind that I am dealing with the threatened destruction of 12 billions of property.[55]

The strongest case for the death-sentence provision came when the committee subpoenaed Howard Hopson, the president of Associated Gas and Electric. After leading investigators on a wild chase through Washington and the nearby countryside, Hopson appeared before the committee. His convoluted description of the system's operations under Black's sharp questioning probably did as much as anything else to turn public opinion against the holding companies. For Associated Gas and Electric exemplified all the worst practices of the holding company. Composed of more than 160 subcompanies, Hopson and his family kept tight control of the two companies that formed the pyramid of Associated Gas and Electric's structure. The variety of stock that the company issued was truly amazing: there were three classes of common stocks, six of preferred, four of preference, seven issues of secured bonds and notes, twenty-four of debentures, and four series of investment certificates. Between 1926 and 1933 Hopson, his family, and an associate received $29,390,198.67 in profits and salaries. Associated Gas and Electric also was the guiding influence behind a $900,000 lobby against the Wheeler-Rayburn bill.[56]

Time magazine reported that Hopson's testimony "dug a pit into which the utility systems of the United States fell and writhed in despair."[57] Although reputable holding-company executives, like Wendell Willkie of Commonwealth and Southern, had no use for Hopson, the latter's testimony seemed to give the lie to Willkie's argument that "utilities were essentially a technical development, devoting their normal energies to engineering and construction work and possessing no

---

55. "Black Committee Hearings," 24.
56. Ibid., 1015-58, 1268, 1285, passim; and the *New York Times,* August 17, 23, 1935.
57. "Complex Rabbit," *Time,* 26 (July 29, 1935), 9.

natural means of articulation."[58] In the end, the public-power enthusiast's thesis that a Power Trust, which threatened to usurp the legitimate functions of government, was the source of all corruption appeared to many to be true. The public and the Black committee glossed over the very real differences that existed within the fellowship of private-utility executives.

Black's methods for ferreting out the evidence against the utility industry and its lobbyists came in for severe criticism. His chief instrument (besides investigators and questionnaires) was the subpoena *duces tecum*—a dragnet subpoena—requiring utility officials to produce all their records and correspondence relative to the holding-company bill. Black used this and the evidence that his investigators had compiled unsparingly. His questions were tough and impersonal; they were designed also to provoke witnesses into making damaging admissions of wrongdoing. A number of prominent critics and defenders of the utility industry complained, both privately and in print, that Black's methods violated the constitutional rights of the witnesses. The one saving grace was that the committee, unlike later investigatory bodies, delved into the witnesses' actions, not their opinions.[59]

The committee's reliance upon the dragnet subpoena provoked a storm of controversy. "The fact about senatorial inquiries," Newton D. Baker complained to Walter Lippmann, "is that they are nearly always partisan."[60] The constitutional rights of the witnesses were being abused amid Black's politicking, he declared. The senator's tactics "constituted a procedure scarcely less ruthless than that of the Hottentots, who I understand execute the victim first and make their inquiry afterwards." William Randolph Hearst, the conservative publisher and New Deal critic, attempted to get a court injunction prohibiting Black from using subpoenas to seize copies of telegrams sent by utility lobbyists.[61] The *Nation* saw Hearst's action as another example of "how under the pressure of a vigorous legislative attack the

58. Willkie, "The Campaign Against the Companies," *Current History*, 42 (May 1935), 119. Joseph P. Tumulty perceived this and warned both Willkie and Gadsden that the public would be little inclined to distinguish between good and bad holding companies. He advised them to issue a statement condemning Corcoran, Cohen, and Charles West for "deliberate misuse of executive power to influence unfairly the legislative action of a coordinate branch of the Government" (Tumulty to Willkie and Gadsden, July 24, 1935, Case Files, box 98).

59. Schlesinger, *Politics of Upheaval*, 322-23.

60. Newton Baker to Walter Lippmann, Feb. 5, 1936, Newton Baker Papers, box 149, Library of Congress.

61. "Congress, Lobbies and the Courts," *Literary Digest*, 121 (Mar. 14, 1936), 6; and "Hearst Telegram, Senate and Courts," ibid., 121 (Mar. 21, 1936), 6.

bourbons always turn to the courts for extreme unction."[62] Black, meanwhile, threatened to "discipline" the court if it interfered with the work of congressional investigating committees. He regarded such inquiries as among the most useful and fruitful functions of the national legislature.[63]

The dragnet subpoena disturbed not only conservatives like Baker, Hearst, and the American Liberty League, but also threatened to divide the liberal community. In April 1936 Roger Baldwin of the American Civil Liberties Union protested against this method of obtaining evidence. However commendable the objective, the union claimed that such methods necessarily struck at the foundations of civil liberty and might be used to justify any kind of unreasonable search and seizure. Black disagreed; he noted that the committee had issued subpoenas only where it had previous information upon which to act. He refused to reveal to Baldwin the nature of such information for fear that the individuals and organizations involved then would have proper cause for complaint. The relevant information, he said, would come out in the committee's public hearings.[64]

Earlier, Walter Lippmann echoed Baldwin's fears in a very strong column. "Today it is Senator Black out after the unpopular utility lobbyists," he wrote on March 5, 1936:

Yesterday it was an Aldermanic committee out after the social workers of New York City. A few weeks ago it was the Nye committee out to prove that Mr. Morgan put us into the war. A few months ago it was a committee out to ruin Chicago University. A few years ago it was a committee out after Jane Addams and John Dewey. Against whom and what will this engine be turned against next? I do not know. But I do know that when lawlessness is approved for supposedly good ends, it will be used for bad ones.

So I say it is high time the legislative investigations were investigated, and that some one had the courage to raise the issue and bring home to the American people that until reasonable safeguards are established in these proceedings, they are tolerating a very dangerous breach in their institutions and in their traditions of how justice is to be administered.[65]

62. Quoted from an editorial comment in the *Nation*, 142 (Mar. 25, 1936), 365.
63. Hugo L. Black, "Inside a Senate Investigation," *Harper's Magazine*, 172 (Feb. 1936), 275-86.
64. Roger Baldwin to Black, Apr. 22, 1935; Black to Baldwin, May 4, 1936, General Files, box 11.
65. *New York Herald Tribune*, Mar. 5, 1936.

The *New York Post* quickly defended Black's committee and its methods against the criticisms of liberals and conservatives. Its editorial, in the opinion of one writer, was the classic statement of the progressive views of the time. Fear that the committee would abuse its powers was balanced against the conviction that assumption of jurisdiction by the courts would render impotent the legislative power of inquiry. Without investigating committees, the *Post* observed, the people would never have known about Teapot Dome, the Klan's racketeering, and the election scandals involving Vare, Smith, and the Senate. "If the American Liberty League has nothing to hide," the editorial continued, "why does it fear this investigation? Why does it not welcome this investigation as a means of clearing itself of suspicion in the public mind? Or does it fear that investigation will confirm suspicion?"[66]

By later standards of conduct, Black may or may not have pushed the investigative power to an extreme. In 1935-36, despite some criticism from the extreme right and the business community, the public consensus seemed to favor having the clay feet of its financial and business leaders bared. "What Senator Black is doing, therefore, constitutes not an arbitrary violation of liberty but one of the indispensable paths to liberty," declared the *Nation*. "There are still a few men in Congress who are taking seriously the task of economic control, who know that the only thing that will have effectiveness as against the massed force of wealth is the massed power of the federal government."[67] In the wake of Walsh, Wheeler, and Pecora, Senator Black's investigation enjoyed, for a short time at least, a large measure of public toleration. Black, evidently, was following the dictim of Woodrow Wilson, who wrote earlier in the century: "If there is nothing to conceal then why conceal it? ... Everybody knows that corruption thrives in secret places, and avoids public places, and we believe it a fair presumption that secrecy means impropriety. So, our honest politicians, and our honorable corporation heads owe it to their reputations to bring their activities out into the open."[68] The committee was bringing into the open what some people had known or suspected all the while, that is, that the "moneyed interests" were behind the efforts to block this legislation. In the South, where the inquiry was often portrayed in terms of the "people" versus Wall Street, the investigation was especially popular.

66. Albert A. Mavrinac, "Congressional Investigations," *Confluence,* 3 (Dec. 1954), 469.
67. Editorial, "Who Are the Tyrants?" *The Nation,* 142 (Mar. 18, 1936), 336.
68. Quoted in Black, "Inside a Senate Investigation," 275.

The committee's period of greatest activity ended in June 1936, though it limped along until December 1940 with different personnel. A final report on its findings never was issued. The attention of the press and the public wearied as other problems, both domestic and foreign, intruded. In the end, the investigation was terminated not because of public indignation at the committee's methods but because of public boredom.

On August 26, 1935, President Roosevelt signed into law the Wheeler-Rayburn bill, including the controversial section eleven death sentence. Where had the industry failed? How, after spending so much money in an elaborate campaign to persuade Congress and the public against the merits of the bill, had the industry lost? The reason is complex, but perhaps it lies in the fact that the private utilities had overplayed their hand. At the same time, industry officials had seriously underestimated the resourcefulness of the administration in striking back and the intelligence of the public. The industry had spent *too* much money in a vulgar and naked show of influence, precisely when the climate of public opinion was distinctly cool to the mystique of the business community's omniscience. The depression and the revelations of the FTC had seriously undermined public confidence in the leadership of the private-utility industry.

Also, the industry had permitted the issue to become bogged down in a sea of emotional outbursts. This was a serious, though perhaps unavoidable, error in the circumstances, for it made itself vulnerable to similar tactics by the Black committee. There is little doubt that the sensational revelations of the lobby investigation, coinciding as they did with the congressional debates and the conference-committee meetings, helped to swing public opinion against the industry. The administration encouraged Black in his investigation because it was confident that, in the long run, opinion would turn in its favor. Quite simply the industry's conservative leaders *had* lost touch with the people whom they were supposed to serve. The more enlightened figures, like Willkie, were never given solid ground on which to take a stand separate from the traditionalists. They were not able to discipline the most offensive companies, like Associated Gas and Electric, or figures in the industry, like Hopson; nor did they present a reasonable and meaningful alternative to the Wheeler-Rayburn bill. Their attitude was more negative than positive, and this steeled Roosevelt in his determination to get the bill through Congress with section eleven intact.

One of the principal assertions that the industry used to combat the legislation, and which the lobby investigation fully documented, was that it would wipe out billions of dollars worth of securities. The extent to which this argument was accurate is worth examining, because the industry ultimately rested its entire defense upon it. The majority of Congress and the public clearly were not persuaded, although it must be conceded that a substantial and highly vocal minority did share this view. An answer to this question is difficult to give because, at the time, neither the industry nor the government had made a systematic attempt to compute which holding-company securities were solid, representing actual investment in plant and operations, and which were paper investments, representing worthless or heavily inflated values. The FTC was making a start in this direction in its long investigation; but it never was asked to ascertain the probable impact of the Wheeler-Rayburn bill on holding-company and operating-company securities. The Black committee lacked the time, the expertise, and the objectivity to go into the matter of securities; it began with the assumption that the leadership of the industry was essentially dishonest or not to be trusted and that most holding-company securities represented inflated values.

The utility industry had taken the position that the proposed legislation would destroy private enterprise in the electric-power field in the United States. This has patently not been the case; nor was there any evidence from the time the legislation was enacted through America's entry into World War II that the industry was in disarray or about to break up because of enforcement of the Public Utility Holding Company Act. The SEC, as a matter of fact, went to great lengths in an effort to reassure the industry that it would implement the law rationally and equitably.[69] On the basis of the best evidence available—the annual reports of the SEC—billions of dollars worth of securities were not lost from the time companies first registered in 1938

69. After passage of the law, the power companies initiated numerous suits attacking the statute as a whole and the constitutionality of section 11-b in particular. For two and one-quarter years thereafter the statute was in a state of suspension. Ben Cohen ultimately devised the strategy whereby litigation was restricted to one suit brought by the government against Associated Gas and Electric. The Supreme Court, in March 1938, upheld the constitutionality of the law and, immediately thereafter, SEC Chairman William O. Douglas canvassed the companies to determine the extent to which they would move forward voluntarily under section eleven. By December 1938, the SEC had received the industry's integration and simplification plans. It found them, in a majority of instances, unsatisfactory and, in 1940, concluded that "we can expect very little more to be done on a voluntary basis." The SEC thereupon instituted dissolution proceedings against virtually every major system. See Manuel F. Cohen, "Federal Legislation Affecting the Public Offerings of Securities," *George Washington Law Review*, 28 (Oct. 1959), 160; and Jerome N. Frank to George W. Norris, Dec. 9, 1939, George W. Norris Papers, tray 66, box 11, Library of Congress.

with the commission. Despite the drastic elimination of inflationary items from plant accounts and increases in depreciation reserves, both of which tended to reduce common-stock equity to an actual investment basis, the capital structures of many companies underwent substantial improvement as a result of the act. After a decade of administering the law, the SEC reported, in 1951, that the financial integrity of the industry was greatly strengthened and that utility investors had received "down-to-the-rails income paying securities of sound utility enterprises."[70]

Meanwhile, during the course of the fight to break up the Power Trust, Roosevelt moved by executive order to relieve one of the worst evils caused by the holding companies' emphasis on profits rather than service. He created the Rural Electrification Administration to lend money at low interest for the construction of power plants and power lines in poor rural areas.

70. U.S. Securities and Exchange Commission, *Seventeenth Annual Report of the Securities and Exchange Commission* (Washington, D.C., 1952), 66-67.

CHAPTER V

Morris L. Cooke and the Origins of the REA

In the course of the legislative fight to break up the Power Trust by striking directly at holding-company control, Roosevelt issued an executive order temporarily creating the Rural Electrification Administration. The history of the REA, with its attempts at both cooperation and coercion, which ultimately led to conflict, in many instances paralleled that of the TVA and must be considered an extension of the struggle to free the consumer from the monopoly of holding-company control. Beyond this, rural electrification had long been one of Roosevelt's favorite projects. The new agency, designed to lend money at low interest so that the poorer rural areas could obtain cheap electrical energy, was to be one of the New Deal's most popular achievements.

When Thomas A. Edison installed the first central-station service in New York City in 1882, he sparked the beginnings of a nationwide urban-electrification movement. Almost simultaneously, he stirred a ripple of interest among farmers in the potential use of electricity for lighting, household, and farm chores. By the close of the nineteenth century, electric power was applied to agriculture on a limited, experimental basis in different sections of the country. The shortage of capital and the primitive state of technology prior to World War I, however, made extensive rural line-building impossible. Moreover, until 1910 the NELA evinced little interest in rural electrification. In that year, Herman Russell of the Rochester (New York) Railway and Light Company urged delegates to the annual convention to devote closer attention to the problems of farm electrification. He foresaw the day when "electric lines in the country will be as common as telephone and telegraph lines are today, and the present investment in our central stations will be employed in making farms more productive, and life more worth living for both the farmer and the company."[1]

1. Quoted in John H. Ronayne, "The Development of Farm Electrification," section

Responding to the challenge, the NELA organized the Committee on Electricity in Rural Districts to gather statistics and report on the progress of farm electrification. In 1911, the committee published its report, an eighty-seven-page document, which marked the first attempt to survey systematically the dimensions of the problem. Its findings, on the whole, were not encouraging for the immediate extension of lines to rural inhabitants. At this stage in the development of rural extensions, the industry's investment in lines, transformers, equipment, and manpower—including the inflationary cost of maintenance—was far greater than any anticipated return. This condition held true over the next two decades, and constituted the most serious obstacle in bringing electricity to every farmer.[2] In between occurred World War I, during which the industry gave priority to the power needs of the producers of war material.

Electrical energy, however, remained the claim of both a rural-agricultural and an urban-industrial society. In 1913, Samuel Insull conducted his famous Lake County experiment, demonstrating for the first time that systematized electric service was technically and economically feasible in large rural areas.[3] During the war numerous articles on the subject began to appear in technical and popular journals; afterward, state conventions heard papers on the farm uses of electricity. Distribution costs were debated, and people talked knowledgeably about the merits of area coverage as opposed to line coverage.[4] In 1923, Grover Neff of the Wisconsin Power and Light Company persuaded the NELA to establish a new national organization: the Committee on the Relation of Electricity to Agriculture (CREA). Composed of agricultural schools, federal and state agricultural departments, farm organizations, equipment manufacturers, and utility men, CREA

2 in *Farm Electrification Manual*, ed. Edison Electric Institute (New York, 1947), 3.

2. Ibid., 4. The CERD asked that the secretary of agriculture have the U.S. Census Bureau compile data on the extent to which farmers currently were using electric power. For the federal government's early interest in the problem of farm electrification, see Murray Benedict, *Farm Policies of the United States, 1789-1950* (New York, 1953), 388.

3. Middle West Utilities, *Harvests and Highlines* (Chicago, 1930). See also the excellent study by Forrest McDonald, *Insull* (Chicago, 1962), 137-45. It is a mine of information on the early problems of electrification in the United States.

4. See, for example, C. M. Harger, "Bringing Electricity to the Farm," *Country Gentlemen*, 88 (Apr. 27, 1918), 11; A. Marpole, "Electricity an Aid in Farming," *Farm Engineering*, 3 (June 1916), 281; and E. N. Cable, "Comforts with Electricity," *American Fruit Grower*, 39 (July 1919), 29.

studied, experimented, and promoted the use of electricity on the farm.[5]

The CREA, from its inception, was the focal point of controversy between those who wanted rural electrification accomplished under private auspices and the advocates of public power. Its champions pointed to its accomplishments as a fact-finding and educational agency, and were proud that it had constructed seven model distribution lines in as many states. Its critics in the public-power movement alleged that its total impact, particularly with the onset of the depression in 1929, was limited. The test projects, they observed, were conducted under ideal conditions, closely supervised by experts, and used large quantities of freely loaned equipment. National rural electrification required massive governmental assistance, for the CREA's models were not typical of existing conditions on the American farm. Even if distribution lines were brought to their doors the majority of farmers lacked the cash required to approach the results achieved in the test projects. To support their claims these critics noted that, as late as 1933, eighteen states, most of them located in the South (which admittedly lagged behind other sections of the nation) still had less than 1 percent of their farms electrified.[6]

This critique of the industry's performance went beyond the isolated example of the CREA. Public-power and farmer organizations were alarmed because the United States was rapidly dividing into two nations: the city dweller, enjoying the luxuries which electricity afforded, and the country poor, who still toiled like peasants in a preindustrial age.[7] They also feared that full electrification of the major farming areas would occur slowly, if the dominant criteria for constructing lines was the profit motive. Until service replaced profit, the rural dweller was doomed to remain the forgotten man. The unfortunate remarks of a few utility leaders conveyed the impression to the public that the industry was motivated solely by greed. "Unless rural service is worth more than it costs, it should not be supplied," declared one

5. Forrest McDonald, *Let There Be Light: The Electric Utility Industry in Wisconsin, 1881-1955* (Madison, 1957), 287.

6. Morris L. Cooke, "The Early Days of the Rural Electrification Idea: 1914-1936," *American Political Science Review,* 42 (June 1948), 437. See also Ronayne, "Farm Electrification," 6-7. By 1935 this assessment of the CREA's performance had broad support from a number of federal agencies which approached it as the handmaid of the private-utility lobby. Federal participation ceased thereafter. See Morris L. Cooke to Paul H. Appleby, Oct. 1, 1935, National Archives, Record Group 221, Rural Electrification Administration, Administrator's File, box 7 (hereafter only the record group, the file, and the box number will be cited).

7. William E. Leuchtenburg, *Franklin D. Roosevelt and the New Deal* (New York, 1963), 12.

utility magnate.[8] Worth was reckoned in terms of financial profit. Public-power propagandists eagerly seized upon such statements as grist for their mills.

Some utility officials were, in fact, under heavy pressure to return larger dividends and many had argued that it was not economically feasible, given the relatively small amount of power used by most farms, to build lines into the countryside.[9] But the indictment that all segments of the industry deliberately dragged their heels must be balanced against the state of technology and other factors pertinent to the industry. An in-depth study of the situation in Wisconsin revealed that seven major obstacles stood in the way of the extension of electric-power lines into rural areas, and that these conditions, in varying degree, held true for the rest of the nation. Three of the obstacles were points to which the industry had to advance before efforts could even seriously be made, and four were tasks to be performed before rural electrification could actually be made feasible.[10]

Among the basic conditions, the first was that urban electrification had to be an accomplished fact or something approximating it. As long as there was a large undeveloped market in the form of potential customers along existing urban lines, it was not to be expected that central-station operators would go in search of customers whom it cost many times as much to connect. Also, urban electrification was necessary as the nucleus for expanding into rural areas in order to reduce the costs of generating facilities to a reasonable figure during the developmental stage of rural electrification. The third condition was one easily forgotten. Companies required not only the ability but also the right to serve an area before service could be extended into it. The presence of numerous companies competing for the same territory acted as an obstacle rather than a stepping stone to rural electrification.[11]

Once these conditions were met, the rural-electrification enthusiast confronted additional barriers. First, he had to persuade his management of the merits of the idea, a formidable task before 1925, when

8. Quoted in Arthur M. Schlesinger, Jr., *The Politics of Upheaval* (Boston, 1960), 380.

9. Exceptions were made where farmsteads were close together, or where there was a considerable demand for power to operate heavy motors, as in the irrigated farm areas of the Far West. See Ronayne, "Farm Electrification," 4; Benedict, *Farm Policies*, 338.

10. For the following synopsis I am heavily indebted to McDonald's case study of the Wisconsin situation in *Let There Be Light*, 278-84.

11. Ibid.

most utility men did not take rural electrification seriously.[12] One official, for example, wrote that "the dominating nature of other problems has given central station men a tendency to treat the rural service problem as a fad."[13] Secondly, he had to learn how to make it technically and economically feasible to both the utility and the farmer. And, in a surprisingly large number of instances, he had to overcome the fear and resistance of the farmers themselves to electricity. The fourth obstacle was the individual state's railroad commission. In its zeal to prevent extravagance and unwarranted investments, it frowned on rural extensions unless they were self-supporting.

Nevertheless, as each year passed the demand of rural dwellers, spurred on by public-power enthusiasts, for electric power grew more urgent. The pressure was acute in a few states, one utility leader observed, "and may soon be acute in others."[14] Farm organizations were beginning to put pressure upon public-service commissions to order the industry to construct distribution lines into the countryside. There even was talk about building the lines themselves, although the industry moved quickly to quash such action. In 1924, the Committee on Electricity in Rural Districts of the NELA instructed delegates on how to discourage agricultural groups from setting up their own poles and operating their own distribution systems.[15] On the whole, however, farmer agitation in the 1920s did not advance much beyond the local and state level.

If electrification of the farm was to occur within the foreseeable future, the public-power lobby argued that government must intervene. In 1923, this premise was dramatized at the state level when Governor Gifford Pinchot of Pennsylvania authorized the first Giant Power Survey.[16] Pinchot, a fiery Bull Moose conservationist, originally intended to make a comparative survey of electric-power rates throughout the

12. Ibid.
13. Quoted in John M. Carmody, "Rural Electrification in the United States," *Annals of the American Academy of Political and Social Science,* 201 (Jan. 1939), 83.
14. Ibid.
15. Cooke, "Rural Electrification Idea," 437.
16. The precedent for this was established in 1914, when Mayor Rudolph Blankenburg of Philadelphia instituted the first successful electric-rate case against the Philadelphia Electric Company. The team of experts that he assembled—lawyers, accountants, and engineers—served in the Power Section of the Emergency Fleet Corporation in World War I where they gained further experience in the technical and financial aspects of the electric-utility industry. During the 1920s they placed this experience at the service of the community and were largely instrument in laying the groundwork for the New Deal's REA. Morris L. Cooke was one of these men. See Cooke, "Rural Electrification Idea," 434-35.

state in keeping with an electoral-campaign promise.[17] Morris Llewellyn Cooke, a Philadelphian of impeccable standing, persuaded him to expand the scope of the investigation and to have it culminate in a plan for the coordinated development of the state's power resources by private companies under state regulation and planning.[18]

An avid proponent of Theodore Roosevelt's New Nationalism, Cooke was a management engineer by profession. He had read and studied the ideas of Frederick W. Taylor, the archpriest of scientific management, in a social context and was sparked by a vision of the state planning and directing the expansion of electric power for use by all citizens regardless of their economic situation. A Jeffersonian in his love of the rural life, he feared that rural America was doomed to remain in the backwater of the onward rush of civilization, unless the fruits of technology could be employed on the farm. He hoped to stem the exodus from the farm to the city by mobilizing technology to preserve the wholesomeness of country life. The Giant Power Survey was the keystone "in the larger game of building the Great State." Cooke wrote to Pinchot that in America "the Great State is going to grow up out of a revived agriculture and a reinspiration in small town life and the utilization of these in placing the government of our individual states on a plane of effective social purpose."[19]

Cooke had been a perennial student of Pennsylvania's utilities and, with the governor's blessing, headed the Giant Power Board. He appointed his staff from many of the same experts with whom he had worked in the Philadelphia rate case.[20] What distinguished these technocrats from others was their sharing of "the public point of view."[21] He also deftly fingered those utility practices which the board eventually investigated. In 1925, Cooke presented its recommendations to the state legislature. The report focused upon the social and economic needs of the commonwealth's citizens and encompassed a broad pro-

17. Cooke to Roy Husselman, Sept. 9, 1922, Cooke to Gifford Pinchot, Feb. 21, 1924, Morris L. Cooke Papers, boxes 24, 25, Franklin D. Roosevelt Library (hereafter cited as Cooke Papers); and Pinchot to Cooke, Mar. 9, 1923, Gifford Pinchot Papers, box 679, Library of Congress.

18. According to Judson King, the term *Giant Power Survey* was coined to distinguish it from *Superpower,* the latter being used by private companies in their expansion along customarily private lines. "It was falsely dubbed public ownership by the utilities," he wrote, "who fought it as vigorously as they did public ownership which once more demonstrates that the utilities are as much opposed to honest regulation as to public operation" (Judson King, "Memo Re: Giant Power Survey Board," n.d., Judson King Papers, box 79, Library of Congress).

19. Cooke to Pinchot, Mar. 10, 1924, Cooke Papers, box 35.

20. See n. 16.

21. Cooke, "Memorandum on Power," Jan. 18, 1923, Cooke Papers, box 38.

gram for holding-company regulation, lower rates, conservation, more efficient utilization of coal for power, and the electrification of farms in the rural counties.[22] The legislature, which was widely believed to be under the thumb of the utilities, did not greet the report enthusiastically. In 1926, the public-service commission attempted to implement one section of the report, when it ordered the private-power companies to construct at their own expense distribution lines into rural areas. The order was ignored with impunity.

Although the legislature defeated every bill to implement the board's proposals, the Giant Power Survey established a pattern of similar activity in other states. In New York, the interest of Franklin D. Roosevelt, the state's Democratic governor, was aroused. By 1930, Roosevelt was in the process of reorganizing the State Power Authority, and he requested assistance from Cooke and the Power Survey experts. With the permission of Governor Pinchot they trekked to New York where they began to study the question of rural-distribution costs in connection with power from the much-talked-about St. Lawrence Seaway. Thus began the close association of Cooke and Roosevelt which later bore fruit in the REA.[23]

Fundamentally, Roosevelt shared Cooke's appreciation of the rural life. He saw in the recommendations of the Giant Power Survey his own vision of a balanced society, rural and industrial, the population decentralized in smaller cities and towns. He also perceived the problems of agriculture in a social context and, like Cooke, desired to rehabilitate farm life. As governor and then president, Roosevelt wanted to reverse the decline not simply in farm prices but in the quality of rural as contrasted with urban living. Nowhere was this sentiment articulated more forcefully than in a 1930 speech to Cornell University undergraduates. On that occasion, he professed as the objective of his administration, "the great fundamental of making country life in every way as desirable as city life, an objective which will from the economic side make possible the earning of an adequate compensation and on the social side the enjoyment of all the necessary

---

22. "Proposals for Legislation," *Report of the Giant Power Board Survey to the General Assembly of the Commonwealth of Pennsylvania* (Harrisburg, 1925), 164 passim. About one-third of the study into the various phases of rural electrification was compiled by Judson Dickerman and others who had been active in the Philadelphia rate case. See also a copy of the report in RG 221, REA Administrator's File, box 31.

23. Pinchot to Cooke, Jan. 22, 1926, Cooke Papers, box 36; and Cooke, "Rural Electrification Idea," 436-42. At about the same time, Cooke met James Delmage Ross, who was to be named administrator of the Bonneville Power Administration.

advantages which exist today in the cities.''[24] Bringing power to the farm was the first step.

Meanwhile, the expansion of the private utilities into the countryside on a broad scale had just commenced in 1930 when the Great Depression aborted it. Cooke, as did many other people, petitioned the federal government to adopt vigorous measures to restore prosperity. He believed that positive government, acting in a democratic manner, could preserve the welfare and thus the liberty of the people. Hence, he proposed a national program to the Hoover administration, patterned after the Giant Power Survey, to take up the slack from private industry. Rural electrification was an enormous field for exploitation as the nation entered a new decade, and there was room enough for private industry, government, or a combination of the two. In the 1930 census of agriculture, for example, only 13.4 percent of 841,310 farms reporting indicated that the owners' dwellings were lighted by electricity and, of 256,663 farms reporting, only 4.1 percent had electric motors for farm work. The South, in all categories of rural electrification, lagged badly behind other sections of the nation. Hoover's secretary, Laurence Ritchey, never appreciated the implications of these statistics, for he brushed aside Cooke's idea without ever forwarding it to the president.[25]

The depression, nevertheless, had acted as a truly catalytic agent. Public-power enthusiasts and rural-electrification advocates concentrated their energies on attaining direct federal assistance. The first indication of the change came when Cooke hitched his plan to the ascending political fortunes of Governor Roosevelt. In 1932, when the governor captured the Democratic presidential nomination, Cooke hoped that his long-standing interest in rural electrification, born of frequent sojourns to Warm Springs, Georgia, in the twenties, would be translated into affirmative action. He suggested during the course of the campaign that Roosevelt capitalize on the present emergency as a means of accomplishing general rural electrification. In this, he had the strong backing of public-power groups, especially the National Popular Government League. Roosevelt was not prepared to commit himself to a definite course of action in advance of his election and,

24. Franklin D. Roosevelt, "Betterment of Agricultural Conditions" (address delivered at the State College of Agriculture, Cornell University, Feb. 14, 1930), in Samuel I. Rosenman, comp., *The Public Papers and Addresses of Franklin D. Roosevelt* (New York, 1938), I, 700-02; Daniel Fusfeld, *The Economic Thought of Franklin D. Roosevelt and the Origins of the New Deal* (New York, 1956), 123, 153.

25. U.S. Department of Commerce, Bureau of the Census, *Fifteenth Census of the United States: 1930, Agriculture* (Washington, D.C., 1932), IV, tables 20, 21.

in the first two years of his administration, one crisis after another prevented him from following up on Cooke's proposal.[26]

In June 1933, Cooke drew up a new memorandum urging the recently inaugurated president to establish a commission to explore the feasibility of national rural electrification. The timing of the proposal, unfortunately, was inopportune; it was mixed in with the numerous panaceas for coping with the economic crisis that had flooded the White House in the early days of the New Deal and, instead of receiving serious consideration, was shunted off to Louis M. Howe.[27] The president's aide passed it along without comment to General Hugh Johnson of the NRA where it was quietly interred. Cooke vented his anger in a letter to Harry Slattery, Ickes' right-hand man in the PWA. "I can easily see," he wrote, "that if my correspondence about the scheme for rural electrification is sent to General Hugh Johnson and by him handed up to the Honorable Bernard [Baruch] or worse still, handed down to one John P. Hogan ... a laugh will result."[28] Apart from Slattery and Secretary Ickes, there appeared to be little enthusiasm for Cooke's idea among presidential advisers.

This setback only inspired Cooke to fight harder for his ideas. His first real break occurred late in 1933, when the president appointed him chairman of the Mississippi Valley Committee of the PWA. In the course of surveying the flood control, conservation, and power problems of the Mississippi valley, he gave a prominent place to rural electrification. Writing to Ickes in 1934, he touched upon the theme which the president had raised four years earlier when addressing the Cornell undergraduates. "My own interest in rural electrification," he observed, "is based on a growing conviction that the gravest of our troubles can be traced to the increasing dominance of 'city people' in human affairs and the lessening of the influence of those in material and spiritual touch with the soil."[29] Cooke wanted to reverse what he saw as an unhealthy trend and believed that he could succeed by making rural electrification a full partner in the president's power policy. Essentially a moderate Progressive, he hoped to enlist the aid of the private-power companies in attaining the goal of national rural electrifi-

26. Kenneth Trombley, *Life and Times of a Happy Liberal: A Biography of Morris Llewellyn Cooke* (New York, 1954), ch. 10.

27. Cooke to Roosevelt, June 5, 1933, Cooke Papers, box 263.

28. Cooke to Harry A. Slattery, June 10, 1933, Harry A. Slattery Papers, box 97, Duke University Library (hereafter cited as Slattery Papers), and as quoted in Jean Christie, "Morris Llewellyn Cooke: Progressive Engineer" (Ph.D. diss., Columbia University, 1963), 208.

29. Cooke to Harold L. Ickes, Feb. 13, 1934, Cooke Papers, box 263.

cation and to persuade a highly suspicious public-power faction within the administration of their goodwill.

The most disheartening obstacle to cooperation was the industry's distrust of the New Deal, a feeling that was more than reciprocated. Roosevelt, as governor, and then in the electoral campaign, had outspokenly criticized certain utility practices, especially the financial abuse of holding companies. Coming on the heels of the TVA legislation, the private utilities might readily interpret government support of rural electrification as another attempt to "socialize" the industry. Cooke, therefore, decided to make informal soundings of the industry's leadership to gauge their reaction to the idea of a partnership with government. Preliminary talks in 1933 led him to believe that the private-power companies had been chastened by recent events, "and the best of them are working hard to build a constructive program."[30]

Cooke's optimism was scarcely warranted from some of the public statements given out by industry officials. In November 1933, George W. Kable, the director of the National Rural Electric Project, told the American Society of Agricultural Engineers that the "utility and manufacturing executive interest is not as keen on rural business as on railway electrification or the urban domestic load." A vice-president of the Philadelphia Electric Company denied that progress in rural electrification had been unnecessarily slow. "Of one thing I am absolutely convinced," he told the Association for the Advancement of Science. "The greatest error we could make would be an impetuous plunge into a national program of complete electrification of the rural and agricultural areas." A few utility spokesmen, more sensitive to the political ramifications of the issue, feared that farm groups might pressure the administration into acting rashly and argued that the industry should seize the initiative from the politicians. The editor of *Electrical World*, however, in a disparaging thrust at the TVA's primitive rural-electrification program voiced the sentiment of the majority. Instead of fooling around with "power yardsticks," he declared, the federal government ought to give all the TVA funds to the utilities and let them run their own program.[31]

Brushing aside public statements of this tenor, Cooke was optimistic that the private industry would participate in the administration-sponsored rural-electrification program. He even formulated a plan

30. Cooke to Ickes, Dec. 14, 1933, in ibid.
31. George W. Kable, "Farm Electrification Steadily Winning," *Electrical World*, 102 (Nov. 4, 1933), 605; H. P. Liversidge, "Gradual Rural Electrification," *Electrical World*, 102 (Jan. 27, 1934), 151; and Editorial, "Farmers Demand Electricity," *Electrical World*, 104 (Sept. 29, 1934), 506.

whereby the utilities and the government would cooperate as equals. This scheme never got off the ground because Ickes flatly declared that he would never work with "the scoundrels."[32] Fearful of risking the support of his one powerful ally within the administration, Cooke discarded the partnership approach for a national plan whereby rural electrification was to be advanced as a wholly public enterprise. Dated February 1934, the revised proposal vested primary responsibility for its execution in the secretary of the interior. Within the department a new section was to be established, "managed by socially-minded electrical engineers, who ... will cooperate with groups within the several states in planning appropriate developments."[33] The Bureau of Reclamation, whose sluggish regulatory activities had angered liberals and delighted the utilities, was cleverly eliminated, as was the army which did not consider rural electrification within its province.[34]

Cooke's new program was posited upon three conditions for success: that the projects were to be self-liquidating and originate with the inhabitants in the area; that it was to be a temporary program, at least until Congress voted regular budgetary appropriations for projects; and that its administrators were to cooperate with the Electric Home and Farm Authority (EHFA) in promoting greater use of electrical appliances and equipment among rural dwellers. Most importantly, Cooke tied the proposed rural-electrification section more closely into the broader policy that was taking shape under the New Deal. This agency, he wrote, must take "an active hand in planning out the rural use of current from such developments as Grand Coulee, Fort Peck, Bonneville, and Boulder Dams."[35]

Cooke fortunately had political instincts, and they warned him that, no matter how desirable a program was on paper, someone certainly would raise objections to it. The body of his proposal anticipated the most likely questions; the "general-welfare" clause cast a wide mantle

32. Cooke to Ickes, Dec. 12, 1933; Ickes to Cooke, Jan. 1934, Cooke Papers, box 263.

33. Cooke, "National Plan for the Advancement of Rural Electrification Under Federal Leadership and Control with State and Local Cooperation and as a Wholly Public Enterprise," Feb. 1934, Cooke Papers, box 230.

34. W. D. Ketchum, "Power Aspects of Federally-Operated Reclamation Projects," *Edison Electric Institute Bulletin,* 3 (Dec. 1935), 449-51.

35. Cooke, "National Plan for Rural Electrification," 13 ff. One of the major impediments to private development of rural electrification had been the farmers' lack of capital. The EHFA was to extend credit for appliances, wiring, plumbing, and various types of electrically driven machinery. Incidentally, these loans served as an inflationary tool to combat the depression among the manufacturers of electrical equipment and were used to win their support of the government's program.

and could easily be used to blanket the program against constitutional doubts. State and local governments were more jealous of their prerogatives, and they might resent the intrusion of the central government. To minimize hostility from this quarter he suggested that the rural-electrification section function through power districts. Cooke apparently had in mind a procedure wherein the rural dwellers of an area voted first to incorporate a district. The district then authorized the acquisition, construction, and operation of electric plants, furnishing power to the inhabitants. In states like Pennsylvania, where the law did not permit power districts, he suggested that the government agency operate through agricultural cooperatives, while exerting pressure upon state legislators to enact enabling legislation.[36] Either way, the initiative for federal assistance originated at the local level.

Cooke's grand scheme would have had little chance of getting off the drawing board, but for the gloomy economic situation in the winter of 1933-34.[37] Nine million men were unemployed; whole families in the nation's urban centers lacked adequate food, clothing, and shelter; local resources could not keep pace with the need; and the administration's détente with the business community (as symbolized in the NRA) was rapidly crumbling. Federal relief on a massive scale remained a critical need. Ickes, meanwhile, had transmitted a copy of Cooke's plan to the president. The vision of electrifying over a million farms, of providing rural dwellers with the conveniences of urban living, and of stemming the flight from the farm to the already overburdened cities struck a responsive chord. Roosevelt, however, was even more intrigued by the possibility of using rural electrification to make inroads on the unemployment-relief problem. In the short run, it was this aspect of Cooke's plan that had the strongest appeal to the president; to Harry L. Hopkins, head of the Federal Emergency Relief Administration; and to Daniel Roper, secretary of the Department of Commerce, and this was the decisive factor in its acceptance. What began as a relatively straightforward work-relief measure took on within six months, broader political, social, and economic implications.[38]

In 1934, however, the principle of rural electrification was still paid only lip service. There appeared to be very little consensus within the administration as to how the program should actually function. And Cooke, because he had been the main protagonist for the program,

---

36. Ibid.
37. For economic conditions see Schlesinger, *Politics of Upheaval,* 2-4, esp. the statement of Henry Morgenthau, Jr.
38. Cooke to Ickes, Oct. 22, 1934, RG 221, REA Administrator's File, box 9.

quite naturally was the target of pressure from both public- and private-power interests who were determined to shape it. During the fall and winter he met with a group of eastern utility executives to discuss the problems of rural electrification.[39] The power companies supplied the government with data about costs, standards, and methods of construction, although they were "much disturbed as to the possible far-reaching effect of Federal activities in rural electrification—even in areas not now having service."[40] The industry saw the economic practicability of extending service to an additional one million rural inhabitants, provided the government extended credit for appliances as the TVA was doing. "But the hitch comes," Cooke declared, "when we suggest that the government may see fit to extend rural electrification beyond the limits which the private companies consider economically feasible, build the lines and lease under conditions which will mean federal control of rates." Cooke attributed the industry's tepid response and desire to limit the program to the fear that federal participation would force rates down, "far below present standards."[41]

Within the government there existed some sentiment for handling the private-power companies pragmatically, that is, to invite their cooperation and face any problems as they arose. Clayton W. Pike, an engineer who had served with the Giant Power Survey, articulated this view. His primary concern was to begin the program without further delay and, in his judgment, the active participation of the industry was vital because of its facilities, data, and experience in constructing such projects. In October 1934, he wrote to Cooke that the opportunity for securing industry support would be enhanced greatly, "if the utilities could be induced to aggressively lead the movement."[42] The structure of the industry in this country inevitably dictated that holding companies would assume control of the program. Pike conceded this, but argued that the long-term social advantages would more than counterbalance the liabilities. His was distinctly a minority view, for such a circumstance was antithetical to the basic premise of the administration's power policy. In reality the NPPC for the past four months had been drafting the holding-company legislation. From the perspective of ardent New Dealers, who could say positively that the private

39. McDonald, *Let There Be Light,* 359-60. The author clearly overstates the case when he says: "In short, the group gave Cooke a thorough grounding in the economics of farm electric service."
40. Cooke to Ickes, Dec. 6, 1934, RG 221, REA Administrator's File, box 9.
41. Ibid. See also Cooke to Ickes, Nov. 19, 1934, in ibid.
42. Clayton W. Pike to Cooke, Oct. 1934, Cooke Papers, box 230.

utilities would not also sabotage the rural-electrification program?[43]

The distrust that poisoned the relationship of the administration and private-power-company executives in the fall of 1934 was so great that Cooke was required to adopt a cautious approach. He did not rule out entirely some form of cooperation, although he conceded that the program would be in jeopardy if he followed Pike's counsel. On October 25, 1934, Cooke approached the president to ascertain "how far we should go at this time in enlisting the interest of the private industry in Rural Electrification."[44] Roosevelt's reply is unrecorded, but it appears safe to assume that he did not rule out a role for the private utilities. And Cooke proceeded on the assumption that national rural electrification would advance as a joint venture involving the Federal Emergency Relief Administration, the PWA, and the private utilities. The essence of the plan—which Cooke called "the only remaining self-liquidating, large-scale immediately available outlet for federal relief expenditures"—was unveiled on October 22. It envisioned a total expenditure of $1.185 billion to bring electricity to 3.5 million farmers over a ten- to twenty-year period.[45]

In the final analysis, rural electrification was sold to the "doubting Thomases" within the administration not on its merits alone but primarily as a work-relief measure. It was incorporated into the Emergency Relief Appropriation bill which was being drawn up for presentation to the Seventy-fourth Congress, and it left the door ajar for those operating companies that wished to participate in the national program. This decision undoubtedly was conditioned by the recommendations of the Mississippi Valley Committee late in October 1934 and the National Resources Committee in December. The latter body, particularly, voiced the desire that the private utilities participate in rural electrification. In addition, strong support of federal leadership emanated from sources outside the administration. The National Grange and American Farm Bureau Federation, the two most influential farm

43. Rosenman, *Public Papers of FDR*, III, 339-41. The NPPC had also assigned Dr. Thomas Norcross to investigate the rural-electrification problem in conjunction with the evolution of a national power policy.

44. Cooke to Roosevelt, Oct. 25, 1934, Franklin D. Roosevelt Papers, Office File 800, Franklin D. Roosevelt Library (hereafter cited as Roosevelt Papers, OF).

45. Cooke, "Electrify Rural America Now," Oct. 22, 1934, National Archives, Record Group 221, Rural Electrification Administration Central File, General Correspondence, 1935-1940, box 18. Cooke arrived at this sum by figuring that construction costs could be slashed 50 percent if the federal agency supervising the program followed the procedure of low-cost loans amortized over twenty to thirty years; if construction were planned on an area basis; if construction techniques, voltage, and line equipment were standardized; and if construction were supervised on a central basis.

organizations, had abandoned the hope that private industry would move into rural electrification on a national scale. Their respective conventions resolved that the federal government should direct and finance the program. Judson King and the National Popular Government League took a similar position. In the Senate, George W. Norris urged the federal government to go it alone.[46] Lilienthal's prediction in 1933 that the TVA legislation was only the beginning "toward no less a goal than the electrification of America" was gradually becoming a reality.[47]

In January 1935, the administration submitted to an unenthusiastic Congress its work-relief bill, the cost of which was reckoned at $5 billion. The legislation, declaring as its goal the reemployment of 3.5 million able-bodied men, included a modest request of $100 million for the employment of workers specifically on rural-electrification projects. The bill passed through the House without difficulty but in the Senate conservatives and liberals attacked it, delaying enactment more than two months. Senate conservatives professed to see in the request, especially the provision granting to the executive broad discretionary power over the expenditure of funds, the makings of a dictatorship. Liberal senators, in contrast, grumbled that $5 billion was a paltry sum to combat nationwide unemployment. Many protested that turning back the unemployables to local poor relief was cruel.[48]

The brunt of the criticism fell upon the relief features of the legislation and, as a consequence, the provision for rural electrification was almost throttled. Fiscal conservatives, including Carter Glass of Virginia, objected to the financial arrangements whereby projects were slated for construction; other senators protested the further encroachment of the federal government in the power field. Later, in meetings of the joint Senate and House conference committee, Senator Royal Copeland, Democrat, of New York, and a foe of the New Deal, attempted to amend the bill in order to prohibit relief agencies from lending funds on nonfederal projects unless more than half the sum was expended for labor employed directly at the site. He also wanted 90 percent of the labor to come directly from the relief rolls of the area.

46. National Resources Board, *A Report on National Planning and Public Works in Relation to Natural Resources and Including Land Use ... With Findings and Recommendations* (Washington, D.C., 1934), 352; Mississippi Valley Committee, *Report of the Mississippi Valley Committee of the Public Works Administration* (Washington, D.C., 1934), 51-52; and Harry A. Slattery, "Autobiography," 154, typewritten copy in the Slattery Papers.

47. David E. Lilienthal, "TVA Seen Only as Spur to Electrification of America," *Electrical World*, 102 (Nov. 4, 1933), 687-90.

48. Schlesinger, *Politics of Upheaval*, 269.

The true purpose of the amendment was to destroy both the rural-electrification program and the PWA, the agency administering relief funds, for there were practically no nonfederal projects that could have mustered so heavy a proportion of labor at the site. Copeland freely admitted that he was aware of this, and that the intent was to prohibit the government from making loans that might compete with the construction plans of the privately owned utilities. The House conferees, meanwhile, refused to report the bill out with Copeland's amendment intact.[49]

On March 25, 1935, the NPPC issued the report of Thomas W. Norcross, chief engineer of the Forest Services, entitled *A New Deal in Rural Electrification–A National Plan*. The report was without doubt the most comprehensive treatise on the subject from the public point of view, and also set the problem in the context of the national power policy. Cooke was very excited about it and wrote to Ickes that "it will set our program ahead by weeks if not by months and will prove an invaluable handbook for those who will have the carrying out of this project."[50] The report and Cooke's warm endorsement of it persuaded Ickes and other administration leaders to take steps to rescue the relief bill from the conference-committee deadlock.

Ickes's intervention averted an impasse that would have doomed the rural-electrification program for at least another year. Working through James Buchanan of Texas, the head of the House conference committee, and Senator James F. Byrnes, he persuaded Copeland and Glass to accept a less-rigid version of the amendment. On April 3, 1935, the committee announced that it had hammered out an agreement. The compromise bill had only a slightly reduced appropriation from the initial $5 billion to $4.8 billion. The REA would observe the same standards under which the entire work-relief program functioned. Only 25 percent of the funds would be spent for labor, although 90 percent of the labor force still would be drawn directly from the relief rolls. Five days later Roosevelt signed the bill into law.[51]

On May 11, 1935, the president issued Executive Order 7037. It established the REA as a temporary agency whose purpose was "to initiate, formulate, administer, and supervise a program of approved projects with respect to the generation, transmission, and distribution

49. Harold L. Ickes, *The Secret Diary of Harold L. Ickes: The First Thousand Days* (New York, 1953), 334-40.

50. Cooke to Ickes, Mar. 25, 1935, RG 221, REA Administrator's File, box 9.

51. The *New York Times*, Apr. 5, 8, 1935; and *Emergency Relief Appropriation Act of 1935*, in *United States Statutes at Large*, 49, ch. 115, 1935.

of electrical energy in rural areas."[52] Three months later, on August 7, the president made what was probably the most far-reaching decision in the history of the REA, when he established its character as a lending agency. From this moment rural electrification became a sound national business investment.[53]

The most pressing task was to translate the REA from a paper organization into a functioning agency, one that would pull its weight in the fight against unemployment and, secondarily, contribute to the national power policy. Even before Congress had enacted the law, Cooke was very busy assembling a staff and hiring field representatives. There was little doubt that he would receive the appointment of administrator; this assumption, in fact, had muted much of the congressional opposition. On the Hill, Cooke had a highly regarded reputation as an administrator who could be entrusted with large sums of money. And, when the president made the appointment official, Cooke established headquarters on Massachusetts Avenue.[54]

From the start Cooke was extraordinarily sensitive to the value of favorable publicity for his fledgling organization. His first act as administrator was to hold a press conference to outline the ambitious goals which the REA intended to attain. Waxing eloquently, he announced that the REA proposed to construct 100,000 miles of power lines, to electrify one million farms, and to provide outlets for hydroelectric power from federal dams. Each project would be self-liquidating over a period of twenty years so that the original monies would be returned to the Treasury.[55] Thus he initiated the first phase in the history of the REA, a period extending through 1937 in which Cooke devoted his energies to promoting the cause of national rural electrification. His remarks, upon close observation, suggest also that Cooke perceived the REA's functions on a more ambitious scale than that of a temporary relief agency.

To this end Administrator Cooke adopted a policy designed to insure the political survival of the REA and the success of its mission. In response to sharp inquiries from Commissioner Elwood Mead of the Bureau of Reclamation, a member also of the NPPC, he revealed that the agency intended to refrain from competing directly with the

52. *Executive Order No. 7037,* May 11, 1935.
53. Harlow S. Person, "The Rural Electrification Administration in Perspective," *Agricultural History,* 24 (Apr. 1950), 73.
54. Ibid.
55. The *New York Times,* May 5, 1935. Cooke also cultivated the support of congressional sympathizers like Senator Norris who regularly received reports on the progress of rural-electrification projects in Nebraska.

private-power companies for territories, and that he would continue to work for their cooperation.[56] A rapprochement did not seem to be beyond the realm of possibility. Early in January 1935, a committee of utility executives had submitted to him a proposal for a one-year program, financed entirely through private funds, to construct 100,000 miles of power lines connecting one-half million new rural customers.[57] Unfortunately, the public-utility holding-company legislation then before the Congress set back the negotiations for joint industry-government cooperation.[58] Even without this obstacle it still was not certain that the majority of utility officials regarded the rural market as a field of enormous future potential. As late as June 1935, one executive wrote that "only in the imagination of these his [Cooke's] champions, does there exist any widespread demand for rural electrification."[59]

Cooke, however, was gambling that the industry's leadership had greater imagination and foresight. In May 1935, he requested that representatives of the fifteen largest companies appoint a committee to assess "the approximate extent to which further development of rural electrification may be affected promptly in cooperation with the Rural Electrification Administration."[60] The meeting, held on May 20, took place in Washington's Lafayette Hotel, and was attended by W. W. Freeman, vice-president of Columbia Gas and Electric Company; Hudson W. Reed, assistant to the president of United Gas Improvement; and others. According to officials of the Wisconsin Power and Light Company, Cooke described the primary objective of the REA as bringing electricity to as many farms as possible and as quickly as possible. He also announced that he expected to loan 95 percent of REA's appropriation to the private utilities at 2 to 3 percent interest because of their greater experience in building rural projects. Municipally owned utilities and farmer-owned distribution cooperatives would receive the remaining 5 percent. To expedite matters he also asked the industry to make a nationwide survey of rural electrical needs and to submit to him a program for utilizing the available funds.[61]

56. Cooke to Elwood Mead, Jan. [?] 1935, RG 221, REA Administrator's File, box 21.

57. Lemont K. Richardson, "The REA Program in Wisconsin, 1935-1955" (Ph.D. diss., University of Wisconsin, 1956), 37.

58. David E. Lilienthal, The Journals of David E. Lilienthal, 5 vols. (New York, 1964-71), I, 46-47.

59. Hudson W. Reed, "Rural Electrification," Edison Electric Institute Bulletin, 3 (June 1935), 182; and Richardson, "REA in Wisconsin," 37.

60. Person, "REA in Perspective," 73 ff.

61. McDonald, Let There Be Light, 360-63.

Whether Cooke ever made such a promise is uncertain, but the utilities drew up their plans on the assumption that they were to receive the lion's share of the funds. There is no record to be found of such an agreement among Cooke's papers or in any government records. In any event, disturbing hints that the industry was critical of the entire idea began to filter back to Washington. For its part, the industry suspected that Cooke was responsible for engineering the destruction of Ohio's state CREA, although there is no persuasive evidence to conclude that he had masterminded this feat.[62] The CREA had dwindled in influence since the depression and, under the New Deal, federal power agencies looked contemptuously upon it as the tool of the industry. In September 1935, Cooke expressed a forthright opinion of it to Paul Appleby of the Agricultural Department. Since the depression, he wrote, the CREA had been directed to brake the widespread demand for rural electrification by claiming that a lot of research was necessary before progress could be made. But Cooke never considered it a serious obstacle to his plans or to his negotiations with the power companies.[63]

On July 22, 1935, two days before the committee of utility executives was scheduled to deliver its report, Cooke warned his staff to be wary of their eagerness to cooperate.[64] Forrest McDonald, using data from the files of the Wisconsin Power and Light Company, has suggested that Cooke, from the outset, intended to trick power-company officials into revealing information on rural electrification to the REA. He also asserted that it would have taken Cooke several years and enormous sums of money to study the question himself.[65] The facts do not appear to warrant such an interpretation. Quite apart from the fact that he attributes to Cooke a Machiavelian technique that is totally out of character, he ignores the administrator's oft-repeated wish, as expressed to his staff, for cooperation with the private utilities.[66] But cooperation was not to be equated with surrender to the private-power

62. McDonald makes this assertion in ibid., 364, but the evidence is tenuous.

63. See Cooke to Paul Appleby, Sept. 5, 1935, RG 221, REA Administrator's File, box 7.

64. Cooke to REA Staff, July 22, 1935, Cooke Papers, Informal Talks File.

65. McDonald, *Let There Be Light,* 364-65.

66. Referring to the private utilities, Cooke wrote, "I am encouraged to think that they are going to do something a little different from what we might have expected," and spoke animatedly about drawing up contracts with them. Later, he was genuinely disappointed that they did not make application for loans from the REA. See Cooke to J. D. Ross, May 27, 1935, Seattle City Lighting Department Records, box 99, University of Washington Library; and "Interview Between Joseph Marion and Boyd Fisher," Dec. 13, 1935, RG 221, REA Administrator's File, box 14.

companies. Further, there is no supporting evidence in Cooke's papers or the files of the agency to support McDonald's contention. And finally, he overlooks one important consideration: Cooke could have obtained most of the technical information that appeared in the final industry report simply by consulting the files of the FPC, the TVA, and the public-service commissions of the states. The U.S. Bureau of the Census also had adequate data on rural electrification, and the Civil Works Administration recently had completed a national survey of the problem.[67] These findings were freely available to Cooke or anyone else. Moreover, the industry's research and findings could easily have been culled from its trade publications: *Electrical World, Public Utilities Fortnightly,* the CREA *Bulletin,* and the *Proceedings* of the NELA.[68]

The committee's report, dated July 24, 1935, failed to strike new ground, and simply reiterated timeworn accusations alleging government interference with private enterprise.[69] Its authors evidently had approached the problem from a narrow perspective, going so far as to divorce the social from the economic problems of the farmer. One statement which Cooke and REA officials seized upon to support this assertion was the declaration that there were few farms which still required electricity for major operations. The committee also wrote that the problem of rural electrification was not one of high rates but of the farmer's inability to finance the wiring of his home and the purchase of electrical appliances. The critique from an economic perspective solely was accurate enough; the problem was that Cooke had advanced beyond this level of analysis, perceiving rural electrification primarily as a social problem. To those whose avowed goal was to electrify all of rural America, and not simply the regions which could afford the cost, the committee was guilty of formalism.

Seen from this perspective, the report was inadequate. The furthest the industry would go was to propose a one-year program whereby it agreed to spend $113,685,000 for the construction of 78,000 miles of new lines to connect 351,000 rural customers. It was also naïve of the committee to believe that Cooke would surrender almost the entire $100 million authorization of the REA to the operating companies, and that the government would provide an additional $125

67. See George W. Kable and G. B. Gray, *Report on Civil Works Administration National Survey of Rural Electrification* (Washington, D.C., 1934).
68. See Richardson, "REA in Wisconsin," 39.
69. "Memorandum of the Rural Electrification Committee of Privately-Owned Utilities to Morris L. Cooke," July 24, 1935, Roosevelt Papers, OF 1570.

million in credit to rural customers to finance the installation of wiring, service contracts, and the purchase of appliances. Politically, it would not have been feasible, for the public-power groups were carefully watching him.[70]

This consideration aside, the crassness of the report outraged Cooke. He pointed out that private industry's financial risk very clearly would be kept to a minimum, whereas, if the program succeeded, it stood to reap a fortune from the reservoir of new customers. He also castigated the committee for its lack of vision, accusing the members of ignoring the potential benefits that a vigorous program of area coverage afforded, while distorting the rate and cost problems. But what grated him most was the audacity of the committee to suggest that the federal government should risk its entire capital appropriation while the industry reaped the profits.[71] Three weeks later, on June 6, 1935, Cooke conferred with national cooperative leaders and challenged them to participate in the rural-electrification program. He evidently intended to move along many fronts, private and public, in order to implement the administration's policy.[72]

Upon reflection, Cooke attributed the hostility of so many prominent utility men to the REA to die-hard opposition to holding-company regulation. And since they would not cooperate, he was unwilling to make a definite commitment to them that the REA would approve their applications for loans.[73] In this respect, he was under some pressure to adopt a hardline toward recalcitrant companies. The industry's negative attitude had deeply distressed Senator Norris, Cooke reported, and he "holds strongly to the view that there should be a radical change in the Administration's attitude toward public utilities." Cooke further informed the president that Norris believed that "it would be a mistake for us to loan money under any circumstances to any private company."[74]

The adoption of a tit-for-tat strategy, hard on the heels of earlier confusions and misunderstandings, cemented the wall of distrust and hostility that divided the private-power companies and the government. Ultimately, the opportunity to advance rural electrification as a joint public and private enterprise was lost. The private utilities, too, were at fault for the missed opportunity. From the start a significant number

70. Ibid.
71. Person, "REA in Perspective," 74.
72. REA, *Press Release No. 13,* June 6, 1935.
73. Ibid.
74. Cooke to Roosevelt, Aug. 2, 1935, RG 221, REA Administrator's File, box 30.

of executives were openly contemptuous of a rapprochement, and the misunderstanding arising from the May 20 conference soured even those who cautiously believed that cooperation was desirable. In June 1935, a supervisor for the Wisconsin Power and Light Company accused Cooke and his associates of deliberately inciting farmers to think that they could have electricity if only they formed cooperatives. And Grover Neff, one of the original members of the utility committee, implored his associates to revive the CREA in order to "checkmate REA's future moves." In December 1935, Neff wrote to Fred Insull: "Our industry is vulnerable on rural electrification."[75]

Soon thereafter, the REA joined other New Deal power programs as objects of vituperation by the private utilities. Their strategy was to forestall it by moving into some profitable areas that hitherto were ignored and to impede the REA's system of area coverage by building lines that attracted just enough potential customers to make the organization of an REA cooperative impossible. "Snake lines," darting out in all directions, and "spite lines," driven carefully through the center of a projected REA district, became potent weapons in the industry's "cream-skimming" policy.[76] The complaints of the government and the private utilities aside, this competition to service rural customers for whatever motive—and both government and industry had a vested interest in wanting to promote rural electrification after 1935—benefited the consumer in the long run. The rural dweller acquired electric power much sooner than he otherwise might have.

In some areas, though, the distinction between nibbling and a normal expansion of the private utilities was a fine one. Cooke was willing to concede the latter almost as much as he was prepared to deprecate the former. A case in point occurred in Ohio, involving the activities of the Ohio Edison Company, a subsidiary of Commonwealth and Southern. Cooke accused it of nibbling on certain territories which the REA believed properly belonged to a rural cooperative. Wendell L. Willkie, the director of the giant holding company, disagreed, and termed Ohio Edison's actions "a normal natural expansion of rural lines." But what is most interesting in his correspondence with Cooke on the subject of "spite lines" is the startling revelation of the poor state of relations that existed between the Roosevelt administration and the private-utility industry. "There are investigations made by

75. Quoted in Richardson, "REA in Wisconsin," 39-40.
76. Raymond S. Tompkins, "The Electrified Farmer in the New Deal Dell," *Electrical World*, 105 (Sept. 14, 1935), 42-44; and United States Rural Electrification Administration, *First Annual Report of the Rural Electrification Administration* (Washington, D.C., 1936).

government investigators," he complained, "their reports are apparently accepted as the facts and actions are taken based upon such reports." The power companies were never given the opportunity to present their side of the picture. "I have had this experience so many times in my relationships with various federal government departments in the last three years that I have almost lost hope of working out sane solutions of the many problems which are arising by reason of the increased governmental activities."[77]

By the end of the year relations between the two rapidly approached the breaking point. The private-utility industry, much to the distress of REA officials, showed not the slightest inclination to borrow any funds from the agency. The strict conditions imposed upon government loans had rendered them unattractive. In July 1935, Cooke had disclosed that "in weighing the relative desirability of loans, it will be necessary for REA to consider carefully existing and proposed rate structures with reference to developing the large use essential to the success of our program."[78] Translated into concrete language, this meant that the industry first had to reduce construction costs to the minimum consistent with good service; it also was expected to simplify and lower rates and eliminate completely capital contributions from consumers toward the extension of service, and lastly the practice of high minimum bills. Few utility companies were prepared to accept these terms, preferring to turn to the money market where companies in good financial standing could take advantage of declining interest rates to obtain funds under more favorable conditions than those offered by the REA.[79]

No matter how equitable Cooke wished to be in dealing with requests for loans from private sources, political considerations dictated in part the imposition of stiff terms. In September 1935, he had circulated a memorandum among his staff which set the pattern. "I understand," he wrote, "that there is still some doubt in the minds of some of the members of the staff as to our attitude toward requests for loans coming from public and non-profit organizations as contrasted with the attitude toward loans to private companies. Obviously, we want to treat everybody fairly, and when I say fairly I mean fairly. But it should be equally obvious that we cannot carry out the obvious

77. Cooke to Wendell L. Willkie, Apr. 22, 1936; Willkie to Cooke, July 5, 1935, RG 221, REA Administrator's File, box 36.

78. REA, *Press Release No. 21,* July 31, 1935.

79. Twentieth Century Fund, *Electric Power and Government Policy* (New York, 1948), 445-46.

legislative intent if, and when there is a clash or near clash of public and private interests, we did not give the public interests preference."[80] Cooke's attitude also was influenced by Senator Norris, who was violently opposed to lending REA monies to the private utilities. In midsummer, he had written to the administrator that, in view of the present state of the industry, "this would be taking a step which cannot be defended upon any ground of either justice or honesty. ... To lend money to a [private utility] to carry on its business is absolutely indefensible."[81] In a tone that was a mixture of embarrassment as well as pride, Cooke replied to the Nebraskan in January of the new year. He pointed out "how small a part the private utilities have played to date and are apparently planning to play in the promotion of rural electrification with Government money."[82]

In fact, REA officials had been quietly reshaping their policy to give principal consideration to nonprofit associations. The first inkling of the shift occurred in a letter which Cooke wrote to C. W. Warburton, director of the Agricultural Extension Service. It was dated June 10, 1935, and declared that county agricultural agents were in a particularly strategic position to encourage group discussions among farmers about the REA program and to promote the formation of viable cooperative projects. Thereafter, farmers' cooperative organizations surged to the front as the leading borrowers. Private-power companies still had not been written off, and in March 1936 Boyd Fisher made a new overture to them. The REA was willing to grant loans to the industry under slightly modified conditions: first, the company must already have demonstrated its capacity to render service; secondly, it had to have ample working capital and was requesting the loan only for the purpose of extending service; and thirdly, it intended to build only where it was not feasible for a cooperative or anyone else to make the proper extension. Even these conditions were unsatisfactory to most companies, and few bothered to apply for funds.[83]

The agency also was experiencing difficulty in functioning as a work-relief agency. In May and June 1935, President Roosevelt had issued executive orders governing the disbursement of relief funds; the orders applied to funds for rural-electrification projects as well. The administration assumed that the REA would follow the normal grant-

80. Cooke to REA Staff, Sept. 13, 1935, RG 221, REA Central File, General Correspondence, 1935-1940, box 18.
81. Norris to Cooke, Aug. 1, 1935, in ibid., box 26.
82. Cooke to Norris, Jan. 1936, in ibid.
83. See Cooke's statement in *Rural Electrification News,* 1 (Oct. 1935), 2; and Boyd Fisher to Cooke, Mar. 5, 1936, RG 221, REA Administrator's File, box 14.

subsidy-loan practice of other relief agencies, channeling funds as quickly as possible into projects which employed the greatest number of workers. To its dismay the staff of the REA learned that it could not proceed on a large scale and still adhere to the presidential directives. These orders had stated that 25 percent of the funds for the agency had to be spent directly on labor and that 90 percent of the labor force had to be procured from the relief rolls and certified by the U. S. Employment Service. In addition, the REA had been strictly enjoined from competing for the privately unemployed.[84] Thus, in most rural areas where projects were likely to be constructed, there was a shortage of skilled electrical workers on the local relief rolls.[85]

The problem was complicated further by the fact that the REA simply did not have adequate funds to perform both its relief and electrification tasks. Lilienthal of the TVA recognized this deficiency almost from the start. In September 1935, he advised Cooke that "the work relief monies to be made available for power projects is going to be very limited," and offered the cooperation of his agency as an intermediary with Secretary Ickes to obtain the release of funds for "must" projects. But he warned Cooke not to run up the bill, "because it would indicate that, unless you get more money than is available, there is not much use in helping you."[86]

The shortage of funds dictated inevitably that preference would be shown to public nonprofit organizations rather than to private borrowers. As mentioned, the thrust of REA activity in the first year was toward promoting cooperatives and working through already established state rural-electrification authorities, power districts, and municipal boards. This policy was fraught with hazards and contradictions because the number of public-power authorities was never substantial enough to make a dent in the unemployment problem. In many instances the public bodies could not muster the resources, the technical competence, or the skilled labor to begin construction immediately. In other areas, local prejudices militated against the expansion of mu-

84. Carmody, "Rural Electrification in the U.S.," 71.

85. Beginning in May 1935 an Advisory Committee on Allotments was instituted. It met every two weeks and unequivocally held fast to the policy that REA funds were to be used to take employable people from the relief rolls. See "Digest of Proceedings of the Advisory Committee on Allotments," May 7, 1935, RG 221, REA Administrator's File, box 38.

86. Lilienthal to Cooke, Sept. 13, 1935, in ibid., box 20. For additional evidence on the paucity of funds see also Lilienthal to Cooke, Aug. 1, 1935 in ibid.; Cooke's request to Secretary Ickes for financial aid from the PWA, June 22, 1935, in ibid., box 18; and Cooke to Ross, [1935], Seattle City Lighting Department Records, box 99.

nicipal plants into nearby rural hamlets. In lieu of an objective analysis of these problems, there was on occasion a tendency for REA officials to attribute their difficulties solely to the fact that the private utilities would not apply for REA loans. Their circular logic smacked of an attempt to conceal their own shortcomings.[87]

The REA, likewise, was beset with internal divisions over policy that made it impossible to adopt a neutral attitude toward the development of projects on which it was asked to lend money. To some degree this was to be expected of an inexperienced agency, but it also led to delay, loss of money, and frayed nerves. Boyd Fisher, the head of the Development Section, took the position that the REA should not aggressively promote cooperatives; it ought to wait for the initiative to come from local sources. He feared—and Cooke shared this fear—that the public would conclude that the REA was guaranteeing *in advance* the loan of money regardless of the quality of the application. He observed that the agency wanted to be able to reject loan applications on their merits without jeopardizing its own status.[88] However, neither he nor Cooke was able to exercise complete control over the quality of the expenditures. In the early days there were few dependable standards to determine whether a project would be self-liquidating; the agency also was under intense pressure to spend quickly its relief allotment.[89]

Moreover, the performance of the REA's field agents was unpredictable. In Wisconsin, where sentiment for public power was at fever pitch, the agents viewed their role as active propagandists to the cooperatives and wanted to channel REA funds almost exclusively to them.[90] This was a far cry from the more limited approach advocated by Fisher and Cooke. In June 1935, Fisher had made it clear that he viewed his role chiefly as a credit agent, rating the soundness of the cooperative's project. His secondary function was to advise citizens seeking to form a cooperative of the agency's standards.[91]

The cumulative effect of these difficulties was that the agency did

87. "Interview Between Joseph Marion and Boyd Fisher," Dec. 13, 1935, RG 221, REA Administrator's File, box 14. Not until Sept. 9, 1935, were the first allocations, amounting to $2,351,355, made from relief funds, none of which went to the private utilities.

88. Ibid.

89. Cooke, "Memorandum Covering Approval of Projects," Dec. 23, 1936, in ibid., box 18.

90. See Fisher to Cooke, June 20, 1935, Cooke to Fisher, July 2, 1935, and M. D. Lincoln to Fisher, Dec. 13, 1935, in ibid., box 14.

91. "Interview Between Joseph Marion and Boyd Fisher," Dec. 13, 1935, in ibid., box 14.

not live up to expectations. The president, especially, was keenly dissatisfied with its failure to make headway in the unemployment crisis; and, after a few months of operation, he threatened to cut off its funds. The special pleading of Cooke alone stayed the president's hand; and yet, even he had to admit that the REA was not performing up to par. Instead, the administrator shifted ground, and talked about its *potential* impact upon the unemployment problem once procedures were adjusted. In April 1936, Cooke told the staff that "the amount of labor which a given distribution line instigates in the houses adjacent to it and in the factories making appliances puts rural electrification in the top class of relief agencies." Then he added, almost as an afterthought: "I should like to have us accent this in every way we can."[92]

Senator Norris put his finger on the crux of the problem, when he observed that, under present conditions, the REA could not perform successfully both of its tasks. The temporary status of the agency, inadequate funding, and the loss of the president's confidence had narrowly defined the parameters of its effectiveness. From the start the Nebraskan had considered the relief aspect of secondary importance to the main purpose, which was to accomplish national rural electrification. In October 1935, he talked openly and forcefully about the desirability of putting the REA on a permanent footing. On October 24, he asked Cooke "what would be involved in the proper extension of rural lines, so that a much larger percentage of rural homes may be electrified, and how soon can this be brought about."[93] Cooke estimated that it would require about $500 million over the next ten years in order to bring electric power to one million new rural customers.[94] Thus began the movement to make the REA a permanent and integral feature of the New Deal's national power policy.

92. Person, "REA in Perspective," 74-75; and Cooke to Staff, Apr. 8, 1936, RG 221, REA Administrator's File, box 18.
93. Norris to Cooke, Oct. 24, 1935, Roosevelt Papers, OF 1570.
94. Cooke to Norris, Oct. 24, 1935, RG 221, REA Administrator's File, box 26.

CHAPTER VI

REA: The Formative Years

Norris's inquiry had given Cooke the opportunity to revive the question of the REA's future. It was not a new topic; in February 1934 Cooke had proposed the establishment of a permanent administration funded by means of a system of banks similar to the federal land banks of the Wilson administration. This suggestion never came to fruition, although the prospect of a permanent agency, as part of a national power policy, exercised a certain fascination. In October 1935, T. A. Panter, one of Cooke's consultants, wrote to him that "even though the work of REA has been in progress but a few months, the majority of the response from the potential rural customers ... has been so great, it is plainly evident that it will be extremely difficult to limit the work to the original program without creating great dissatisfaction." He proposed, therefore, a plan whereby the REA would undertake a complete national rural-electrification program, executed in three stages, for about $1.3 billion.[1]

Refusing to commit himself to any one plan, Cooke, at that time, kept his options fluid. Nevertheless Panter's memorandum, Norris's prodding, and the growing pressure upon the president in late 1935 to adopt a more radical social program kept alive discussion of the agency's future. Roosevelt had reluctantly reached the conclusion that the REA was only marginally effective as a program to combat unemployment but his progressive-humanitarian and political instincts told him that the REA was popular. As a result, he joined Cooke in framing a carefully worded reply to Senator Norris, setting forth the administration's attitude on the matter. Their recommendation was similar to the one put forth by Norcross in his report to the NPPC. The key paragraph asserted that federal participation in a comprehensive rural-electrification program of long-range rather than of a temporary work-relief character was economically and socially justi-

---

1. T. A. Panter, "Suggested Program for a More Complete National Rural Electrification with Tentative Recommendations and Appropriate Estimates of Costs," Oct. 29, 1935, Morris L. Cooke Papers, box 324, Franklin D. Roosevelt Library (hereafter cited as Cooke Papers).

fiable. Norris was given the green light to draft legislation incorporating the REA as an ongoing feature of the New Deal.[2]

In January 1936, with administration backing, he and Representative Sam Rayburn introduced the REA bills. The long-term issues of public versus private and cooperative versus private development of power once again confronted Congress. And yet, neither bill elicited the savage opposition of Congress or the utility industry as had the TVA bill or the holding-company bill's "death sentence." Quite the contrary; public discussion in the industry's technical journals, *Electrical World* and *Public Utilities Fortnightly,* was nearly nonexistent in comparison with the flood of vituperative articles denouncing the TVA and the Public Utility Holding Company Act. The United States Chamber of Commerce sent to each senator a perfunctory statement arguing against the legislation, but its protest was all the more remarkable for being solitary.[3]

Debate in Congress centered chiefly upon the mechanics of the legislation; even its critics were ready to concede the principle of rural electrification. Representative Charles Wolverton, an archfoe of public power, captured the mood of the House when he observed that "the purpose of the proposed legislation is to establish a permanent and comprehensive national policy for rural electrification." The absence of overt protest from the utility industry was puzzling, especially to Henry Luckey of Nebraska who anticipated a repetition of the massive lobbying of 1935. His efforts to suck the industry's defenders into debate were unavailing. James Wadsworth of New York, one of the severest critics of the Public Utility Holding Company Act, reassured his colleagues that they would not be in for "any such performance as featured that occasion." He reminded them that the industry had evinced no opposition to the legislation "whatsoever."[4]

In a literal sense, of course, Wadsworth's statement was accurate. There had been no phalanx of criticism in part because the legislation was drawn carefully in order to deflect the shafts of its enemies. The REA, for example, was rigorously enjoined from competing with exist-

2. See Jean Christie, "Morris Llewellyn Cooke: Progressive Engineer" (Ph.D. diss., Columbia University, 1963), 235. Under the new proposal the REA would construct projects on an area basis in order to take advantage of the economics of mass production.

3. Morris L. Cooke to John P. Robertson, Mar. 2, 1936, National Archives, Record Group 221, REA Administrator's File, box 26 (hereafter only the record group, the file, and the box number will be cited). Robertson was private secretary to Senator Norris.

4. *Congressional Record,* 74th Cong., 2d sess., 80 (Apr. 9, 1936), 5284, 5293-94 ff. Even the warning of Representative Schuyler Merritt of Connecticut against creeping bureaucratic socialism did not arouse a storm of opposition to the bill. See ibid., 5279.

ing private-utility systems. And, by offering the promise of a whole new market for electrical appliances, the bill dulled the hostility of one segment of the industry, that is, the manufacturers of electrical equipment and appliances. Also, Senator Black's lobby investigation had momentarily placed the utilities on the defensive. But it was the *Kiplinger Washington Letter* which most likely touched upon the true reason: the power companies were absolutely confident that the Norris and Rayburn bills "will prove to be another New Deal flop."[5] Its canvass of utility opinion revealed that the industry's leadership believed that the REA would never succeed in persuading farmers to go into debt for electricity when, if they were patient, the power companies would get their lines out to them. In retrospect, it is clear that the industry seriously underestimated the sentiment among rural dwellers for obtaining power immediately. And low-interest loans were to make it financially attractive for them to borrow from the REA.[6]

When the bill came up to the Senate floor for debate, Norris employed all the timeworn arguments of the public-power lobby to persuade his colleagues to vote for it. He introduced little new information on the subject, other than what was culled from the practical experience of the agency in its relatively brief year of operation. His most compelling argument for a permanent agency incorporated a nostalgic concern for the yeoman farmer with self-interest and sound economics. Electricity was the touchstone for industrializing the farm and securing the rural dweller's competitive footing vis à vis the urban worker and businessman. In the race for a fair share of the national income, Norris declared, power on the farm made all the difference in the world. It also opened up to American manufacturing and industry a market that was unlimited in its potential. So politically popular was rural electrification that the Committee on Agriculture and Forestry endorsed S. 3843 without the formality of a hearing. And when Norris declared that he had neither heard nor knew of any objection to the principle of rural electrification, his observation went unchallenged.[7]

The legislative path, however, was not altogether smooth. This was evident from the stormy meetings of the joint conference committee which met to reconcile differences between the Senate and House bills. The issues in dispute ranged over a broad spectrum; their resolu-

5. Francis X. Welch, "World Wide Electrification," *Public Utilities Fortnightly,* 17 (Mar. 12, 1936), 389-91.
6. The *New York Times,* May 31, 1936.
7. *Congressional Record,* 74th Cong., 2d sess., 80 (Apr. 9, 1936), 2753 ff., 2818-19, 3302-07, 3317. See also U.S. Congress, Senate, *Senate Report 1581,* 74th Cong., 2d sess. (Washington, D.C., 1936).

tion would shape thereafter the character of the REA. The most important questions included whether the agency should be structured along
partisan political lines; whether it might invite applications for loans
from the private-power companies; whether such loans should not be
reserved exclusively, or at least preferentially, for public agencies and
cooperatives; and how much interest should be charged on loans. Toward the close of April, Norris, appointed head of the Senate conference, met with the House conferees, determined to resist any watering
down of his bill. For the next three weeks the future of government
participation in rural electrification in the United States hung in the
balance. Meeting after meeting of the committee broke up in angry
accusations; the press reported that the conferees had come perilously
close to blows on more than one occasion.[8]

From the sidelines the administration nervously followed the melee,
fearful that the REA would be the prime casualty and with it the
goal of national rural electrification. Norris balked at any compromise
that opened the agency to political influence; he warned his House
counterparts that the REA's future effectiveness was limited if it had
to rely upon the favor of the administration in power. His opposition
to lending public monies to the private-utility industry persisted, despite
the more flexible approach of Sam Rayburn. And, agreeing with economists and financial experts who maintained that interest rates on loans
had to be high enough to make the program self-liquidating, he resisted
the advances of House conferees, who were under pressure themselves
from the public-power and farm blocs and from farmer organizations,
to fix very low rates. By May the conference committee had reached
an impasse. At the critical moment administration officials stepped
in to break the deadlock.[9]

The initial movement toward compromise came from the president
through his legislative leaders in the Congress. The president signaled
to them his desire to keep the agency out of politics, and they, in
turn, instructed the House conferees to give way on the administrative
issue. Cooke thereupon intervened with Norris, persuading the Nebraskan that he could yield on the remaining points without sacrificing
any substantive principle. Interest rates on REA loans were set at
a rate equal to the average rate of interest payable on federal obligations

8. Ibid., 5273-79. Led by John Rankin of Mississippi, a group of public-power radicals
in the House had tried to ban the use of REA funds for loans to private-utility corporations.
See also Marquis W. Childs, *The Farmer Takes a Hand* (New York, 1952), 66-70;
and United States Rural Electrification Administration, *Proceedings and Address, Sixth
Annual Staff Conference, April 15-18, 1941* (Washington, D.C., 1941), 20.
9. The *New York Times*, May 5, 1936.

having a maturity of ten years or more. In practice this meant that the rate was set at about 3 percent.[10] The conference also agreed that the utilities should be eligible to apply for loans but under the same conditions as cooperatives and other public agencies. This concession was window dressing, Cooke pointed out, because the REA intended to grant loans according to the percentage of farms covered in a given area and not merely on the basis of miles of line constructed. Cooke expected that the emphasis upon area coverage would discourage the private-power companies from heavy borrowing; later events demonstrated that his analysis was correct.[11]

Once the principle of preference for nonprofit agencies was established, Norris dropped his opposition. The conference wrote its report embodying the new agreements and recommended that Congress enact the legislation. Within a few days the House and Senate acted, the vote being unrecorded. On May 20, 1936, a pleased president signed it into law.[12]

The establishment of the REA as a regular agency galvanized the operating companies into strenuous opposition. In southern states, where holding companies were particularly influential, the industry's leaders were fearful that the new emphasis upon farmers' cooperatives might serve as a stepping stone to organized political activity, much as the Populists had used the farmer's Alliances in the 1890s. Often they resorted to disreputable tactics in order to forestall cooperative formation. In Texas, the first cooperative was quashed when a Department of Agriculture agent, who had participated in its organization, was induced to hand over his maps to the Texas Power and Light Company. The utility, which hitherto had refused to service the area, then built the lines itself. In Madison County, Iowa, the problem was to organize the farmers. The power companies there had persuaded them that a rural electric project was a very complicated and expensive affair, one that could be managed by the companies alone.[13]

10. Cooke to Franklin D. Roosevelt, May 7, 1936, Cooke Papers, box 147; George W. Norris, *Fighting Liberal* (New York, 1945), 322-23.
11. Cooke to Roosevelt, May 7, 1936, in Cooke Papers, box 147. On March 24, 1936, Cooke wrote that REA loans would go to private companies only on an area basis "to avoid helping companies pick the most profitable lines and thus making it more difficult for those who are left over to get service" and "to develop the technique by which companies will be forced to take the lean with the fat in the same way that cooperatives do" (Cooke to Earl H. Barber, Mar. 24, 1936, RG 221, REA Administrator's File, box 3).
12. Cooke to Roosevelt, May 19, 1936, in RG 221, REA Administrator's File, box 30.
13. See, for example, John Carmody to Clay L. Cochran, Jan. 26, 1955, John M. Carmody Papers, box 83, Franklin D. Roosevelt Library (hereafter cited as Carmody

The problem of "spite lines" also persisted. Cooke made repeated efforts to halt their construction but, on the whole, he was not successful. The time lapse between the planning and actual construction of lines occasionally made it unclear whether a utility was deliberately bent on wrecking a cooperative or just happened to be setting poles in territory that was under consideration for an REA project. The same was true when the REA operated in territory claimed by private industry; the result was increased friction between the government and the utilities. The Johnston County Electric Corporation, an REA undertaking in North Carolina, was a case in point. Its power was derived from Electric Bond and Share's subsidiary, the Carolina Power and Light Company. In January 1937, Cooke wrote to C. F. Groesbeck that it was the REA's fixed policy not to compete where private industry had set up its poles. In this instance the company had waited until after the farmers had established their own organization and applied for REA funds. Cooke may have been correct, but he could never be certain without first examining the company's records. The most he could do was to issue a warning. "But I would be falling down on my job," he told Groesbeck, "if I did not from time to time remind you higher ups what is going on in certain areas and at the same time express the opinion that it cannot go on forever."[14]

When they were not building "spite lines," the utilities resorted to other obstructive tactics. They launched a clever, and wholly legal, campaign to subject REA cooperatives to the jurisdiction of state public-service commissions. In Pennsylvania, Virginia, North Carolina, and wherever the commissions were notoriously hostile to public bodies, the aim was to destroy the movement by involving farmers in costly and time-consuming litigation. Nowhere was this opposition stronger or more determined than in Massachusetts. Its Department of Public Utilities rendered an unfavorable ruling which destroyed the largest cooperative, composed of seven hundred farmers, in the northwestern part of the state.[15] Marion L. Ramsay, the muckraking

Papers); and J. Long to Boyd Fisher, May 8, 1936, RG 221, REA Administrator's File, box 14.

14. Cooke to C. F. Groesbeck, Jan. 4, 1937, in RG 221, REA Administrator's File, box 12.

15. The REA thoroughly botched the cooperative movement in Massachusetts, which played directly into the hands of the private utilities and forced the administrator to defend a cooperative that he knew to be poorly organized and run. Earl Barber, an REA consultant, described the situation in the Bay State as follows: "Carmody knew Cooke had left him a pup, but for face-saving purposes [he] was willing to go through with it if the thing would pay its bare operating expenses but not amortization. If the DPU [Department of Public Utilities] had taken the responsibility for refusal, and be-

author of *Pyramids of Power*, angrily watched what was occurring and argued that commission control was never intended to apply to nonprofit bodies such as municipal electrical plants or cooperatives. Ramsay's reports alerted Senator Norris and the public-power organizations to this newest strategem.[16]

Cooke complained also that the power companies were tampering with rates as a means of bringing the cooperatives to heel. "It seems fair to advise you and a few other men of standing in the private electric industry," he wrote to Willkie and Groesbeck, "that the cooperatives to be financed by this Administration are not receiving the service in the matter of wholesale rates to which they feel themselves entitled and which would accord with the industry's protestations of goodwill and cooperation."[17] His criticism was equally biting in memoranda circulated privately to his staff whom he urged to be "polite in one case and rough in another" in order to force down rates. "Normally in negotiating a contract," he told Harry Zinder, "a good buyer respects the interests of the man from whom he is buying, but this seems out of the question in dealing with an industry whose present day conduct is so largely influenced by its narrow past."[18]

The rate problem had arisen in part because of the REA's decision to concentrate its limited resources upon the distributive aspects of electrification. It was also the policy of the administration to stimulate the widest possible use of power by forcing down rates. "In the interest of spreading our loan funds as wide as possible, as well as in the interest of cooperating with the industry," Cooke observed, "we have not wished to finance any considerable number of generating plants. We have felt we could do better by financing distribution lines and getting the energy from existing sources." This policy could be maintained only if the industry quoted rates to REA projects based upon cost plus a *reasonable* profit. The agency had determined after extensive cost-analysis investigation that a wholesale price of two cents per kilowatt hour met this criterion. The operating companies either were quoting prices well above this figure or were simply refusing

---

haved in a diplomatic manner, I guess he would have heaved a sigh of relief. But when the DPU went out of its way to give REA a wanton booting, Carmody very properly booted back" (Barber to Judson King, Jan. 25, 1938, Judson King Papers, box 18, Library of Congress [hereafter cited as King Papers]).

16. Marion L. Ramsay to Norris, Feb. 14, Mar. 8, 1937, George Norris Papers, tray 80, box 8, Library of Congress (hereafter cited as Norris Papers).

17. Cooke to C. F. Groesbeck and Wendell L. Willkie, Dec. 3, 1936, RG 221, REA Administrator's File, boxes 12 and 36.

18. Cooke to H. Zinder, Feb. 13, 1937, in ibid., box 5.

to make any tenders. "This experience indicates plainly that too many companies are either reluctant to supply our cooperatives or are quoting more or less arbitrary prices," Cooke declared. "You know of course that the wholesale price is vital to us because unless it is reasonably low many thousands of farmers cannot be served at all, or could be served only at the price of unduly restricting their use of electricity and jeopardizing our loans."[19] The wholesale-rate problem continued to fester and exacerbate relations between the industry and the government; but, as late as June 30, 1941, the REA had financed power generation for only 4 percent of its borrowers.[20]

The harrassment of the private utilities was not wholly to blame for the REA's failure to progress beyond the promotional stage of rural electrification. Its basic difficulties, after May 1936, continued to be of an internal nature, arising from questions of policy which had never been resolved satisfactorily during the agency's tenure as a relief body. As early as April 1935, the staff had broken into factions over policy toward the private-power companies; this division inevitably manifested itself in the slowness with which loan applications were processed, especially those of the operating companies. On one side were staff members who argued that the REA was essentially a lending agency, and that it ought to leave the actual construction work to others. This group cannot be labeled neatly "proindustry," or "anti-public power"; it more accurately represented the desires of those individuals who hoped to heal the breach between industry and government. S. N. Tideman represented their point of view. On April 29, 1935, he wrote to Cook, explaining his attitude: "I believe that private initiative should be given a fair field to cooperate, and that government generosity to rural electrification will meet with public approval provided that all classes of enterprise competent of useful functioning are encouraged rather than suppressed."[21]

Arraigned against him were Deputy Administrator John M. Carmody and Boyd Fisher, the chief of the REA's Development Section. Carmody shared to a degree the public-power viewpoint; his attitude toward the industry was influenced by its attacks upon the TVA and the holding-company legislation. Fisher, likewise, was suspicious of the

19. Cooke to Groesbeck, Oct. 23, Dec. 3, 1936, in ibid., box 12.
20. The private utilities supplied 49.7 percent, with the REA, municipal plants, TVA, public-power districts, and other public bodies accounting for the remaining 50.3 percent. See Twentieth Century Fund, *Electric Power and Government Policy* (New York, 1948), 447, table VIII-2.
21. S. N. Tideman to Cooke, Apr. 29, 1935, RG 221, REA Administrator's File, box 31.

industry, although his dealings with it were always properly correct. But, by virtue of his position in the REA, he also had a vested interest in wanting to participate in the construction phase of rural-electrification projects. Both men demanded that the federal government assume the primary responsibility for financing, planning, and constructing projects. They were also the instigators of the cooperative approach.[22]

The repercussions of this schism were iniquitous, infecting the entire staff and affecting adversely the agency's efficiency as a relief body. The divisions persisted even after the REA was set up on a permanent footing, until Cooke retired voluntarily in 1937. The conflict over the manner in which projects were handled is a good illustration. Neither Craig Winder's Projects Section nor the Development Section people could agree on the proper disposition of a project application, each department taking it in turn as its exclusive possession and formulating policy without regard to anyone else. In extreme cases each section corresponded independently with the applicant and denied its information to the other. Boyd Fisher complained later that decisions sometimes were made on the basis of personal attitudes, or else an applicant's project had to run the gauntlet of one department which favored cooperatives and then another which preferred any private project to any cooperative. From 1935 through 1937 inefficiency, as opposed to systematic discrimination, was often at the root of the REA's mishandling of loan applications from private companies.[23]

Cooke's position, initially, was to ride the middle ground. What appeared as indecisiveness to critics within the REA and the public-power movement was mistaken for hostility by the private utilities. Actually, he had never surrendered the conviction that the industry would collaborate with the REA, although he was well apprised that the Edison Electric Institute, the successor to the old NELA, opposed the New Deal's power policy. Addressing the institute's 1936 convention, W. W. Freeman, a utility executive, expressed doubt about the entire REA program. He declared that "it is evident that what the industry must regard from its own experience as an exceedingly optimistic experiment is being undertaken by the Federal Government without any admitted doubts of assured success."[24] Cooke brushed aside Freeman's distortion and clung to the hope that the industry's

22. Carmody to Cochran, Jan. 26, 1955, Carmody Papers, box 83; and Boyd Fisher to Cooke, June 11, 1936, RG 221, REA Administrator's File, box 14.
23. The intensity of the hostility which this rivalry created is well portrayed in James H. Boyle to Fisher, July 2, 1935; Fisher to Cooke, June 11, 1936; and Carmody to REA Staff, Dec. 4, 1936, in RG 221, REA Administrator's File, boxes 14 and 18.
24. See Foster Adams to Cooke, July 30, 1936, in ibid., box 1.

more enlightened leaders would come to terms with the REA. On May 27, 1936, he circulated a memorandum to his staff emphasizing this position. "As our program widens geographically the opportunity grows for possible clashes between public, cooperative, and private interests. We want to encourage the accommodation of these interests in every proper way," he wrote. Nirvana was still in the future, but he instructed the staff "to refrain from any criticism of the private interests irrespective of how provocative the immediate situation may seem to be."[25] Only after he realized that the progressives in the industry were not about to apply for loans did he turn gradually to the cooperatives. In January 1937, few newspapers or public-power men detected this shift of emphasis; they continued to portray the administrator as tepid toward cooperatives.[26]

The REA's inability to advance substantially toward national rural electrification from 1935 to 1937 may also be attributed to its dismal relationship with the EHFA.[27] Reorganized as a public corporation in 1935, it was expected to initiate a national campaign to persuade consumers to purchase more electrical appliances. The EHFA also was empowered to make credit available to its customers for wiring and other purposes requiring the use of electrical energy on the farm. Successful execution of its assignment would stimulate the demand for electricity in rural areas and thereby facilitate the agency's task. Thus, the EHFA had a large role in influencing the downward trend of electric rates. Unfortunately, the tightfisted fiscal policies of its director, Jesse H. Jones, conflicted with the aims of the REA, and it never lived up to expectations. Cooke complained to Jones that the EHFA had fallen down on the job. "But this work has really never started," he wrote in November 1935. "We are just about where we were when the organization was incorporated. In fact, I think we have lost some of the impetus which we inherited."[28] Cooke eventually resigned from the agency's board of directors in disgust and spoke about having the REA build its own merchandizing organization. This bottleneck in getting money to farmers to purchase wiring, water sys-

25. Cooke to REA Staff, May 27, 1936, in ibid., box 14.
26. See, for example, the Chambersburg, Pa., *Public Opinion,* Jan. 20, 1937, in Carmody Papers, box 82.
27. The evidence is overwhelming but see William A. Weaver to Cooke, Oct. 22, 30, 1935; Cooke to David E. Lilienthal, and to Roosevelt, Nov. 18, 1935; Zinder to Cooke, Jan. 2, 1936; and Cooke to Roosevelt, Jan. 16, 1936, in RG 221, REA Administrator's File, boxes 12, 20, and 30.
28. Cooke to Jesse H. Jones, Nov. 18, 1935, Cooke Papers, box 324.

tems, and appliances plagued the REA until 1937 when its new director, Carmody, cut the fiscal knot.[29]

Underlying these irritations there remained one unalterable fact. Despite its elevation in status the REA was strapped with a tight budget. Congress had allocated to it for the fiscal year 1936-37 the sum of $50 million, an amount hardly calculated to achieve national rural electrification in the immediate future.[30] The question confronting Cooke, therefore, was whether to continue to beat the bushes for new project proposals or to stand still and cease developmental work. This, in turn, raised other fundamental questions that the administrator had to decide.[31] The REA could easily have adopted the policy of discouraging new proposals simply by calling in its field agents. It had on hand requisitions for projects totaling $112 million, or two and one-quarter times as much money to spend as it was allocated, and a year ahead of it in which new requests were certain to come.[32]

Boyd Fisher, however, built a persuasive case for an alternative policy. Since the REA already knew the sums of money it could allot for projects in each of the thirty-four states participating in the program, he proposed to make in-depth studies to determine fairly precisely which counties were suitable for development, and to determine in advance their legal, economic, and social problems. Without waiting for the initiative of the local people, he would conduct the investigations quietly. "Let us then suddenly go about the formation of the cooperative, incorporating, securing franchises, etc.," wrote Fisher, "and let us be prepared to push through the allotments, making contracts, etc., so that construction can begin immediately before the power companies have the chance to wean away or secure any prejudiced assistance from the public service commissions."[33] Fisher did not expect this course of action to surprise the power companies; he thought it would increase the prestige of the REA as an agency competent to construct lines. It would also refute the timeworn accusation that government was unable to move expeditiously.

Continuing, Fisher approached the ten-year goal of nationwide electrification in three phases. The REA would disburse funds over

29. "Cooke Quits the E.H.F.A.," *Electrical World*, 105 (Dec. 7, 1935), 2908. That Cooke was bluffing in his threat to build generators is evident in letters written afterward. See Cooke to Carmody and to Emil Schram, Jan. 5, 1937, RG 221, REA Administrator's File, box 5.
30. Fisher to Correspondents, Development Section, May 8, 1936, RG 221, REA Administrator's File, box 14.
31. Cooke to Fisher, May 25, 1936, ibid.
32. Fisher to Cooke, May 19, 1936, ibid.
33. Ibid.

a three-year period, instead of the current year-by-year allotment. Plans could then be drawn on the basis of a $150-million expenditure instead of the present $50 million. During the first year, one-third of the total funds was earmarked for construction in the most profitable territories, in the second year the next third in somewhat less profitable territories, and in the last year the final third in areas that, because of the sparsity of population, were the least profitable. By retaining the element of flexibility the benefits would outweigh the shortcomings. The cooperatives could husband their resources, developing utilities in the most lucrative territories before spreading into thinner areas. This procedure afforded the government a measure of protection for its loans against default, and leverage whereby the cooperatives would be kept on good behavior for at least two years longer. The winning argument, in the long run, was that the plan enabled the cooperatives to stake a claim to the most desirable territories and prevented the private-power companies from anticipating the REA's future growth by building "snake" and "spite" lines.[34]

The burden of deciding between these two radically different courses of action, either of which would shape the REA's character for many years, weighed heavily upon Cooke's shoulders. The path of retrenchment, at least until Congress increased the appropriation, was seductive; it offered a ready explanation for the agency's inability to deliver on its promise to supply power to every farm. To his credit Cooke perceived that the REA could not pursue the easy path without dimming, or destroying altogether, the hopes of millions of rural dwellers. Hence, he adopted Fisher's basic proposals.

The fruit of this decision was not observable until after Cooke retired. His critics dwelt upon the problems he left behind, and gave credit to his successors for the actual construction of large numbers of REA projects. However, the obstacles he encountered cannot be minimized or ignored; many were endemic to a new bureaucratic organization with a lack of experience or precedent to guide it. There is little evidence to support the contention of some public-power enthusiasts that he was using his position to further his political ambitions.[35]

34. Ibid. Allocations were to be made on the basis of ability to pay, initiative in forming cooperatives, and the level of service a state was receiving from the private-utility industry.

35. See, for example, the letter of Judson King to J. D. Ross, Dec. 14, 1938, King Papers, box 19. King wrote: "... but I must say to you in all kindness that I consider him a dangerous man in the public service and he must lay aside his ambitions for a high post in the government where he can affect our power policy and its administration."

In February 1937, the president regretfully accepted Cooke's resignation. Cooke was sixty-four years old and was anxious to make one more trip to Europe. The president appointed John M. Carmody, deputy administrator since the birth of the REA, his successor.

Without Cooke's faith in the New Deal's power policy there would have been no REA in 1935, and no decision to expand the program in the face of financial and other obstacles. In the space of two energetic years, he had proven that national rural electrification was desirable and technically feasible, thanks largely to the risk capital advanced from the federal treasury.[36] The stage of promotion was drawing to a close; beginning early in 1937, the REA embarked upon the actual construction of projects in all sections of the country, again, because Cooke had decided to push forward. To nurture this phase of the program to maturity, the REA, perhaps, did require the firm hand of a younger, dynamic, and more decisive administrator, who could quell bureaucratic rivalries and get down to the fundamentals of the program—the wiring of homes, installation of plumbing, and electrification of farm equipment.

Carmody was admirably suited for this task and brought impressive credentials to the office. Like Cooke, he had read Taylor; by training, he was an industrial engineer. He had served industry as the editor of *Factory and Industrial Management* and government as a member of the National Mediation Board and National Labor Relations Board.[37] His appointment, moreover, afforded no comfort to the private-power companies, for their leadership considered him an ally of Norris, Lilienthal, and the public-power crowd. Even the press interpreted his promotion as the start of a new and aggressive era in national rural electrification. "Young liberals in the REA dissatisfied with Morris Llewellyn Cooke's regime were praying for the Carmody appointment," wrote one Pennsylvania newspaper. In all internal rows Carmody had favored an aggressive policy in the development of rural cooperatives as purchasers of juice. "He has demanded lower and lower rates in negotiations with private companies for the sale of power to rural consumers." And he was expected "to weed out several subordinates suspected of sabotaging REA out of their sympathy for the private utilities."[38]

36. The REA, for example, successfully reduced the cost per mile of construction lines in rural areas from $2,500 to less than $1,500 within a year of its existence.
37. "Roosevelt Appoints Carmody REA Head," *Electrical World*, 107 (Feb. 20, 1937), 660.
38. See the Chambersburg, Pa., *Public Opinion*, Jan. 20, Feb. 13, 1937, Carmody Papers, box 82. Similar sentiments were expressed in other newspapers; the clippings may be found in the same box.

Carmody did nothing to shake this image and later wrote: "I gave recalcitrant private utilities no quarter."[39]

Reorganizing the REA's staff and boosting morale held first priority. Carmody attained both objectives, he recalled later, "by the simple procedure of dissolving internal factions and organizing the staff to fight the enemy instead of wasting their energy fighting among themselves as they had been doing for a year or so." The surgery was perhaps not as neat and clean as he suggested, but his forceful leadership suffused new vitality throughout the agency, and encouraged the personnel to deal confidently with the problems that had plagued Cooke's administration. He also moved swiftly to clarify the REA's guidelines. In what amounted to the second fundamental policy decision—the first having set the lending character of the agency—he announced that henceforth the REA would look to cooperatives to hasten the distribution of electric power to all rural dwellers.[40]

Had Cooke made this decision a year earlier he would have encountered stiff opposition. The Cooperative League of the United States, at that time, opposed closer ties with the federal government. Circumstances were different now; its members were restless because of the power companies' slow rate of progress. James Warbasse, the league's spokesman, eagerly endorsed the use of cooperatives.[41] The decision, however, did not spell the end of engineering, fiscal, or legal problems.

By June 1937, the REA had loaned only $59 million, and delays in processing loan applications persisted. In Pennsylvania's Crawford and Erie counties, projects which had commenced with much fanfare under Cooke were trying to pull themselves out of a hole because of mysterious and unexplained delays in their loan requests. "It is the same miserable tale which you and I have heard from all sections of the country," Judson King complained to Norris.[42] This criticism from friends of the administration worried Norris, and he made inquiries to ascertain their accuracy. In March 1937, he had suggested to Carmody that the delays might have been attributable to members of the staff "who are moved in their official acts by the desires and requests of private utility officials."[43] The implication here was unmistakable:

39. Quoted in Arthur M. Schlesinger, Jr., *The Politics of Upheaval* (Boston, 1960), 384.
40. Carmody to Cochran, Jan. 26, 1955, in ibid., box 83; and Harlow S. Person, "The Rural Electrification Administration in Perspective," *Agricultural History*, 24 (Apr. 1950), 75-78.
41. Schlesinger, *Politics of Upheaval*, 384.
42. King to Norris, Sept. 22, 1937, Norris Papers, tray 69, box 3.
43. Norris to Carmody, Mar. 13, 1937, ibid., tray 80, box 8.

Carmody had better move quickly to put the REA's house in order. The delays in Pennsylvania happened to be a special case. Harlow S. Person, the REA's chief economist, touched upon the fundamental problem when he noted that in the past few farmers or rural dwellers had had any experience with the REA-type cooperative. Unlike earlier cooperatives, the federal government, rather than the individual participants, was advancing the entire capital outlay for plant construction. The REA cooperative functioned both as collateral for the loan and as the potential supplier of revenue for repayment of the debt. The agency discovered that few farmers had the professional skill to plan and execute a self-liquidating project within the twenty-year time limit. Nor did they possess the legal training to meet the statutory requirements of public-service commissions or to fight the obstructive tactics of the private utilities.[44]

In the early days of the REA the emergence of this new type of borrower had been only dimly perceived. The credit problem was entirely different from that of other government agencies; it was interwoven in the fabric of REA activities, from helping the farmers to organize a legally acceptable borrower, through designing and constructing lines that would provide the maximum possible security in a physical plant, to aiding the borrowers in becoming successful managers (which constituted the real security of the loan). Bankers' customary criteria of credit rating had little or no bearing on the REA credit problem.[45] Perceiving that flexibility and innovation were essential, Carmody decided to reverse the earlier policy espoused by Cooke and Fisher: the REA would reach down into the grass roots of rural America, something it had never done before. By 1938, it had dispatched hundreds of agents into the field to guide local borrowers in the mechanics of applying for loans and in working up suitable projects.[46]

The field agents also provided the administrator with a direct pipeline to the cooperatives, and Carmody often used this channel, bypassing state and regional associations he did not consider reliable, to communicate his directives. He maintained the nonpartisan character of the REA but, like Cooke, he was also attuned to shifting political currents. He knew how to cultivate the agency's friends in Congress and the public-power movement; he was adept at mobilizing the press and state and local political support to attack the industry's "spite-line"

44. Person, "REA in Perspective," 75-78.
45. Harlow S. Person to Norman J. Wald, June 27, 1940, RG 221, REA Administrator's File (Harry S. Slattery), box 69.
46. Person, "REA in Perspective," 75-78.

tactics. In June 1938, he focused upon the worst offender, Electric Bond and Share. Its affiliates included the Carolina Power and Light Company, Minnesota Power and Light, the Idaho and Nebraska power companies, the Texas Electric Service Company, Pacific Power and Light, Texas Power and Light, and the Houston Lighting and Power Company. He accused it of "anti-social behavior" for ordering subsidiaries in Florida, Mississippi, Colorado, and Kansas to build competing lines in cooperative territory. In so doing, he held up to public condemnation the very same holding company which the SEC just happened to be investigating for violations of the Public Utility Holding Company Act.[47]

In extreme instances where power companies refused to lower rates for cooperatives, Carmody threatened to construct his own generating plants. Much of this was rhetoric for public consumption; few generators were built, whereas "spite-line" activity diminished only with the approach of World War II and after the most desirable territories had already been staked out. Also, the companies steadfastly refused to adopt the REA's "area-service" policy, forcing the agency to turn to the state public-service commissions wherein each case was determined upon its merits. Nevertheless, a discernible pattern was emerging by 1940. Where a state had a strong tradition of civic consciousness, or a well-organized public-power movement, the commission was likely to rule in favor of the cooperatives,[48] and REA projects benefited from politicians anxious to establish "little New Deals" in their states. In Pennsylvania, Carmody worked through the Democratic governor to prevent a hostile state legislature from limiting cooperative activity. In Michigan, Arkansas, and elsewhere, the pattern was identical, that is, Carmody cooperated with friendly governors or legislators to reorganize utility commissions and hinder legislation detrimental to REA programs.[49]

Given the remarkably successful record of the REA during Carmody's tenure, it seems inappropriate for the administration to tamper with it, particularly at a time when other New Deal programs were

47. *New York Herald Tribune,* June 24, 1938, newsclipping in Carmody Papers, box 92; and "Statement Concerning Opposition to REA-Financed Cooperatives on the Part of Companies Affiliated with the Electric Bond and Share Company Throughout the Country," Apr. 8, 1941, RG 221, REA Administrator's File (Slattery), box 85.

48. Ibid. See also Twentieth Century Fund, *Electric Power and Government Policy,* 458-59, for the manner in which various states attempted to resolve the dispute.

49. Carmody to Cochran, Jan. 26, 1955, Carmody Papers, box 83; and Frank Hook to Roosevelt, n.d., Franklin D. Roosevelt Papers, Office File 505, Franklin D. Roosevelt Library (hereafter cited as Roosevelt Papers, OF).

faring poorly. By 1940, however, the agency had lost its autonomous standing, Carmody had resigned in protest, and the European war was making deep inroads into the supply of material, especially copper wiring, that was essential to the progress of rural electrification. This shift in the agency's fortunes commenced with the abortive efforts of Louis Brownlow, after 1937, to streamline the operation of the executive departments in the interest of greater efficiency and economy. The Brownlow Committee's recommendations, as one scholar has noted, aimed at no less than a New Deal revolution in governmental administration. Coming on the heels of the president's ill-fated scheme to reform the Supreme Court, the committee's proposals were attacked in Congress by a coalition of fiscal and ideological conservatives, anti-New Deal Democrats, special-interest groups, bureaucrats whose empires were targeted for dismantling, and just plain folk who believed that Roosevelt wished to institute a totalitarian dictatorship.[50]

In 1939, the administration submitted a modified and less-ambitious version to Congress which later was referred to as Reorganization Plan No. 1. To preserve its integrity the president's advisers agreed to work without publicity and to unveil the whole plan rather than the details in piecemeal fashion. Unfortunately, the press published presumably confidential information and soon was speculating about which agencies were earmarked for elimination, for transfer to other departments, or for reduction of staff. Rumors and uncertainty fostered an atmosphere of suspicion and recriminations within the administration. The REA was dragged into the controversy once the issue became one of whether it and the other power agencies should be incorporated into existing executive departments, or whether their effectiveness hinged upon remaining autonomous. The dispute outwardly concerned rival approaches to efficient public administration; the wrong decision, however, might have an adverse impact upon the national power policy.[51]

The REA moved into the center of a bureaucratic feud that had bitter personal undertones. Harold Ickes, ever since national defense had become a matter of concern, had taken the position that the president should appoint him sole coordinator of the national power policy. Intermittently, he also had advocated the creation of a Department

50. The details of the Brownlow Committee's activities are ably recounted in Barry Dean Karl, *Executive Reorganization and Reform in the New Deal* (Cambridge, Mass., 1963), and Richard Polenberg, *Reorganizing Roosevelt's Government* (Cambridge, Mass., 1966), chs. 2, 7-9.
51. The primary emphasis of the revision was fiscal savings rather than administrative reform. See Polenberg, *Reorganizing Roosevelt's Government*, 133, 167, 185-87.

of Conservation with himself as the director. Although his genuine concern for the future of public power was not in question, the secretary's appetite for interfering in the affairs of other governmental agencies was insatiable, and the heads of other departments resisted it. Secretary of Agriculture Henry A Wallace, particularly, refused to stand aside while Ickes added the REA to his fiefdom. He had neither forgotten nor forgiven Ickes for trying to purloin the National Forest Service from Agriculture.

If there was to be any shuffling, Wallace was determined to come out on top of the deck. In the spring of 1939, he maneuvered himself into a more tenable political position, enabling him to resist Ickes's imperialism while advancing his own claim against the REA. His argument was simplistic but logical: an agency having the word "rural" in its title must pertain to farming and therefore belonged in the Department of Agriculture. The scale was tipped against Ickes when the heads of the other power agencies united in order to preserve their own integrity. Senator Norris also joined in, though he clearly opposed the transfer of the agency either to Interior or Agriculture. He was too late, for the pendulum had swung in the opposite direction and, by a circuitous procedure, the REA found itself in the clutches of Agriculture. Sometime between the president's approval of the reorganization plan and its submission to the Senate, an unidentified person had added the REA to the list of transfers to Agriculture. Under the rules of debate in the Senate the list could not be altered, thereby sealing the fate of the agency. Carmody later attributed the REA's loss of autonomy to unnamed presidential advisers, not to the president himself or even to Wallace.[52]

When the time approached to execute the reorganization order, Senator Norris entered a last plea to spare the REA. On June 5, 1939, he sent a letter to the White House by special messenger. Having fathered the REA, Norris took a proprietary interest in protecting its independence; he predicted that "great damage" would befall the agency as a consequence of the transfer. "The REA," he wrote eloquently, "is one place in your Administration where your noble ideals have been carried to perfection. ... It is one thing, a great thing, where the farmers of America are brought into perfect accord in their fight for common justice against the private power monopoly." Carmody was correct, he wrote, in claiming that "much of the work of

52. David E. Lilienthal, *The Journals of David E. Lilienthal*, 5 vols. (New York, 1964-71), I, 129-30; and Carmody to Paul L. Kelley, Mar. 21, 1945, Carmody Papers, box 84.

this organization ... will to a great extent be frustrated and destroyed."[53]

Reorganization had assumed its own momentum, and the president decided that he could not grant a reprieve without fomenting political rebellion in other quarters. Carmody, too, believed that he had no other choice but to tender his resignation; it was his judgment that the REA's mission was incompatible with the loss of autonomy. "When an independent agency is incorporated into another agency," he later wrote with remarkable prescience, "it loses its personality and is exploited by those who know nothing about its purpose but only wish to exploit it for their own prestige or profit."[54] On September 7, 1939, Harry A. Slattery was appointed to succeed him as administrator; the transfer to Agriculture was completed.[55]

Slattery came to the REA with the impeccable credentials of a Theodore Roosevelt conservationist, a Progressive, and a staunch New Dealer. Born in Greenville, South Carolina, of Roman Catholic parentage, he earned a law degree from the George Washington University in 1909, when insurgency was hitting its stride in Congress, and immediately entered a career of public service. His first employment was as secretary to Gifford Pinchot, chief forester during the stormy years of the Taft administration. From 1912-23, he served as secretary and counsel for the National Conservation Association; during the war years he was a special assistant to Interior Secretary Franklin K. Lane. The twenties was not a hospitable era for Progressives in Washington and Slattery went into private law practice, while continuing his interest in conservation and public power. As counsel for the National Boulder Dam Association and the National Conservation Commission, he was active in the passage of federal coal- and oil-leasing measures, federal water-power and forestry legislation, and the Alaskan coal and home-rule acts. He is credited with playing a prominent role in uncovering the Teapot Dome oil frauds. In 1933, Ickes invited him to be his personal assistant, and in 1938 the president appointed him undersecretary of the interior. Public-power enthusiasts confidently expected him to continue in Carmody's aggressive footsteps.[56]

Their optimism quickly dissipated when Slattery began to encounter

53. Norris to Roosevelt, June 5, 1939, in ibid.
54. Carmody to Kelley, Mar. 21, 1945, in ibid.
55. "Government Power Bodies Due to Be Consolidated," *Electrical World,* 112 (Sept. 1939), 6-7.
56. Biographical data was derived from Harry A. Slattery's "Autobiography," a type-written copy of which is among the author's papers in the Duke University Library. See also "Who's Who in REA," RG 221, REA Administrator's File (Slattery), box 97.

difficulties shortly after Henry Wallace resigned from Agriculture to become Roosevelt's vice-presidential running mate. This was late in 1940. Until then, Slattery had maintained cordial relations with his superior, despite the minor irritations that attended the transfer of the REA.[57] Wallace had made every effort to accommodate Slattery. At a meeting of the joint committee to integrate the REA into the department on April 30, 1940, Ralph W. Olmstead declared: "Our job is to take a very good operating agency and fit it into the pattern of the Department in respects as will improve relations and increase efficiency without ill-effects on operations."[58] In December, Wallace told Slattery that he wished to have each staff office in the REA headed by a man who was mutually acceptable to the administrator and to the departmental staff officer assigned to work with him.[59] Earlier, he praised Slattery's administrative talents to the president.[60]

The designation of Claude Wickard as Wallace's successor ruptured this easy relationship.[61] Whether from insecurity or poor counsel, the new secretary determined to make a public show of his authority over the REA and to treat it like any other bureau of the department. In so doing, he antagonized Slattery, who felt that Wickard had ignored the REA's previous history of autonomy. Slattery also felt that Wickard had little appreciation of the work that the agency was doing; later, he suspected him of employing REA field agents as fund raisers for the Democratic party, thereby jeopardizing the status of the agency under the law.[62] The first indication of trouble came in February 1941. Wickard assigned Paul Appleby of Agriculture to ride herd over the REA's activities.[63] He also spread the rumor that the agency was in administrative chaos and experiencing great fiscal difficulties. If his analysis was correct, the responsibility for permitting this condition to develop should have fallen upon Wallace, as Slattery's boss, as

57. Person to Slattery, May 9, 1940; U.S. Department of Agriculture, "Organizational Survey of the Rural Electrification Administration," Apr. 1, 1940, Harry A. Slattery Papers, box 107, Duke University Library (hereafter cited as Slattery Papers).

58. Quoted in George E. Chamberlain to Person, May 5, 1940, in ibid.

59. Henry Wallace to Slattery, Dec. 2, 1940, in ibid.

60. Wallace to Roosevelt, Mar. 9, 1940, in ibid., box 60.

61. For a more sympathetic attitude toward Wickard see Dean Albertson, *Roosevelt's Farmer: Claude R. Wickard in the New Deal* (New York, 1955), 387. It should be noted, however, that the author does not offer any documentation, not even from the secretary's own papers, on this point.

62. In 1943, Wickard became cochairman of a committee to raise funds for the Democratic party; the other cochairman was Robert E. Hannegan, the party's national chairman. See the *St. Louis Post-Dispatch,* Oct. 16, 1943.

63. "Interview with Vice-President Wallace," Feb. 8, 1941, Slattery Papers, box 108.

well as upon the administrator. Whether the situation was actually as gloomy as Wickard portrayed is highly doubtful; nevertheless, Appleby proceeded on this assumption and decided to move Slattery and his people out and to replace them with loyal Wickard men.[64] Shortly thereafter, the history of the REA degenerates into a story of petty bureaucracy, constant spying investigations, and politics.

Appleby soon learned that Slattery's resignation would not be easily accomplished. Early in 1941, Appleby attempted to separate Slattery from his public-power allies by offering the administrator's post to ex-Senator James Pope, a Democrat long identified with public power in the Pacific Northwest. Under other circumstances this might have been an admirable choice, but Pope saw through the scheme and declined the offer.[65] Norris, meanwhile, had contacted Congressman John Rankin, head of the power bloc in the House, and together they prevailed upon Slattery to remain in office. Appleby's high-handedness had so incensed them that both men petitioned the president to restore the REA's independence.[66] Their plea went unanswered, but Wickard was put in the embarrassing position of either proving the incompetence of his administrator and firing him or of renouncing his aide who, presumably, was acting under orders.[67] Instead, Wickard moved cautiously, searching for evidence of incompetence while systematically stripping Slattery of his administrative powers.

In his autobiography Slattery later wrote that Wickard had illegally used REA funds to finance Agriculture's Division of Investigation. He alleged further that its chief activity in 1941 was to spy on himself and the agency's activities for the secretary. After a flurry of work, the investigators failed to unearth evidence of malfeasance or corruption. Slattery, meanwhile, accused the secretary of deliberately hiring men from private-utility backgrounds in order to discredit the agency. Over the next year and a half the two men traded charges and counter-charges acrimoniously until senatorial interest was stirred.[68]

64. Ibid.
65. "Memo of a Conversation with Norris," Feb. 20, 1941, ibid.
66. "Memo of a Conversation with Claude Wickard," Feb. 20, 1941, ibid.; Slattery, "Autobiography," in ibid.
67. "Memo of a Conversation with Claude Wickard," Feb. 20, 1941, ibid.
68. The New York Times, Mar. 14, 1944. Wickard had failed to prove incompetence on Slattery's part. In 1944 a Senate committee investigating the REA's difficulties asked Wickard why he had not fired the administrator three years earlier, if the charges made against him were true. The secretary was unable to provide a satisfactory answer, but replied that Pearl Harbor had come along "and it was obvious that the REA program would be greatly curtailed and I thought that, with the administrative load reduced, things might work themselves out."

Having failed in their attempt to remove him, Wickard and Appleby deprived Slattery of his authority with the active encouragement of the National Association of Rural Electric Cooperatives and its executive officer, Clyde T. Ellis.[69] The association was established originally to promote cooperatives in the Tennessee valley and elsewhere. By 1941, egged on by anti-Slattery men in the REA, it was functioning as a political lobby, pressuring members of Congress whenever the matter of rural electrification arose.[70] Slattery had incurred its enmity when he vetoed a scheme to utilize the membership and surplus funds of REA customers to establish a private rural-electrification insurance plan.[71] The opportunity for revenge came in 1943 when the association supported Wickard's appointment of a political lame duck, William J. Neal, the defeated Democratic candidate for the governorship of New Hampshire, as deputy administrator.

Neal ostensibly was given "coordinate authority" to oversee the REA's affairs. In fact, he took over both personnel and decision-making. Loan applications, allotments for rural lines, the hiring and firing of staff, promotions and demotions—all passed through his hands. Slattery's worst fear seemed to have materialized; decisions affecting the program were being made on a political basis.[72] Worse still, the conflict spilled over into the president's relations with Congress, when Jonathan Daniels, an executive assistant, tried to force Slattery to resign.[73] In the end, Slattery held on to his post until 1945, long after his usefulness to the REA had come to an end.[74]

69. Even Lilienthal, who had an amicable relationship with Wickard, considered the association something of a Frankenstein.

70. Lilienthal, *Journals*, I, 586-87.

71. *St. Louis Post-Dispatch*, May 26, July 29, Aug. 31, Oct. 16, 1943, and Mar. 4, 1944.

72. The appointment was particularly questionable because Neal had been president of one of the worst-managed of all REA systems, one which was $180,000 in the red in its operations and owed $38,000 to the government on its loan. See Slattery, "Autobiography," esp. the chapter entitled, "Make REA Independent Again," Slattery Papers.

73. Daniels concluded, without divulging his reasons, that Slattery was an inefficient administrator, and on three separate occasions he asked him to resign. In addition, he suggested that Norris might take the position, in spite of his advanced age. Apparently Daniels intended to have the senator act as a figurehead, while the day-to-day operation of the REA would be entrusted to a younger man. The Senate, which was investigating the question, threatened to provoke the constitutional issue of executive privilege by holding Daniels in contempt. The entire controversy must also be seen as part of a broader effort on the part of the legislative branch of the government to recoup some of the powers it had abdicated to the executive during the crises of depression and war. See the *New York Times*, Feb. 17, 1944.

74. Ibid., and Mar. 8, 1944. His ability to function at a high level diminished as the controversy was prolonged during the war years. After his voluntary retirement Senators Norris and Henrik Shipstead unsuccessfully introduced legislation to restore

Whether the REA would have functioned any more effectively under a new administrator is highly doubtful. In 1941, the agency was reacting to the national-defense emergency. On the occasion of its sixth anniversary—April 9, 1941—the president congratulated Slattery and his staff for their splendid work and identified the progress of rural electrification in the United States with the preservation of democratic principles.[75] Slattery responded by asserting that the REA would facilitate the development of the national defense power network. He envisaged the placing of electrical outlets in every part of the country so that military agencies and defense plants could make connections promptly with power sources. The potential contributions of the REA to national defense were many: it might build a power base for processing critical protein foods, serve as a labor-saving facility to alleviate the shortage of rural workers, service the power needs of military camps and defense plants located in rural areas, and provide the power for decentralized industry.[76]

Slattery also was alert to the political value of the agency's expanded role in national defense. He knew that any agency peripheral to the war effort was doomed to suffer a diminution of funds and staff, leading eventually to the shriveling of its functions. Rural electrification by 1941 was big business; Slattery aimed to protect his agency's interests. In addition, he was not eager to have the private utilities move in after the war.

The shortage of copper wiring and restrictions on the use of other vital war materials in 1941 inevitably set parameters on the REA's participation in national defense.[77] And, although the president established committees for the purpose of anticipating wartime power needs, the REA's contribution to preparedness was hardly tapped. Slattery attributed this situation to the jealousy of other government agencies; he also accused the War Production Board, which came to exercise final judgment in such matters, of having succumbed to the influence

---

the REA's autonomous status. President Truman, much to the consternation of congressional liberals, appointed Wickard as administrator of the REA after his original choice, Aubrey Williams, was rejected by the Senate. See also ibid., Jan. 23, Mar. 3, and July 3, 1945.

75. Roosevelt called for the further expansion of rural lines "as a vital necessity for national defense." Roosevelt to Slattery, Apr. 9, 1941, RG 221, REA Administrator's File (Slattery), box 77.

76. For additional details on the power network for national defense see chapter 9.

77. On the question of wartime shortages of vital materials for the REA's program, see Slattery to Jesse L. Maury, July 11, 1941, RG 221, REA Administrator's File (Slattery), box 65. Maury was chief of the Non-Ferrous Metals Section, Civilian Allocations Division, Office of Price Administration and Civilian Supply.

of the private utilities seeking to discredit the REA.[78] Among the agencies having the power to utilize its cooperation, he wrote to Senator Norris, "there is not a disposition to employ that cooperation somewhere in nearly all of these agencies—usually not at the highest levels but at levels more easily permeated by representatives of private electric companies." The attitude had "a detrimental effect on the REA program of the Congress."[79] And after the Pearl Harbor attack, the full consequences of remaining on the periphery of defense planning were apparent; it took all of Slattery's talent to keep the rural-electrification program from collapsing altogether.

The first indication that the REA was losing status in the defense emergency came late in 1941 with the decision to transfer its headquarters from Washington to St. Louis. The following year, with the United States fighting on two fronts, the agency was required to cut back its personnel and to reduce expenditures. Reorganization was voluntary, controlled, and planned; nevertheless, it was geared to the preservation of only the most critical functions to keep the agency alive. Dr. Harlow S. Person, who directed the streamlining operation, conceded as much.[80] "If circumstances—some outer force—were to step in and compel reorganization," he told a staff conference, "it would in all probability, because without understanding of REA functions and activities, be ruthless and destructive of that integral whole which can be adjusted to present conditions yet remain ready for full activity after the war, when the REA type of activity will be one of the major resources for rehabilitation of the national economy."[81]

The war and the reorganization process took a high toll in morale and efficiency. The dispute with Secretary Wickard, paralleling as it did the war years, merely exacerbated the REA's difficulties. Person, keenly attuned to everything that went on in the agency, concluded that the deterioration of *esprit* from the high point under Carmody was the result of "the changes in the character of our work created

78. Slattery to Norris, Nov. 18, 1942, ibid.

79. Slattery to Norris, Nov. 5, 1941, ibid.

80. "The reorganization task of REA, then, is one of preserving the main structure of REA," Person wrote, "but within that frame of carefully distinguished functions that REA should continue a greater or less degree of activity and should be allowed to sleep, and of not filling positions as personnel are drafted to the military and other war agencies. ... We must let some of our staff go to places of greater present need, and let their positions sleep—i.e., remain open but not filled—in the expectation that when the war is over they will come back to REA to participate in that larger normal activity which lies ahead" ("Transcript of Dr. Person's Remarks at Staff Conference Held August 19, 1942," ibid., box 29).

81. Ibid.

by war duties.'' Insecurity of employment, reminiscent of the early depression years, stalked the agency; every section head and division chief tried to maintain his unit intact ''by explaining whenever possible and thus justifying the preservation of his own Division.'' Nevertheless, reports came in from the field that the program was in deep trouble. One project attorney was under indictment for allegedly accepting a bribe from a Japanese; another spent his time riding around Kansas with representatives of the Kansas Power and Light Company. In Georgia and Texas field agents too often were seen in the company of private-utility men.

Slattery believed that the utilities had infiltrated their own people up and down the line in the REA, and that this was ''one of the reasons why we're having some of our difficulties.''[82] This observation was accurate to a degree; although a great many public-power enthusiasts shared the belief that private industry was waiting to subvert the national power policy under the guise of the war emergency. The problems of the REA were more fundamental, as Carmody's worst fears for its welfare after the transfer to Agriculture materialized. After its successful growth record in peacetime, the agency was standing still during the war years; neither Slattery nor anyone else, including the president, was able to arrest the cancerous hold of politics and war-induced problems. In this respect at least the REA was not unique; its difficulties were endemic to bureaucratic government. The TVA, earlier, had weathered its internal leadership crisis and was contributing mightily to the war effort. In 1939, the Bonneville Power Administration had experienced a similar ordeal, aggravated also by the defense problem. The war simply brought to public attention the tensions that had long been building in the REA.

82. ''Minutes of the Meeting of the Administrator's Staff Conference,'' Oct. 28, 1942, ibid.

CHAPTER VII

"A Great Natural Undertaking": The Bonneville Project

Bonneville Dam was the first of the federal projects designed to improve navigation and to develop hydroelectric power on the Columbia River. Located forty-two miles upstream from Portland, Oregon, the dam spans the river where it cuts a rugged canyon through the Cascade Mountains. The Roosevelt administration conceived the project as an integral part of the New Deal's program for the conservation and development of the nation's natural resources in the interest of all the people of America.

Bonneville also was the fulfillment of the president's campaign promise to the citizens of Portland and the Pacific Northwest, in 1932, of a great power development on the Columbia River that would forever be a national yardstick. As part of the national power policy the project was intended to stimulate the greatest use of hydroelectric power in the homes, stores, factories, and on the farms of Oregon, Washington, and Idaho. The PWA made the initial allotment for construction in the summer of 1933; the Army Corps of Engineers completed construction four years later. In the interim, the central consideration of the administration and public-power enthusiasts was to set the cost of energy at the lowest rates that would pay off indebtedness on the plant and still have Bonneville serve as the national yardstick.[1]

As early as 1935, two years before the completion of the dam, bills were introduced in Congress providing for an organization charged with the responsibility of marketing and selling all of the power to be generated. The most ambitious legislation of this kind was offered

1. The *New York Times,* July 29, Sept. 30, 1933; and U.S. Department of the Interior, *The Bonneville Project: A Great National Undertaking,* pamphlet, dated May 1938, Seattle City Lighting Department Records, box 134, University of Washington Library (hereafter cited as Seattle City Lighting Records).

by Senator James P. Pope. Pope was anxious to guarantee the benefits of cheap power and water for his constituents, and he proposed the establishment of a Columbia Valley Authority (CVA) to embrace the entire Pacific Northwest.[2] Modeled after TVA legislation, S. 869 ran afoul of the Army Engineers and the Bureau of Reclamation. Both agencies had looked upon the power market of the region, which was not being served by private industry, as their particular preserve. To protect this arrangement and to neutralize the momentum that was building for a CVA, each agency sought its own alternative to the Pope bill.[3]

An opportunity arose when Oregon's two Republican senators, Charles McNary and Frederick Steiwer, who questioned the need for a CVA, but who wanted to get on with the task of marketing power, approached them and the FPC for advice. The product of their discussions was a substitute bill, S. 3330, introduced in the Senate on July 29, 1935.[4] The McNary-Steiwer bill quickly won the endorsement of local chambers of commerce and private-power companies; it was uniformly condemned by public-power groups.[5] Congressman Walter M. Pierce of Oregon, an outspoken proponent of a valley-type authority for the region in 1935, charged that the bill shortchanged the public interest. Bonneville's transmission lines, he wrote to Senator Norris, would carry power only to heavy industry and the private utilities at tidewater, and would deprive all of the inhabitants of the region of the benefits of cheap power.[6] Congress adjourned before acting upon either bill, thereby giving the public-power organizations time to recoup and to reformulate their position.

When Congress reassembled in January 1936, Senator McNary again

2. *Congressional Record,* 74th Cong., 1st sess., 79 (Jan. 14, 1935), 407. Representative Knute Hill of Washington introduced an identical but less well known bill (H.R. 2790) which was never reported out of committee. See also Charles McKinley, *Uncle Sam in the Pacific Northwest* (Berkeley, Calif., 1952), 157-58.

3. Ibid. One of the chief objections to the Bureau of Reclamation was its habit, under previous administrations, of charging all the traffic would bear for power generated at irrigation sites. See Basil Manly to Franklin D. Roosevelt, May 29, 1936, Franklin D. Roosevelt Papers, Office File 360, Franklin D. Roosevelt Library (hereafter cited as Roosevelt Papers, OF).

4. *Congressional Record,* 74th Cong., 1st sess., 79 (July 29, 1935), 11944.

5. Roosevelt gave his approval upon the recommendation of the three agencies involved. In his haste to settle the marketing question it is doubtful that he gave close attention to the details. See Roosevelt to Royal S. Copeland, July 26, 1935, Roosevelt Papers, OF 25-N.

6. Walter M. Pierce to George W. Norris, Nov. 15, 1930, George W. Norris Papers, tray 81, box 4, Library of Congress (hereafter cited as Norris Papers).

raised the Bonneville issue.[7] In the interim, the Pope bill was shelved at the request of the president. Roosevelt had instructed the National Resources Committee to investigate the future development of the Columbia River area and had counseled Pope that there was "plenty of time" to consider a CVA arrangement.[8] The McNary-Steiwer bill of the previous session appeared to have a clear field until, on March 5, 1936, Democratic Senators Homer T. Bone and Lewis Schwellenbach of Washington introduced legislation distinctly more solicitous of the public-power aspects of Bonneville.[9] To effect a compromise that both senatorial delegations could endorse, the views of the FPC and the Army Engineers once again were requested. Their approach was to treat the Bonneville project as an isolated venture: the army would generate power and construct the high-transmission lines, while the FPC was authorized to market the energy and set the rates. As a concession to Bone and Schwellenbach, the principle of giving preference to publicly and cooperatively owned distribution systems was firmly established.[10] These compromises were embodied in S. 4695, which all four senators sponsored late in May.[11]

Prior to congressional hearings on the bill, the National Resources Committee submitted to President Roosevelt a report of the Pacific Northwest Regional Planning Commission.[12] The report, dated December 28, 1935, and endorsed by labor, agricultural, and some professional groups, stopped short of proposing a CVA for the region.

7. The McNary-Steiwer bill was reintroduced a week before the Bone-Schwellenbach bill (see below, n. 9). See *Congressional Record,* 74th Cong., 2d sess., 80 (Apr. 29, 1936), 6325.

8. See Pacific Northwest Regional Planning Commission, "Summary of Results of Informal Hearings," *Columbia Basin Report* (Washington, D.C., 1936), Appendix Z-e, 21.

9. The bill in question was S. 4178. See Homer T. Bone to Roosevelt, Mar. 3, 1936, Roosevelt Papers, OF 360.

10. U.S. Congress, Senate, Hearings before a Subcommittee of the Committee on Agriculture and Forestry on Senate bills 869, 3330, 4178, and 4566, *Navigation and Flood Control on the Columbia River and Its Tributaries,* 74th Cong., 2d sess., May 7-9, 13, 1936 (Washington, D.C., 1936), 9-15 (hereafter cited as *Navigation and Flood Control Hearings: Bonneville, 1936*).

11. Similar legislation was sponsored in the House. See U.S. Congress, House, Hearings before the Committee on Rivers and Harbors on House bills 12875, 12895, and 12899, *Columbia River (Bonneville Dam) Oreg. and Wash.,* 74th Cong., 2d sess. (Washington, D.C., 1936), 4 ff. (hereafter cited as *Columbia River: Bonneville Dam*).

12. The Pacific Northwest Regional Planning Commission represented the state planning boards of Washington, Oregon, Idaho, and Montana. When it first canvassed the public in early 1935, it found little enthusiasm for a grid-transmission system, uniform rates, or a regional administrative authority. Public hearings were responsible for awakening and polarizing opinion on these issues. See National Resources Committee, *Regional Planning,* Part I: *Pacific Northwest* (Washington, D.C., 1936), xxiv.

Professor Charles McKinley of Reed College had strongly shaped the commission's recommendations, and he argued that a CVA, with its "ameliorative and philanthropic tasks," was not germane to the Pacific Northwest where hydroelectric power and its distribution were the central issues. McKinley also rejected the proposal to have the agencies which had built Bonneville and Grand Coulee assume responsibility for marketing the power. His recommendations included three major points:[13]

1. The establishment of a new agency, wholly controlled by the government, to dispose of Bonneville power
2. The adoption of a uniform-rate policy throughout the grid-transmission system
3. The application of a TVA-type, three-man administrative board, that is, "moving administrative power away from the palace and out into the fields and hills."[14]

The National Resources Committee advised the president to implement the recommendations, but Secretary of War George Dern balked at having the engineers confined solely to the task of generating power at the dam. Dern also defended the engineers' demand that mileage rates should be set for power from the Columbia River dams rather than the uniform "postage-stamp" rates advocated by the committee.[15] He refused to sign the covering letter that accompanied the committee's

13. See esp. "Organization for the Operation of Public Works," National Resources Committee, *Regional Planning*, pt. I, 175-92; and Herman C. Voeltz, "Genesis and Development of a Regional Power Authority in the Pacific Northwest, 1933-1943," *Pacific Northwest Quarterly*, 53 (Apr. 1962), 67-68.
14. The phrase is from David E. Lilienthal, *The Journals of David E. Lilienthal*, 5 vols. (New York, 1964-71), I, 342. By 1937, McKinley was advocating a power authority for Bonneville. This authority would be organized as a public corporation which would function not on the basis of annual congressional appropriations but as an independent federal unit. The Treasury Department would handle the funds, but, after an initial revolving fund of $500,000, the authority would pay its own way from revenues. Other functions such as reclamation and erosion control would be left to the proper governmental bureaus already engaged in these activities. Their work was to be coordinated with the Columbia Power Authority through the regional planning board and the National Resources Committee, while the FPC would advise only on rate structure. See "Report to the Hon. Harold L. Ickes ... of a Conference of Engineers and Economists on Bonneville Power," June 19, 1937, Seattle City Lighting Records, box 77.
15. "So far as the Bonneville project is concerned," the report maintained, "this latter zone system would be peculiarly ill-advised; first, because it would encourage the use of this energy in the heart of the Columbia River Gorge, where the topography and physical environment is primarily suited for recreation purposes and not for the building of industrial cities. There already exist within the Portland-Vancouver-Longview region many towns and cities now being served by expensive governmental functions—highways, schools, sewers, fire-police protection, etc., adequate to take care

report. Roosevelt, however, knew as early as March 16, 1936, that the committee was not unanimous in its advice.[16] He was forced, in the circumstances, to weigh other considerations, for to go along with the report as it stood might push the War Department even further into the arms of those already opposed to the legislation. On the other hand, the early completion of the dam necessitated immediate action to create a marketing agency for the power that would issue shortly from Bonneville. The president chose to compromise on the original report; his suggestion was that Congress should establish an *interim* agency to distribute the energy until it legislated a permanent arrangement.[17] Later, this decision became the focal point of controversy.

Early in May, a subcommittee of the Senate commenced hearings on the various legislative proposals for the Pacific Northwest. Frederic A. Delano, the chairman of the National Resources Committee's advisory committee, agreed to testify as its first witness. His testimony largely set the direction which the hearings were to take. He observed that the National Resources Committee did not believe that the present Congress was legislating irrevocably for Bonneville, "but that it would set up or suggest an organization which would explore the question, and perhaps at the next session of Congress further develop it."[18] For this reason, he was asking Congress to establish a temporary agency in line with the president's recommendation.[19] Later, Congress could adopt legislation to put the power program of the region on a permanent, businesslike basis.[20]

Other witnesses, however, raised the really substantive issues for the future of public power. Professor McKinley addressed his remarks to whether Bonneville's rates should be uniform or reflect transmission distance, and whether the federal government or the private utilities should construct and operate the transmission lines. The thrust of his testimony, advocating regional-power development similar to the

---

of the needs for considerable enlargments to their populations. It would be exceedingly wasteful, from the point of view of public economy, to encourage the building of new industrial towns next to the site of the Bonneville Dam. From the point of view of ultimate regional cohesion and goodwill, a policy based upon similar rates for large areas possesses distinct advantages" (National Resources Committee, *Regional Planning,* pt. I, xvii).

16. Frederic A. Delano to Roosevelt, Mar. 16, 1936, Roosevelt Papers, OF 2882-B.

17. *Columbia River: Bonneville Dam,* 33; and McKinley, *Uncle Sam in the Pacific Northwest,* 160-61.

18. *Navigation and Flood Control Hearings: Bonneville, 1936,* 17.

19. For the interchange between Delano and Senator Charles McNary see ibid., 18-19.

20. Daniel M. Ogden, Jr., "The Development of Federal Power Policy in the Pacific Northwest" (Ph.D. diss., University of Chicago, 1949), 223.

Ontario hydroelectric project, which was established in 1906 as a cooperative wholesale purchasing and transmission agency for independent municipal distributors, was in keeping with a national power policy. "My belief," he told the subcommittee, "is that the Bonneville development, if undertaken without a complete envisaging of the program presented by the Regional Planning Commission's report, is likely to work against the ultimate development of that program." McKinley prescribed a central-grid system for the region, triangular in shape with Puget Sound, Portland, and Spokane forming each apex. Ultimately, the supergrid would be extended eastward across the mountains to Fort Peck, then down toward the Idaho-Snake River country, and finally south toward the California border. Grand Coulee would be tied into it as soon as construction there was completed.[21]

As the hearings progressed, the existence of a split between Oregon's congressional delegation and the chairman of its Super-Power Commission, John J. Lewis, was evident. Lewis demanded a New Deal for the citizens of the Pacific Northwest and the formation of an agency that was not susceptible to pressure from the privately owned power companies. He condemned the rate provisions of the McNary-Steiwer bill and predicted that, if the engineers or the FPC did not push rate reductions aggressively, the local citizens would retaliate. "It is my personal opinion," he declared, "that the United States Army Engineers of this division and district [Portland] are under the indirect control of or are dominated by the private power interests. Their plans do not conform to the needs of this community because they cannot see the great market for power."[22]

Lewis's accusations were in part confirmed by the testimony of Colonel Thomas M. Robins of the Corps of Engineers. His statements differed little from those of W. D. B. Dodson, vice-president of Portland's conservative Chamber of Commerce. Dodson had testified that Bonneville ought to be left to private enterprise, and he condemned the Pacific Northwest Regional Planning Commission for being "too visionary, possibly not sound in getting constructive action on the thing." A backbone transmission system, minus the rate differential for the private utilities and industries, who were the purchasers of the largest blocks of energy, was not feasible. And McKinley's proposal

21. *Navigation and Flood Control Hearings: Bonneville, 1936*, 98. J. D. Ross, SEC commissioner, and the chairman of Washington's State Planning Council both agreed with McKinley that rates should be uniform and the government should construct the distribution lines in order to spread the benefits of cheap power as widely as possible. See ibid., 111, 121-29.

22. Ibid., 144.

of a uniform-rate structure, he declared, would not repay the original investment because there were not enough customers in the public market to justify it. Unmistakably, the McNary bill, vesting control of transmission in the army, would result in preferred treatment for Portland and the private utilities. The social objectives of the administration could easily be overlooked.[23]

The engineers' report to Congress was nearly identical, having declared that it would not be economically feasible to set uniform rates for the entire region because "it costs money to transmit power." The corps found that "the recommendation for the construction of a superpower network of transmission lines by the Government is questionable.... If you superimpose an enormous transmission system or grid over that country with its present small population, relatively speaking, and large distances that you have to cover, and average up the cost so that it is the same all over, it will make your cost so much that you will never be able to sell to industry, and if you don't get industry, you don't get people, and if you don't get people, you can't sell power."[24]

In retrospect, it is evident that the Corps of Engineers simply could not comprehend the importance of providing low-cost power for the economic development of the Pacific Northwest. The standard which it had proposed for rate-making gave slight emphasis to any social or economic objective that might be attained through an imaginative power policy; it recognized only the one necessary factor of reimbursement. "The Corps' representatives," one scholar has written, "were among the calamity howlers of the thirties who feared the New Deal was erecting great white and power-full elephants in the West."[25]

The Senate and, later, the House committees on flood control and navigation eventually reported out a modified version of the engineers' recommendations, but Congress again failed to act. Bonneville legislation was trapped in the logjam, as each house hurriedly concluded its business in preparation for the forthcoming congressional and presi-

23. Ibid., 208-19, 234-36 passim.

24. Secretary of War George Dern to chairman, National Resources Committee, Apr. 11, 1936, National Archives, National Resources Planning Board, Flood Control General (old file unnumbered). See also *Columbia River: Bonneville Dam;* and U.S. Congress, House, Hearings before the Committee on Rivers and Harbors on House bill 7642, *Columbia River (Bonneville Dam) Oreg. and Wash.,* 75th Cong., 1st sess., March-June 1937 (Washington, D.C., 1937), 52-60 ff. (hereafter cited as *Columbia River: Bonneville Dam,* 1937 Hearings).

25. Arthur Maass, *Muddy Waters: The Army Engineers and the Nation's Rivers* (Cambridge, Mass., 1951), 199.

dential elections.[26] After the ballots had been counted, it was evident that the returns implied more than the reelection of President Roosevelt. In the Pacific Northwest, the voters had decided upon the future disposition of hydroelectric power from federal dams on the Columbia River. Their ballots had failed to ratify a decision in favor of either private or public construction and operation of transmission lines. In the aftermath of the election, the federal government moved into the vacuum that existed, becoming the sole agency that was in a position to decide the matter.[27]

The first significant move toward establishing a new agency occurred shortly after the election. Again, it was the result of pressure from General Markham, who warned that the dam was nearing completion and that it was urgently necessary to provide legislation for the distribution of its power.[28] On January 16, 1937, the president appointed an "informal" Committee on National Power Policy (CNPP) to recommend legislation specifically for Bonneville and, more generally, to formulate a national policy for the generation, transmission, and distribution of electrical energy.[29] With respect to rates, the president was quite explicit; he desired the policy to be uniform, "as far as practicable or advisable." This did not mean "identical rates in every part of the country," he wrote to Morris L. Cooke, a member of the committee, but uniformity of policy. "This policy, once established, will apply to existing projects, such as Boulder Dam and portions of the TVA and to all new power developments as they are completed during the next few years."[30] In addition, he expected the committee to bring in its report within two weeks, which Ickes thought was "a pretty tall order" considering the magnitude of the task.[31] The abbreviated time limit, in fact, made any serious consideration of a national power policy out of the question.

It appears likely that the president intended the CNPP to be distinct and apart from the earlier NPPC which had responsibility for holding-

26. *Columbia River: Bonneville Dam,* 1936, 35, 53-54; *Congressional Record,* 74th Cong., 2d sess., 80 (June 6, 1936), 9177-78.

27. Ogden, "Power Policy in the Northwest," 230-32.

28. Edward Markham to Roosevelt, Jan. 18, 1937, Roosevelt Papers, OF 25-N.

29. Roosevelt to Ickes, Jan. 16, 1937, National Archives, Record Group 48, Office of the Secretary of the Interior, File 1-310, pt. 2, Bonneville General, box 3099. Also in the Roosevelt Papers, OF 235, 466-B. The initial suggestion for such a committee came from Ickes, McNinch, and Manly.

30. Roosevelt to Morris L. Cooke, Jan. 16, 1937, Seattle City Lighting Records, box 81.

31. Harold L. Ickes, *The Secret Diary of Harold L. Ickes: The First Thousand Days,* 3 vols. (New York, 1953-54), II, 50.

company legislation. In practice, however, few substantive differences existed between the two bodies, with the CNPP acting as a kind of rump committee of the larger body. Sharing five of the same members as the NPPC, it afforded a measure of continuity of ideas, agencies, and personnel that was vital to the formulation of the New Deal's power policy.[32] Even SEC Commissioner James M. Landis, not a member of the original NPPC, was admirably suited for the task; he had been one of the original drafters of the Public Utility Holding Company Act.[33]

On January 25, the committee, using the McNary bill as its basis for discussion, met with the senators from Washington and Oregon to devise a satisfactory compromise for marketing Bonneville power. The discussion was heated and, at the outset, Ickes declared that he was "not entirely satisfied" with the attitude of the Army Engineers on power and refused to delegate to them exclusive authority to run the power plant, locate markets, and negotiate contracts. He demanded to know whether McNary would insist upon having his bill as it stood. The Oregonian, however, seeing that he could not dissuade Ickes, relented and explained that army control had been simply a means by which expenses could be held down. He did not consider this provision a *sine qua non*. Once this point was clarified to Ickes's satisfaction, the conference progressed smoothly.[34]

Frederic A. Delano of the National Resources Committee announced that he had received a letter from the president. Its gist was that the president had decided to dissolve the power-pool committee of government and private-utility executives which had been formed in the early days of the administration. The decision struck a responsive chord from the committee which, at the suggestion of McNinch, amended section six of the McNary bill to preclude future pooling at Bonneville. Before the meeting adjourned to meet again the following day, the committee reached a consensus on several other aspects of the legislation.[35]

Prior to its second meeting, some members of the committee closeted themselves with the president for a general discussion of power policy.

32. Ickes drew no distinction between the two committees. See ibid., II, 59-60; and Ickes to Roosevelt, May 20, 1937, National Archives, Record Group 48, Records of the National Power Policy Committee, Classified File, Bonneville Dam, box 24 (hereafter cited as NPPC Records, CF).

33. See NPPC Records, CF, Bonneville Dam, box 24; and Ickes, *Secret Diary,* II, 50.

34. Ickes, *Secret Diary,* ibid., II, 60-61.

35. McNinch to Norris, Feb. 25, 1937, Norris Papers, tray 81, box 4; and Ickes, *Secret Diary,* II, 60-61.

Roosevelt reaffirmed his desire for a bill and a statement of national policy by the following week. To the surprise of those present he also unveiled a proposal to divide the nation into eight great districts, each having a valley authority to implement sound conservation policies and the entire structure capped with a new Department of Conservation. The prospect of little TVAs strung across the country, broached originally by Thomas G. Corcoran and Harry Slattery, intrigued Roosevelt and he promptly enlisted the support of Senator Norris, father of the original valley authority. The president closed the conference with the announcement that he would send a special message to Congress on the subject and therefore wished the committee to draft legislation for this purpose.[36]

This additional assignment further complicated the original mandate of the committee. With only one week remaining, it was expected to dispose of Bonneville, draft a valley-authorities bill, and compose a state paper setting forth the New Deal's national-power-policy goals. Rather wisely in view of the magnitude of the assignment, its members decided to postpone the latter, at least until the Department of Conservation had become a reality. In the interim, the committee proceeded with the Bonneville bill because of its urgency; it agreed, however, to word it in such a way as to avoid any conflict with a future statement of policy. From the perspective of the present, though, the committee also forfeited a sterling opportunity to articulate a broad national power policy for the American people. Morris L. Cooke of the REA recognized this at the time; he alone continued to work on this particular aspect of the president's order.[37]

As the deadline approached, the committee worked feverishly to complete the draft of its bill. On February 9, 1937, it submitted its Bonneville legislation with a preliminary statement to the president.[38] The covering letter unanimously endorsed the regional viewpoint of the Pacific Northwest Regional Planning Commission. The bill itself vested all phases of power development in a civilian administrator and recommended a uniform-rate structure in order to encourage the widespread use of power. To advance rural electrification it also

36. For the history of the little TVAs proposal see the incisive analysis of William E. Leuchtenburg, "Roosevelt, Norris and the 'Seven Little TVAs'," *Journal of Politics*, 14 (Aug. 1952), 418-41; and McAllister Coleman to Norris, Nov. 22, 1937, Norris Papers, tray 80, box 6.

37. Ickes to Roosevelt, Feb. 9, 1937, Department of the Interior Records, General Administrative File 1-310, pt. 2, box 3099 (hereafter cited as Interior Department Files, GAF); see also copy in Roosevelt Papers, OF 2575.

38. Ibid.

strongly suggested giving preference to publicly and cooperatively owned distribution agencies. Only at one point did the committee's bill depart significantly from the planning commission's report, and that was on the status of the new agency. Whereas the latter envisioned an independent corporation, the former recommended that the Bonneville Power Administration be made a bureau of the Department of the Interior. The committee believed that the agency should control generation at the damsite and the transmission and distribution functions.[39] The bill, in other respects, was a compromise made possible by its temporary nature. Commissioner Frank McNinch made this perfectly plain in a letter to Senator Norris. "Because of the temporary character of this recommended legislation," he declared, "it was possible for the committee to compose differences of opinion."[40]

With the committee's report in hand, President Roosevelt summoned the congressional delegations of the Pacific Northwest to a White House conference scheduled for February 18, 1937. At that time, he went over each section of the Bonneville legislation with them, and further urged them to incorporate the committee's recommendations into the legislation which they planned to introduce. By acting as he did, the president had made four policy decisions that were to prove crucial to the future development of Bonneville:

1. That power from the dam would be marketed separately from privately produced power
2. That the publicly and cooperatively owned distribution systems would receive preference
3. That the federal government, rather than private enterprise or local government, would construct the backbone transmission system
4. That a new civilian agency to market power from the dam would be established within the Department of the Interior.

The decision as to whether rates would be uniform or reflect transmission distance was vested in the administrator, but with the admonition that "the widest possible use of available electrical energy" was desired. Locating the new agency in Interior, where Secretary Ickes was able to maintain a watchful eye, ultimately guaranteed the policy of uniformly low rates.[41]

The next day Congressman Martin Smith of Washington introduced

39. *Columbia River: Bonneville Dam,* 1937 Hearings, 141-43; and "Progress Report from the Committee on National Power Policy, the Bonneville Project," Feb. 24, 1937, NPPC Records, CF, box 24.
40. McNinch to Norris, Feb. 25, 1937, Norris Papers, tray 81, box 4.
41. Ogden, "Power Policy in the Northwest," 233-34.

the committee's draft bill to the Congress as H.R. 4948.[42] The president followed up his action with a special message to the House strongly endorsing the bill and the entire work of the committee.[43] Outside the Congress, reaction to the message and the legislation was mixed; press comment was more a reflection of whether a paper was for or against public power, and the extent of its commitment to New Deal policies generally. The Knoxville, Tennessee, *News-Sentinel* predicted that the citizens of the Pacific Northwest would enjoy the same benefits as those of the Tennessee valley; the Portland, Oregon, *News-Telegram* urged strict government supervision of rates. However, whether the president had actually articulated a national power policy by endorsing the legislation was uncertain. The critical *Philadelphia Inquirer* viewed his message as "the frankest definition of his national power policy he has yet expressed," and warned that taxpayers elsewhere would have to subsidize the lower rates that soon were to be enjoyed by the citizens of the Pacific Northwest. The Buffalo, New York, *Express,* however, insisted that Roosevelt should have formulated the national power policy *first*, in order to have Bonneville conform to it.[44]

Morris L. Cooke, who was working on this particular aspect of the presidential request, shared the *Express's* sentiment.[45] After Smith introduced H.R. 4948, he reopened the matter of formulating a national power policy. In light of the instructions to draft a valley-authorities bill, Cooke wrote that "it appears even more imperative that a tentative definition of power policy be made." He feared that the authorities bill, which clearly carried serious policy implications, might cause future embarrassment, unless that policy were spelled out now. His own concept of a proper policy embraced flood control, low-water control, navigation, irrigation, and soil conservation. In addition, forestry, recreation, and electric-power production rounded out his schema. The generation and sale of power (in keeping with the recommendation of the Mississippi Valley Committee), however, was the coordinating agent of this policy, the thrust of which was to elevate the social income and living standard of millions of Americans.[46]

42. *Congressional Record,* 75th Cong., 1st sess., 81 (Feb. 19, 1937), 1451. Smith had reintroduced his 1936 bill as H.R. 92 on Jan. 1, 1937. There is no evidence that the House seriously considered it. See ibid., Jan. 5, 1937, 25.
43. The *New York Times,* Feb. 25, 1937.
44. These press clippings and others are in Interior Department Files, GAF 1-310, pt. I, box 366.
45. Cooke to Roosevelt, Feb. 20, 1937, Roosevelt Papers, OF 2575.
46. Cooke to the Committee on National Power Policy, Feb. 19, 1937, Interior Department Files, GAF 1-310, pt. I, box 366.

Cooke's memorandum waited upon the return of Secretary Ickes, who was completing an inspection tour of Interior Department programs in the West, for a reply. On March 3, 1937, he assured Cooke that each member of the committee agreed that "the formulation of a national power policy is the most important part of our assignment," but also reminded him that the president had first requested the Bonneville and little TVAs legislation. For this reason, he wrote, "every effort was made ... so to frame our recommendations with regard to Bonneville that they would not be incompatible with any national policy which might subsequently be promulgated."[47] Unfortunately, the opportunity to define such a policy was lost, as Cooke came to realize, in the debate over Bonneville and the conservation-authorities legislation.[48] The committee qua committee never again met to analyze, discuss, or formulate a policy having the balance and breadth of vision that Cooke desired. Overlapping, competing jurisdictions; bureaucratic rivalries; and, in the end, Ickes's attempt to establish himself as "power czar" confused administration policy. Coordination and planning were lost sight of in the turbulent days prior to America's entry into World War II.

The immediate task at this point was to steer H.R. 4948 past the shoals of committee hearings and on to the floor of the House. The opposition already was assembling, preparing to advance familiar arguments against the bill. The new Secretary of War, Henry L. Woodring, testified on behalf of the Corps of Engineers. He protested against the corps's relegation to the innocuous task of overseeing navigation, flood control, and the fish ladders at the dam. Monotonously, he droned on that the engineers, having built the dam, should be invested with unitary authority to produce, transmit, and sell the power. His prime concern was to protect the interests of the engineers, unlike the private utilities and industries of the Pacific Northwest, particularly in and around Portland, who expected to receive block sales of power from the corps at preferred rates. Secretary Ickes, who defended the committee's decision to invest the civilian administrator with integrated control over Bonneville's power, firmly rebuffed Woodring's arguments. Shortly before the hearings, he analyzed the situation in the Pacific Northwest from the viewpoint of the public-power enthusiast. "From information that we get," he recorded, "the power interests

47. Ickes to Cooke, Mar. 3, 1937, in ibid., pt. 2, box 3099.
48. In the end, as Leuchtenburg and others have noted, neither a Department of Conservation nor the little TVAs materialized. See Leuchtenburg, "Roosevelt, Norris and the 'Seven Little TVAs'," 44.

in the Northwest are opposed to the Administrator who is to make contracts for Bonneville power, to be named by the Secretary of the Interior. They want the War Department to have charge of this phase of the administration, as was provided in the original [McNary] bill. It will be interesting to see how this works out."[49]

As the hearings progressed, they increasingly focused upon the question of who should be responsible for operating the generators at the dam, the engineers or the civilian administrator. The implication, which everyone understood, was that the victor would determine the rate schedule, thereby fixing policy for many years to come. Thus, the public-power proponents within the administration were surprised when the chief of the Army Engineers, General Edward Markham, testified that the president had decided to allow his people to generate the power and deliver it at the switchboard to the administrator for disposal. The House subcommittee interpreted his testimony to mean that the president was repudiating the recommendation of his own advisory group to unite these functions in the civilian administrator. If he had altered his thinking on this point, might he not have done so on the important matter of rate-fixing?[50]

This turn of events so disturbed Ickes that he immediately dispatched a memorandum to the president. He demanded a clarification of the general's testimony, and further reminded his boss that he had endorsed the committee's recommendations without reservation. "The Power Policy Committee is somewhat embarrassed as to the position it should take in this matter if its views should be sought by the House Committee," he wrote, "inasmuch as General Markham has given that Committee the impression that you have approved the amendment proposed by him."[51] To Congressman Joseph Mansfield, the chairman of the House Committee on Rivers and Harbors, he proclaimed his support of the original bill in order to attain "the goal of a wide distribution of the benefits of this project."[52]

As a matter of fact, the president's bow to the Army Engineers

49. Ickes, *Secret Diary*, II, 86. Ickes's distrust of the loyalty of the engineers to the New Deal's power policy persisted long after he left office. In 1951, he wrote: "No more lawless or irresponsible Federal group than the Corps of Army Engineers has ever attempted to operate in the United States, either outside of or within the law" (see his foreward to Maass, *Muddy Waters*, xiv).

50. For Markham's testimony see *Columbia River: Bonneville Dam*, 1937 Hearings, 5-6, 40.

51. Ickes to Roosevelt, Mar. 20, 1937, NPPC Records, CF, box 24; also the copy in Seattle City Lighting Records, box 81.

52. Ickes to Joseph J. Mansfield, Mar. 22, 1937, Interior Department Files, GAF 1-310, pt. I, box 366.

was only the first of several blows to the committee's prestige. On March 24, 1937, the president figuratively washed his hands of the bureaucratic wrangling; he informed Ickes that, insofar as he was concerned, he could live with either two organizations at Bonneville or a single operating staff under the administrator, "whichever was finally agreed upon." Then he went off on a tour of the West, leaving the committee and the engineers to fight it out between them.[53] He also undercut the prestige of the committee by going outside of it. Upon his return to the Capitol, Roosevelt immediately summoned Senator Norris to the White House to discuss the valley-authorities legislation. After the conference of March 31, Norris told reporters that the agenda had included national power and flood-control planning; he revealed also that he would draft the legislation for the regional authorities. Not a word was said of the CNPP.[54] The president, apparently having second thoughts, told newsmen that he intended to "boil down" *various* proposals for regional authorities. The damage was done, however, for the *Washington Post* reported on May 1 that the president was expected to support the Norris bill.[55] This succession of body blows, while the committee hearings on H.R. 4948 were in progress, was simply too much for Ickes and the committee to sustain; the members finally agreed "to put it squarely up to him [the president] whether our usefulness is not at an end."[56] The president did not formally disband the committee, but he did leave its authority in question.

The hearings, meanwhile, graphically illustrated the intimate bond that existed between the nature of the Bonneville administration and the type of a rate structure that the people of the Pacific Northwest could expect. A civilian agency, whose administrator was appointed by the secretary of the interior, virtually assured the adoption of a uniform-rate schedule. On the other hand, the Corps of Engineers, which had made no secret of the fact that it believed that a sufficiently large public market did not exist, could be expected to endorse the differential-rate policy favored by private industry. Colonel Robins revealed as much, when he testified that the engineers proposed to build only two short transmission lines from Bonneville, the main line connecting Portland, and to give industry at the damsite preferred bus-bar sale. Governor Charles A. Martin of Oregon, a retired army

53. Roosevelt to Ickes, Mar. 24, 1937, NPPC Records, CF, box 24; copy in Seattle City Lighting Records, box 81.
54. The *New York Times*, Apr. 1, 1937.
55. See "Press Conferences of the President, 1/1-6/30/37," Roosevelt Papers, President's Personal File (hereafter cited as PPF), 1-P.
56. Ickes, *Secret Diary*, II, 129-30.

general and a Democrat critical of the Roosevelt administration, supported Robins's testimony; he also insisted that there was no power market among domestic consumers in the region. Martin further warned the House committee that the Bonneville investment could be repaid only by encouraging new industries which made heavy use of electricity to come into the area, and that this could be accomplished only through a system of preferred rates.[57]

The commercial and private-power interests in and around Portland warmly endorsed this testimony. Their attitude was that a uniform-rate policy would set Bonneville power beyond the limits deemed commercially attractive and, in the long run, this would discourage the location of new industries.[58] This argument very often coincided with a more general criticism of New Deal policies and revealed a trace of envy which the civic leaders of Portland felt toward Seattle, their more heavily industrialized neighbor to the north. W. D. B. Dodson of the Portland Chamber of Commerce, for example, testified that blanket rates would destroy the prospects for new industry, and then went on to declare that "those who view the heavy industrial development of our neighbors, with their success in all economic and social things, and then declare for a policy which would prevent our reaping what benefits power offers, are controlled by unholy and un-American principles."[59]

On May 10, 1937, Ickes appeared before the committee in order to rebut the testimony of General Markham.[60] He read into the record a formal statement reaffirming the recommendation of the CNPP that there should be no partition of federal authority over the generating, transmitting, and marketing phases of Bonneville power. The memorandum, drafted by Ben Cohen, Joel D. Wolfsohn, and James Delmage Ross, strongly endorsed the concept of a uniform-rate structure.[61] Ickes then deferred to Ross on the more technical aspects of rate-making. Ross was well versed in the subject, having gained broad experience as superintendent of the Seattle City Lighting Department and as a member of the SEC. Unofficially, he also was acting as a lobbyist

---

57. *Columbia River: Bonneville Dam*, 1937 Hearings, 58-60, 63-71.

58. For this and similar arguments see ibid., 83-104, 104-21, 199-204, 204-12, 284-99, 299-305.

59. Ibid., 305-25, esp. 323.

60. See the *Seattle Star*, May 10, 1937, in Robert W. Beck Papers, box 16, University of Washington Library (hereafter cited as Beck Papers); and *Columbia River: Bonneville Dam*, 1937 Hearings, 143-65.

61. See Wolfsohn to Ickes, May 5, 1937, Interior Department Files, Classified Files, box 24, and the seven-page statement attached to the letter.

for the bill at the behest of the Washington Public Ownership League.[62] Ross approached the whole question of rate-making from the standpoint of a national power policy, for he clearly suggested in the course of testifying that he did not look upon Bonneville as an isolated generating plant, but as the first in a regionwide multistation system to provide cheap power to all the people of the Pacific Northwest.[63]

The testimonies of Ickes and Ross had favorably impressed the committee and even won the praise of public-power enthusiasts. John Rankin of Mississippi joined with former governor Walter M. Pierce, who represented the sparsely settled eastern section of Oregon in Congress, in support of the recommendations of the CNPP.[64] Strong sentiment also was building at the grass-roots level in favor of H.R. 4948 as it was originally proposed. In Oregon and Washington, politically influential "Commonwealth Federations," composed of state Grange organizations and local units of the American Federation of Labor, closed ranks to lobby for cheap public power.[65] Their pressure gradually had an effect upon the congressional delegates of the Pacific Northwest; Steiwer, Bone, and finally McNary swung their support to the bill, with its provision for a civilian administrator, as the most efficient means of marketing Bonneville power.[66]

The question that still remained, however, was whether the House committee could report out a bill reconciling the engineers' and FPC's differences before the session ended. Afraid that a continuation of further interagency bickering would kill the chances of any legislation, Senator Homer T. Bone proposed a compromise. The "Bone Formula," as it was popularly known, assigned to the Army Engineers the responsibility for operating the dam and its power-generating facilities. The engineers would deliver the current to the substation, at which point the civilian administrator was to dispose of it, set the rates, and otherwise supervise the system. In addition, the administrator

62. *Columbia River: Bonneville Dam,* 1937 Hearings, 177-78.

63. See the Washington Public Ownership League circular letter of Apr. 26, 1937, in Beck Papers, box 16; also the telegrams between Ross and Beck, Apr. 20, 1937, in ibid.

64. Ickes, *Secret Diary,* II, 137-38; *Columbia River: Bonneville Dam,* 1937 Hearings, 180-98, 239-67.

65. The *Oregonian,* May 2, 1937; Carl D. Thompson to the Hon. Joseph J. Mansfield, May 1, 1937, Seattle City Lighting Records, box 79; and Frederick J. Chamberlain and the Washington Public Ownership League to Senator Norris, June 10, 1937, Norris Papers, tray 81, box 4.

66. U.S. Congress, Senate, Hearings before Commiteee on Commerce on Senate bill 2092, *Completion and Operation of the Bonneville Project,* 75th Cong., 1st sess., June 29, 1937 (Washington, D.C., 1937), esp. 11-16 (hereafter cited as *Senate Hearings on S. 2092*).

had the authority to operate or close down the generators in order to control power production. Preference in the sale of power under the "Bone Formula" was explicitly given to publicly owned systems and agricultural cooperatives at the expense of the private utilities and industry.[67]

Bone's "Formula" was a compromise only in the broadest sense. For, while it accepted the recommendation of the CNPP and the National Resources Committee to create a new marketing agency and the War Department position on the daily operation of the dam, enough safeguards were written in to prevent the engineers from hamstringing the administrator. In surrendering its control over transmission and distribution, the corps had also forfeited influence on the essential question of rate-making.[68] Given the opposition to it within the Roosevelt administration and among public-power groups, this was probably the best the War Department could hope for. Woodring conceded as much, when he announced that the "Bone Formula" was the most satisfactory solution. President Roosevelt agreed with his assessment and, in the spring of 1937, he gave the green light to its supporters to substitute a compromise bill in lieu of H.R. 4948.[69]

Secretary Ickes, however, was less than enthusiastic about the "Bone Formula," for he viewed it as a needless concession to the engineers. "I do not trust the Army Engineers on power," he confided to his diary, "and, moreover, I do not think that, as a general policy, they ought to be permitted to extend their powers and jurisdiction as they would, if this bill should pass as amended."[70] In the Pacific Northwest also, there were signs of dissatisfaction. The Oregon and Washington Grange organizations, working with Robert W. Beck of the Seattle City Lighting Department, sought to dilute the Bone compromise in order to enhance public-power control and further diminish the influence of the Army Engineers.[71] Ickes's reservations about the "Bone Formula," prompted in part by the utilities' irritating practice of hiring retired army engineers whose knowledge of government policies and operations often was useful, were communicated to the other members of the CNPP. That body had barely recovered from the president's unexpected announcement that Senator Norris would draft the "little

67. Beck to Ross, Apr. 28, 1937, Seattle City Lighting Records, box 48.
68. Ogden, "Power Policy in the Northwest," 244.
69. Roosevelt to Homer T. Bone, June 7, 1937, Roosevelt Papers, OF 360.
70. Ickes, *Secret Diary*, II, 129-30.
71. See Beck to Ross, Apr. 28, 1937, Seattle City Lighting Records, box 48.

TVAs" legislation and also write the statement on power policy.[72] Its members reconvened in order to discuss the committee's future usefulness in the light of all that had occurred recently; they finally agreed to stand behind the original bill (H.R. 4948) and to try to persuade the president to withdraw his endorsement of the "Bone Formula." Ickes took the initiative in the countercampaign by writing letters to Mansfield and Senator Royal Copeland, urging them to instruct their committees to reject any Bone compromise bills.[73]

As the hearings continued into June, proponents and critics of the Bone compromise reached an impasse, and there seemed little hope that the House committee would report out any bill. In an effort to avert this, the forces of moderation—the congressional delegates of the Pacific Northwest and Chairman Mansfield of the Rivers and Harbors Committee—swung into action. On June 23, Mansfield introduced an amended version of H.R. 4948 which substantially embodied the Bone Formula's recommendation that responsibility for generating power should be vested in the Corps of Engineers.[74] Meanwhile, the Oregon and Washington Granges and the Commonwealth Federations had been assured that the amended bill would not in any way diminish the opportunity to attain cheap public power. They dropped their opposition and endorsed the new bill, H.R. 7642. Before Ickes or the committee could dissuade the president, the House committee conducting the hearings unanimously reported out the Mansfield bill to the Committee of the Whole; it was placed on the calendar for a vote on June 24. On July 23, 1937, the House voted on H.R. 7642, but not before Congressman Rankin made two abortive attempts to substitute the original bill, minus the Bone compromise, for the Mansfield bill. Ickes, by this time, was thoroughly discouraged and made almost no effort to give Rankin assistance. In the end, the compromise bill passed with only one-fifth of the House in attendance, and without the formality of a roll-call vote.[75]

Unlike the extended House queries, the Senate considered only one bill, S. 2092, which was endorsed by each senator of the Pacific Northwest except Idaho's Borah. The opposition to the Bone compromise had slackened by now, and after only two days of hearings the com-

72. The *New York Times*, Apr. 1, 1937; "Transcript of Presidential Press Conference," May 1, 1937, Roosevelt Papers, PPF, 1-P.

73. For Ickes's opinion of the Honeyman bill (H.R. 6151) and the Bone bill (S. 2092) see Ickes to Mansfield and to Copeland, May 6, 1937, NPPC Records, CF, box 24.

74. *Columbia River: Bonneville Dam*, 1937 Hearings, 513; *Congressional Record*, 75th Cong., 1st sess., 81 (July 26, 1937), 7622-24.

75. Ickes, *Secret Diary*, II, 165.

merce committee recommended the bill to the full Senate. On August 9, S. 2092 passed the Senate; three days later a joint conference committee reconciled minor differences between the House and Senate versions. On August 20, 1937, President Roosevelt signed the Bonneville Power Act.[76]

The legislation established temporarily the Bonneville project administrator's office in the Department of the Interior; the implication was that a more permanent arrangement would be made after the construction of Grand Coulee Dam was completed. The Corps of Engineers bore the responsibility for generating power at the dam, but Congress had vested the authority to dispose of the energy and set rates in the civilian administrator.[77] The selection of the administrator by Secretary Ickes signaled the victory of the public-power point of view in rate-making and was a setback for the private utilities and their chamber-of-commerce allies. The Bonneville Power Act, containing a provision for the interconnection of federal projects, also gave to public-power enthusiasts a lever by which they were able to take control of energy produced at Grand Coulee away from the Bureau of Reclamation. The president's role in the legislative process is more difficult to assess. It is true that, had it not been for his active though tardy intervention, buttressed by the studies and recommendations of the National Resources Committee and its regional agency, the legislation would have lacked many features of a regional program.[78] But the president also blew hot and cold on regional planning; he stopped short of committing his support to legislation that would have provided permanent unified control of power policy along TVA lines for the Pacific Northwest. As a result, the temporary nature of Bonneville's administration inevitably carried in it the seeds of bureaucratic discontent and interagency rivalry for control of the program.

One last point should also be mentioned. The manner in which Norris and the "little TVAs" bill were abandoned, after unduly raising the hopes of public-power supporters, did not bring credit upon the administration.[79] At the same time, the president callously dashed the author-

76. The official title, "Bonneville Power Administration," was not adopted until Feb. 21, 1940. Previously it was referred to as the Bonneville Power Authority, the Bonneville Administration, or simply as Bonneville. For purposes of brevity I have used either the official title or BPA throughout.

77. Ogden, "Power Policy in the Northwest," 244.

78. McKinley, *Uncle Sam in the Pacific Northwest,* 161-67.

79. Opponents of the bill included Secretary of Agriculture Henry Wallace and the Army Corps of Engineers. The fact remained, nevertheless, that the president in the end took no stand at all. See Leuchtenburg, "Roosevelt, Norris and the 'Seven Little TVAs'," 433.

ity of his own advisory committee, undermined its prestige, and forsook the opportunity to articulate—really for the first time—a coherent, integrated national power policy that might have served the people and the country in the ensuing decades.

Toward the close of September 1937, President Roosevelt journeyed to the Pacific Northwest, where he officially dedicated Bonneville Dam. He delivered a strong speech for the occasion, reaffirming his desire to have the administrator distribute the power widely and at the lowest rate consistent with sound fiscal policy. The address was hardly calculated to please the Portland Chamber of Commerce, Governor Martin of Oregon, or the private-power companies, who were aware that a movement already was afoot to foist upon them J. D. Ross as Bonneville's first administrator. The press, in fact, had spent the past few weeks openly speculating whether Ross would receive the appointment. And when Roosevelt arrived at the damsite, he was greeted with the placards of public-ownership groups proclaiming: "We Want Ross."[80]

The private utilities, meanwhile, had shifted their attention to the appointment of the administrator, for they recognized that he would be in the position of setting the rate schedule for Bonneville power and thereby determine policy. Governor Charles Martin of Oregon and the chambers of commerce, above all, were determined to block the appointment of J. D. Ross. His advocacy of "municipal socialism" as head of the Seattle City Lighting Department led them to believe that he would impose uniform rates and construct a regional grid in the Pacific Northwest. During the summer and early fall, they fabricated the allegation that Ross, if appointed, would be biased in favor of Washington at the expense of the Rose State. The charge actually was calculated to turn popular support in Oregon, which looked upon Bonneville as the key to industrialization, against Ross.[81] Ross also encountered hostility from the public-power supporters of the Grand Coulee project, who feared that his candidacy would eclipse their own plans for reclaiming the Columbia basin.[82] Others, however, looked upon the administratorship as the fountainhead of patronage and new jobs. This latter element was manifested in the opposition of the Jackson Club of Oregon, the Democratic party's unofficial high command, to Ross. Its members bluntly inquired of the state's eastern congressman, Walter M. Pierce, who was a Ross supporter: "Which state

80. The *New York Times*, Sept. 29, 1937.

81. See the circular letter of the Peoples' Power League, Sept. 20, 1937, Seattle City Lighting Records, box 78.

82. Ogden, "Power Policy in the Northwest," 245.

do you represent in Congress, Washington or Oregon?"[83]

All the while, Ross was playing his cards close to his chest. He refused to confirm or deny that he was seeking the position, nor would he commit himself in advance on the rate question, which the mayor of Portland, Joseph Carson, and others wanted in return for their support.[84] Ross referred such inquirers to his public statements, which suggested at most that he believed in the general desirability of low rates. On the other hand, he was quick to criticize his opponents. On July 21, for instance, Ross accused Governor Martin and Portland's commercial interests of plotting "to bottle up the power output from Bonneville Dam" so that "present exorbitant rates charged by the private companies would not be affected."[85] Meanwhile, the public-power groups of the Pacific Northwest, labor unions and agricultural Granges, and Senator Norris worked feverishly to line up support for his nomination.[86] They were able to seize the advantage because the private utilities had no candidate of Ross's stature, reputation, and ability.

From every indication Ross was the logical choice for the position. He shared the president's belief that cheap electric power would unlock the door to a higher living standard for all Americans. Philosophically, he had incorporated into his own thinking the basic goals and humanitarian concerns of the "city-building" idea. This concept applied a millennial vision to local needs, for it saw cheap electricity as a gift of nature which could be brought into every home to lighten man's burdens. The first step toward bringing this idea to fruition was to establish a unified national rate schedule that would effect a decentralization of population and industry from the overcrowded urban centers. Ross, as superintendent of Seattle's municipal power plant in the 1920s, exerted his energies to this end. The extent to which he was successful was a tribute to his intimate knowledge of the region and its inhabitants, their confidence in him, and his appreciation of the engineering and financial problems of the electric-utility industry.[87]

Although the utilities and conservative local politicians opposed

83. See the *Portland Star*, July 20, 1937, news clipping in NPPC Records, Cohen File, box 9.

84. Ross to Joseph Carson, July 27, 1937; Ross to J. F. Hosch, Aug. 9, 1937; Beck to Pierce H. Parott, Aug. 5, 1937, all in Beck Papers, box 16.

85. The *Oregonian*, July 22, 1937.

86. See Claude McColloch to Ickes, Oct. 15, 1937, Seattle City Lighting Records, box 78.

87. For Ross's philosophy and career as director of the Seattle City Lighting Department see J. D. Ross, "Should All Electric Utilities Be Governmentally Owned and Operated?" *Congressional Digest*, 15 (Oct. 1936), 240-42; Wesley A. Dick, "The Gene-

Ross's nomination to the post, there were other considerations in his favor. He was a close personal friend of the president, an acquaintance that went back to the governorship when Roosevelt first demonstrated a keen interest in developing the St. Lawrence Seaway for its energy potential.[88] Also, the president had erred in appointing Ross to a vacancy on the SEC in 1935. The industry generally had received the appointment "as an indication of the aggressive attitude which the Federal agency is supposed to pursue in its new duties."[89] But the law was tied up in litigation from 1935 to 1938, thereby making Ross's appointment somewhat meaningless.

Ross disliked Washington, D. C. and yearned to return to the Pacific Northwest where he could tramp through the forests, climb mountains, and fish in the deep, blue lakes. The tediousness of the commission's work and his own lack of a judicial temperament added to his discomfort. Thus, when the position of Bonneville administrator materialized, he accepted it without hesitation. He looked upon it as a new opportunity to experiment with his "city-building" idea. The president offered the administratorship to Ross upon the recommendation of his advisers and over the protests of Governor Charles Martin of Oregon and the private utilities. Ickes alone of administration officials was not entirely pleased with the selection because he saw in Ross a potential rival for the president's ear. And though he kept silent, he confided to his diary that he still would have the right to select an Oregon man as assistant administrator, "to maintain political and geographical harmony in the region." Ross's appointment, however, was fraught with pitfalls. He was expected to work hand in glove with Secretary Ickes, win over the local public-power groups, and earn the confidence of the private utilities. The outlook for the Bonneville project was less placid than Ickes's diary entry suggested.[90]

sis of Seattle City Light" (Master's thesis, University of Washington, 1964); and William O. Sparks, "J. D. Ross and Seattle City Light, 1917-1932" (Master's thesis, University of Washington, 1964).

88. For a brief but incisive background and history of the St. Lawrence power project see James M. Burns, *Roosevelt: The Lion and the Fox* (New York, 1956), 112-15; and Frank Freidel, *Franklin D. Roosevelt: The Triumph* (Boston, 1956), 43-46, 112. Roosevelt, who was governor at the time, proposed that the state be authorized to make contracts with transmission and distribution companies, "under which a fair price to the consumer will be guaranteed, this price to make allowances only for a fair return to the companies on the actual capital invested in the transmitting and distributing of this particular power energy" (quoted in Burns, *Lion and Fox*, 113).

89. Ross occupied the seat held formerly by Ferdinand Pecora. See *New York Herald Tribune*, Aug. 24, 1935; and Ralph F. De Bedts, *The New Deal's SEC* (New York, 1964), 184.

90. Ickes, *Secret Diary*, II, 228.

CHAPTER VIII

The Bonneville Power Administration: The Formative Years

To Ross the great barriers of steel and concrete at Bonneville and Grand Coulee were symbols of comfort in the home, convenience on the farm, and progress in the factory. Power for every bungalow, ranch, and industry had become a crusade as well as a career for him. As he assumed the duties of administrator on November 1, 1937, the tasks before him were fivefold: to organize the staff and formulate policy, particularly on the matter of resale rates; to promote utility districts; to get distribution lines out to the customers; to establish a good working relationship with the private- and public-power groups in the region, as well as with his superior, Secretary Ickes; and to prepare the way for a permanent agency to administer the project after Grand Coulee was completed. Each assignment claimed the full energy of first Ross and then his successors prior to American entry into World War II.[1]

Two weeks after he had established the offices of the Bonneville Power Administration (BPA) in Portland's Failing Building, Ross described the challenge and the opportunity that awaited him. He noted that public interest in the distribution of power was running high, even before installation of the initial two generators was completed, and he intended to capitalize on it. If excitement were translatable into affirmative action, he wrote to Senator Norris, then "we will have a real yardstick from generating plant to customer" in keeping with the president's directive. Ross was optimistic that he could swing public support to his policies, just as he was certain that, in time, he could induce industry and private-utility companies to purchase energy from Bonneville. The agency had an opportunity to encourage industry to hire a large number of unemployed workers, and he was willing to

1. The *New York Times*, Mar. 15, 1939.

allocate to them up to 20 percent of the power at the dam. He would not, on the other hand, encourage "those manufacturers who do not employ considerable labor to seek Bonneville power." The administrator, from the outset, intended to be scrupulously fair in his dealings with industry and the power companies, but he was not willing to sacrifice the social objectives of the New Deal which Bonneville power represented.[2]

Ultimately, of course, Bonneville did become the matrix of cheap power for the Pacific Northwest. In 1937, however, a dark cloud hovered over the project. For no one could be absolutely certain that a large public market for the energy existed. No one except Ross, who was convinced that the market existed; his optimism rested heavily upon a preliminary report of the Oregon market that the Bonneville Commission had written in 1934.[3] Other federal agencies in the region, which had assured Ross of their willingness to cooperate, and the private utilities did not exhibit the same confidence. "I appear to be about the only one who is enthusiastic that there is plenty of market," he confessed to Senator Norris. Even if a market did not exist, he was ready to create one. "I think the market is about what you make it," he declared, "and we are certainly going to succeed in making a market here. The trouble is—the one big trouble—lack of funds to get the lines quickly to the people."[4]

This obstacle notwithstanding, Ross moved with maximum feasibility to integrate the objectives of the Bonneville legislation into the national power policy.[5] The components of that policy were similar to those being implemented in the Tennessee valley: construction of a regional grid, establishment of uniformly low power rates, and long-range planning for soil conservation, rural electrification, and farmer settlement. Cheap electric power, upon which rested the success of the New Deal program in the region, proved especially difficult to attain, for it was tied to the rate question. And when Ross delayed announcement of

2. J. D. Ross to George W. Norris, Nov. 20, 1937, George W. Norris Papers, tray 81, box 4, Library of Congress (hereafter cited as Norris Papers).

3. Bonneville Power Commission, "Report on the Market for Bonneville Power in the State of Oregon, Submitted June 5, 1934," Seattle City Lighting Department Records, box 134, University of Washington Library (hereafter cited as Seattle City Lighting Records).

4. Ross to Norris, Nov. 20, 1937, Norris Papers, tray 81, box 4; see also Ross to Charles H. Martin, Feb. 23, 1938, and Martin to Ross, Mar. 7, 1938, Seattle City Lighting Records, box 72.

5. For evidence of Ross's influence upon the attitudes of Roosevelt and Ickes toward the Bonneville project, see Robert W. Beck to Ross, Oct. 22, 1937, in Seattle City Lighting Records, box 48.

Bonneville's rate schedule several weeks, he was subjected to criticism. Public-power enthusiasts immediately became alarmed; some even accused him of deviating from the president's policy. Others feared that he intended to give preferential rates to private industry.[6]

In truth, neither explanation sufficed. Ross was waiting for the FPC to complete its analysis of the Bonneville's rates before revealing his own decision. In September 1936, President Roosevelt had instructed the FPC to commence rate studies. His only guideline at the time was to draw the attention of the commission to the recommendations of the Pacific Northwest Regional Planning Commission. Those recommendations had stressed "the importance of a rate structure which will not lead to the future congestion of industry close to the generating units, but in preference distribute the benefits of the Columbia River over as wide an area as practicable."[7] The FPC had gone straight to Ross and the Seattle City Lighting Department for information upon which to determine a proper allocation of costs to power development at Bonneville.[8] Not until early February 1938 did the FPC complete its investigation. The circumstances surrounding the delay were unknown to outsiders, however, as many congressional liberals threatened to cut off funds to Ross unless Bonneville power was kept for the "people" and denied to the private interests.[9]

This misunderstanding as to the administrator's actions unfortunately exacerbated hostility toward the private-power companies. And worse, it created bitter divisions within the ranks of public-power men. Judson King of the National Popular Government League lamented that the continuation of the schism could prove the death knell of public power in the Pacific Northwest. He strongly endorsed Ross's decision to sell power to the private companies, and condemned the alleged champions of the public interest for not having thought "the thing through or faced the necessity of amortization and what must be done to repay government loans." They had failed to recognize that even the large

6. Daniel M. Ogden, Jr., "The Development of Federal Power Policy in the Pacific Northwest" (Ph.D. diss., University of Chicago, 1949), 248; and L. C. Kramien to Harold L. Ickes, Apr. 23, 1937, Norris Papers, tray 81, box 4.

7. Franklin D. Roosevelt to Frank McNinch, Sept. 8, 1936, National Archives, Record Group 48, Office of the Secretary of the Interior, Classified File, Bonneville Dam, box 24; Ickes to Forster, Aug. 25, 1936, Franklin D. Roosevelt Papers, Office File 25-N, box 6A, Franklin D. Roosevelt Library (hereafter cited as Roosevelt Papers, OF); and Lester S. Wing to Ross, Oct. 13, 1936, Seattle City Lighting Records, box 96.

8. Clyde L. Seavey to Ross, Dec. 27, 1937, in Seattle City Lighting Records, box 96.

9. See the report of the Federal Power Commission, "Allocation of Costs to Initial Power Development," Feb. 8, 1938, in ibid.

municipal plants of Seattle, Tacoma, and Los Angeles could not sell electricity as cheaply as they did without simultaneously selling larger blocks to private industry at still lower rates. Defending Ross's silence on the rate question before all the facts were in, King urged the administrator to propagandize the need for a balanced load on any public utility.[10]

The president's commitment to the broadest distribution of cheap power among the citizens of the Pacific Northwest placed Ross in a difficult situation. The more electric-power consumers there were, the more feasible it became to reduce unit costs to the point where everyone might participate in its benefits. Kenneth S. Wingfield, assistant director of the PWA's Power Division, whom Ickes had sent west to survey the potential public market, believed that the prospects for expansion were bleak. "Apparently existing public bodies can provide little if any market by the fall of 1937 for Bonneville power," he had reported to his superior, Clark Foreman.[11] The Army Engineers also assumed that power from Bonneville's first two generators would go exclusively to private companies.[12] Indeed, there were no more than twenty-one municipal distribution systems in Washington, and only ten in Oregon. Seattle, Tacoma, and Eugene, the only cities of any size with public power, had their own plants. The organization of public utility districts (PUDs) was proceeding rapidly in Washington but very slowly in Oregon. In any event, none were expected to be ready before the fall, according to Wingfield's report.

The PUD was an elective unit of local government whose boundaries generally coincided with an entire rural county. Endowed with substantial powers to borrow money, incur debt, levy taxes, and issue bonds, it was organized to market hydroelectric power on a nonprofit basis. It also had the potentially awesome power to acquire by condemnation any private utility within the district. The fiscal agent for the districts in 1937, and the man chiefly responsible for selling the bonds which financed their activities, was Guy C. Myers. Myers, who maintained an office at 35 Wall Street in New York City, had excellent contacts in eastern financial circles and acted as a liaison for Ross. His asso-

10. Judson King to Ross, Feb. 20, 1938; and King's memorandum to Ross, "Necessity of a Balanced Load and Sale of Public Power to Big Industry and, Where Necessary, to Private Utilities," Feb. 12, 1938, in Judson King Papers, Container 19, Library of Congress (hereafter cited as King Papers).

11. Kenneth S. Wingfield to Clark Foreman, Feb. 11, 1937, National Archives, Record Group 48, Records of the National Power Policy Committee, Classified File, Bonneville General Correspondence I, box 23 (hereafter cited as NPPC Records, CF).

12. Glen H. Smith to Ross, Oct. 18, 1937, Seattle City Lighting Records, box 48.

ciation with the Bonneville administrator originated in the early years of the depression, when Ross was experiencing difficulty placing the bonds of the Seattle City Lighting Department. Myers came to the rescue and later performed a similar service for the Washington and Oregon PUDs. For this service he received a commission of 2.5 percent of the value of the bonds that were sold. While Myers was the financial whiz, Houghton, Coughlin, Cluck & Schubat of Seattle handled the legal aspects of forming districts.[13]

In 1937 and early 1938, the districts were in their infancy and experiencing many difficulties. Jack R. Cluck of Houghton, Coughlin, Cluck & Schubat described some of the administrative and legal problems that confronted them. "Experience with other districts has demonstrated the advisability of a responsible committee making a close check of each step of the proceedings leading up to the organization of a district," he wrote to John M. Reynolds of the Kitsap County district. "We have found defects in the election procedure of four or five districts thus far, making litigation necessary which otherwise could be avoided, and rendering one or two of the districts subject to the serious danger of being held invalid and non-existent in the counties."[14] The result was that the districts were not yet ready to provide the market for power that Ross hoped for.[15] In the circumstances, the administrator found himself subjected to intense pressure to fix rates beneficial to private industry. On May 4, 1937, Governor Charles H. Martin of Oregon, who was anxious to develop private industry based on cheap power in his state, warned Secretary Ickes that, unless such plants were established along the Columbia to utilize huge quantities of power, "Bonneville will turn out to be a gigantic failure—a failure which will have a disastrous effect on the completion of the Grand Coulee and further development of the upper Columbia."[16] Martin strongly opposed reliance upon cooperatives and utility districts over privately owned distribution outlets.

Martin's letter also suggested the divergence of opinion in the region that existed on the power issue. He, and the business interests who

13. See the article of Richard L. Neuberger, "Power Policy," in the Oct. 22, 1938, issue of *Collier's,* 12-13, in the Robert W. Beck Papers, box 7, University of Washington Library (hereafter cited as Beck Papers). Also, Jack R. Cluck to Richard L. Neuberger, Nov. 24, 1937, and Cluck to John C. Fischer, Nov. 29, 1937, in the Houghton, Coughlin, Cluck & Schubat Archive, box 13, University of Washington Library (hereafter cited as HCC&S Arch.).

14. Cluck to John M. Reynolds, Sept. 25, 1937, HCC&S Arch., box 13.

15. See Cluck to Llewellyn Evans, Nov. 3, 1937, in ibid. Evans was chief engineer for the TVA.

16. Martin to Ickes, May 4, 1937, NPPC Records, CF, Bonneville, box 23.

endorsed him, tended to view Bonneville chiefly from the perspective of economics, that is, how the state could best utilize the cheap power to attract industry and turn a profit for private enterprise. Martin tipped his hand when he suggested that the government should not construct transmission lines into areas which were unable to afford them. Had the proposal been adopted, a fatal blow almost certainly would have been administered to the rural-electrification program.[17] The Roosevelt administration, in contrast, was not ignoring the economics of Bonneville; indeed, cost figured prominently in its thinking. But the social cost of denying a higher standard of living to every inhabitant of the region weighed more heavily. When Congress was deliberating on the Bonneville bill in 1937, Ross placed the social functions before any other. "After all," he declared, "Bonneville is a financial institution. It is also humanitarian. I think the humanitarian use is by far the greater. It is not just what the electricity costs; it is what our people can do with it that constitutes the help to humanity and makes it a real success."[18] Ickes evidently agreed, for he refused to bind Ross to a switchboard rate that would favor private industry at the damsite. "Certainly the benefits of these great national projects should be distributed as equitably and as widely as possible among the people of the Northwest," he replied to Martin.[19]

The governor, nevertheless, had raised a legitimate point, for the government's financial stake in the success of the venture was considerable. Ickes deferred giving him a direct answer in May, arguing that it was wiser to delay a decision on rates pending the appointment of an administrator.[20] Ross's appointment resolved the matter, for he clearly expressed his conviction that Bonneville and other public plants were fully able to pay their own way and that, under a reasonable schedule of payments, the government would receive back its investment.[21] "I would like to do a really constructive work in as short

17. Ickes to Martin, May 13, 1937, in ibid. Cluck wrote to Robert W. Beck: "Frankly, Bob, my hunch is that several of the power companies here will adopt the outward appearance of conciliation, but will exhaust every recourse through other agencies to cause embarrassment to the districts and every one connected with them .... At the same time, I notice that certain propaganda agencies are being established for the obvious purpose of discrediting the district commissioners and their advisers" (Cluck to Beck, Oct. 23, 1937, HCC&S Arch., box 1). See also Stephen B. Kahn to the editor, *Daily Oregonian,* July 1, 1937, Seattle City Lighting Records, box 70.

18. Ross to Paul R. Kelty, Aug. 6, 1937, Beck Papers, box 16.

19. Ickes to Martin, May 13, 1937, NPPC Records, CF, Bonneville, box 23.

20. Ibid.

21. Ross to Ickes, Oct. 11, 1937, Department of the Interior Records, General Administrative File 1-310, pt. 2, Bonneville General, box 3099 (hereafter cited as Department of Interior Files, GAF). Ross suggested 4 percent interest and a forty-to-fifty-year

a time as possible," Ross told Ickes, "because none of us know what the National bill will be, and it would be a fine thing if we could get the ball rolling in good shape before that time."[22]

Ross's statement, uttered shortly before the public announcement of his appointment as administrator, indicates that the rate question was foremost in his thoughts and that he viewed its resolution as the key to Bonneville's success. On October 27, 1937, he discussed the subject with the president, pointing out its implications for the national power policy. Ross also was gravely concerned about accusations from a hostile press that other sections of the country which did not share the benefits of Bonneville power nonetheless were expected to foot the bill. Boulder Dam, for instance, had repaid the government 4 percent, whereas the TVA because of its originally experimental nature returned no interest. Such allegations, if they persisted, could damage the reputation of the project and the president's policy. Hence, Ross was anxious to create as soon as possible a "yardstick" rate for Bonneville power that could then be applied to all federal hydroelectric projects. Roosevelt eventually endorsed the yardstick idea, and even hinted to the press that he might employ it nationally to attain a uniform-rate structure.[23]

Delay in resolving the rate issue during the winter of 1937-38 was caused in part by demands upon Ross's time to attend to organizational problems and to preliminary planning for the purchase of utility properties. Opposition, meanwhile, also mounted from Los Angeles, where municipal-power enthusiasts feared that Bonneville's rate differential in the Pacific Northwest might weaken their own position; from Boulder Dam, because of Bonneville's advantageous interest and amortization features (3.5 percent over forty years); and from the private utilities, who had dug into their treasuries to finance the candidacies of conservative, anti-public-power men in recent primary elections.[24] Ross's response was swift; he instructed his staff to avoid entangling the project in local politics—an order which Stephen B. Kahn, public relations director of the project, and lesser figures ignored—but permitted it to assist districts, in which the initiative originated at the local level,

amortization period, the latter taking the place of depreciation. He also believed that it made little difference whether Bonneville and Grand Coulee were given a 30 percent write-off since he was confident that each plant would quickly pay its own way.

22. Ibid.

23. Ibid.; also Ross to Roosevelt, Dec. 22, 1937, Roosevelt Papers, OF 2882-B, box 3.

24. Ross to Nathan Margold, Mar. 1, 1938, Interior Department Files, GAF 1-310, pt. 3, box 3100; and Frank Fitts to Cluck, Jan. 30, 1938, HCC&S Arch., box 13.

to exercise "their rights, to take advantage of Bonneville power, before January 1, 1941."[25] He also conferred repeatedly with the president about the tie line to Grand Coulee. When funds became available again, after the economic recession of 1937 passed, he started to draft a master plan for a transmission-grid system, premised upon the maximization of the resources of the region.[26]

John C. Fischer, the project's general counsel, thought that Ross was pursuing "his usual very cagy tactics."[27] For he repeatedly offered to purchase the Puget Sound Power and Light Company in a move that kept the atmosphere of Washington and Oregon bubbling. At the same time, he rushed the formation of power districts so that they would be ready to acquire all the properties of Puget Sound, when the company decided to sell.[28] The acquisition, Fischer had observed, would not merely add new outlets for the power that soon would fall from Bonneville's generators, it would bring "the power companies of Oregon to their knees." In any event, he was satisfied that the administrator was "such a marvelous strategist that he will outmaneuver his opponents."

Fischer's analysis was highly perceptive. Early in March 1938, Ross unveiled a plan to hold public hearings on the rate question in order to give Pacific Northwest residents the opportunity to express their sentiments.[29] He invited Claude Draper of the FPC to attend the hearings, and decided that the initial testimony would be taken in Salem and Olympia. The third hearing, as a matter of protocol, would have to occur in Boise, the capital of Idaho, a city located in the southern part of the state, well beyond any immediate prospect of receiving Bonneville power economically. Rate hearings then were conducted in Pendleton, Walla Walla, Spokane, and Yakima prior to Portland itself on March 17. The response was "splendid," Ross informed Ickes, and "the public seemed to appreciate the innovation." By having the public voice an opinion, Ross had shrewdly outmaneuvered his critics; for, by the time the commercial and private-utility interests of Portland advanced their plea for rates reflecting transmission

25. Ross to Cluck, Apr. 17, 1937, in HCC&S Arch., box 12.
26. U.S. Bonneville Power Administration, "History of the Bonneville Power Administration," 3 vols. (1945), I, 9. Lilian Davis edited the unpublished, typewritten copy which is on deposit in the BPA Library. The pagination is not always consistent.
27. Fischer to Joel D. Wolfsohn, Mar. 7, 1938, NPPC Records, CF, Bonneville, box 23.
28. Cluck to Ervin E. King, Apr. 23, 1938, HCC&S Arch., box 13.
29. The *Oregonian,* Mar. 8, 1938; and U. J. Gendron to Ross, Mar. 4, 1938, Seattle City Lighting Records, box 65.

distance, the burden of testimony was overwhelmingly against them.[30]

Once the testimony was taken, Ross conferred with the project's advisory committee.[31] In April, it agreed unanimously that the government should receive a return upon its investment of 3.5 percent, and an additional 1.183 percent for amortization, over a forty-year period. There was some minor disagreement over the charge per kilowatt hour per month, but a compromise was soon effected. "I urged holding the price up a little, namely to $15 and $18 until we got started, and see how everything goes," Ross informed Ickes, "but we all finally agreed on $14.50 and $17.50."[32] Of the two generators soon to be installed, the output of one was reserved solely for public consumption, the other would be shared by the private-power companies and industries situated at the dam. "We are taking the attitude," Ross declared, "that since the private companies serve thousands of people they come ahead of industry at the Dam."[33]

Privately, Ross believed that public ownership was the only feasible solution to attaining the lowest possible light and power rates. The experience of thirty-seven years in public power had taught him that the private utilities would never reduce rates to the point where they should be. The introduction of competition by a public plant did drop rates to a great degree, but there still existed double costs on account of having two systems. Public monopoly was the answer, Ross wrote to his executive assistant, U. J. Gendron. "Therefore the purchasing of a private power concern that wishes to sell, not only ends a controversy in which neither side can win, but it follows the most economical line and brings the lowest possible rates for light and power."[34]

The FPC, meanwhile, approved on June 8, 1938, the rate schedule. Ickes agreed that the rates were reasonable and observed that the broad-based sale of power "will be a boon to the whole of the Northwest and will justify completely, I am sure, the decision of the President and the Administration in developing this great project."[35] Elsewhere, disclosure of the rate schedule was accorded widespread approval, particularly among the public-power groups. Stephen B. Kahn declared that "practically everyone is satisfied with the rate schedule Mr. Ross

30. Ross to Ickes, Apr. 20, 1938, NPPC Records, CF, Bonneville, box 23.
31. The committee was composed of representatives from the Departments of Agriculture and War, the Federal Power Commission, and the Grand Coulee project.
32. Ross to Ickes, Apr. 20, 1938, NPPC Records, CF, Bonneville, box 23. Ross wrote: "I am afraid that if it goes any lower in proportion at the Dam that we will be flooded with a lot of requests for plants that we cannot satisfy for lack of power."
33. Ibid.
34. Ross to Gendron, Dec. 23, 1938, Seattle City Lighting Records, box 65.
35. Ickes to Ross, Apr. 27, 1938; "History of the BPA," I, 21.

has proposed—except the Portland Chamber of Commerce."[36] Ross's optimism was tempered by the realization that Bonneville's work was just beginning. "Our greatest effort," he wrote to Ickes, "is to get our lines to the market which is waiting."

It was at this point that the project encountered new obstacles. Ross had expended nearly the entire initial appropriation upon the rate studies, planning, and staffing. Funds were low for financing other essential tasks. The PUD commissioners, meanwhile, admonished him to exert pressure upon Ickes to release PWA funds for line construction and the purchase of properties.[37] Ickes and the PWA, however, were very skeptical of the worth of the districts, and of their tie-in through Myers to the eastern bankers, and demanded to know all the details before they would authorize the release of funds.[38] Meanwhile, Jack Cluck, attorney for the Washington districts, corresponded in the spring of 1938 with the RFC and with the state's congressional delegation, urging that funds be made available to the districts for the acquisition of utility properties.[39] In March, four of the districts (Pacific, Cowlitz, Pierce, and Wahkiakum) asserted their intention to establish a public-power pool and to acquire 30,000 kilowatts of energy. Afterward, another eighteen districts formed a superpower association to hook up with Bonneville and with public plants in Tacoma and Seattle and to buy private-utility properties. Puget Sound Power and Light was first on its list.[40]

The private utilities, naturally, resisted any effort to force them out of business. Robert W. Beck had the impression, after discussing the matter with Myers, that the companies and the men who ran them did not want to sell. "I know the pressure that Myers has to bring through banks, insurance companies, investment trusts, and large security holders to force these companies into line," he wrote to Cluck. "That is why one seldom gets past the front door in trying to arrange a purchase of a company."[41] Beck had this experience in Nebraska, and each time he wired Myers to open the door for him. Myers, meanwhile, urged Ross to take a more aggressive line toward the companies in Washington and Oregon; he went so far as to tell the administrator

36. Kahn to King, May 23, 1938, King Papers, Container 21; and Cluck to Ross, May 16, 1938, HCC&S Arch., box 13.

37. Cluck to Ross, Jan. 25, 1938; C. C. Hockley to Cluck, Feb. 7, 1938, HCC&S Arch., box 13.

38. Beck to Ross, Jan. 17, 1938, Oct. 12, 1938, Seattle City Lighting Records, box 49.

39. See, for example, Cluck to King, Apr. 27, 1939, HCC&S Arch., box 13.

40. "History of the BPA," I, 26-27.

41. Beck to Cluck, Oct. 19, 1937, Seattle City Lighting Records, box 57.

to throw a fright into the private utilities, if need be, in order to persuade them to relinquish their properties to the districts.[42] In November 1937, for example, he drafted a letter for Ross that was to be sent to George O. Muhlfeld, the president of Stone and Webster. "The situation in Nebraska, as I view it, is one that is very dangerous for the power companies, placed as they are between the power districts and the urge for municipal ownership," the letter read. "It is my opinion that you should seriously consider the sale of your property, even though the price may not be as high as you expected. In the long run I think you will be better off than to enter into a long competitive battle, which would be very costly. I am sure that the solution to your problem there is the disposal of your property as soon as possible."[43] The three-year battle to acquire Puget Sound Power and Light, however, demonstrated that the utilities would not easily succumb.[44]

In the circumstances Ross was forced to resort to makeshift financial arrangements to keep the project operative until the next congressional appropriation. The RFC, for example, agreed to release funds for line construction but not for the acquisition of properties, a policy it adhered to through the summer of 1938. Cluck was convinced that, if this policy persisted, the districts would receive no funds "until the Bonneville lines were constructed, which will be some time in the future."[45] To expedite matters Ross asked Ickes for a PWA loan to permit the agency to clear rights-of-way as quickly as possible.[46] Shortly thereafter, with the assistance of Guy Myers, Robert W. Beck, and the eastern bankers, he financed the construction of a 220,000-volt line to tap Grand Coulee as a market for Bonneville power.[47] Perhaps the most important breakthrough occurred in late May, when Ross signed exclusive contracts to provide power to private utilities, without alienating the support of Norris and other public-power advocates.[48] Beginning in August 1938, with national defense figuring prominently in the thinking of administration officials, he investigated for the presi-

42. Guy C. Myers to Ross, Jan. 31, 1938, in ibid.
43. See Myers's draft letter of Nov. 16, 1937, in ibid.
44. In Nebraska, the power companies went into court to secure injunctions to forestall both the formation of districts and the acquisition of properties. See Ross's description of the Central Nebraska Public Power and Irrigation Districts in Ross to Roosevelt, Mar. 3, 1938, Roosevelt Papers, OF 284.
45. See Cluck to King, Apr. 27, 1939, HCC&S Arch., box 13.
46. Cluck to Ross, Apr. 14, 1938, in ibid.; and Ross to Ickes, Apr. 20, 1938, NPPC Records, CF, Bonneville, box 23.
47. Ross to Cluck, May 31, 1938, HCC&S Arch., box 13.
48. The *Oregonian*, May 26, 1938.

dent the feasibility of linking together the power resources of the whole country. A nationwide grid system, linked together by means of underground cables, was designed, which, if implemented, would protect the nation's electrical supply in the event of war.[49]

Ross remained at the helm of Bonneville all through the first critical year, and continued to demonstrate its economic and social potential. In the short time that he was administrator, Bonneville's appropriations eventually increased thirty-six-fold. His death following abdominal surgery in the Mayo Clinic on March 14, 1939, therefore, came as a deep shock to his many friends, and especially to the president with whom he had formed a very close friendship.[50] Even his critics mourned his passing; the private utilities respected him because he had always dealt strictly but fairly with them.[51] Ross had known how to operate in the tangled network of bureaucracy that was the New Deal. The *Oregonian* of Portland editorialized that the secret of Ross's success had been to persuade the federal government to invest in distribution lines so that Bonneville would have to find or create power users. "As matters stand," it declared, "it is certain that the Administration at Washington, D.C., and the power bloc in Congress—affrighted at the idea of having Bonneville a failure after such huge expenditures for distribution lines—will bring tremendous pressure upon the Bonneville administrator to force adequate sales at any and all costs, and by any and all means."[52]

Ross had pointed Bonneville toward a particular goal, but, as the *Oregonian* perceived, he also had created a pattern that would prove difficult for his successor to alter, should circumstances warrant. He had been a first-rate engineer, a business organizer of high ability, and an evangelist of public power all in one.[53] And yet, for all his positive qualities, Ross never learned to delegate authority as administrator; nor did he devote much time to the staff-line problems within his own organization. The agency functioned as a monolith with only one purpose, and that was to get out the lines to deliver power to

49. "History of the BPA," I, 20.
50. See the letters and obituary notices of Ross's death in the Guy C. Myers Papers, Package C, box 1, University of Washington Library (hereafter cited as Myers Papers).
51. On this point see the unidentified newspaper clipping, dated Mar. 25, 1939, in the King Papers, Container 22; and The *Oregonian*, May 26, 1939.
52. Describing his attitude toward the private utilities, Ross declared: "My job is to get something done for the people of the West. I can't do it by laying down to the power companies. Neither can I do it by frightening them for malice or spite, or for a few pennies" (quoted in Carl Dreher, "J. D. Ross, Public Power Magnate," *Harper's Magazine*, 181 [June 1940], 56).
53. Ibid.

the people of Washington and Oregon. Myers very clearly put his finger on the root problems that surfaced once Ross's strong hand was removed. "When it came to Bonneville," he wrote, "he did not have time to build up the organization he would eventually have had, as many were forced upon him from Washington and through friendship. . . . Mr. Ross was well-aware of the inefficiency of the Bonneville personnel and talked to me about it many times, but as his first job was to construct lines . . . to deliver Bonneville power, he did not let the personnel bother him too much."[54]

Myers was inclined to believe that Ross eventually would have dealt with the petty jealousies and rivalries within the organization. Unfortunately, he did not live to do so, and some of this dissatisfaction erupted into the open. The Land Division, to cite one illustration, bitterly resented remarks to the effect that it had not furnished the information and legal descriptions necessary for acquiring rights of way, and that it was delaying the work of the Construction Division by not providing land which could be taken over for clearing.[55] John C. Fischer, the BPA's general counsel, also came in for extensive public criticism in the Pacific Northwest. Monroe T. Sweetland, executive secretary of the Oregon Commonwealth Federation, speaking for himself and Richard L. Neuberger, a young freelance journalist active in behalf of public power, urged the president's aide, James Rowe, to replace "the ineffectual and incompetent" Fischer. He attributed Bonneville's problems to Fischer's failure "to gear-in with the long time public ownership movement in Oregon."[56] Sweetland already was lobbying for the appointment of another native to succeed Ross. Robert W. Beck of Tacoma, or a "stalwart progressive" like Clark Foreman, was quite acceptable to him.[57]

The search for Ross's successor lingered on through the spring of 1939, leaving the organization rudderless at a critical moment. Lilienthal judged correctly that Roosevelt was looking for a second Ross, "one who could take on the Bonneville Administrator's work, who would be someone we could trust."[58] Ickes, meanwhile, refused to accept responsibility for the confusion that occurred while the search continued, but he did exercise a negative veto over the appointment of

54. Myers to Dreher, Aug. 15, 1939, Myers Papers, box P1.
55. "History of the BPA," I, 16.
56. Monroe T. Sweetland to James Rowe, Mar. 16, 1939, NPPC Records, Cohen File, box 6.
57. Sweetland to Benjamin V. Cohen, Mar. 27, 1939, in ibid.
58. David E. Lilienthal, *The Journals of David E. Lilienthal,* 5 vols. (New York, 1964-71), I, 107-08.

a new administrator.[59] Ickes considered Beck definitely unacceptable, since he, along with Myers and Acting Administrator Charles E. Carey, had criticized publicly the decision of the Washington PUDs to reverse Ross's policy of patient negotiations and to substitute in its place condemnation proceedings against the private systems. The PUDs had branded his criticism as "vicious" and "misleading" and argued that the companies would not come to a fair price unless they knew they would be condemned. E. K. Murray, a commissioner, demanded that Ickes investigate Beck, Myers, and Carey, and that he dissociate himself from their accusation. He could not believe that the secretary "would want to place the districts in a position where they would have to deal with the power companies on the power companies' own terms."[60] Ickes fired Beck immediately thereafter.[61]

Several candidates were considered in passing, although none was available or satisfactory to the president. Clark Foreman, of Interior's Power Section, refused to leave Washington, D. C., to head up the project whereas Ickes's candidate, John Carmody, would not give up the reins at the REA, even on a temporary basis, to take the assignment. Leland Olds of the FPC, ex-Senator James P. Pope, and Dr. Paul J. Raver, a lesser-known utility commissioner from Illinois, were also mentioned as possible candidates.[62] On April 26, 1939, the president and Ickes sat down with the list of candidates and eventually settled upon Julius Krug of the TVA. Krug, however, turned out to be unavailable; he was involved in litigating Commonwealth and Southern properties for the TVA and Lilienthal was unwilling to part with him for at least three months more. Rather than leave the post vacant that length of time, the president agreed to the appointment of Frank A. Banks, an Ickes candidate, as interim administrator.[63]

Banks's appointment evoked mixed reaction from the press. Formerly chief construction engineer at Grand Coulee and a member of Bonneville's Advisory Committee, his paper credentials were impressive. The press, however, unaccountably identified him and his

59. Ickes to Roosevelt, Apr. 22, 1939, Roosevelt Papers, President's Secretary File (hereafter cited as PSF), box 23.

60. Seattle *Post-Intelligencer,* Apr. 28, 1939; and E. K. Murray to Ickes, Apr. 28, 1939, HCC&S Arch., box 13.

61. Beck attributed his dismissal to the political influence of King, Cluck, Murray, Herman Lafke, and the Washington Commonwealth Federation, working through Homer T. Bone. See Beck to Thompson, Mar. 29, 1940, Beck Papers, box 7. I have been unable to locate further information about Thompson.

62. Tex Goldschmidt to Jerome N. Frank, Mar. 28, 1939, NPPC Records, Cohen File, box 6.

63. Lilienthal, *Journals,* I, 107-08.

assistant, Barry Dibble, with the Bureau of Reclamation, an agency which Ickes usually viewed with a jaundiced eye because of its pre-New Deal reputation for being overly solicitous of the private utilities. Almost immediately a number of papers instituted a campaign to persuade the president to make his appointment permanent because they believed that he would put an end to the PUDs. The *Oregonian* editorialized that his retention as permanent administrator "would imply a valid and important change in general administration policies respecting that project," and would encourage "the thought that Bonneville and Grand Coulee are to be administered as true business enterprises and not as promoters of political theory and economic experiment."[64]

Between May and September 1939, Banks communicated frequently with Ickes, totally reversing the state of affairs under Ross, whose correspondence was infrequent and confined largely to periodic general summaries. "From the perhaps extreme autonomy of the Administration under its first Administrator," wrote one observer, "BPA during the months that Mr. Banks was Acting Administrator, voluntarily attached itself more and more firmly to the Washington Department, a natural result of the fact that Mr. Banks had for years been with the Bureau of Reclamation, which was within the Department."[65] The Oregon *Daily Journal* saw evidence in this close relationship of Ickes's determination to run Bonneville personally—now that Ross no longer stood between him and the president. The paper noted that Banks had displaced or demoted the three men closest to Ross—Carey, Beck, and Fischer—while Congressman Pierce and Senator McNary had attempted to amend the Bonneville Power Act to place the appointment of the chief engineer, assistant administrator, and chief counsel in Ickes's hands.[66] Banks's action simply undermined morale and confused procedures and responsibilities. Ickes's man clearly was not working out as the secretary had expected. Lawrence Fly, who replaced Fischer as chief counsel, complained to Ben Cohen that "the organization as a whole needs drive." Banks was adept at firing people, he thought, but the "greater immediate need is for intelligent hiring"

64. The *Oregonian,* May 6, 1939.

65. "History of the BPA," I, ch. 4, p. 33.

66. See "The Bonneville Housecleaning," *Oregon Daily Journal,* May 22, 1939. Ickes, at a hearing before the House Committee on Rivers and Harbors, asked Congress to give him full control over Bonneville and to extend beyond January 1, 1941, the 50 percent reserve power for public bodies. He declared that he was charged with responsibility for the project but had no authority to appoint any officers except the administrator. In addition, he supported Senator Charles L. McNary's amendment that provided for the appointment of an assistant administrator. See the "History of the BPA," I, ch. 4, p. 33; and Ickes to Cluck, May 15, 1939, HCC&S Arch., box 13.

and a "shaking up" of divisions and procedures.[67]

Shortly after taking up the administrator's post, Banks found himself at odds with the Washington and Oregon PUDs. He had not been party to Ross's strategy and did not believe that the administrator should continue to promote vigorously the formation of new districts. On June 12, 1939, he expressed support for their goals but cautioned that the BPA would not fight their battles. "We won't take sides between districts and private utilities," he told the annual conference of Washington PUD commissioners. "The Bonneville administration is a federal enterprise and will give assistance and information equally to all."[68] Because of the waxing strength of the districts in the Pacific Northwest, the time for neutrality, if it ever existed, was past. The administrator no longer could remain aloof from local politics, as Ross had tried to do, nor did the districts expect him to. In the spring and summer of 1939 the region was alive with debate on the future course of public power. In Portland, Sweetland, Neuberger, state senator Harry M. Kenin, and the Oregon Commonwealth Federation demanded Banks's support in the forthcoming municipal election. There, the issue was whether to purchase the Northwest Electric Company as the first step in forming the Portland utility district.[69]

Banks refused to campaign for the districts, while his decision to continue selling power to the private companies drew down the wrath of public-power enthusiasts. Unable to make headway with him, they took their complaints directly to Ickes, alleging that the administrator was betraying the national power policy. They demanded that Ickes order Banks to stop selling power to the private utilities. Ickes, however, resisted their pressure and continued to support Banks, for he recognized the economic necessity of the government selling as much power as it could in order to recoup its investment. This was apart from the fact that he would have had to concede that he had erred in the appointment. "I cannot agree with the implications of your letter," he replied to Senator W. E. Burke of Oregon, "that Bonneville power should not be sold to private agencies pending the development of a public market." The power ought to be sold "in the most advan-

67. Lawrence Fly to Cohen, July 18, 1939, NPPC Records, Cohen File, box 6. Compare this with the rather placid account in the semiofficial "History of the BPA," I, ch. 4, pp. 3-4.

68. The *Oregonian*, June 13, 1939.

69. Ibid., June 11, July 2, 1939; on this point see U.S. Congress, Senate and House, Joint Hearings before Subcommittee of the Senate Committee on Commerce and the House Committee on Rivers and Harbors on Senate bill 2430 and House bills 6889 and 6990, *Columbia Power Administration*, 77th Cong., 2d sess., June 3-19, 1942 (Washington, D.C., 1942), esp. 560 ff.

tageous manner possible so as to avoid waste."[70]

The administrator, meanwhile, did continue the policy of encouraging the districts to institute condemnation proceedings against the power companies. This decision further exacerbated tensions within the BPA, dividing the staff and public-power men in the region. Now that Ross was dead and unable to oppose him, Ickes applauded the decision, as did Jack Cluck, and the Washington and Oregon Commonwealth Federations.[71] Arraigned against Banks before they were systematically removed had been Beck, Carey, and Myers. In June 1939, the issue surfaced again, and this time John Fischer joined the opposition. In April, Beck and Carey had expressed the opinion to Puget Sound district commissioners that federal authorities in Washington, D. C., "connected with the formulation of what might be called a national power policy had expressed themselves as being opposed to the institution of condemnation proceedings."[72] The principle at issue was one of fair play and peaceful negotiations with the private systems as against "ruthless methods which would precipitate the people of the Northwest into bitter strife and turmoil."[73] Conceding that the public agencies would be unable to purchase more than 10,000 kilowatts by 1940 because they had so few distribution systems, they argued nonetheless that condemnation proceedings would tie up acquisitions in endless litigation. And Myers warned of the adverse effect of this policy upon the sale of district bonds in the New York money market.[74] Fischer assured his own removal when he forthrightly declared that Banks "had completely reversed J. D.'s program."[75]

The position of the acting administrator grew increasingly untenable during the summer of 1939 as Bonneville succumbed to near administrative paralysis. The districts attacked Banks for not doing enough to help them fight the power companies, while members of his staff criticized him for undoing Ross's work. News of the trouble in the

70. Ickes to W. E. Burke, July 7, 1939, Interior Department Files, GAF, 1-310, pt. 1, box 3115.

71. Cluck to Homer T. Bone, May 5, 1939, HCC&S Arch., box 13.

72. Cluck to King, Apr. 20, 1939, in ibid.

73. Significantly, Beck inquired publicly why Ickes had not reprimanded him for similar statements while Ross was alive. "Is it because Mr. Ickes did not agree with the policies of Mr. Ross? Was and is it because Mr. Ross' lips are forever silent that Mr. Ickes has the courage to challenge the Ross policies and to belittle and frustrate his accomplishments by humiliating and discharging a trusted lieutenant of J. D. Ross as I am widely known to have been?" (see Beck's statement of May 6, 1939, in ibid., box 1).

74. Myers to Cluck, Apr. 30, 1938, in ibid., box 4; also Beck to Cluck, Apr. 20, 1938, in ibid., box 1.

75. Fischer to Myers, June 12, 1939, Myers Papers, box P1.

Pacific Northwest very quickly reached Ickes who, by mid-July, dispatched a team of lawyers to investigate the BPA. Herbert S. Marks actually took over as general counsel for a time and was empowered to reorganize the administration. He was also instructed to bypass the administrator, if need be, and to refer his recommendations directly to the secretary. Within a few weeks of his arrival, Marks had a fairly accurate picture of conditions at Bonneville. On August 9, 1939, he complained to Cohen that the problems were much worse than he had imagined. He was very discouraged and described his efforts to patch up the program as "a hopeless slaughter."[76] He also communicated his despair to Ickes. "While we have been at work only a few weeks," he wrote, "it has become increasingly evident that the condition of the organization and the attitude of the public towards it are far worse than the gloomy picture which I had been given initially, and that the prospects of remedying the situation are becoming less favorable with each day."[77]

Marks attributed the deterioration of Bonneville to shockingly poor administrative procedures which had become institutionalized under Ross and which were resistant to reform. Inept leadership merely compounded the troubles. "But most important," he wrote to Ickes, "there was strong reason to doubt the sympathy of the present Administrator with the policy ... requiring that preference be given to the public agencies over private utility companies." Marks was referring to the distribution of power, and Banks's tendency to go further in the direction of the private-power companies than even Ross. This policy, he wrote, was being thwarted "at the very time when vigorous action is most necessary to effectuate it," for significant matters that would affect long-term policy relative to contracts, rates, and general attitudes loomed ahead. Neither he nor his assistant, Allen Hart, felt that they could go on working for Banks much longer, because "he fails to command our confidence and seems to entertain, however sincerely, a point of view which we regard as inconsistent with the policy expressed in the Bonneville Act."[78]

In the last analysis, Marks's recommendation left Ickes with no real alternative. Banks had to be replaced with a permanent administrator who was in accord with and able to implement the fundamental purposes of the Bonneville legislation. Marks reverted to Julius Krug,

76. Herbert S. Marks to Cohen, Aug. 9, 1939, NPPC Records, Cohen File, box 6.
77. Marks to Ickes, Aug. 9, 1939, in ibid. (Contrast this with the account in the "History of the BPA," I, ch. 4, pp. 33 ff.)
78. Ibid.

Ickes's original candidate. Although Krug was reluctant to abandon the TVA in the final stages of litigating the Commonwealth and Southern properties, Marks argued that "there was from the standpoint of national power policy an even greater immediate need for his services ... at the Bonneville Project."[79] Drastic surgery, according to Ickes's investigator, had become a precondition for retaining the services of highly competent engineers, rate experts, and attorneys of the caliber of William T. Martin. The latter, prior to coming to the BPA, had negotiated on behalf of the TVA the power contracts with Commonwealth and Southern.

Paradoxically, Banks had found little favor among the private-power companies, which accused him of stalling negotiations to sell power from the second of Bonneville's two generators. Considering the intense hostility of the local PUDs to the policy, this conclusion was wholly predictable even though it may not have been entirely accurate. Banks had been proceeding cautiously, but only because he was afraid that the companies would resell the power to local customers at exorbitant rates. The problem of resale rates was still up in the air. Ickes, moreover, had admonished him that the first contracts would be eyed with intense interest. Nebraska utility officials were closely following their progress, and other states were expected to take their cue from the results in Seattle and Portland. "Actually the contracts are going to be important, not only as establishing precedents for subsequent contracts ... in the Northwest and elsewhere," Ickes declared, "but also because of their effect upon the Government's bargaining position in dealing with the private power industry."[80]

Ickes was determined to exercise a tight rein over the negotiations on resale rates. Clark Foreman and FPC Commissioner Olds collaborated on a memorandum setting forth in detail the guidelines which Banks should observe when negotiating with Portland General Electric and the Northwest Electric Company. According to the document, each contract should provide for the progressive reduction of resale rates over a five-year span, publication of the specific schedule of each intervening year, and the "objective" rate schedule that was to be attained at the end of the fifth year.[81] If Portland General Electric balked at the progressive rate reduction, Ickes advised Banks to contact the subsidiaries of Electric Bond and Share, "as the Bond and Share

79. Ibid.
80. Ickes to Frank A. Banks, Aug. 17, 1939, Interior Department Files, GAF 1-310, pt. 1, box 3115.
81. See "Memorandum on Resale Rates in Bonneville Power Contracts," in ibid.

people are familiar with and seem not unsympathetic to the idea."[82] In either case, he expected that Banks would submit to him for approval any contract that was negotiated.

Before the negotiations had proceeded very far, Ickes reached the limit of his patience and acted upon Marks's recommendation. He relieved Banks as acting administrator of the BPA on August 21, 1939, and announced the appointment of Dr. Paul J. Raver as his permanent replacement.[83] Raver was a relatively unknown quantity among public-power men, but Ickes had followed his career closely from the time they were in Chicago together. A professor of engineering and public utilities at Northwestern University, and a former chairman of the Illinois Commerce Commission, he had been a part of the Chicago group, which included Ickes, that had spearheaded the attack upon Samuel Insull and Middle West Utilities. When the appointment was disclosed, the people at Bonneville greeted it enthusiastically.[84] William Martin wrote to Ben Cohen: "We are all very pleased with the selection of the new Administrator and with his plans for obtaining the necessary personnel for establishing a strong organization here."[85]

Elsewhere, the appointment was greeted warmly though for an entirely different reason. The *Wall Street Journal,* New York's *Herald Tribune,* and other papers identified with private power promptly announced that the new administrator would give a "conservative cast" to Bonneville. Judson King, however, discarded such talk and declared that it was intended "to poison the minds of Progressives in the Northwest against Raver and make it more difficult for him to proceed." He reassured Jack Cluck that the administrator would cooperate with the forces working for public power in Washington and Oregon, "and that he will not sell you down the river."[86]

The warmth of the enthusiasm for the appointment was tempered, however, by an awareness of the serious difficulties that awaited Raver. Alluding to the confusion that had characterized Banks's tenure, Martin listed the roadblocks that stood in Raver's path before he could sell power to the private utilities. Then he described to Cohen the tack that the new administrator should (and did ultimately) adopt in order to increase Bonneville's revenues. He wrote that Raver should go through with the Portland General Electric contract and, at the same

82. Ickes to Banks, Aug. 17, 1939, in ibid.
83. The *Oregonian,* Aug. 22, 1939.
84. Harold L. Ickes, *The Secret Diary of Harold L. Ickes: The First Thousand Days,* 3 vols. (New York, 1953-54), III, 42.
85. Martin to Cohen, Aug. 22, 1939, NPPC Records, Cohen File, box 6.
86. King to Cluck, Sept. 11, 1939, HCC&S Arch., box 4.

time, persuade private industry to increase its power load substantially above current levels. His advice, however, also was to discourage long-term contracts in the future. "It seems to me," Martin concluded, "that if the public ownership movement is to have any chance of success out here, we should adopt the above policy and then exert every effort to further the development of the public utility districts and the proposed municipal plants in the rest of the country."[87]

When Raver arrived in Portland in mid-September, he found the building program well advanced, but few power contracts signed.[88] His maiden speech, a public relations gesture, attempted to sidestep the distribution controversy and to reassure the power companies that he would not use Bonneville to destroy legitimate private enterprise. He pleaded for time to acquaint himself with grass-roots sentiment and to correct the agency's organizational problems.[89] His talks with representative groups in Oregon and Washington led him to believe that the "people will be firmly behind the Project."[90]

Three weeks later, Raver received his initiation into the morass of New Deal politics. Administrator Harry Slattery of the REA accused him of indifference while the Washington Water Power Company systematically wrecked cooperatives in the eastern part of the state. This type of interagency conflict persisted throughout Raver's early tenure. In January 1940, for example, Dr. Harlow S. Person of the REA recorded a strong difference of opinion with Raver over the resale-rate schedule and the disposal of revenues accruing from power sales to REA-financed cooperatives. His comments left little doubt that the REA would fight to retain jurisdiction over both rates and revenues.[91] The Bureau of Reclamation, by contrast, was long oriented to private interests; it demanded that the administrator increase the rate schedule in order to repay the government's investment as quickly as possible and return taxes to local treasuries.[92] Secretary Ickes, meanwhile, pursued his imperialistic scheme to bring all facets of the national power policy under his jurisdiction by continually manipulating his office to deprive the BPA of its autonomy.[93]

87. Martin to Cohen, Aug. 22, 1939, NPPC Records, Cohen File, box 6.
88. "History of the BPA," II, intro., 4.
89. Ibid., II, chs. 1 and 3; and the *Oregonian*, Sept. 17, 1939.
90. Paul J. Raver to Ickes, Oct. 10, 1939, NPPC Records, Cohen File, box 6.
91. See "Minutes of the Meeting of Jan. 17, 1940," ibid., GCF, box 21.
92. Ibid. (See also Water Conservation Conference, *Newsletter*, I [June 29, 1943], 3, in ibid., box 26.)
93. For evidence see Philip J. Funigiello, "Kilowatts for Defense: The New Deal and the Coming of the Second World War," *Journal of American History*, 56 (Dec. 1969), 614 ff.

The PUD commissioners, shortly thereafter, angrily denounced the administrator for confining BPA assistance to technical problems. And a disillusioned faction of public-power enthusiasts interpreted Raver's listlessness as an attempt to appease the private-power interests. Judson King, however, thought that Raver was acting under orders from the president. "It is the old story," he wrote, "that the President is being influenced to pull his punches and adopt an 'appeasement policy' in response to the urgings of some government men who are playing more or less with the private interests—Bond and Share in particular at the moment."[94]

Raver was not indifferent to the criticisms but deeply resented the innuendo that he was sacrificing the goals of the public-power movement. Problems existed, but he attributed them largely to the absence of first-class department heads. But here, too, he was optimistic that he was making "some progress."[95] Replying to a letter of Judson King, he vented his anger against the superguardians of public power, who denied him credit while seizing upon his mistakes. "Despite all criticisms to the contrary," he observed, "in my opinion the public ownership movement has been materially strengthened within the last two months."[96]

The administrator's performance, indeed, was promising. Raver had shifted the agency's emphasis to give preference to power sales, savings, and regional planning for power use. He also had negotiated four new contracts to sell energy, had effected a lower resale-rate schedule which was incorporated into every contract with the private-power companies, and had reemphasized the importance of the BPA as a unit in regional and national planning. By the end of the year, the record was to be even more impressive: a contract with Portland General Electric worth $500,000 in revenues and enough contracts pending to enable the agency to sell the entire output of the next two generators yet to be installed; a substantial increase in the amount of RFC funding; and the more extensive use of REA distribution outlets. The BPA also had erected a 75,000-kilowatt backbone transmission line from the dam to the St. John's substation to serve Forest Grove. The rates of this small community in Oregon already were well below those of Tupelo, Mississippi, the showcase of the TVA.[97]

94. King to Raver, Oct. 20, 1939, King Papers, Container 22.
95. Raver to Ickes, Oct. 10, 1939, NPPC Records, Cohen File, box 6.
96. Raver to King, Oct. 16, 1939, King Papers, Container 22.
97. "History of the BPA," II, intro., 1 ff; and Raver to King, Dec. 4, 1939, King Papers, Container 22.

These positive accomplishments, unfortunately, went unheralded because of the controversy centering upon the PUDs.[98] Raver unwittingly fed the dispute by calling the attention of Bonneville's Advisory Committee to their allegedly dismal performance. He attributed their deficiencies to the absence of aggressive leadership, originating in the relatively poor caliber of the commissioners who tended to rely upon the administrator for direction.[99] Like his predecessor, Banks, he fought in vain to keep the BPA from becoming entangled in the conflict between public- and private-power groups. In February 1939, for example, he told Jack Cluck that, while he sympathized with the efforts of the Washington PUDs to take over the Puget Sound Power and Light properties, he would leave the method of acquisition up to the commissioners. "In the meantime, however, I have neither recommended nor approved any particular plan of procedure and I have no intention of taking any part in the matter until the Commissioners have indicated their unity."[100]

Another of Raver's decisions—not to proceed beyond encouraging abler men to stand for district elections—alienated many who expected him to campaign actively against the private utilities. The dispute became public in April 1940, when an editorial critical of Raver's attitude appeared in the *Nation,* a leading liberal magazine. The anonymous author contrasted unfavorably the present administrator's neutrality with Ross's lifelong devotion to public ownership. He accused Raver of suborning the Bonneville Power Act, which gave preference in the sale of power to publicly owned systems, and blamed the resignation of Herbert Marks to his "disgust with Raver's policies." The writer concluded his diatribe with a call for a new administrative body for the project, specifically a valley-type authority.[101]

The anonymous critic was Richard L. Neuberger, future editor of the *Oregonian;* a close friend of Senator Norris, Jack Cluck, and the public-power lobby; and an ambitious young man. Neuberger, in his private correspondence, was far more vehement in his denunciation of Raver, especially for the administrator's hands-off policy in the forthcoming Portland PUD election. He wrote to John P. Robertson, Norris's private secretary, on April 11: "It shows that I was wrong

98. For Raver's review of the history, progress, and obstacles of the BPA see his address of May 6, 1940, in Interior Department Files, GAF 1-310, pt. 6, Bonneville, box 3100.

99. See, for example, his comments in "Minutes of the Meeting of January 17, 1940," NPPC Records, GCF, box 21.

100. Raver to Cluck, Feb. 21, 1939, HCC&S Arch., box 19.

101. [Richard L. Neuberger], Editorial, *The Nation,* 150 (Apr. 20, 1940), 499.

about the Bonneville Administrator, Raver, and that he is not going to help the public power movement. That is a great tragedy." He added that neither Roosevelt nor Lilienthal had been neutral in PUD elections, "but this Bonneville Administrator is."[102]

The editorial, which was intended to force the administrator to take a new tack, miscarried.[103] For, as the controversy persisted, Raver replied vaguely that he would be guided by the "wishes of the people and Congress."[104] Left to their own devices, the public-power forces in Oregon experienced a crushing defeat in the PUD elections of May 1940. In retrospect, the factors accounting for the defeat were more complex than Raver's lack of positive assistance. The issue of municipal versus district ownership in Portland, the effective use of propaganda against the district concept, and two rate reductions, shrewdly timed to go into effect shortly before the elections, played a role in the private utilities' victory. Raver, nonetheless, received the onus of blame and, from that moment, his standing among public-power enthusiasts in the region diminished.[105]

Whether Raver's course was politically feasible given the federal government's investment in the region is open to question. His aloofness, however, sustained the efforts of those who were opting for a modification of Bonneville's administrative status. Between 1940 and 1942 Congress debated, but never enacted, bills governing the disposition of the project. Representing the preferences of their sponsors, the bills took the form of a comprehensive valley authority, a power agency alone, and the incorporation of the BPA into an enlarged Department of the Interior. Senator James Pope revived the proposal for a Columbia Valley Authority, taking heart from the oft-repeated statements of the president that he desired a comprehensive plan for the Pacific Northwest.[106] But, as Herman C. Voeltz has indicated, opposition to a centrally directed valley authority was considerably stronger in the region in 1939-40 than it had been previously. The private utilities, predictably, fought against any extension of public power, but the main source of hostility at the end of the decade came from residents who, although sympathetic to public power, preferred local control

102. Neuberger to John P. Robertson, Apr. 11, 1940, Norris Papers, tray 70, box 1.

103. Neuberger to Robertson, Apr. 22, 1940, in ibid.

104. "What the Administrator Says About Bonneville: An Interview with Dr. Paul J. Raver," *Electrical World*, 84 (Jan. 1940), 28.

105. Ogden, "Power Policy in the Northwest," 324-28; the *Oregonian*, Apr. 10, May 2, 1940; and *Columbia Power Administration*, 560.

106. See, for example, the *Oregonian*, Feb. 5, 1941.

to more federal interference. David Eccles, Oregon's representative on the Pacific Northwest Regional Planning Commission, was particularly vocal on this point.[107]

The issue, in 1940, shifted from a CVA to a power authority alone, as the public-power groups of the Pacific Northwest eschewed comprehensive resource planning for the more limited objective of increasing power generation at the dams. Congress gave impetus to this movement in 1937 when it considered several bills to reorganize the BPA into a government corporation concerned exclusively with power generation and distribution. None of the bills would have established a full-fledged authority but, because they used the term in their titles, they aroused strong reactions from opponents. Similarly, the proposed legislation of 1940-43 evoked all the emotions, fears, and prejudices that the earlier TVA legislation had. In the process, it very bitterly divided the public-power movement into warring factions.[108]

Senator Homer T. Bone introduced, on September 30, 1940, the first of the CVA bills, S. 4390, which was premised upon the single-administrator principle and placed the proposed Columbia River Power Administration in the Department of the Interior.[109] Ben Cohen had drafted the legislation with assistance from Marvin Hart and Bill Youngman of the FPC. Ickes, in the interim, prevailed upon Bone to introduce the bill in the Senate on behalf of the department, although the senator's own commitment to it was tepid. The bill had the immediate effect of polarizing public-power enthusiasts into two camps. Those who believed that a greater degree of centralization of control, as embodied in the bill, was essential to a uniform power policy supported it. The largest number of people, however, opposed the Bone bill. Local inhabitants of the Pacific Northwest and critics of Ickes's imperialism in Washington, including Senator Norris and David Lilienthal, were united in their opposition to the further extension of control of power facilities by a remote, highly centralized, and largely unresponsive bureaucracy.

The critics of S. 4390 met in Washington, D.C., on November 27, 1940, to plot their strategy.[110] The group included ten of the most prominent state and national figures identified with the public-power movement: Judson King, Harry Slattery and Bob Craig of the REA,

107. Herman C. Voeltz, "Genesis and Development of a Regional Power Agency in the Pacific Northwest, 1933-1943," *Pacific Northwest Quarterly,* 53 (Apr. 1962), 69.
108. Ibid.
109. See Homer Bone to Clark Squire, Apr. 13, 1942, HCC&S Arch., box 15.
110. See King to Norris, Nov. 28, 1940, Norris Papers, tray 69, box 3.

FPC Commissioners John Scott and Frank McNinch, Congressmen John Rankin and Walter M. Pierce, California's Jerry Voorhis, Sam Thompson of the National Planning Board, Gerald Cruise of the New York Power Authority, and Gifford Pinchot. Their greatest fear was that the president would endorse the Bone bill: "What is feared, however," wrote Judson King to Senator Norris, "is that the Ickes, Cohen crowd may bring pressure to bear on the President to get him to make some commitment or public statement about the matter any time now, and we feel this would be very undesirable."[111] The bill as written had very little chance of passing Congress; nevertheless, the opposition group saw in it an opportunity to rewrite its major provisions along the lines of a true Columbia River-TVA.

Roosevelt, initially, was sympathetic to the Bone bill, which would have vested in Ickes the authority to name the administrator. The Morgan-Lilienthal feud, Raver's difficulties with the public-power groups, and the rapid spread of war in Europe in 1940 had led him to believe that centralization of the decision-making process would resolve future problems. Senator Norris, however, had taken a long-range view of the Bonneville question; he concluded that the single-administrator principle would have unfortunate consequences for the nation's power program. His opposition was not directed against Ickes personally, but was grounded in more fundamental considerations. He explained to Judson King that a member of the cabinet was, as a rule, appointed for political reasons and therefore should not have control over legislation of the kind proposed in the Bone bill. As a political appointee, the cabinet member could not divorce himself completely from executive control; therefore Norris believed that "we ought to go as far as we can to have an independent, non-political board of administration." He preferred the establishment in the Pacific Northwest of a three-man board for Bonneville, the principle that had brought local autonomy to the Tennessee valley.[112]

Norris was convinced that Ickes believed that, "as a matter of right, this authority ought to be given to him." But he had just returned from a trip to Grand Coulee, Bonneville, and Shasta dams, and had talked widely with people interested in the power question. "I could not help but be impressed by the general opposition of all those who talked with me to the control of these projects by the Secretary of the Interior," he wrote to Lilienthal. The sentiment against Ickes was very strong, and he predicted "a bitter fight ahead" if Ickes succeeded

111. Ibid.
112. Norris to King, Dec. 3, 1940, Norris Papers, tray 69, box 3.

in his objective. "I dislike this," he declared, because it is a "fight among friends, and I think never ought to be begun, but the more I think of it, the more I feel that it cannot be avoided."[113] Although he was convinced that Ickes could not possibly be appeased in this matter, Norris spearheaded the bitter fight that resulted in the defeat of the bill.[114]

The Public Power Association of the Northwest, thereafter, came forth with a substitute plan that essentially embodied the principle of local control. However, it also incorporated the model of TVA's governing board to give control of power distribution to local agencies. Three of the five governors were to have been appointed by the PUDs; the federal government was to have selected the other two candidates. The proposal never really enjoyed wide currency in part because Roosevelt hinted, in the spring of 1941, that he was now considering a TVA setup for the region. The press, in fact, was speculating openly that Lilienthal had already drafted the legislation.[115]

Ickes, however, had not abandoned the principle of a single administrator whom he would appoint and control. In the spring of 1941, he renewed his fight to have the president endorse it. Robert W. Beck reported that Washington's congressional delegation was beginning to lean toward Ickes's viewpoint simply to end the dispute. Oregon's delegation, on the other hand, was adamantly against centralization.[116] In fact, the division described by Beck was less clearly defined, for Norris reported that Bone, after the defeat of S. 4390, was now in favor of the TVA approach. Opinion in Oregon, he noted, was probably divided between the two proposals.[117] In any event, Representative Knute Hill of Washington introduced, on June 23, 1941, H.R. 5129, which basically was a restatement of the previously defeated Bone bill. Hill's motive was fairly uncomplicated; he was less interested in the type of agency to administer the Bonneville project than in ending the deadlock. He wanted the power districts to resume the

113. Robert W. Beck declared: "It seems to me that the Secretary may be more interested in getting the power into his hands than anything else" (Beck to W. J. McKeen, June 13, 1941; also Beck to Harlan Plumb, Mar. 27, 1941, Beck Papers, box 16). Governor Charles A. Sprague preferred local control to either a CVA or centralized authority for Bonneville. See Sprague to Beck, May 31, 1941, in ibid.

114. Norris to Lilienthal, Jan. 6, 1941; Lilienthal to Norris, Dec. 30, 1940, Norris Papers, tray 69, box 4.

115. See the *Seattle Star*, Apr. 15, 1941, and the article, "Independent Authority Favored for Northwest," *Electrical World* (Mar. 8, 1941), n.p., clippings found in the Beck Papers, box 16; also Lilienthal, *Journals*, I, 268-69.

116. Beck to J. W. McArthur, Mar. 20, 1941; Morris to Beck, Mar. 18, 1941, Beck Papers, box 16.

117. Norris to Lilienthal, Jan. 6, 1941, Norris Papers, tray 69, box 4.

purchase of utility properties free of any bureaucratic encumbrances.[118]

Ickes fought hard for the Hill bill despite the fact that his critics were firmly entrenched in opposition. His plea that centralization was essential to cope with the war emergency cut no ice with them. Their usual retort was that authority had already been centralized in Washington to the point that it impeded the war effort. Ultimately, they expressed their hostility in the form of a measure sponsored jointly by Senator Bone and Congressman Martin S. Smith. Introduced on April 14, 1941, the Bone-Smith bill (S. 1852 and H.R. 5583) would have established a Columbia Power Authority independent of the Department of the Interior but based on the TVA principle of a three-man board. Norris, Lilienthal, Leland Olds, Arthur B. Langlie (Washington's governor), the Oregon State Grange, and the American Federation of Labor lined up in support of the legislation. Efforts to work out a compromise between the Hill and the Bone-Smith bills failed however, as did similar attempts in the following year.[119]

Meanwhile, the European conflict overshadowed the bureaucratic divisions within the BPA, the antagonism between Administrator Raver and the "Old Curmudgeon," and the war of attrition between PUD enthusiasts and the private-power companies. As a member of the National Power Policy and Defense Committee (NPPDC), Raver asserted vital leadership in preparing Bonneville and Grand Coulee power to be the cornerstone of an integrated defense network in the Pacific Northwest. In July 1942, the war made its greatest impact upon all prospective power legislation for the region and initiated a new, often stormy, relationship between public and private power. Under the impetus of the War Production Board, order 1-94 interconnected the federal system of Bonneville and all other major electrical systems in the area.

What Roosevelt had resisted in peacetime, as scholars have noted, the war accomplished. Although BPA officials were never very enthusiastic about the interconnection order, as federal agents they had no option except to implement it. In the Pacific Northwest, however, advocates of public power regarded interconnections as a serious threat to, if not an outright defeat of, all regional-power-authority legislation. And in Washington, D.C., Secretary Ickes perceived in the order and its sponsor, the War Production Board, further evidence that the

118. Ibid.
119. Voeltz, "Development of a Regional Power Agency," pp. 71-74, n. 45.

private utilities would employ the war emergency to subvert the national power policy.[120]

In the next chapter it will become apparent that the threat of war, from about 1938 onward, posed a serious obstacle to fulfilling the broader objectives of the public-power enthusiasts. This, in turn, made it increasingly difficult to realize the goal of a national power policy.

120. Ibid., 74-76.

CHAPTER IX

Kilowatts for Defense

Prior to the U. S. declaration of war against the Central Powers in April 1917, President Woodrow Wilson established the Council of National Defense (CND) to plan and direct a war-preparedness program.[1] The CND, however, proved to be cumbersome and unable either to devise a workable plan for assaying the nation's natural and industrial resources or to employ them effectively. Hence, in July 1917, Wilson abolished the CND and transferred its coordinating functions to a newly created War Industries Board (WIB). Bernard M. Baruch, a prominent businessman and philanthropist, assumed the leadership of the WIB and, in this capacity, exercised virtually dictatorial powers over the wartime economy.

Under Baruch's aggressive direction, the WIB quickly recognized the strategic uses of materials such as copper, lead, and zinc. The board established subdepartments for the purpose of acquiring these metals and allocating their use according to a predetermined system of priorities.[2] Inexplicably, neither the CND nor the WIB initially took steps either to ascertain the nation's electric generating capacity or to determine the energy needs of the industrial-war-material centers. Nor did they draft a schedule to govern the assignment of existing power supplies or to procure additional energy.[3] Colonel Charles Keller of the Army Corps of Engineers, in 1921, undertook to examine the reasons why the government had been so ineffectual in this area. He submitted his analysis of the wartime power shortage to Secretary of War John W. Weeks. Keller's report declared unequivocally that the basic deficiencies of the national defense power program had originated in the failure of Congress and other governmental agencies to formulate a comprehensive national power policy. Nearly a year and

1. The story of the council as seen by its secretary is told in Grosvenor B. Clarkson, *Industrial America in the World War* (Boston, 1923).

2. See Bernard M. Baruch, *American Industry in the War: A Report of the War Industries Board* (New York, 1941); and Gerald D. Nash, "Experiments in Industrial Mobilization: WIB and NRA," *Mid-America*, 45 (July 1963), 157-74.

3. Charles Keller, ed., *The Power Situation During the War* (Washington, D.C., 1921), 1.

a half into the war, the nation still had not been able "to proceed to the execution of a comprehensive program for taking care of our ascertained power needs of the near future."[4] He attributed this state of affairs to the constricted authority granted to WIB's Power Section, which functioned solely as "an investigating, planning, advisory and supervisory body" at a time when financial, labor, and business conditions rendered it increasingly more difficult for the private utilities to finance plant expansion except on prohibitive terms.[5]

Ultimately, of course, only better interconnection of the existing power facilities and the expansion of generating capacity could have ameliorated the shortage. The Power Section did order some interconnections toward the war's end, but they were too late and not on a scale to permit adjacent systems to take advantage of their diverse loads. Keller concluded, however, that the most serious obstacle had been the absence of a broadly comprehensive plan to develop and interconnect the nation's steam and hydraulic resources, "so as to serve not only the immediate war needs, but also to supply the general public in times of peace with the greatest efficiency and economy."[6]

Although the government had given little serious consideration to the construction of a unified power grid, it was a topic much in the minds of the engineers.[7] W. S. Murray, a consulting engineer from New York City, suggested in 1919 that the WIB conduct a study of the electric-power supply of the northeastern Atlantic seaboard, where the bulk of the nation's industry and population was concentrated.[8] The proposal was widely publicized and discussed but finally languished with the end of hostilities. Soon thereafter, Murray and nine other prominent engineers conducted a symposium that led to a paper which he delivered before the American Institute of Electrical Engineers. The timing of Murray's paper, which predicted enormous savings in coal from the efficient integration of the area's power supply, was opportune because, in February 1920, the United States experienced a dire shortage of fossil fuel. The crisis, in retrospect, had commenced in the last year of the war but was intensified by a wave of postwar strikes. Against this background, Congress authorized the

4. Ibid., 18.
5. Ibid., 18, 126.
6. Ibid., 13-14, 18-19.
7. Forrest McDonald, *Insull* (Chicago, 1962), vii; "Proposals of Colonel Charles Keller for Dealing with the Problems of War Power Supply," Sept. 7, 1939, Federal Power Commission Records, National Power Policy Committee File, no. 17-37 (hereafter cited as FPC Records, NPPC File).
8. See the excellent summary in Forrest McDonald, *Let There Be Light: The Electric Utility Industry in Wisconsin, 1881-1955* (Madison, 1957), 182-85.

expenditure of $125,000 for Murray and the Geological Survey to investigate the problem.[9]

Murray's report, *A Superpower System for the Region Between Boston and Washington,* was issued in June 1921 coinciding with the publication of Colonel Keller's report. In it, he described the concept of a unified electric-power supply that was to capture the imagination of the public and utility officials during the next two decades. The essence of the superpower system was the blanketing of the country with huge interconnected electric-utility systems, power being generated only in extremely large stations situated preferably at the mouths of coal mines and transported along high-voltage transmission lines or grids to the centers of consumption.[10] Both Murray's and Keller's recommendations led logically to national planning for the construction of a national power system to meet the future energy needs of the country. "There should be a close economic relation established between the generation of power, the conservation and transportation of fuel, the improvement of navigable conditions on rivers and the control of floods," Keller declared, as he requested Congress to appropriate funds and to enact legislation to give substance to a national power policy.[11]

Congress never acted upon Keller's proposal. In fact, it offered, on more than one occasion in the 1920s, to sell its wartime power facilities, notably at Muscle Shoals, to private interests. It also defeated a bill, in 1919, that would have authorized the expenditure of $175,000,000 for the construction of power plants. The reason was clear: Presidents Harding and Coolidge considered federal planning socialistic, whereas President Hoover cast a jaundiced eye upon Norris's proposals to have the federal government develop a regional power program in the Tennessee valley.[12] In the absence of federal commitment, the private-power companies had a clear field to satisfy the superpower craze that swept every city, village, hamlet, and crossroads.

Nonetheless, the near-disastrous experience of World War I was not forgotten in high government circles; Major Charles F. Lacombe, also of the Army Engineers, had observed that the unexpected collapse of the Central Powers in 1919 alone had diverted public attention from

---

9. Ibid., 182-83.
10. Ibid., 183-84.
11. Keller, *Power Situation During the War*, 21.
12. See Johnny B. Smallwood, Jr., "George W. Norris and the Concept of a Planned Region" (Ph.D. diss., University of North Carolina, 1963), esp. chs. 6 and 7.

the critical power deficit.[13] As fascism in Europe and Asia disturbed the tenuous peace of the 1930s, the recommendations of Keller and his aides conditioned the Roosevelt administration's thinking. Gradually, steps to combat another potential wartime power shortage were woven into the fabric of the New Deal's national power policy.[14]

The kaleidoscopic crises of the mid-thirties, beginning in the fall of 1935 with Italy's invasion of Ethiopia and climaxing with Hitler's outrageous demands upon Czechoslovakia in 1938, seriously undermined America's confidence in the capacity of the League of Nations to preserve peace. The deteriorating international situation, meanwhile, precipitated a sharp debate in this country between the nationalists, or the America First Committee, and the advocates of collective security on the issue of American policy toward belligerents. Despite their differences, both factions agreed that the United States, for reasons that suited their own objectives, should rebuild its defense posture but, at the same time, avoid war.[15]

Concern for the national defense even carried into the deliberations of the NARUC. It issued a warning to the nation, in 1938, to use to advantage every opportunity to increase its power-generating capacity before another world war occurred. Noting that there was a time lag before a steam or hydraulic plant went from blueprint to construction, the association warned that "it would be disastrous to await the actual coming of a war crisis to take necessary steps in this direction." The primary responsibility for averting a wartime power shortage rested, in the first instance, with the federal government, it declared, but "the Public Service Commissions of the several states are directly and deeply interested in this problem."[16]

The association's warning, if directed to the administration, was belated and somewhat superfluous. For President Roosevelt had instructed the FPC, on March 18, 1938, to cooperate with the War Department in a survey of the nation's power facilities and generating

13. Charles F. Lacombe, "Report to the Chief of Engineers, United States Army," in Keller, *Power Situation During the War*, Appendix A, 48-49.

14. For evidence see "Proposals of Colonel Charles Keller for Dealing with the Problems of War Power Supply," Sept. 7, 1939, FPC Records, NPPC File, no. 17-37; and "Federal Control of Electric Power Industry During the First World War," n.d., Leland Olds Papers, box 61, Franklin D. Roosevelt Library (hereafter cited as Olds Papers).

15. See Robert A. Divine, *The Reluctant Belligerent: American Entry Into World War II* (New York, 1965), ch. 3, p. 4.

16. National Association of Railroad and Utility Comissioners, "Report of the Committee on Generation and Distribution of Electric Power," *Proceedings* (Washington, D.C., 1938), 656.

capacity. Cautious about giving the impression that he was committing the country to a war posture, Roosevelt, nevertheless, invoked his authority as commander in chief to make certain that adequate electrical energy was available to the nation in the event of war. Four months later, having completed their inspection, the two governmental agencies submitted a confidential report. Their findings revealed the existence of a situation "so serious as to require immediate attention."[17]

The joint memorandum of the FPC and the War Department opened with a quick review of the current status of the power industry. It noted that the utility industry appeared to be recovering from the sharp economic recession of 1937, but that recovery, paradoxically, presented an obstacle to the organization of a national defense power program. "Should the durable goods industry also resume productivity in the wake of the recession," the memo stated, "there would be greater demands for electric power in 1939 and 1940, far exceeding any previous power needs and in most areas of the country exceeding the ability of the utilities to provide this power for normal peacetime uses."[18] If a wartime load were superimposed, "widespread and critical shortages of generating capacity would occur."

The experience of World War I was instructive on this point. Between late 1917 and the closing months of the war, the generation of electric power had failed to keep abreast of its demand in the highly industrialized urban centers where the war-material factories were located. Shortages of fossil fuel in the severe winter of 1917-18 had intensified the power shortage and this occasioned protests from the industries located in and around Niagara Falls, the New England states, New Jersey, Pittsburgh, and the Philadelphia-Wilmington-Baltimore industrial complex. Similar grumblings echoed from the factory centers of the Midwest and the Pacific coast.[19]

Besides the failure of advanced planning, the power crisis of World War I had been the product of other factors. Government orders for turbogenerators for the Navy and munitions plants, for example, claimed highest priority in the allocation of electrical energy thereby denying it to other vital segments of the war economy. In addition, the performance of the private utilities was less than satisfactory. All too frequently, they had been reluctant to incur the high costs of ma-

17. Federal Power Commission and War Department, "Confidential Memorandum on Shortages of Electric Generating Capacity for War-Time Needs," July 1, 1938, George W. Norris Papers, tray 72, box 2, Library of Congress (hereafter cited as Norris Papers).
18. Ibid.
19. Keller, *Power Situation During the War*, 1.

terial, labor, and interest rates characteristic of plant expansion in a period of inflation, when the demand for energy might be only temporary. The actions of state-utility commissions, particularly their rigid interpretation of regulations and reluctance to allow private utilities to increase rates as rapidly or as highly as their counterparts in other industries, had discouraged, in some instances, voluntary plant expansion. "The rate of return which would be allowed on additional investment became a controlling factor to the extent that new capital was not to be had without adequate assurances as to the soundness of the enterprise," Major Lacombe had reported.[20]

To alleviate the shortage of power in a particular center the army, navy, or the Emergency Fleet Corporation had to install generating machinery directly into the plants that held government contracts for war material. In other localities, where generating capacity was inadequate to fulfill army contracts, the secretary of war eventually prohibited the placing of new orders without the approval of the WIB's Power Section.[21] The Fuel Administration, likewise, recommended that the government let contracts only in areas where sea, rail, or road transportation was available.[22]

The WIB, by October 1918, had abandoned the effort to expand total generating capacity across the nation and resorted to the rationing of electrical energy. It arranged industries into categories according to their relative importance to the prosecution of the war, the most vital receiving top priority.[23] The remaining groups were rationed according to a complex formula and, insofar as it was used, this proved satisfactory and inconvenienced the more important industries to the smallest extent.[24] The entire procedure, however, had been makeshift and not very satisfactory, as the FPC-War Department memorandum indicated. Both agencies warned that the manufacturers of generating equipment would be unable to combat a power shortage in the event

20. Ibid., 39.
21. Ibid., 44. Lacombe wrote that the government department most interested in the output of a particular district where shortages existed "would contract for electric energy to be sold by it in turn to its contractors for supplies in such a way as to provide funds for the building and development of additional plants, parts of plants, and interconnections found necessary."
22. Ibid., 42, 68.
23. Ibid., 48. Included in the highest-priority category were the small household consumers of electricity on the theory that the possible saving of energy by curtailing their consumption would not justify the loss to morale and the industrial unrest that might occur in its wake.
24. The WIB, in addition, appointed power administrators for the Niagara Falls and Pittsburgh regions, and President Wilson requisitioned the entire output of the Hydraulic and Niagara Falls power companies. See ibid., 51.

of war unless the government initiated immediately an accelerated program of plant expansion and placed orders for new generators.

Most of the war material required to meet the needs of the national defense emanated from the expansion of existing industrial plants rather than from the construction of new ones. Geographically, the nation's war-industries complex was located east of the Mississippi River and north of the state of Tennessee. Within this triangle, and with the addition of heavily industrialized St. Louis, Missouri, and Birmingham, Alabama, were the fifteen principal centers for the production of war material. Together they accounted for 45 percent of the total installed capacity of the United States. Taking these facts into consideration, the FPC and the War Department recommended that the available power load be diversified as far as possible among existing plants and factories within this critical area, and that priority be accorded to plants contracted to produce war material.

Both agencies agreed that, if war were to come to the United States, the crucial year probably would be 1940. If the world did not go up in flames before then, the chances were good that the United States could continue along its peaceful course. Even then, however, it still had to meet the increased demand for power that the normal growth of the economy and the population would necessitate. The FPC estimated this at 1,146,000 kilowatts, but if the country was at war in 1940, closer to 5,000,000 kilowatts of power would be required to supply the fifteen centers. Financing normal growth of the system was calculated at $172 million, but this figure would sharply rise in the event of war to a staggering $733 million.

The consequences of not having available the additional power in the war-material centers were far too serious even to contemplate. The nation would have to resort to costly and uneconomic alternatives, the FPC and War Department noted. War orders, for example, would have to be reallocated to industrial plants where surplus power existed, but which were less suitable for production or remote from the major centers of transportation and communication. "Doubt may be expressed that such expedients, at whatever cost, could fill the need," their memo stated. "It is possible that the shortage of power may be a limiting factor in a national effort to meet a major emergency."

In addition, rapid expansion of power capacity was hindered by a more immediate impediment. Three plants, General Electric, Westinghouse, and Allis-Chalmers, produced 95 percent of the steam turbines and generators for the utility industry. A sharp recession in 1937, unfortunately, had compelled the private utilities to suspend or cancel orders for additional generating equipment. The manufacturers, in turn, were in the process of laying off their highly skilled employees. If this situation continued, a crisis would develop in the industry's ability to expand its generating capacity to meet either wartime or peacetime needs. "If additional orders are not received, and work on suspended orders is not resumed within the next few months," both agencies warned, "the manufacturers indicate that they will probably lay off first, apprentice labor, and second skilled labors and designers; with the result that when the expected period of rapidly expanding business in 1939 and 1940 is reached, it would find the principle [*sic*] manufacturers of this equipment without adequate skilled labor to turn out this machinery as rapidly as needed. If this country should become involved in a major war, the situation would be critical."[25]

The FPC and the War Department were determined to avert this crisis. They recommended that the federal government initiate a series of conferences with the manufacturers of generating equipment and also with representatives of the major public- and private-utility systems serving each of the fifteen war-material centers. In cooperation with the government they were to ascertain their present and future power requirements so that steps could be taken to insure an adequate power supply for national defense.

The problem of financing plant expansion, which had been a major obstacle during the first war, also was anticipated. Both agencies proposed to utilize financial "pump-priming" techniques to underwrite the costs of expanding power capacity.[26] They recommended that the federal government place orders with the manufacturers of generating equipment for the machinery to construct modern standardized steam plants. Financing this equipment was to come from RFC loans to a public corporation established for this specific purpose. The equipment then would be leased to private industry. An alternative proposal was to have the RFC simply make the loans directly to the utilities for plant expansion.

From 1938 until the outbreak of war in December 1941 this latter proposal was the source of bitter dispute within the administration. Key figures in the public-power movement, especially Interior Secretary Ickes, believed that private industry would use the government's money and the war emergency to undermine the New Deal's power

25. FPC-War Department, "Confidential Memorandum on Shortages of Electric Generating Capacity for War-Time Needs," July 1, 1938, Norris Papers, tray 72, box 2.

26. See, FPC-War Department, "Confidential Memorandum, Temporary War Reserve of Electric Power," n.d., Norris Papers, tray 72, box 2.

program. World War I had demonstrated that the possibility certainly existed and the threat could not be ignored or minimized.[27] Other government officials in the FPC and in the TVA weighed it against what they perceived to be a more serious danger—confronting the nation with a major war without its having the electric energy to run the defense industries.

Two rival plans for insuring an adequate power supply emerged in the summer of 1938. One, sponsored by the FPC, contemplated the construction of an interconnected network of high-capacity transmission lines, supplemented by the expansion of hydroelectric and steam-electric power. For the latter objective the FPC expected to utilize the St. Lawrence, the Niagara, the Great Lakes, the Susquehanna, and the Tennessee waterways. The other, advocated by the army and the navy, proposed to eliminate the more expensive high-voltage network in favor of a plan to increase generating capacity by building new steam plants in each of the fifteen centers. The War Department believed that the surplus funds could better be employed in rearming the army and the navy, a task which certainly deserved high priority. The FPC, however, objected to the elimination of the grid system and further argued that it could see no reason why its more comprehensive program should be sacrificed because in the past the military had done a poor job of looking after its armaments.[28]

The FPC's plan gradually emerged as the preferred approach. It was more comprehensive in scope and more dutifully attentive to the economics of the problem in the long run. "It is a national power policy—logical, practical, serving the needs of peace and ready for the emergency of war," the commission argued in clinching its case. Its plan did not simply take into account a war situation but was drafted as the superstructure "for a continuing national power program adaptable to meet any peacetime needs that may hereafter arise." An equally important consideration bearing upon the selection of the FPC's proposal was that it preserved the government's stake in the power field. "The network," it declared flatly, "should be constructed, maintained and operated by the Federal Government as a national defense measure and operate as a common carrier system during peacetime, transmitting power between industrial centers and between sources of power supply

27. See Paul A. C. Koistinen, "The 'Industrial-Military Complex' in Historical Perspective: World War I," *Business History Review,* 41 (Winter 1967), 378-403; and Robert Cuff, "A Dollar-a-Year Man in Government: George N. Peek and the War Industries Board," ibid., 404-20.

28. "Memorandum to the National Defense Power Committee," Aug. 12, 1938, Olds Papers, box 61.

and market.'' To round off its case the commission proposed that the federal and state governments join hands in building hydroelectric plants, leaving to private industry, assisted by low-interest RFC loans, the construction of steam plants in the coal fields.

The commission was careful here also to protect the government's interest in power. There was no reason why the private-utility companies could not enter the field of hydroelectric production, if the federal government were given prior jurisdiction over the use of such power in wartime. The War Department conceivably could use its own engineers to construct the plants and then lease them to the utilities. Whichever program was finally adopted it still would take up to five years to complete. Therefore, both the War Department and the FPC urged the president to submit enabling legislation to the Congress without further delay.[29]

This was the extent of progress made down to September 1, 1938. On that date President Roosevelt convened a conference at the White House to establish a more formal apparatus to plan the national defense power program. The National Defense Power Committee (NDPC) was established to examine the proposals of the various agencies concerned and was instructed to draft enabling legislation and to recommend budgetary appropriations.[30] Its chairman was Louis Johnson, the assistant secretary of war. Johnson's appointment reflected both the military implications of the power issue and his temporary ascendancy in government circles in matters relating to the national defense.[31]

The White House conference, followed by newspaper speculation about a power shortage, inevitably captured the interest of the leaders of the public-power movement in and out of the government. They viewed the national defense power issue as a mixed blessing. On September 8, 1938, Judson King of the National Popular Government League wrote a long letter to Senator George W. Norris, the foremost proponent of public power in the country. The recent talk concerning a national defense power network, King observed, "has equal pos-

29. FPC-War Department, "Confidential Memorandum on Power Program for National Defense," Aug. 12, 1938, Norris Papers, tray 72, box 2.

30. Louis Johnson to George W. Norris, Sept. 7, 1938, Norris Papers, tray 72, box 2; "Committee to Study Power Supply Facilities for War Emergency," Electrical World, 110 (Sept. 17, 1938), 7. Other members of the NDPC included Frederic A. Delano of the National Resources Committee, Secretary Ickes, Power Commissioner Basil Manly, SEC Commissioner William O. Douglas, and Assistant Secretary of the Navy Charles Edison.

31. Eliot Janeway, The Struggle for Survival (New Haven, 1951), 26.

sibility for good and for evil, depending on how it is handled."[32] He was inclined to be pessimistic, however, fearing that the utilities would use the war emergency to foist on the public again the already discredited "pooling" plan.[33] Unlike the British, who meant by pooling the fusing of public and private agencies under the management and control of a joint board, the private utilities looked upon it as a license to dominate the superpower network for their own benefit. King therefore advised Norris to remain alert for any sign of a power grab.

From sources present at the White House conference King also had been informed that no consideration was given to two questions of critical import for the public-power movement: What would be done with the reserve power in peacetime, and what would be the fate of the transmission network in the event there was no war? Speaking for an important segment of the public-power community, he declared that the states, municipalities, and agricultural cooperatives ought to have "preferential right" to use the grid. This apparently was not to be the case however, because an engineer connected with the project, who also was anonymous and who shared their philosophy, informed King that the government was planning to sell publicly produced power under contract to private utilities. If this information was correct, and King had no reason to doubt it, it would put "a hell of a crimp" in the public-power movement.

Reflecting upon the matter privately, the director of the National Popular Government League found it difficult to believe that President Roosevelt would consent to such a scheme. "On the other hand," he noted, "since it would save the private utilities millions of dollars for investment for new plants and slow down the public ownership program, they would be bold enough to attempt it and they would have the help of a lot of men inside the Government." At the very least, King admonished Norris, there was "enough queer stuff going on to put us on guard, to watch this thing just as carefully as we did the pool business."[34]

As the NDPC organized, the public-power men watched nervously, looking for the slightest hint that the private-power companies were ready to move under the guise of the emergency to undo the New Deal's program. On September 26, 1938, with the Sudeten crisis hanging fire, the NDPC arrived at three important decisions: to review at

32. Judson King to Norris, Sept. 8, 1938, Judson King Papers, box 18, Library of Congress (hereafter cited as King Papers).
33. King to J. D. Ross, Mar. 24, 1938, King Papers, box 19.
34. King to Norris, Sept. 8, 1938, King Papers, box 18.

once the scope of its task, to speed to completion the investigatory studies initiated by the War Department and the FPC, and to consult with representatives of the utilities in the war-material centers in order to avert a shortage.[35] Meanwhile, on October 12, the Federal Emergency Relief Administration of the PWA entered the picture. It announced the allocation of $200,000 to study the feasibility of constructing a public-works power network.

The decision to involve private industry in the defense power program and the later announcement of the PWA alarmed the public-power faction. John W. Scott, an FPC commissioner and acquaintance of Judson King, was alarmed, fearing that a conspiracy was in the making to elbow aside the public-power group's interest. He wrote to King advising him that the time was ripe "to make inquiry at Army and P.W.A. as to the plan and to get the Thermopolye Boys busy."[36] King's response took the form of a confidential memorandum to thirty or forty influential people revealing what allegedly were the "true facts" about the defense emergency. In addition, he used the National Popular Government League's bulletin to alert public-power proponents to this latest insidious power grab.[37]

At the root of this suspicion was the fact that the public-power men never trusted Louis Johnson. Johnson had been a commander of the American Legion, a corporation lawyer, and the West Virginia associate of New Deal Senator Harley Kilgore. Roosevelt appointed him assistant secretary of the army in 1938 to rejuvenate the War Department. From that office he came to direct the NDPC. Politically Johnson was somewhat reckless, and under his chairmanship the committee was becoming almost a partnership between himself and the most suspect figures in the utility industry.[38] The public-power groups were absolutely certain that he was deceiving the president and was supplying the Power Trust with the information that they were currently using to create the elaborate propaganda campaign for "peace with the power companies." King's informant implied that Johnson was to blame for misrepresenting the power emergency. "I won't go into details," King wrote to Senator Norris, "but simply say that the facts revealed bear out your prediction that the power trust would move

35. "Agenda for September 26 Meeting ... On Power for National Defense," Sept. 24, 1938, National Archives, Record Group 48, National Defense Power Committee Files, 1938-1941, General File, box 8, folder 107 (hereafter cited as NDPC Files, GF).
36. John W. Scott to Judson King, Oct. 12, 1938, King Papers, box 18.
37. King to Scott, Oct. 18, 1938, King Papers, box 18.
38. Janeway, *Struggle for Survival,* 26, 69-71.

heaven and earth to horn in on this national defense necessity."[39] In the end King fully expected them to double-cross the president.

The European crisis that was unfolding late in the autumn of 1938 overshadowed his warnings. It also was responsible for promoting regular conferences of the NDPC in order to hasten power planning. On September 27, 1938, the committee met; the presence of Thomas G. Corcoran, the president's representative, suggested the urgency of the problem. Johnson's opening remark, that the "situation gets worse the deeper we get into the picture," conveys the gloom that prevailed at the conference.

In the course of the meeting a division of opinion materialized. The chief point of contention was whether and to what extent the federal government or private enterprise should assume the burden of financing the defense power network. The earlier doubts clearly had not been resolved. Nevertheless, Johnson argued that private enterprise basically should undertake the financing and constructing of the network, with as little duplication of facilities as possible by the federal government. He was well aware that he was going out on a limb. As an olive branch to the spokesmen for the public interest on the committee, he requested the members to authorize him to inform the private-power companies that their work "has got to be done under the most minute and exact governmental supervision," because ultimately it would have a bearing upon the rates paid by the consumer.

Two of the more outspoken proponents of public power at the conference, Basil Manly of the FPC and Secretary of the Interior Ickes, questioned the feasibility of Johnson's proposal. Manly, more so than Ickes, conceded that the private utilities would have to participate in the program of necessity, but neither one was as optimistic as Johnson about the extent of cooperation the government would receive. Ickes was convinced that the utilities would demand a *quid pro quo:* a promise from the government to discourage future municipal-ownership movements. This could have a detrimental impact upon such programs as the one currently underway at Bonneville. Johnson, however, prided himself on his extensive and influential contacts in the business community, and assured the committee that such promises would not be forthcoming. "We aren't going to make any deals with any of these utilities whereby this Committee is going to undertake to work out any of their other governmental problems," he declared. Ickes, for the moment at least, was inclined to go along with Johnson's idea, for he shrewdly perceived that, once the industry had been appealed

39. King to Norris, Oct. 28, 1938, King Papers, box 18.

to in the name of patriotism and national defense, it "would be in a bad position to refuse cooperation."

Finally the committee drew up a list of key executives in the private-utility industry with whom it should confer. The lingering distrust, born of frequent conflict since 1933, still existed. Only utility men cleared by the SEC and from whom the government might expect fair play were invited to come to Washington. Corcoran suggested that Johnson ought personally to telephone each official and arrange a meeting for the following day. It was clear that he still harbored some misgivings because he commented that a conference as quickly as possible would prevent the industry from coordinating its strategy *against* the government. In this atmosphere of suspicion and doubt the meeting took place.[40]

On September 28, 1938, representatives of the private utilities met in Washington with Johnson and the NDPC. Some of the more prominent utility executives, including C. F. Groesbeck of Electric Bond and Share and Wendell L. Willkie of the Commonwealth and Southern Corporation, were excluded. Although the atmosphere was relaxed, almost cordial, it soon was evident that the industry feared the government was using the war emergency to expand its regulatory powers. To set their minds at ease on this point Power Commissioner Manly assured the executives that the FPC was authorized to effect temporary interconnections without changing the intrastate character of individual systems. Therefore there was no reason to fear that intrastate companies would come under the permanent jurisdiction of the Public Utility Holding Company Act. Their other main concern was that, if war did not occur, the emergency expansion of plant capacity, with the huge investment of capital that entailed, might prove to be an economic liability. Hobart Porter of the American Water Works and Electric Company thereupon suggested that the government might finance, build, and lease new generating units to the private utilities until such time as their loads justified purchase by the industry. At that point Corcoran revealed to those present that the RFC was considering the possibility of financing plant expansion, although a firm decision had not yet been made.[41]

For the remainder of the year the question of who should finance plant expansion and on what terms was the primary obstacle to industry-

40. "Minutes of the Meeting, September 27, 1938," NDPC Files, GF, box 108, folder 107.

41. "Record of Conference with Utility Executives, Sept. 28, 1938," NDPC Files, GF, box 108, folder 107.

government cooperation. The utilities wanted to protect themselves from overexpansion financially and in the construction of new plants. On the other hand, they also tended to underestimate the normal increase in consumer demand for electric power. In October, Floyd L. Carlisle of the Niagara-Hudson Power Corporation moved to break the stalemate, this time proposing that the RFC finance the expansion program on terms comparable to the public sale of bonds.[42] In November, J. C. Damon, another utility official, told Commissioner William O. Douglas of the SEC that the industry looked upon the financial provisions of the Public Utility Holding Company Act as an obstacle to its cooperation in the defense program.[43] Investors, he wrote, were reluctant to add higher fixed charges to their investments for power that would be used only in the event of war. At the very least, they would demand a rate increase to offset any financial burdens. The committee agreed to take these matters under advisement and, late in 1938, established a subcommittee of Douglas, Manly, and Ben Cohen, one of the architects of the holding company act, to delve into the feasibility of RFC financing.

A second obstacle to cooperation resulted from the fact that the public-ownership movement had entered a new phase. Vigorously expanding, it no longer justified itself simply as a reform. Its proponents now affirmed that the movement was indispensable to the national security. This development startled a number of utility executives who had never accepted the New Deal's power program to begin with. There was some indication that they were willing to cooperate with the NDPC, if it could be manipulated in such a way as to divert the public-power movement. Indeed, the entire response of the industry was ambivalent: behind the scenes most utility men were anxious to cooperate in the defense program but, for public consumption, the industry adhered to the position that it possessed all the resources to meet the nation's power requirements in the event of war. It did not deviate from this public position until the war exposed the emptiness of this boast.[44]

To the public-power people this claim was further evidence of the industry's irresponsibility. Commissioner Scott called Judson King's attention to an article in the *Washington Times*. A survey of the nation's

---

42. "Minutes of the Meeting, October 25, 1938," in ibid.
43. J. C. Damon to William O. Douglas, Nov. 26, 1938, in ibid. See also, "Government Competition Still Threat to Utilities," *Electrical World*, 112 (Oct. 21, 1939), 1173, which suggests that the industry never fully conquered its fear.
44. Janeway, *Struggle for Survival*, 234-35.

power resources for an emergency, it reported, was expected "to force a sharp change in S.E.C. efforts to impose the 'death sentence' on scattered utility groups." This conviction prevailed apparently among a number of utility executives, although the administration had done nothing to give it credence. If anything, the president was intent upon implementing the holding-company legislation. Yet neither Scott nor King, whose fears of a sellout persisted, was satisfied. Indeed, Scott warned King that "eternal vigilance is the price of safety."[45]

Within the NDPC, members expressed a similar concern. On October 13, 1938, Johnson assured Ickes that the utilities would not be permitted to use the war emergency to undermine the New Deal's power program. "We have kept steadily in mind and have definitely advised the representatives of the utilities that, in any plan by which the Government would aid in providing new generating capacity, either by lease or otherwise, provision would be made for the protection of consumers, both as to rates and service," he wrote.[46]

Johnson's explanation was not wholly acceptable to the members, and the committee vetoed his suggestion that he arrange a press conference to announce the existence of a rapprochement between the government and the industry. More and more, he was losing touch with the committee's true sentiments.[47] On November 3, 1938, to cite one example, Leland Olds recorded the details of his conversation with J. D. Ross and Judson King. Both men "felt emphatically" that any power facilities built with government money should be owned and controlled wholly by the government. They were realists, however, and recognized the folly of attempting to thwart the defense power program for the sake of "some completely idealistic conception of a public power system." Ross suggested, and King agreed, that they use their influence to write into the committee's final plans safeguards to protect the "forward movement" toward public power during the war emergency.[48]

While King was consulting with Johnson, corresponding with Scott, and speaking with Olds, he was keeping Senator Norris apprised of

45. See the *Washington Times,* Sept. 13, 1938, newspaper clipping, and Scott to King, Oct. 12, 1938, in King Papers, box 18. In fact, however, President Roosevelt in 1940 instructed the SEC to begin "death-sentence" proceedings against Electric Bond and Share. See "Defense Work Won't Halt Death Sentence," *Electrical World,* 114 (July 27, 1940), 222; and the *Wall Street Journal,* June 18, 1940.

46. Johnson to Ickes, Oct. 13, 1938, NDPC Files, GF, box 8, folder 107.

47. "Minutes of the Meeting of October 25, 1938," in ibid.

48. Olds, "Memorandum of Conversation with J. D. Ross and Judson King," Nov. 3, 1938, Olds Papers, box 61.

the committee's work. On November 3, 1938, his vigilance returned dividends. Writing from McCook, Nebraska, Norris raised the whole issue of the committee's work and the administration's power policy in a letter to President Roosevelt.[49] From newspaper articles appearing in the *Wall Street Journal,* the *Journal of Commerce,* the *Baltimore Sun,* and the *New York Times,* the senator was led to believe that the public interest in the national defense power emergency was being treated in a cavalier manner. The articles, he wrote, "clearly indicate that the plan about to be proposed to you does not take into consideration any expansion of the Government utility development but the thing seems to be that the private companies shall make the development with Government aid." If the reports were accurate, he declared, the president seemingly had backtracked on his initial thinking. The expansion of the public-power sector, particularly the Gilbertsville Dam on the Tennessee River, had been envisioned in preliminary planning. Judging again from press accounts, Norris concluded that the administration had decided to forgo making public power an integral part of the defense program. "In other words, it narrows down to the proposal of the Government loaning money through the RFC to the private utility companies." Had Roosevelt forgotten that it was the private-power companies who cost the government millions of dollars litigating the TVA? "I hope," he admonished, "no approval to any plan will be given by you which is one-sided and unjust to the Government."[50]

Norris sent a carbon of his letter to King who read it with "great pleasure." In response he wrote to Norris that Ross, Olds, and Frank Walsh of the FPC were strongly opposed to lending money to the utilities or going into partnership with them if it might subvert the New Deal's power policy. The private utilities were perfectly free to finance their role in the defense power program, he observed, but the federal government must continue to supervise them.[51]

King's commentary and Leland Olds's memorandum of a conference with Louis Johnson on November 3, 1938, provide a detailed account of the progress made by the government in its efforts to bring the industry into defense planning. Olds had asked Johnson whether the publicly announced decision of the utilities on October 28 to construct one million kilowatts of new capacity to meet peacetime requirements

49. Norris to Roosevelt, Nov. 3, 1938, FPC Records, NPPC File, no. 17-37.
50. Ibid. See "RFC Ready to Lend Utilities $250,000,000 for Program," *Electrical World,* 110 (Nov. 12, 1938), 1380.
51. See King, "Memorandum Re: Letter of Senator Norris to President Roosevelt," Nov. 3, 1938, and King to Norris, Nov. 9, 1938, King Papers, box 18.

represented any real concession on their part. He suspected that it might have been a play for public support and that they intended to expand their generating capacity in any event. Johnson emphatically declared that their action represented the first break in the industry's front against the president. Until now, it had not undertaken much plant expansion, even though the curtailing of service threatened the welfare of the communities for which the utilities were responsible. Private-power companies, Johnson noted, had discontinued orders for turbines, generators, and other electrical equipment. This practice was followed by a number of companies that could well have afforded to invest in plant expansion despite the depression. Given this situation, he told Olds, the NDPC bluntly told the companies that they would have to assume collective responsibility for the immediate completion of a program to provide an additional one million kilowatts of power.

Olds's memorandum shed light on the tension that existed between the industry and the administration. The executives of the privately owned utilities, Johnson stated, at first had balked at the government's insistence that the industry assume collective responsibility. They had wanted each local company to be held accountable for producing its share of the added power without reference to other companies in adjacent geographic areas. The committee rejected this plan outright, Olds was informed, and warned the industry that, if it did not act in concert, the federal government was prepared to finance, construct, and operate its own power plants in direct competition. It was warned also that the regulatory agencies, meaning primarily the FPC, would stretch their powers to the extent that it was necessary to prevent a power shortage. Finally, skilled electrical workers also were not going to be laid off. In the face of these bold threats, opposition collapsed. The committee, Johnson concluded, had made no other concessions to the utilities.[52]

Essentially Roosevelt passed on the same information to Norris. On November 10, 1938, the FPC's staff drafted a reply for the president's signature. Branding the newspaper accounts "completely misleading" and "entirely erroneous," the tone of the letter was conciliatory and retraced the administration's relations with the power industry. Since the onset of the depression, the private utilities had constructed few generating plants in the war-material centers, but now the NDPC had decided to have "a showdown with the utilities as to their ability and willingness to finance and construct the generating plants" to meet

52. Olds, "Memorandum of Conference with ... Louis Johnson," Nov. 3, 1938, Olds Papers, box 61.

consumer and defense needs. Some companies, Roosevelt wrote, had indicated that they would need financial assistance from the government. They were instructed to apply to the RFC for loans which would be granted "only where there is a clear showing that a government loan is justified and that the utility company cannot finance necessary construction from its own resources or by the sale of securities in the open market."

The Nebraskan also was advised that the federal government distinguished between peacetime and wartime power requirements. In the latter circumstance, Norris was told, the government unambiguously saw its responsibility and intended to pursue an expanded program on the Tennessee, St. Lawrence, and Niagara rivers. Norris had not read this in the newspapers because the NDPC was unwilling to disclose this phase of its program before presenting it to Congress. "On the basis of past experience they felt that to do so would only subject it to attacks and distortion by the utility propagandists and make more difficult its consideration by Congress."

The president's letter apparently satisfied Norris and Olds that the administration was not sacrificing its power program to the war emergency. Olds, nevertheless, reiterated to Johnson that he must be careful not to make any commitments detrimental to the president's power policy for the public-power people already were in a highly agitated state. "I pointed out," he wrote later, "that in terms of the eventual success of the necessary legislation every effort should be made to carry the public power group along, because if they believed the program had elements contrary to the governmental interest in power, they represented sufficient strength to defeat legislation in Congress."[53] Johnson replied that, with Corcoran looking over his shoulder, the president's power policy was in no danger of being compromised.[54]

During the winter of 1938, Olds became more closely involved in defense power planning. Ben Cohen, speaking on December 20, 1938, for Ickes and himself, asked Olds to participate in future conferences of the NDPC in order to lend his expertise to matters bearing on policy. Olds assumed responsibility for interpreting the FPC's technical data, but the committee also expected him to offer recommendations for disposing of the high-transmission network in the event that war

---

53. Roosevelt, "Memo to FPC, Nov. 8, 1939"; FPC Staff, "Draft of Reply for Signature of the President," Nov. 10, 1938. FPC Records, NPPC File, no. 17-37.
54. Olds, "Memorandum of Conference with ... Louis Johnson," Nov. 3, 1938, Olds Papers, box 61.

did not occur.[55] Resolution of this issue, he recognized, would exercise a determining influence on the direction of the New Deal's power policy and on the government's relations with the private utilities.

He had barely received this assignment before the FPC's engineers thrust before him their own solution. Under the direction of Thomas R. Tate, the engineers had prepared a series of confidential working papers. They concluded that Congress should incorporate a Defense Power Corporation, wholly owned and operated by the federal government, to produce power for defense needs.[56] Private industry figured hardly at all in their calculations, except that the corporation would use public and private companies as distribution outlets.

The plan, if adopted, presaged a radical shift in the relationship between the industry and the government and in the structure of private enterprise as traditionally conceived by the utility industry. Perceiving this, Olds cautiously backed away from their recommendations, declaring that the NDPC "needed a more concrete picture of alternative plans as a basis for any decision."

In the interim, Power Commissioner Manly cut through the bureaucratic red tape that delayed Olds's investigation. Johnson permitted him to examine the committee's confidential data so that he would have a basis for offering informed recommendations. After a long and difficult week studying and analyzing reports, charts, and production figures, Olds presented his own assessment of the situation to Manly. The national defense power network, he wrote, would demonstrate its economic feasibility in peacetime only to the extent that it also provided for the development of hydroelectric power. The federal government would have to expand the TVA and utilize more fully power from the St. Lawrence, Niagara, Susquehanna, and Cumberland rivers. Such a network, relying heavily upon the expansion of steam-generating capacity, he added, would cost the taxpayer a great sum of money.

Olds sent an identical recommendation to Cohen for transmittal to the NDPC. He emphasized that his recommendations went beyond what the committee had been considering and admitted that the cost of the program was in excess of the sums originally projected. But

55. See Olds, "Memorandum ... with Reference to the NDPC," Jan. 23, 1939, in ibid.

56. Thomas R. Tate to the Program Subcommittee of the NDPC, Dec. 13, 1938; "Outline of an Organization to Design, Conduct, and Operate a National Defense Network," Dec. 15, 1938; Scott to Federal Power Commissioners, Dec. 23, 1938, in FPC Records, NPPC File, no. 17-37.

Olds insisted that the use of hydroelectricity would prove the more economical, on an annual-cost basis, to the United States.

Cohen conceded that Olds's recommendations were sound, but they were also too expensive for the administration. Because of the state of mind of Congress and the people, he observed, such expenditures were "politically impossible." Olds suggested that, if politics was the only consideration, the president should bypass Congress and take his plan directly to the people. Cohen disagreed and, as a result, Olds's report never came before the committee.[57]

As the international situation deteriorated in the spring of 1939, the NDPC moved briskly to complete its survey of wartime-power requirements. Johnson had hoped to deliver his report to the president quickly, but he failed because of dissension within the committee and delays by essential industries in reporting their projected power needs. "Nevertheless," he wrote to Power Commissioner Clyde L. Seavey in April 1939, "it is of vital importance from a national standpoint that this work should be completed, if it is humanly possible, within the next two months."[58]

While Johnson pushed the committee to complete its work, his own position grew increasingly vulnerable. Gradually at first, and then with sheer boldness, Secretary of the Interior Ickes challenged his command of the defense power program. The ploy he used was to persuade the president to resurrect the NPPC, the executive committee that had been suspended since 1936.[59] Ickes, as secretary of the interior, was chairman of the NPPC. With assistance from Cohen, the legal counsel for both the Interior Department and the NDPC, Ickes's Machiavellian stratagem succeeded. On June 16, 1939, Cohen drafted an executive order for the president's signature. It centralized in the Department of the Interior the work of all government bureaus and committees involved in peacetime and wartime power planning. To soften the blow Cohen shrewdly had the order redesignate the NPPC as the National Power Policy and Defense Committee (NPPDC).[60] This was the first clear indication that Ickes wanted the president

57. Olds, "Memorandum ... with Reference to the NDPC," Jan. 23, 1939, Olds Papers, box 61.

58. Johnson to Seavey, Apr. 27, 1939, FPC Records, NPPC File, no. 17-37.

59. See above, ch. 2.

60. "Draft of Executive Order ... Establishing a National Power Policy and Defense Committee," June 16, 1939, National Archives, Record Group 48, Department of the Interior Records, General Administrative File 1-288, pt. 4 (hereafter cited as Interior Department Records, GAF).

to appoint him "power czar," with exclusive jurisdiction over matters hitherto dispersed among various government agencies.[61]

When conservation or the future of public power was at issue, Ickes responded almost instinctively. The utility industry, according to him, intended to take advantage of the war emergency in order to place its henchmen in key governmental agencies. From these posts they would undermine the president's power policy. David E. Lilienthal, Olds, Johnson—even Norris, Ickes feared—had been duped. After years of fighting the industry tooth and nail, especially the Chicago Insulls, he could not conceive of circumstances in which its executives might sincerely cooperate with the government.[62]

Ickes's maneuvering succeeded in part because of the hostility of the public-power people toward Johnson and the near completion of the power surveys. Johnson himself surmized that the NDPC's future was precarious and, despite evidence to the contrary, wrote to Seavey that the members had brought their work to a "successful conclusion."[63] President Roosevelt, in October 1939, transferred the committee's functions *in toto* to the newly christened NPPDC. Johnson was efficiently dispatched from his chairmanship and Ickes accepted the mandate to pursue "immediate concrete action necessary to meet power needs as estimated by the National Defense Power Committee."[64]

The secretary's naked grab for power sowed discord throughout the administration. It was the catalytic agent that bared the divergent attitudes toward public power held by architects of the New Deal's policies. Ickes sought to use the war emergency to direct the forward momentum of the public-power movement. He equated its progress with the interest of his own office, and he regarded the heads of independent agencies as opponents. This was unfortunate because Olds, Lilienthal, and Norris were fully cognizant that war might destroy the public-power movement. Nor did they have any illusions about the willingness of the utilities to cooperate. But national defense held priority over public power; and, if the government had to enlist the

61. This conclusion is based upon a reading of the extensive correspondence in the Harold L. Ickes Papers, Library of Congress.

62. M. Judd Harmon, "Some Contributions of Harold L. Ickes," *Western Political Quarterly,* 7 (June 1954), 238-44.

63. Johnson to Seavey, July 1, 1939, FPC Records, NPPC File, no. 17-37.

64. Roosevelt to Ickes, Oct. 13, 1939, Interior Department Records, GAF 1-288, pt. 4.

aid of the industry in order to expand generating capacity, they voted to incur the risk. Besides, at the moment Ickes's empire building seemed the greater threat.[65]

While this bureaucratic infighting raged, control of the program threatened to become an end in itself. Ickes was not able to pick up where Johnson had left off; the merger of the two committees simply compounded fundamental differences of opinion. Olds, who became vice-chairman under Ickes, continued to confer with the utilities on the matter of interconnections. He and Lilienthal preferred to secure their voluntary cooperation, whereas Ickes did not hesitate to threaten them with the big stick.

The NPPDC, meanwhile, weighed possible courses of action under existing statutes to speed the interconnections. Cohen noted that under section 202-c of the Water Power Act the FPC, upon a declaration of war or national emergency, could order "such temporary interconnections of facilities and such generation, delivery, interchange, or transmission of electrical energy as in its judgment will best meet the emergency." Although neither state actually existed in 1939, Cohen thought that the purposes of section 202-c could still be accomplished if the private utilities collaborated willingly. Olds was more hopeful that the private-power companies would cooperate. "In other words," he reported to the FPC, "the foundations might be laid, for carrying out this provision, by negotiations directed to securing the voluntary action by the companies." He conceded, however, that the commission could, as a last resort, exercise its authority to compel connections and "a closer approach to the integrated operation."[66]

In the winter of 1939-40, the NPPDC held formal conferences with utility representatives from the war-material centers. As chairman, Ickes struck a note of cordiality whenever he welcomed the delegates; but more than once he implied that the government would enter the power business if necessary. "I need not add," he concluded his address of December 5, "that the more the industry is prepared to do to meet this problem of national defense, the less the government eventually will have to do."[67] Away from the conference table, he continued his running feud with the Chamber of Commerce, going as far as to impugn its patriotism. He accused its directors of promoting

65. David E. Lilienthal, *The Journals of David E. Lilienthal,* 5 vols. (New York, 1964-71), I, 366.

66. Olds to Federal Power Commissioners, Oct. 24, 1939, FPC Records, NPPC File, no. 17-37.

67. See Ickes's speech of Dec. 5, 1939, to utility representatives in ibid.

hostility between the industry and the government for reasons best known to themselves.[68]

Minor irritations aside, the conferences progressed smoothly through the new year. Even Ickes felt obliged to remark to the president on the cooperation that the committee was receiving, although privately he and the engineering staff believed that the power companies were too conservative in their estimate of wartime power requirements. They also continued to be skeptical of the economic feasibility of the high-transmission network, but did not flatly rule it out.[69] This was a remarkable admission from one who congenitally distrusted the private-power interests.

Nevertheless, the discussions also revealed that fundamental and possibly irreconcilable differences existed. Neither side appeared prepared to sacrifice what it considered basic to its interests. On March 12, 1940, for example, the industry's leaders held a private dinner conference in New York City to which they invited Olds, Cohen, and a government engineer, E. F. Scattergood. Their reservations about constructing the high-transmission network differed little from those put forth a year earlier. A few were skeptical that it could be built in time to meet an emergency; some questioned the economic feasibility of the idea; and others pointed to the problems of integrating it into existing systems. Behind each question was the fear that the agency administering the program would become another regulatory body and extend its tentacles to rate-making. Olds, Cohen, and finally Scattergood tried to convince them otherwise; but when the evening ended the only concession they received was the industry's promise to restudy the proposal.[70]

Nevertheless, the NPPDC decided to forge ahead with its report for the president. Jerome Frank of the SEC and REA Administrator John Carmody made some last minute suggestions which found their way into the report. On May 28, 1940, the document was completed; the committee's recommendations complemented the administration's power policy as it had evolved since 1933 in public statements, statutes, and the rulings of regulatory agencies. The report consisted of eleven interrelated points, each of which was intended to assure the nation

68. The Chamber of Commerce held consistently to the position that private enterprise was fully able to meet wartime power needs without government interference. See Ickes to U.S. Chamber of Commerce, Dec. 12, 1939, Interior Department Records, GAF 1-288, pts. 3-4.

69. See the memorandum marked "Confidential," Ickes to Roosevelt, Feb. 1, 1940, in ibid.

70. Minutes of the Meeting of Apr. 2, 1940, Olds Papers, box 61.

of an adequate power supply in a national emergency. Part one gave to the president sweeping authority to plan, finance, and construct an integrated network and to require private industry, where necessary, to participate in order to insure a continuous and reliable supply of power to industrial centers. Part two of the report recommended that the committee appoint a special adviser who was also a technically trained executive in good standing with the private utilities. His function was to advise the agency administering the program. "He would not function as a representative of the power industry, but would be expected to place his experience in the private field at the service of the government on a full-time basis."[71]

The report had not reached the president's hands before personal and ancient bureaucratic divisions within the NPPDC flared anew. Someone, whether deliberately or unwittingly, had leaked information about the committee's activities to the press. In April 1940, for example, a reporter for the *Buffalo News* published a detailed account of the March 12 conference. The meeting had been intended as a private affair, and its public revelation stirred up a hornet's nest. Ickes, Cohen, and Abe Fortas, chief of the Power Division of the Department of the Interior concluded that Olds was responsible. They suspected him of attempting to steal the credit for establishing the program in order to further his political ambitions. Michael Strauss, a member of Cohen's staff, used the incident to pillory the committee. "All this gives a very dangerous vulnerability to continuing the present publicity policy of the National Power Policy and Defense Committee," Strauss wrote. "In the absence of the 'no comment' policy ... the Committee is at the mercy of its attackers. I presume that there are plenty of power interests that will take advantage of this situation and grind their own axes."

Unfortunately for the future harmony of the administration, neither Ickes nor Cohen was able to produce solid evidence to support his charges against Olds. Worse still, both had to admit that there were at least a half dozen other pipelines from the committee to the press.[72]

Meanwhile, Olds, Lilienthal, and Norris bitterly resisted Ickes's efforts to excise them from participating in important decisions relating to the defense power program. To the dismay of the president and the bewilderment of the industry, the committee was stuck on dead center. For more than a year this infighting consumed the energies

71. "Re: Emergency Power Supply Program," May 28, 1940, copy in ibid.
72. See Michael W. Strauss to Benjamin V. Cohen, Apr. 1, 1940, Interior Department Records, GAF 1-288, pt. 4, for evidence of friction among NPPDC members.

of ranking administration officials, and the committee's planning ground to a halt.[73]

Frustrated by this turn of events, Roosevelt in the summer of 1940 turned to the FPC as the pivotal agency to speed the program to completion. Increasingly, he viewed the NPPDC as too unwieldy a body with too many competing interests ever to fulfill its task. From then until December 7, 1941, the committee functioned as a lame duck. It was not abolished, but neither did it accomplish much.

The FPC, by contrast, was staffed with dynamic administrators and engineers, men who had the technological expertise and the experience to cope with the anticipated wartime power shortage. "The scope of the Commission's activities since 1933," wrote Commissioner Clyde L. Seavey to the attorney general on September 6, 1939, "and, more particularly, its national power survey, its work on the power aspects of the flood control program, and its cooperation with the War Department in the National Defense Power Committee, have equipped it with a body of well-organized data and trained staff of technicians offering the government the possibility of carrying out a national defense power program promptly and efficiently."[74]

On June 14, 1940, Roosevelt instructed the FPC to prepare plans for supplying the war-material centers with adequate power. There was little that Ickes could do to reverse this decision, although until America entered the war, he schemed to absorb the commission into the NPPDC. He also plotted to undercut the authority of the newly established Office of Production Management (OPM) and its chief, Julius Krug. Thwarted in this, he concocted an elaborate plan whereby the president would place every independent governmental agency concerned with power under his jurisdiction. When this maneuver failed, he deluged the president with letters denouncing the "cabal" of administration and congressional friends for betraying the New Deal's power policy. More specifically, he accused Olds, Lilienthal, Norris, Krug, Bernard Baruch, Judge Samuel I. Rosenman, and Budget Director Harold Smith.[75]

Despite his intriguing (indeed, largely because of it), Ickes failed to attain the accolade of coordinator of power. His frenetic activities, instead, forged an alliance of convenience among the heads of rival

73. See Ickes to Roosevelt, June 7, 1940, July 3, 21, 1941, in ibid. See also Lilienthal, *Journals*, I, 365-66, 376-77; Harold L. Ickes, *The Secret Diary of Harold L. Ickes: The First Thousand Days*, 3 vols. (New York, 1953-54), III, 578-79.
74. Seavey to Attorney General, Sept. 6, 1939, FPC Records, NPPC File, no. 17-37.
75. Ickes to Roosevelt, July 3, 1941; draft letter for presidential signature, July 3, 1941, Interior Department Records, GAF 1-288, pt. 4.

bureaucracies, congressional leaders, and private-utility executives to frustrate his power grab. Lilienthal of the TVA, for example, branded Ickes's request as "one of the most brazen documents" he had ever laid eyes upon ("the last word in the personal conception of government") and feared that the business community would construe the appointment as "a signal that the Administration was about to open fire" upon it. Norris unequivocally told the president that he "didn't want to see Ickes have anything to do with power."[76]

Roosevelt never intended to name Ickes "Coordinator of Power," or to place him in charge of "hard fuels," or to give him membership in the "War Cabinet"—other positions to which he aspired. He had taken the measure of his cabinet officer and, in the present crisis, had found him wanting. Ickes was acutely conscious that the president had lost confidence in the NPPDC and, in effect, had repudiated him. However sincere his desire to protect the administration's power program, the secretary was a disruptive presence in a situation that demanded harmony, coordination, and swift, decisive action.[77]

The president handled the entire affair in a typically Rooseveltian manner. Rather than order Ickes to confine his activities to the Interior Department or to abolish the NPPDC, Roosevelt skirted the bureaucratic disputes. On June 14, 1940, he undercut both his secretary and the committee when he instructed the FPC to assume direction of the planning for the war-material centers. Then he let Norris, Lilienthal, and others convince him that Krug was "right" on power and that the OPM already was functioning as a "power coordinator."[78]

Unfortunately, Roosevelt's serpentine maneuvering left the official status of the NPPDC vague. Rather than apply the *coup de grâce,* the president permitted it to linger, while Ickes pleaded in vain for a more influential voice in defense planning. On July 16, 1941, communications between the secretary and the "cabal" terminated abruptly when the FPC disclosed the outlines of its defense power program.[79] The plan, which evolved from conferences with the OPM, vested final power authority in the FPC and provided for RFC financing of plant expansion.

76. Lilienthal, *Journals,* I, 360-63, 366.
77. Ickes, *Secret Diary,* III, 586-88, 604-05, 607; Janeway, *Struggle for Survival,* 125-26.
78. Lilienthal, *Journals,* I, 362-63, 365.
79. See FPC Release no. 1637, July 16, 1941, Gifford Pinchot Papers, box 1963, Library of Congress; Twentieth Century Fund, *Electric Power and Government Policy* (New York, 1948), 737-38; and Leland Olds, "Forecasting Defense Power," *Electrical World,* 114 (Nov. 2, 1940), 55-58.

Once the news media published it, "all hell" broke loose in Washington.[80] "I further cannot agree to a plan," Ickes railed in a letter to Olds, "which is so designated as to make more difficult the carrying out of the public power program of this Administration as embodied in the Holding Company Act, the Rural Electrification Act, the Bonneville Act, and in the statements of the President."[81]

When his protests failed to influence the president, Ickes retreated to his office and sulked. He refused to attend cabinet meetings and complained to his intimates, Cohen and Harry Slattery, that Roosevelt did not have confidence in him. He threatened to resign, but thought better of the idea. Not only would the exercise of authority—which Ickes enjoyed—be denied to him but also, and this was the crucial consideration, there would be no one left in the administration to carry forward the public-power movement. He finally decided to bide his time—calculating that sooner or later the FPC and the OPM would have a falling out—and await the opportune moment to press his claims on the president.[82]

Meanwhile, America's relations with Japan deteriorated as the war in Europe entered its second year. By October 1941, the FPC had begun to coordinate its war functions more closely with the OPM.[83] Then, on December 7, the Japanese attacked Pearl Harbor. After the initial shock, the president invoked the commission's plan of July 16 in order to secure power for the war-material centers. Three weeks later, Charles W. Kellogg of the Edison Electric Institute reported the existence of a power shortage.[84] Predicated on the assumption that the United States required five years to build up its power capacity and to link together the major industrial centers, the FPC's timetable had been upset by the Japanese attack.

The suddenness of the attack also exposed the weaknesses, the confusion, and the delays that had attended national defense power planning. Nor did the president move swiftly and decisively to halt the bureaucratic and personality conflicts that delayed execution of the defense power program. Granted that Roosevelt was under pressure from isolationists, from Congress, and from his executive officers, Ickes was not wholly mistaken when he observed that the president

80. Lilienthal, *Journals*, I, 364.
81. Ickes to Olds, July 24, 1941, Interior Department Records, GAF 1-288, pt. 4.
82. Cooperation between the OPM and the FPC did not, in fact, last long. "The rivalry between the two civilian agencies of Government concerned with overall defense power administration has become exceedingly bitter, and has ... produced adverse reactions in the Congress" (Ickes to Roosevelt, Dec. 31, 1941, in ibid.).
83. Twentieth Century Fund, *Electric Power and Government Policy*, 352-53.
84. The *New York Times*, Dec. 20, 1941.

could have put a stop to all the internal hair-pulling long ago—if he had wanted to do so.[85]

Ickes's conviction that the fundamental issues in the controversy centered on the future course of the New Deal's power program revealed a certain prescience. From his perspective, the private utilities in the name of national defense threatened to subvert the forward progress of the public-power movement, whose impetus had accumulated over a decade of agitation. During the war years the strategic importance of the TVA, the most celebrated of the public-power projects, in the development of atomic energy justified the secretary's confidence in public power.

The tragedy in all the bureaucratic wrangling was that Ickes's opponents were no less attached to the president's power policy. Indeed, many of them occupied important positions and upheld that policy. They read the situation in terms of priorities: the advancement of public power per se in the context of 1941 was less immediate than was the need to supply the war-material centers with adequate power. They concluded that this priority could not be attained without cooperation from the private-utility industry. They, too, acknowledged the threat to the administration's power policy, but they vowed to guard against it.

Private industry, no less than the administration, bears responsibility for the power shortage that developed. Its executives had not been entirely candid with the government or the American people. Publicly and repeatedly they had given assurances that the industry could meet all the power requirements in a war emergency if only the government would not interfere. They failed to deliver on their promises. Despite warnings from the FPC, the industry's engineers had continually underestimated the nation's wartime power needs.

In the final analysis, the nation entered World War II with its power system ill-prepared to meet the demands made upon it. However, the war did not undermine the public-power movement as Ickes feared. Five years of global warfare, the development of atomic energy, the unstable peace following 1945, and the expansion of the economy made it possible for both the public- and private-utility industry to prosper.

---

85. The bureaucratic rivalry may be pieced together from the correspondence in the Harold L. Ickes Papers in the Library of Congress. His letters to Cohen and Harry Slattery, especially, reveal the secretary's despair, almost bordering on hysteria, at the president's apparent loss of confidence in his ability to run the defense power program. The author has not been able to locate copies of the letters in the Harry Slattery Papers, Duke University Library.

CHAPTER X

Conclusion

A columnist for the *Washington Post,* commenting upon the controversy surrounding the holding-company bill, observed that "when and if the true history of the New Deal is ever written, not the least extraordinary part of the tale will tell of the origin of legislation." Federal interest in the electric-power field, as the foregoing account indicates, was not a new phenomenon in 1933. The "corporate revolution" did not occur in the electric-power industry until after World War I. The public-utility law, meanwhile, lagged behind the spectacular innovations in technology and growth which made the industry an integral component of the national economic network. State and federal governments treated the industry as a local enterprise, ignoring the interstate and nationwide web of electric-utility holding-company activity.[1]

The FTC's investigation of holding-company mismanagement, the agitation for federal development of the Muscle Shoals power site, and the depression forced the federal government to reexamine its position vis-à-vis the electric-power industry. Reconstruction of that legislation which New Dealers considered essential to a national power policy indicates that President Roosevelt persuaded Congress to reexamine the whole relationship between private enterprise and the public welfare. He also capitalized on mounting public sentiment to implement a new federal power program, the touchstones of which were unemployment relief and a back-to-the-farm movement. Ironically, neither brought the recovery the president hoped for. Unemployment persisted, whereas the quaintly idealistic proposal to relieve the woes of a population concentrated in the cities was overwhelmed in the ultimate assumption of initiative by a remote and centralized bureaucracy.

The sharpest pressure for federal power legislation in the 1920s seems, in retrospect, to have come from the predominantly rural sec-

1. The *Washington Post,* Apr. 4, 1935, newsclipping in National Archives, Record Group 46, "Senate Special Committee to Investigate Lobbying Activities," Case Files, box 97; and Adolph A. Berle and Gardiner C. Means, *The Modern Corporation and Private Property* (New York, 1932).

tions of the nation which had a long history of antimonopoly, anti-Wall Street sentiment. The rural south, Plains states, and Pacific Northwest had been the last to benefit from central-station electrical service. Roosevelt successfully translated their discontent into votes for his power program. Urban congressmen also voted for federal power legislation primarily because they looked upon it as a work-relief measure, or because they expected to receive rural votes for urban programs. The pattern was reflected most clearly in the congressional voting on the TVA and holding-company bills, but could also be seen in the balloting for rural electrification and Bonneville power legislation. In every instance, though, the administration had to overcome the opposition of Republican and Democratic legislators who opposed the New Deal's spending programs on political or ideological grounds. Opposition to the extension of the federal power program, as in the case of the ill-fated "little TVAs" bill, and to bureaucratic centralization grew increasingly sharp in Congress and the states after 1937.

Initially, the underlying motive in the New Deal's program was the desire to weave the legislation into a coherent national power policy, break the monopoly of the private utilities over the generation and distribution of electrical energy, and provide unemployment relief. During his 1932 presidential campaign, Roosevelt told students of Oglethorpe University, in Atlanta, Georgia, that he was in favor of a "larger measure of social planning."[2] Fresh from victory, the allure of social planning persisted in the early years of the New Deal. The president persuaded Congress to enact the TVA legislation as a controlled experiment in social planning. It was Roosevelt's hope, and that of Senators Norris, McNary, Dill, and others, that the lessons of the TVA could be applied in building a network of power systems involving the river valleys of the nation. In the same spirit, he established the NPPC in 1934. Building upon the success of the TVA, the NPPC was expected to bring, among other benefits, abundant electricity at the lowest rates to the consumer. To execute this mandate the committee first had to curb holding-company abuses.

Almost immediately, federal holding-company regulation became the nucleus of the power program. It was a determined, and largely victorious, attempt to bring the utility law in line with actual practice. But the Brandeisian, antibigness philosophy that permeated it; the president's renewed interest in industry self-regulation after 1935; and the fractiousness of the public-power movement militated against the classi-

2. Samuel I. Rosenman, comp., *The Public Papers and Addresses of Franklin D. Roosevelt,* 13 vols. (New York, 1938-50), I, 639-46.

cal concept of central planning in the electric-power industry.

Public-power-conscious officials were themselves a complex lot, motivated by diverse and sometimes conflicting interests. The extremists among them saw experiments like the TVA, rural-electrification projects, and Bonneville Dam as intermediate measures on the road to full-fledged public power. The moderates conceived of the New Deal power program as a "yardstick"—a public enterprise that would, by competing with private producers, force them to bend more toward the needs of the consumer. Morris Cooke, J. D. Ross, and Ickes envisioned the TVA and federal holding-company legislation as the core of a policy that ultimately would embrace the resources and power needs of whole regions of the country. Lilienthal eschewed comprehensive resource planning for the more practical and limited objective of greater efficiency in producing low-cost electricity.

The entire movement was, in truth, anything but monolithic. And this fact, in turn, rendered the Roosevelt administration ultimately unsuccessful in its larger goal which was to reconcile economic individualism in the power business with collective organization, while preserving the traditional democratic heritage. For New Dealers were advocating, at one and the same time, regulated monopoly, regulated competition, trust-busting, and economic planning. Policies that promoted competition were interspersed with those that would have limited or destroyed it. This made it difficult, if not impossible, for any real consensus on power policy to emerge.[3]

Intraregional differences over federal construction and distribution plans made New Dealers painfully aware of how divided they were. In the Pacific Northwest, for example, there was conflict between the residents of Idaho, eastern Montana, and eastern Oregon, who wanted water for storage and reclamation, and the inhabitants of the more populous urban centers, who wanted water for hydroelectricity. Politics figured importantly in the actions of bureaucrats like Ickes and Gifford Pinchot, who had old political scores to settle. To them holding-company magnates were monopolists who used their treasuries and taxpayers' money to influence politics and legislation. The New Deal afforded them the opportunity to break the utilities' monopoly power once and forever, and to promote the centralists' dream of an enlarged Department of Conservation. Their tactics, frequently heavy-handed and embarrassing to their colleagues, were justified as being in the public interest.

3. Ellis W. Hawley, *The New Deal and the Problem of Monopoly* (Princeton, 1966), vii, 472-73, 484, 490.

The competition among those New Dealers who favored a rational, government-sponsored business community, those who hoped to restore a freely competitive system, and those who envisioned a form of democratic centralism in which the monopoly power of the utilities was transferred to the state, unfortunately, precipitated fierce and continuing struggles for control of the power program. In the Far West and South, public-power men came to doubt the efficacy of increased federal activity. By 1940, there was growing sentiment among people who basically sympathized with the New Deal that the bureaucratic bickering and centralization of programs were counterproductive; these people favored district, state, and regional initiative in power matters. They had allies within the administration, most notably David Lilienthal, the employees of the TVA, and possibly even the president. As one New Deal program after the other was mired in red tape, or torn by internal dissension, those proponents of local autonomy (or "grass-roots democracy") openly challenged the dominant position of the Interior Department and Secretary Ickes, who collectively personified centralized bureaucracy emanating from a remote source. The furious, often emotional, struggle between the decentralizers and centralizers of power policy seriously fragmented the public-power crusade even prior to the outbreak of World War II. The war, paradoxically, facilitated the accommodation of public and private power that Roosevelt earlier had showed signs of wanting.

As the legislative history of the holding-company, the rural-electrification, and the Bonneville bills also suggests, the president's policy toward the electric-power industry underwent several important modifications in accordance with what seemed politically necessary at a given time. With characteristic pragmatism, Roosevelt was willing to take something much less than the regional valley network. On the other hand, he was frankly biased against federal involvement in essentially parochial enterprises, such as the Skagit valley project sponsored by local interests in the Pacific Northwest. And, switching his original stand on complete holding-company elimination, he agreed to permit first-degree holding companies to function where they were economically and geographically essential to good service. He also allowed Bonneville to sell power to private companies over the objections of public-power enthusiasts.

While his enmity toward individual utility magnates and their creature, the holding company, was very nearly instinctual, Roosevelt also recognized that in selling power the federal government had to act in a commercial rather than an eleemosynary capacity. The guiding principle in financing the New Deal's power projects was to treat them as self-supporting enterprises which, though not operated for profit, were expected to earn from revenues all proper charges against them. The program was experimental, shifting, and opportunistic in the espousal of public enterprise and the spending that had to accompany such governmental activity.[4]

There is no evidence at all to indicate that the president seriously considered nationalizing the electric-power industry. He even left unexplored the vast implications of the TVA's "yardstick" concept. Philosophically, Roosevelt was a "liberal-conservative," not a radical. In August 1939, he summed up his beliefs and, in a sense, those of the New Deal in a letter to the president of the Young Democratic Clubs. The president contrasted himself with radicals who wanted "to tear up everything by the roots and plant new and untried seeds." What he wanted, he said, was "to use the existing plants of civilizations, to select the best of them, to water them and make them grow—not only for the present use of mankind, but also for the use of generations to come."[5] A believer in private enterprise, his tactics were pragmatically designed to reestablish the credibility of the industry in the eyes of the public and to make it serve the best interests of the nation, the consumer, and itself. In order to do this, Roosevelt perceived that the countervailing power of the government was necessary to force the industry to toe the mark.

The president's treatment of the NPPC, by contrast, was a classic illustration of his slipshod approach to administrative procedures, which kept New Deal bureaucrats in an almost constant state of tribal warfare and seriously divided public-power enthusiasts. After drafting the holding-company bill, Roosevelt lost interest in the original mandate of the committee, which was comprehensive resource and power planning projected on a national scale. The explanation for the inability of the NPPC to provide the kind of planning its Progressive sponsors in the PWA originally envisioned is twofold: the president's commitment to national planning, which had characterized the emergency legislation of the Hundred Days, visibly waned in 1935, as the nation seemed headed for economic recovery; also he believed it to be politically impossible to establish the centralized mechanism that an ecological approach to a national power policy demanded.

The explanation also relates to the noninstitutional nature of the

4. Charles H. Pritchett, "Administration of Federal Power Programs," *Journal of Land and Public Utility Economics,* 18 (Nov. 1942), 382.

5. Quoted in John W. Caughey and Ernest R. May, *A History of the United States* (Chicago, 1964), 569.

committee. Although it had been established by executive order, Roosevelt's interest in the NPPC seemed to be only peripheral. This was in keeping with his pragmatic approach to policy-making, that is, of not committing himself to any single government body or individuals but evolving policy after long and frequently intense intramural debate. The committee also lacked congressional sanction; thus, its vigor was inversely related to the degree of support that was forthcoming from the president. It existed upon the suffrance of the president and on organizational charts, but the membership did not hold any formal conferences until two years after the holding-company legislation. Its work in the defense program then was quickly superseded by the NDPC and the FPC.

The lack of statutory and institutional status; waning presidential interest; the inability of member agencies to transcend and, if necessary, to sacrifice their individual stakes in the power program; and Roosevelt's refusal to define the jurisdiction of the committee, or of any agency concerned with the power program, rendered true central planning an impossibility. Amid all the debates over different issues, a real policy did not emerge—only a series of piecemeal, *ad hoc* arrangements. This absence of an announced, well-defined, coordinated policy rendered the New Deal's attack even more disturbing to the private-utility industry than it might have been. Morris L. Cooke recognized this at the time he urged the creation of a committee that could formulate and articulate a comprehensive policy statement. "Electric power is as basic to the New Deal as soil conservation, land use or credit and in many highly significant moves of the Administration is so recognized. Yet there is no adequate national power policy coordinating isolated moves and without this it is small wonder that some of these moves seem opportunistic if not illogical and give rise to unwarranted criticism," he wrote to Ickes.[6]

The unity that existed in the New Deal's power policy came from individuals whose generalized commitment to cheap electricity for the consumer brought them together on specific issues. While their goal was usually the same, they differed—frequently violently—over the best means of attaining it. The president's role at times was to balance contending interests in order to reach a consensus. By 1941, the administration had come to recognize, but failed to cope with, the elemental fact that electric-power production and distribution were activities of

6. Morris L. Cooke to Harold L. Ickes, Apr. 6, 1934, National Archives, Record Group 48, National Power Policy Committee Records, General Classified File, box 7 (hereafter cited as NPPC Records).

increasing complexity and importance to the nation. Instead of integrating public- and private-generating facilities into a national grid system, adjusting production to consumption, and placing equitable restraints on the accumulation of profits, the NPPC was shouldered aside, while waste and useless duplication abounded.

When the president's interest in industry self-regulation was rekindled, after 1935, it was inevitable that planning would fall from favor. The comprehensive approach to resource planning that Arthur Morgan and Morris Cooke envisioned, which embraced the unification of the supply of current, standardization of the national rate structure, flood control and navigation, rural electrification, conservation and reforestation, and the efficient utilization of human resources, did not proceed beyond a limited, almost haphazard, basis. The TVA, as early as 1935, was concentrating upon only two aspects of the national power policy: the increased production of electricity from public- and private-generating facilities, and the lowering of rates to promote greater consumption. The failure to move beyond this point was at the crux of the feud between Lilienthal and Morgan.

The last bit of evidence that the NPPC never functioned in the capacity of a central planning agency comes from the FPC. The commission was authorized, in 1935, to divide the United States into electric-power regions and to effect, voluntarily or by compulsion, "the interconnection and coordination of power facilities within such districts." The FPC tentatively established power regions in 1936, and sent a map and an order to state commissions for their recommendations. Four years later, the FPC had completed preliminary studies for only one-half of the forty-eight supply areas. As late as 1948, no regions had as yet been established.[7] The concept of a national power grid had fallen before the decision to build a series of regional and local grids.

The Public Utility Holding Company Act of 1935, meanwhile, had raised fundamental questions about the nature of the American economy. The problems of economic concentration and oligopoly, the social control of vast wealth and the relationship of the national government to private enterprise, and the responsibilities of the corporation to its investors and the public were among the issues implicit in the legislation. Its enactment signified the determination of the Roosevelt administration to exercise regulatory authority over one segment of

7. U.S. Federal Power Commission, *Annual Report of the Federal Power Commission for 1935* (Washington, D.C., 1935), 3. Cf. the reports for 1936-40 and Twentieth Century Fund, *Electric Power and Government Policy* (New York, 1948), 183.

the national economy. Ben Cohen, in an off-the-record letter to Wendell Willkie, succinctly stated that the aim was to preserve the credit and credibility of the industry. "If we want to avoid the sort of regulation which we both abhor, we have simply got to simplify the rules of the game," he wrote. "I for one am not interested in regulation which absorbs the energy of the industry in debating the rules of the game. We need that energy in playing the game, in operating and developing the industry. I, like you, want to see business run as a business and not as a lobby. I don't believe in government by favor and I don't believe in business by favor. I don't believe in a benevolent paternalism public or private."[8]

The 1935 act, as it passed through the legislative process, retained the fundamental provisions that Cohen had written into it. It regulated the financial practices of interstate holding companies and limited systems to those that were economically and geographically integrated as determined by the SEC. But it was also an accommodation between two courses of action: it did not go as far as to require the complete elimination of holding-company systems, despite Cohen's predilection for regulated competition and economic freedom for the small entrepreneur; nor did it permit the economic concentration of properties into fewer and fewer systems to proceed unchecked. The SEC was to allow parent and grandfather companies but not great-grandfather companies.

The law also fell far short of nationalizing holding-company systems as the radical public-power enthusiasts desired, or of returning them to local control as the Brandeisian philosophy dictated. At most, the "death sentence" played a role in the ultimate success of managerial dominance instead of financial dominance in the electrical industry. By the close of 1941, dissolution proceedings were pending against the fourteen largest holding-company systems.[9] As America entered World War II, the problem confronting the American people was how the SEC might reorganize the private holding-company systems, in a manner consistent with democratic government, to achieve optimum coordination with the industrial needs of the nation.

8. Benjamin V. Cohen to Wendell Willkie, Mar. 21, 1935, NPPC Records, Cohen File, box 10.

9. Their consolidated assets aggregated $10,219,000, or 67 percent of the consolidated assets of all registered holding-company systems. See U.S. Securities and Exchange Commission, *Annual Report of the Securities and Exchange Commission for 1942* (Washington, D.C., 1942), 73; and Robert Blum, "SEC Integration of Holding Company Systems," *Journal of Land and Public Utility Economics*, 17 (Nov. 1941), 438.

Unlike the holding-company problem, the rural-electrification program, by 1941, was making dramatic progress. The percentage of farms in the United States participating in central-station service increased from 10.9 percent in 1935 to about 25 percent in January 1940, or about two and one-half times greater than when the REA was established. The rapid increase reflected the work of both the REA and the private-power companies. The federal program stimulated the interest of the latter in rural electrification on a scale more extensive than previously. In particular, competition from the REA induced the power companies to offer more reasonable terms to farmers and to build in rural areas where service had been denied earlier except at exorbitant rates.

The work was far from completed in 1941; more than five million farms still remained without electric service. And yet Norris was substantially correct when he told the president that the REA was the most popular of all New Deal programs. Statistics clearly attested to the magnitude of its success.[10] Nevertheless, REA officials feared with some justification that, if the federal government curtailed its program, the private utilities might revert to their former apathetical

10. By February 1, 1940, there were 462,817 consumers connected and receiving electricity from REA-financed systems, with an additional 400,000 customers to be added after the completion of current projects. The amount of REA allotments dramatically illustrated the importance of federal intervention. The initial sum of $15,050,000 in June 1936 went to sixty-six customers. But by February 1940 allotments totaling $269,396,793 had been granted to 689 borrowers, primarily cooperative associations, in forty-five states. Progress in line construction was equally spectacular, averaging 9,838 miles of line per month in the eight-month period ending March 1, 1940. Financially, the greater number of REA borrowers was in excellent condition and showed assuring prospects of being able to repay their loans. In addition, the REA made contributions to the technology of the industry with the introduction of the cyclometer meter, a low-cost transformer, and cheaper line-building techniques.

All things considered, the private-power companies and satellite industries benefited in the long run from the expansion of the federal program. In 1940, REA borrowers purchased wholesale electric power from the companies in the amount of $3 million. This was new business, for which the power companies incurred no selling or developing expense. The additional business, moreover, contributed to their uniformly high power-and-load factors which, in turn, increased efficiency and reduced generating costs. The REA also created a new market for the manufacturers of line-construction materials. Toward the close of 1941 federal funds for construction, wiring, and plumbing required manufactured items aggregating in excess of $200 million. The statistics relative to the REA cited herein are from National Archives, Record Group 221, Records of the Rural Electrification Administration, Slattery Office File, box 30 ("Increase in Rural Electrification in the United States," memo dated March 1940) (hereafter cited as REA Records). For evidence of diminishing "spite-line" tactics, see Grover C. Neff, "Some Problems and Opportunities in Rural Electrification," *Edison Electric Institute Bulletin,* 7 (Apr. 1939), 140.

attitude. "There is no doubt that some rural line would continue to be built, but rural electrification would no longer be the dynamic force of a growing social and economic program for the farmer," they advised.[11]

The impressive accomplishments of the REA program were paralleled on a slightly lesser scale in the Pacific Northwest. There, in the evolution of the Bonneville Power Administration, the propaganda and pressure politics of policy-making officeholders, office seekers, organizations of citizens, and investors came sharply into focus. The Bonneville story illustrated some of the major ideas behind federal power policy in the 1930s. The focus of ideological conflict there was the dispute between those whose approach had rested upon more generalized principles of planning and resource development and the advocates of power generation. This conflict, as in other New Deal power programs, was fought at the bureaucratic level and centered upon emphases, priorities, and choices of time and circumstance in establishing programs and policies. New Dealers were human also, and so personal competitiveness, personality clashes, and status rivalries existed in the Bonneville project, as in other power programs, including the REA. Problems of interprogram conflict, as between the Bonneville project and the REA program again, also emerged, as the work of the one agency impeded or broadened the mission of the other.[12]

Having made these observations, one must, in fairness, also conclude that Bonneville evolved into the same kind of success, on a larger scale, that Ross had demonstrated at the Seattle City Lighting Department. The resale-rate structure was paying out as early as November 1940.[13] Consumers responded to rate reductions as Ross predicted they would and as the experience of the Seattle City Lighting Department confirmed. Commercial and residential customers in Cascade Locks, Forest Grove, Canby, and Skamania greatly increased their consumption of electric energy. Bonneville demonstrated that the publicly owned distributing systems could break away from the traditional requirement that customers must earn their deductions before receiving

11. "Increase in Rural Electrification in the United States," Mar. 1940, REA Records, Slattery Office File, box 30.

12. For these insights I am indebted to Elmo R. Richardson's critique to author, Sept. 3, 1970, and to Charles E. Jacobs, *Leadership in the New Deal* (Englewood Cliffs, N.J., 1967), 1-34.

13. See Barclay J. Sickler, "Bonneville Resale Rates Pay Out," *Journal of Land and Public Utility Economics,* 16 (Nov. 1940), 487-92.

them.[14] To the degree that it did so, the project became a model for the private utilities to emulate.

Toward the close of 1940, the BPA began to play a more vital role in the preparations for national defense. Ickes appointed Dr. Raver to the NPPC; soon thereafter his counsel was heard in the deliberations of the NDPC. Bonneville and Grand Coulee quickly became the cornerstones of an integrated defense power network embracing the Pacific Northwest. Shortly after the attack on Pearl Harbor, the transmission and sale of power had become a major war industry.[15]

Private industry availed itself of the presence of an inexpensive and reliable quantity of electric energy to mesh its operations with the defense network. Its relationship with the BPA was not always smooth; it could hardly have been otherwise with Ickes maintaining a hawklike vigilance against the power companies. Contract negotiations, on both sides, were hard and often stormy. But the bureaucratic divisions, the early antagonism between Administrator Raver and the "Old Curmudgeon," and the war of attrition between PUD enthusiasts and the private-power companies receded into the background as the war took precedence. The struggle against the common foe forged, temporarily, an alliance between the federal government and private enterprise, a rapprochement made all the more possible because the president shelved the New Deal for the duration.

After eight years of the New Deal, what was the status of the private-utility industry? Despite the efforts of the Edison Electric Institute and its predecessor, the NELA, to speak in its behalf, the industry clearly was not the giant monolith its critics described. It might better be termed an estate with many different mansions, for honest differences of opinion existed among holding- and operating-utility executives on the administrative, financial, and technological aspects of the industry's operations.

Wendell Willkie, one of the more articulate and enlightened executives, though not necessarily the most popular figure in the industry, delineated the situation most accurately.[16] He, along with other progressive executives, had come to recognize certain basic facts about the relationship of the industry to the public and to the federal government. The ease with which public-ownership propaganda, antiutility legislation, and rate attacks gained momentum since the late 1920s was

14. Ibid.
15. Vernon M. Murray, "Grand Coulee and Bonneville Power in the National War Effort," ibid., 18 (May 1942), 131-42.
16. Wendell Willkie, "The Strength That Comes from Adversity," *Electrical World,* 114 (June 3, 1939), 68-69.

evidence that the industry had not always maintained the best relationship with its customers. A number of its financial operations were of doubtful character, to say the least; nor had all companies been as alert as they should have in matters of management efficiency. There was a tendency to consider rates sacred, not to be dropped except as return became too large. Worse still, the industry placed too much reliance upon legal processes rather than popular goodwill to protect its rights and privileges. Likewise, it depended too heavily upon state and federal connections to nullify or soften potentially hostile legislation.

If these were the facts of the situation, as Willkie recounted them, had the progressively managed power companies learned anything after nearly a decade of conflict with New Dealers? Certainly, they ought to have been aware that, although utilities were in a sense monopolies operating under government regulation, they had no inherent rights or privileges. They existed solely by the will of the people. As long as the public felt that it could get more desirable service, everything considered, from privately owned utilities, it would continue to permit their operation. But if the public believed otherwise, the fault was not with it, but with the utilities. Either they had not performed properly, they had become callous to the public interest, or—and this seemed to hold true in most cases—they had neglected to cultivate the public mind.

The rate attacks and increased taxes meant that management had to learn to operate more efficiently. A utility earned its rate of return through superior performance; it was not a reward to be guaranteed through regulation. Rates, then, were not sacred, but were subject to the will of the people to pay. The old theory that companies could lower rates only after a certain reasonable return was exceeded gave way slowly and painfully to the theory that return did not become the province of management until the public, through its appointed regulatory bodies, decided what it was willing to pay. By 1941, as a consequence of the federal government's greater attention, operating ratios were lower, new investment was kept under better control, and the industry was in a healthier operating and fiscal position.

The more perceptive utility executives also had come to realize that legal precedent or lobbying activity did not always afford shelter. Liberalization of judicial thinking during the New Deal era had uprooted a number of old ideas governing utility operations. A power company, for example, no longer had the exclusive right to serve a particular territory. And whatever the value of lobbying for the legislative process, the FTC revelations and the Black Committee's investigation served to bring its more aberrant aspects under control. This latter was the case, at least temporarily, in the electric-power industry. Willkie, Grover Neff, Samuel Ferguson, and others had every reason to be confident that the private-utility industry was fundamentally sounder in 1941 than it was a decade earlier. At the time of the American entry into World War II, the companies had been able to refinance their debt at the lowest rates in their history.[17]

Not every utility official accepted the altered terms under which he was expected to conduct business. Kendall K. Hoyt, a serious student of the private-power industry, analyzed the impact of federal regulation and federal power programs. His appraisal was less optimistic, noting that many executives (whom he did not identify) adopted the attitude that the industry's growth potential was being retarded "owing to the difficulty in securing capital, which has been frightened away by the Federal program."[18] Whereas Willkie confidently saw the tide of public opinion running against left-wing New Deal policies after 1939, Hoyt's executives fixed their gaze upon the depressed levels of utility stocks, the trials of securing equity money, and the "economic unsoundness of the entire multiple purpose of the Tennessee River system and its rubber yardstick rate structure."[19] Likewise, they ignored the philosophical divisions and lack of cohesiveness among New Dealers.

Willkie accurately perceived that the pendulum of opinion was swinging away from the public-power enthusiasts. "The utility industry is the sole master of the situation," he wrote. "It has been on the defensive; it has been fighting a rear guard action. That's wrong." He concluded that the industry "must stand and fight for its right to exist as a private enterprise." The public was tiring of the incessant attacks upon the industry; evidence of the shift in sentiment was numerous and everywhere. Senator Alben Barkley of Kentucky, a staunch supporter of the Roosevelt administration, pledged that the government would no longer construct competing public-power facilities until *after* it had made a fair offer to buy private properties. The recession in 1938, the clamor that public funds be expended where they would do the most good for unemployment and farm relief, growing economic sentiment, the threat of a congressional investigation of the TVA, the growing rebelliousness of a Democratically controlled Congress,

17. Ibid.
18. Kendall K. Hoyt, "Political and Economic Factors in the Slackening of the Federal Power Program," *The Annalist,* 53 (June 8, 1939), 798-800.
19. Ibid.

the disastrous PUD elections in 1940-41, and opposition to a Columbia Valley Authority in the Pacific Northwest from *friends* of the New Deal suggested considerable disenchantment with the extension of public power.[20]

Other considerations weighed against the frequently mentioned proposal to place all government agencies active in the power program into a single, centralized corporation or an enlarged Department of Conservation. It was not only inconsistent with the extant policy for private-power systems, which were being broken into smaller and, hopefully, more rational units, but also contrary to the philosophy of the most successful public-power project—TVA—whose directors had preached the gospel of grass-roots administration of federal programs. The acceleration of public-power programs across the country might also have been accompanied by increased centralization, at a time when domestic and international burdens on Washington already were overwhelming.[21]

The federal power program, in effect, had reached the point where it was more advantageous to gain the cooperation of the private utilities. A *modus vivendi* and a respite from the interminable litigation seemed particularly desirable as war drew closer to America's shores. The president himself seemed to be coming around to this conclusion. He transmitted to Congress, in 1939, a report of the New York Power Authority which recommended the pooling of public and private power to secure lower rates.[22] The administration, previously, had shied away from pooling agreements in the TVA area and the Pacific Northwest because of pressure from the public-power lobby. The approach of war hastened the evolution of a new working arrangement, one not altogether inconsistent with the Rooseveltian policy of low rates for the consumer.

The transformation from overt hostility to arm's-length toleration has been described in connection with the plans for averting a wartime power shortage. The role assigned to the REA in the war effort afforded further evidence of a *modus vivendi*. Writing to Agriculture Secretary Claude Wickard in 1942, the president directed the executive agencies to employ the cheapest sources of power, consistent with war require-

20. Willkie, "Strength That Comes from Adversity," 69.

21. See Herman Pritchett, "Why Reject a Government Corporation Into Which All the Agencies Would Be Placed to Form a National Power Policy?" *Journal of Land and Public Utility Economics,* 18 (Nov. 1942), 380-81.

22. The *New York Times,* May 27, 1939.

ments, in supplying electricity to defense plants.[23] The FPC was expected to advise public- and private-power-generating agencies of the prospective location and requirements of plants on or near their systems. In a negative sense, by failing to push the goals of public power to the fullest extent possible, when he could have taken advantage of the emergency situation, Roosevelt indicated that he accepted the new relationship. Orderly business procedures dictated that the plants were to purchase the power directly from the nearest supplier, at a reasonable rate. "Adoption of my suggestion," the president wrote, "will not discriminate in favor of public or private power, but will accord with sound business practice."[24]

In reducing the status of the public-power movement to parity with the private industry, the president retarded its momentum. The likelihood of war, along with internal divisions that became more pronounced as the crusade moved from one triumph to another, and the declining public interest in new experimentation after 1937 deflected the New Deal from expanding public power into new areas. Public power would not enjoy a resurgence in some areas of the country until after 1945, when peace had returned. The years 1940 and 1941, however, were particularly trying for the movement because most public-power programs were beset with bureaucratic troubles, just when the president demanded a higher degree of coordination of generating facilities. This fact, as much as any other, impelled him to work out a new relationship with the private utilities.

In so doing, Roosevelt and the New Deal encountered a further dilemma. Inviting the private-power companies to participate in defense planning risked subornation of everything the administration had worked to attain in the power field. Excluding them would precipitate the very shortage it hoped to avert. Secretary Ickes readily perceived this quandary; his suggestion that the president appoint him "power czar" was designed not only to extend the influence of his own department but also to enable him to exercise vigilance to protect the public interest.

Ickes has figured prominently in the foregoing narrative and some assessment of his role is in order. If Roosevelt was the high priest of the New Deal, the Old Curmudgeon was its principal gladiator.

---

23. A copy of the letter was sent to the secretaries of war and the navy, to the director of the War Production Board, to the chairman of the Defense Power Committee, and to Rear Admiral Emory S. Land of the Maritime Commission. See Franklin D. Roosevelt to Claude Wickard, Sept. 26, 1942, REA Records, Administrator's File, box 77.
24. Ibid.

He ruled Interior with an iron hand and, on occasion, was guilty of unfairness and oversuspiciousness toward his subordinates.[25] His accomplishments, however, were undeniable: he restored the prestige of the Interior Department from the low esteem into which it had fallen in the 1920s, he publicized conservation and public power, he exercised a tight rein on the Army Corps of Engineers, he administered the vast public-works program, and he brought a high degree of morality, honesty, and a passion for public service to government.[26] No objective observer should minimize the importance of his work, but in the sphere of power policy the positive contributions must be balanced against the negative ones.

From the inception of the New Deal, Ickes always wanted the best for the president's power program. He pursued power not exclusively for its own sake but because he felt certain that he was more capable of using it wisely in the public interest than were others.[27] Lack of success did not embitter him; it steeled his fiber and he attempted to wrest still more power. But, as the bureaucratic conflicts persisted into 1941, the means and the end became so entangled in his mind that he was scarcely able to distinguish between them. The repeated threats to resign his cabinet post and long periods of depression because the president would not heed his advice were manifestations of this confusion. The sad truth is that Ickes was a power seeker and, no matter how honorable his intentions, his imperious meddling did disrupt the administration, did create enemies needlessly, and did impede efforts to build up the nation's wartime power reserves.

By the close of the period, the early optimism of public-power enthusiasts that the New Deal would produce a rationally planned national policy to serve the present and future needs of the people had given way to bitter quarreling. Senator Norris's prediction, in 1924, that electricity would become one of the vital factors shaping human existence was accurate, but efforts to bring electricity to the people at absolute cost, free from the intervention of profit-making and profit-

25. Saul K. Padover, "Ickes: Memoir of a Man Without Fear," *The Reporter,* 6 (Mar. 4, 1952), 36-38.
26. M. Judd Harmon, "Some Contributions of Harold L. Ickes," *Western Political Quarterly,* 7 (June 1954), 238 ff.
27. For a more sympathetic appraisal of Ickes see Lippmann's obituary in the *New York Herald Tribune,* Feb. 7, 1952. Marquis W. Childs has pointed out, correctly I think, that Ickes was not consciously motivated by a Machiavellian desire for power. See Childs, *I Write from Washington* (New York, 1942), 61, as quoted in Harmon, "Some Contributions of Harold L. Ickes," 239.

taking middlemen, failed.[28] They failed because Roosevelt rebuffed attempts to nationalize the industry and to put his own house in order. The president insisted upon close public regulation of utilities, with profits limited to the level of prudent investment and the threat of government ownership as a club to insure fair prices. As one scholar has observed, he probably never grasped, let alone accepted, the full implications of a centralized economy in which government exercises positive controls.[29] If he did, he knew it was politically explosive, and the president could not be induced to think outside of a political context. Planning remained an ideal forever compromised in practice, and the national power policy a hope dashed.

28. Such a plan would have required nationalization of the electric-utility industry. See Norris's revealing letter to Christian A. Sorenson, Feb. 17, 1924, reprinted in James A. Stone, ed., "The Norris Program in 1924," *Nebraska History,* 42 (June 1961), 140.
29. Paul K. Conkin, *The New Deal* (New York, 1967), 39.

Bibliography

Index

Bibliography

PRIMARY SOURCES

MANUSCRIPTS

Duke University Library
    Harry A. Slattery Papers
Franklin D. Roosevelt Library
    Morris L. Cooke Papers
    Leland D. Olds Papers
    Herbert Pell Papers
    Franklin D. Roosevelt Papers
Library of Congress
    Newton D. Baker Papers
    William E. Humphrey Papers
    Harold L. Ickes Papers
    Judson L. King Papers
    George W. Norris Papers
    Gifford W. Pinchot Papers
    Thomas J. Walsh Papers
University of Washington Library
    Robert W. Beck Papers
    Guy C. Myers Papers
    [James D. Ross Papers] Seattle City Lighting Department Records

ARCHIVAL RECORDS

Bonneville Power Administration Archives
    U.S. Bonneville Power Administration. *History of the Bonneville Power Administration.* 3 vols. N.p., n.d.
Federal Power Commission Archives
    Records of the Federal Power Commission
Franklin D. Roosevelt Library
    Proceedings of the National Emergency Council (microfilm)
National Archives
    Records of the Department of Commerce
    Records of the Department of the Interior
    Records of the National Defense Power Committee
    Records of the National Power Policy Committee
    Records of the Rural Electrification Administration
    Records of the United States Congress, House of Representatives, Committee on Interstate and Foreign Commerce, Wheeler-Rayburn Files

Records of the United States Congress, Senate, Committee on Interstate
Commerce, Wheeler-Rayburn Files
Records of the United States Congress, Senate, Special Committee to
Investigate Lobbying Activities, Wheeler-Rayburn Files
University of Washington Library
Houghton, Coughlin, Cluck & Schubat Archive

ORAL INTERVIEWS

Benjamin V. Cohen. Washington, D. C. May 12, 1965
Burton K. Wheeler. Washington, D. C. May 12, 1965

PUBLISHED WORKS

American Bar Association. *Annual Reports*. Baltimore: Lord Baltimore Press,
1933-34.
Black, Hugo L. "Inside a Senate Investigation." *Harper's Magazine*, 172
(Feb. 1936), 275-86.
Blum, John M. *From the Morgenthau Diaries*. 2 vols. Boston: Houghton
Mifflin, 1959, 1965.
Carmody, John M. "Rural Electrification in the United States." *Annals of
the American Academy of Political and Social Science*, 201 (Jan. 1939),
82-88.
Cooke, Morris L. "The Early Days of the Rural Electrification Idea, 1914-
1936." *American Political Science Review*, 42 (June 1948), 431-47.
Couzens, James. "Why the Couzens Bill Will Not Undermine the Powers
of the State Commissions." *Public Utilities Fortnightly*, 6 (Aug. 7, 1930),
131-40.
Davis, Ewin L. "The Influence of the Federal Trade Commission's Investi-
gations on Federal Regulation of Interstate Electric and Gas Utilities."
George Washington Law Review, 14 (Dec. 1945), 21-29.
DeVane, Dozier A. "Highlights of the Legislative History of the Federal
Power Act of 1935 and the Natural Gas Act of 1938." *George Washington
Law Review*, 14 (Dec. 1945), 30-41.
Ickes, Harold L. *The Autobiography of a Curmudgeon*. New York: Reynal
& Hitchcock, 1943.
————. *The Secret Diary of Harold L. Ickes: The First Thousand Days*.
3 vols. New York: Simon & Schuster, 1953-54.
Kable, George W., and Gray, George B. *Report on Civil Works Administration
National Survey of Rural Electrification*. Washington, D.C.: Government
Printing Office, 1934.
Keller, Charles, ed. *The Power Situation During the War*. Washington, D.C.:
Government Printing Office, 1921.
Landis, James M. "The Legislative History of the Securities Act of 1933."
George Washington Law Review, 28 (Oct. 1959), 29-39.
Lilienthal, David E. *The Journals of David E. Lilienthal*. 5 vols. New York:
Harper & Row, 1964-71.
Mississippi Valley Committee. *Report of the Mississippi Valley Committee
of the Public Works Administration*. Washington, D.C.: Government
Printing Office, 1934.

Moley, Raymond. *After Seven Years*. New York: Harper, 1939.

National Association of Railway and Utility Commissioners. *Proceedings*. Washington, D.C.: Government Printing Office, 1930-38.

National Resources Board. *A Report on National Planning and Public Works in Relation to Natural Resources and Including Land Use ... With Findings and Recommendations*. Washington, D.C.: Government Printing Office, 1934.

National Resources Committee. *Regional Planning*. Part I: *Pacific Northwest*. Washington, D.C.: Government Printing Office, 1936.

Nixon, Edgar B., comp. *Franklin D. Roosevelt and Conservation*. 2 vols. Washington, D.C.: Government Printing Office, 1957.

Norris, George W. *Fighting Liberal: The Autobiography of George W. Norris*. New York: Macmillan, 1945.

Pacific Northwest Regional Planning Commission. *Columbia Basin Report*. Washington, D.C.: Government Printing Office, 1936.

Pecora, Ferdinand. *Wall Street Under Oath*. New York: Simon & Schuster, 1939.

Person, Harlow S. "The Rural Electrification Administration in Perspective." *Agricultural History*, 24 (Apr. 1950), 70-88.

Pinchot, Gifford. "The Long Struggle for Effective Federal Water Power Legislation." *George Washington Law Review*, 14 (Dec. 1945), 9-20.

Porter, John Sherman., ed. *Moody's Manual of Investments: Public Utility Securities*. New York: Moody's Investor Service, 1930.

Report of the Giant Power Board Survey to the General Assembly of the Commonwealth of Pennsylvania. Harrisburg, Pa., 1925.

Rosenman, Samuel I., comp. *The Public Papers and Addresses of Franklin D. Roosevelt*. 13 vols. New York: Random House, 1938-50.

Truman, Harry S. *Memoirs*. 2 vols. New York: Doubleday, 1955.

Udell, Gilman G., comp. *Laws Relating to Securities Commission Exchanges and Holding Companies*. Washington, D.C.: Government Printing Office, 1964.

U.S. Chamber of Commerce. *Muscle Shoals, a Groundwork of Fact: Special Report of the National Water Power Policies Committee*. Washington, D.C.: Chamber of Commerce, 1930.

U.S. Congress. House and Senate. *Congressional Record*. 77th Cong., 1st sess. 1941.

———. *Joint Resolution No. 329*. 68th Cong., 2d sess. 1925.

U.S. Congress. House. *A Bill to Reorganize the Federal Power Commission. ...* Hearings on H.R. 11408. 71st Cong., 2d sess. 1930.

———. *Columbia River (Bonneville Dam) Oreg. and Wash.* Hearings on H.R. 12875, 12895, and 12899. 74th Cong., 2d sess. 1936.

———. *Columbia River (Bonneville Dam) Oreg. and Wash.* Hearings on H.R. 7642. 75th Cong., 1st sess. 1937.

———. *Committee Report on S. 2796*. House report on 1318. Union calendar no. 451. 74th Cong., 1st sess. 1935.

———. *Public Utility Holding Companies*. Hearings on H.R. 5423. 74th Cong., 1st sess. 1935.

———. *Report of the National Power Policy Committee*. House doc. no. 137. 74th Cong., 1st sess. 1935.

U.S. Congress. Senate. *Committee Report on S. 1725.* Senate report 621. Union calendar no. 651. 74th Cong., 1st sess. 1935.

————. *Completion and Operation of the Bonneville Project.* Hearings on S. 2092. 75th Cong., 1st sess. 1937.

————. *Electric Power Industry, Control of Power Companies.* Senate doc. no. 213. 69th Cong., 2d sess. 1927.

————. *Electric Power Industry, Supply of Electrical Equipment and Competitive Conditions.* Senate doc. no. 46. 70th Cong., 1st sess. 1928.

————. *Investigation of Public Utility Corporations.* Senate report 225. 70th Cong., 1st sess. 1928.

————. *Investigation of Public Utility Holding Corporations.* Hearings on S. Res. 83. 70th Cong., 1st sess. 1928.

————. *Navigation and Flood Control on the Columbia River and Its Tributaries.* Hearings on S. 869, 3330, 4178, and 4566. 74th Cong., 2d sess. 1936.

————. *Public Utility Holding Companies.* Hearings on S. 1725. 74th Cong., 1st sess. 1935.

————. *Senate Special Committee to Investigate Lobbying Activities.* Hearings purs. to S. Res. 165. 74th Cong., 1st sess. 1935-38.

————. *Stock Exchange Practices.* Hearings purs. to S. Res. 84. 72nd Cong., 2d sess. 1932-33.

————. *Summary Report of the Federal Trade Commission ... on Economic, Financial and Corporate Phases of Holding and Operating Companies of Electric and Gas Utilities.* Senate doc. 92, pt. 73-A. 70th Cong., 1st sess. (1928). 1935.

U.S. Congress. Senate and House. *Columbia Power Administration.* Joint Hearings on S. 2430 and H.R. 6889 and 6890. 77th Cong., 2d sess. 1942.

U.S. Department of Commerce. Bureau of the Census. *Fifteenth Census of the United States: 1930, Agriculture.* Vol. IV. Washington, D.C., 1932.

U.S. Federal Power Commission. *Annual Reports.* Washington, D.C., 1933-41.

————. *Holding Company Control of Licensees of the Federal Power Commission.* Washington, D.C., 1932.

U.S. Rural Electrification Administration. *First Annual Report of the Rural Electrification Administration.* Washington, D.C., 1936.

————. *Proceedings and Address, Sixth Annual Staff Conference, April 15-18, 1941.* Washington, D.C., 1941.

U.S. Securities and Exchange Commission. *Annual Reports.* Washington, D.C., 1942, 1952.

U.S. Statutes At Large. 64th Cong., 1st sess. Vol. 39, pt. I. 1916.

NEWSPAPERS

New York Herald Tribune. 1925-35, 1952.
The Kiplinger Washington Letter. 1934-35.
New York Times. 1925-41.
The Oregon Daily Journal. 1939.
The Oregonian. 1938-41.
St. Louis Post-Dispatch. 1941-44.
The Wall Street Journal. 1925-41.

SECONDARY SOURCES

Albertson, Dean. *Roosevelt's Farmer: Claude R. Wickard in the New Deal.* New York: Columbia University Press, 1955.

"Annual Convention of the N.A.R.U.C., The." *Public Utilities Fortnightly,* 10 (Dec. 8, 1932), 706-09.

Arkwright, Preston K. "What About Holding Companies?" *The Fifth District Banker,* 2 (July 1930), 8-9.

Ascher, Charles S., ed. "The University of Virginia Regional Roundtable." *City Planning,* 7 (Oct. 1931), 261-63.

Barnes, Irston R. *Cases on Public Utility Regulation.* New York: F. S. Crofts, 1938.

Barnes, Joseph. *Willkie.* New York: Simon & Schuster, 1952.

Baruch, Bernard B. *American Industry in the War: A Report of the War Industries Board.* New York: Prentice-Hall, 1941.

Beard, Charles A. "The New Deal's Rough Road." *Current History,* 42 (Sept. 1935), 625-32.

Beck, Sir Adam. "Ontario's Experience." *The Survey,* 51 (Mar. 1, 1924), 585-90, 650-51.

Bellemore, Douglas H. "The Public Utility Holding Company." Ph.D. dissertation, New York University, 1938.

Benedict, Murray. *Farm Policies of the United States, 1789-1950.* New York: Twentieth Century Fund, 1953.

Berle, Adolph, and Means, Gardiner C. *The Modern Corporation and Private Property.* New York: Macmillan, 1932.

Blanchard, Frank L. "Customer Ownership of Public Utilities." *The Fifth District Banker,* 2 (July 1930), 13-14.

Blood, William H., Jr. "The Present Status of Public Utility Regulation in the United States of America." *Stone & Webster Journal,* 45 (Dec. 1929), 740-49.

Blum, John M. *Joe Tumulty and the Wilson Era.* Boston: Houghton Mifflin, 1951.

Blum, Robert. "SEC Integration of Holding Company Systems." *Journal of Land and Public Utility Economics,* 17 (Nov. 1941), 423-39.

Bonbright, James C., and Means, Gardiner C. *The Holding Company.* New York: McGraw-Hill, 1932.

Brandeis, Louis D. *Other People's Money.* New York: F. A. Stokes, 1913.

Buchanan, Norman S. "The Origin and Development of the Public Utility Holding Company." *The Journal of Political Economy,* 44 (Feb. 1936), 31-53.

Burns, James M. *Roosevelt: The Lion and the Fox.* New York: Harcourt Brace, 1956.

Cable, E. N. "Comforts with Electricity." *American Fruit Grower,* 39 (July 1919), 29.

Cameron, H. M. "The Holding Company at the Crossroads." *Electrical World,* 99 (Feb. 20, 1932), 344-55.

Carlisle, Floyd L. "The Control of Public Utility Corporations." *National Electric Light Association Bulletin,* 17 (Nov. 1930), 679-81.

Carosso, Vincent P. *Investment Banking in America: A History.* Cambridge, Mass.: Harvard University Press, 1970.

Caughey, John W., and May, Ernest R. *A History of the United States.* Chicago: Rand McNally, 1964.

Chamberlain, Joseph P. "Regulation of Public Utility Holding Companies." *American Bar Association Journal,* 17 (June 1931), 365-68.

Chambers, Clarke A. *Seedtime of Reform.* Minneapolis: University of Minnesota Press, 1963.

Chase, Stuart. "Upward and Onward." *New Republic,* 45 (Dec. 2, 1925), 35-36.

Childs, Marquis W. *The Farmer Takes a Hand.* New York: Doubleday, 1952.

Christie, Jean. "Morris Llewellyn Cooke: Progressive Engineer." Ph.D. dissertation, Columbia University, 1963.

Clapp, Gordon R. *The TVA: An Approach to the Development of a Region.* Chicago: University of Chicago Press, 1955.

Clarkson, Grosvenor B. *Industrial America in the World War.* Boston: Houghton Mifflin, 1923.

"Close Supervision of Utilities Urged Before Investment Bankers." *Electrical World,* 101 (June 3, 1933), 708-09.

Clough, Ernest T. "Holding Company Bonds Have Investment Merit." *Barron's,* 11 (Aug. 19, 1931), 3-8.

Cohen, Manuel F. "Federal Legislation Affecting the Public Offering of Securities." *George Washington Law Review,* 28 (Oct. 1959), 119-76.

"Commissioners' Attitudes on Wheeler-Rayburn Bill." *Public Utilities Fortnightly,* 16 (Nov. 7, 1935), 654-56.

"Committee to Study Power Supply Facilities for War Emergency." *Electrical World,* 110 (Sept. 17, 1938), 7.

"Complex Rabbit." *Time,* 26 (July 29, 1935), 9.

Conkin, Paul. *The New Deal.* New York: Thomas Y. Crowell, 1967.

"Congress, Lobbies and the Courts." *Literary Digest,* 121 (Mar. 14, 1936), 6.

Cooke, Morris L. "The Long Look Ahead." *The Survey,* 51 (Mar. 1, 1924), 600-04, 651.

"Cooke Quits the E.H.F.A." *Electrical World,* 105 (Dec. 7, 1935), 2908.

Cornwell, Elmer, Jr. *Presidential Leadership of Public Opinion.* Bloomington: Indiana University Press, 1965.

Coughlan, John P. "Public Utilities and the Public." *National Electric Light Association Bulletin,* 19 (Dec. 1932), 711-14.

Cuff, Robert. "A Dollar-a-Year Man in Government: George N. Peek and the War Industries Board." *Business History Review,* 41 (Winter 1967), 404-20.

Danielian, N. R. "From Insull to Injury: Study in Financial Jugglery." *Atlantic Monthly,* 151 (Apr. 1933), 497-508.

Davis, G. Cullom. "The Transformation of the Federal Trade Commission, 1914-1929." *Mississippi Valley Historical Review,* 49 (Dec. 1962), 437-55.

De Bedts, Ralph F. *The New Deal's SEC.* New York: Columbia University Press, 1964.

"Defense Work Won't Halt Death Sentence." *Electrical World,* 114 (July 27, 1940), 222.

Delano, Frederic A. "Regional Planning Next!" *National Municipal Review,* 13 (Mar. 1924), 144-45.

Dick, Wesley A. "The Genesis of Seattle City Light." Master's thesis, University of Washington, 1964.

Divine, Robert A. *The Reluctant Belligerent: American Entry Into World War II.* New York: Wiley, 1965.

"Does the Electrical Industry Want Holding Company Control?" *Public Utilities Fortnightly,* 10 (Aug. 18, 1932), 215-17.

Donovan, William J. "Is the Interest of the Public Inconsistent with the Interest of the Utilities?" *Stone & Webster Journal,* 46 (June 1930), 715-24.

Dreher, Carl. "J. D. Ross, Public Power Magnate." *Harper's Magazine,* 181 (June 1940), 46-60.

Droze, Wilmon H. *High Dams and Slack Waters: TVA Rebuilds a River.* Baton Rouge: Louisiana State University Press, 1965.

"Editorial." *Public Service News,* 12 (Jan. 1, 1935), 4.

Elsbree, Hugh L. *Interstate Transmission of Electric Power: A Study in the Conflict of State and Federal Jurisdictions.* Cambridge, Mass.: Harvard University Press, 1931.

"Executives Storm House Committee to Stop Bill." *Newsweek,* 5 (Apr. 13, 1935), 32-33.

"Extending Control Over Public Utility-Affiliate Financial Transactions." *Harvard Law Review,* 46 (Jan. 1933), 508-15.

Ferguson, Samuel. "How to Remove Popular Misunderstandings of Utilities." *Electrical World,* 102 (Dec. 2, 1933), 729-31.

Filler, Louis. *A Dictionary of American Social Reform.* New York: Greenwood Press, 1963.

Finlayson, Ranald A. "The Public Utility Holding Company Under Federal Regulation." *The Journal of Business of the University of Chicago,* 16, supp. (July 1946), 1-41.

"First Blood in the Power War." *New Republic,* 54 (Feb. 9, 1928), 56.

Friedel, Frank. *Franklin D. Roosevelt: The Triumph.* Boston: Little, Brown, 1956.

Fusfeld, Daniel G. *The Economic Thought of Franklin D. Roosevelt and the Origins of the New Deal.* New York: Columbia University Press, 1956.

Galbraith, John K. *The Great Crash 1929.* Boston: Houghton Mifflin, 1955.

Geddes, Patrick. *Cities in Evolution: An Introduction to the Town Planning Movement and to the Study of Civics.* London, 1915.

Gerhart, Eugene C. *America's Advocate: Robert H. Jackson.* Indianapolis, Ind.: Bobbs-Merrill, 1958.

Gilman, W. C. "Financial Practices of Few Endanger Utilities' Credit." *Electrical World,* 99 (Jan. 16, 1932), 134-36.

Glaeser, Martin G. *Public Utilities in American Capitalism.* New York: Macmillan, 1957.

"Government Competition Still Threat to Utilities." *Electrical World,* 112 (Oct. 21, 1939), 1173.

"Government Power Bodies Due to Be Consolidated." *Electrical World,* 112 (Sept. 1939), 6-7.

"Governor's Theories About Power." *Review of Reviews,* 88 (Dec. 1931), 32.

Gruhl, Edwin. "The Electric Dollar." *National Electric Light Association Bulletin,* 17 (July 1930), 431-35.

Gulick, Charles A. "Holding Companies in Power." *New Republic*, 47 (May 26, 1926), 25-28.

Hagenah, William J. "Public Utility Regulation and Its Accomplishments." *National Electric Light Association Proceedings*, 86 (1929), 85.

Hannah, James J. "Urban Reaction to the Great Depression." Ph.D. dissertation, University of California, 1956.

Harger, C. M. "Bringing Electricity to the Farm." *Country Gentlemen*, 88 (Apr. 27, 1918), 11.

Harmon, M. Judd. "Some Contributions of Harold L. Ickes." *Western Political Quarterly*, 7 (June 1954), 238-52.

Hart, Joseph K. "Power and Culture." *The Survey*, 51 (Mar. 1, 1924), 627-28.

Hawley, Ellis W. *The New Deal and the Problem of Monopoly*. Princeton: Princeton University Press, 1966.

Hayes, Henry R. "Public Confidence in the Power Industry." *National Electric Light Association Bulletin*, 18 (Feb. 1931), 77-80.

Hays, Samuel P. *Conservation and the Gospel of Efficiency*. Cambridge, Mass.: Harvard University Press, 1959.

"Hearst Telegram, Senate and Courts." *Literary Digest*, 121 (Mar. 21, 1936), 6.

Herring, Pendleton. "The Federal Trade Commissioners." *George Washington Law Review*, 8 (Jan.-Feb. 1940), 339-64.

Hicks, John D. *Republican Ascendancy, 1921-1933*. New York: Harper, 1960.

Hooker, H. Lester. "The Raid of the Radicals on State Regulation." *Public Utilities Fortnightly*, 6 (Dec. 25, 1930), 771-83.

Hoyt, Kendall K. "Political and Economic Factors in the Slackening of the Federal Power Program." *The Annalist*, 53 (June 8, 1939), 798-800.

Hubbard, Henry Vincent. "Planning the City and the Region—Then and Now." *The American City*, 43 (Sept. 1930), 99-100.

Hubbard, Preston J. *Origins of the TVA*. Nashville: University of Tennessee Press, 1961.

Insull, Martin J. "Holding Companies and Their Relation to Regulation." *National Electric Light Association Bulletin*, 17 (July 1930), 419-23.

"Insull Crisis Dramatizes Plight of Investment Holding Groups." *Business Week*, 137 (Apr. 20, 1932), 18-19.

Jacob, Charles E. *Leadership in the New Deal*. Englewood Cliffs, N.J.: Prentice-Hall, 1967.

Janeway, Eliot. *The Struggle for Survival*. New Haven: Yale University Press, 1951.

Jenkins, John W. "Legislative History of the Federal Water Power Control." *Congressional Digest*, 13 (Oct. 1934), 227-31.

" 'Jim' Reed's Opening Blast." *Literary Digest*, 95 (Oct. 29, 1927), 10-11.

Jones, W. A. "A National Viewpoint of Utility Problems." *Electrical World*, 96 (Oct. 18, 1930), 731-32.

Kable, George W. "Farm Electrification Steadily Winning." *Electrical World*, 102 (Nov. 4, 1933), 605.

Karl, Barry D. *Executive Reorganization and Reform in the New Deal*. Cambridge, Mass.: Harvard University Press, 1963.

Ketchum, W. D. "Power Aspects of Federally-Operated Reclamation Projects." *Edison Electric Institute Bulletin*, 3 (Dec. 1935), 449-51.

King, Judson. "Letter to Members of the League." *National Popular Government League Bulletin,* 94 (Feb. 1932), 1-6.

———. *The Conservation Fight.* Washington, D.C.: Public Affairs Press, 1959.

Kirkendall, Richard S. "The Great Depression: Another Watershed in American History." In *Change and Continuity in Twentieth Century America,* edited by John Braeman et al., pp. 145-90. Columbus: Ohio State University Press, 1964.

Koenig, Louis. *The Invisible Presidency.* New York: Rinehart, 1960.

Koistinen, Paul A. C. "The 'Industrial-Military Complex' in Historical Perspective: World War I." *Business History Review,* 41 (Winter 1967), 378-403.

Laidler, Harry W. *Concentration of Control in American Industry.* New York: Thomas Y. Crowell, 1931.

Landis, James M. *The Administrative Process.* New Haven: Yale University Press, 1938.

"Lauds Holding Company Aims." *Barron's,* 10 (Sept. 15, 1930), 27.

Lay, David. "The Association of Commissioners Grows a Left Wing." *Public Utilities Fortnightly,* 8 (Nov. 12, 1931), 579-85.

Lee, Ivy L. "The Man Behind Steps Out: A Study in Public Relations." *Public Utilities Fortnightly,* 5 (Feb. 6, 1930), 141-50.

"Let Correction Come from Within the Industry." *Electrical World,* 98 (Aug. 1, 1931), 188-89.

Leuchtenburg, William E. "Roosevelt, Norris and the 'Seven Little TVAs'." *Journal of Politics,* 14 (Aug. 1952), 418-41.

———. *The Perils of Prosperity, 1914-1932.* Chicago: University of Chicago Press, 1958.

———. *Franklin D. Roosevelt and the New Deal.* New York: Harper & Row, 1963.

———. "The New Deal and the Analogue of War." In *Change and Continuity in Twentieth Century America,* edited by John Braeman et al., pp. 81-144. Columbus: Ohio State University Press, 1964.

Lewis, Ben H. "The Bogie of Federal Regulation." *Public Utilities Fortnightly,* 12 (Aug. 21, 1933), 252-59.

Lief, Alfred. *Democracy's Norris.* New York: Stackpole Sons, 1939.

Lilienthal, David E. "The Regulation of Public Utility Holding Companies." *Columbia Law Review,* 29 (Apr. 1929), 404-40.

———. "Recent Developments in the Law of Public Utility Holding Companies." *Columbia Law Review,* 31 (Feb. 1931), 189-207.

———. "Regulation of Public Utilities During the Depression." *Harvard Law Review,* 46 (Mar. 1933), 745-75.

———. "Four Point Program for Legislation." *Electrical World,* 101 (Apr. 1, 1933), 423.

———. "TVA Seen Only as Spur to Electrification of America." *Electrical World,* 102 (Nov. 4, 1933), 687-90.

———. "Birchrods? Legislative Suggestions for Regulating the Public Utility Industry and Its Alter Ego, the Holding Company." *State Government,* 5 (Feb. 1934), 39-41.

———. *TVA: Democracy on the March.* New York: Harper, 1944.

Lippmann, Walter. *Interpretations, 1933-1935.* New York: Macmillan, 1936.

Liversidge, H. P. "Gradual Rural Electrification." *Electrical World,* 102 (Jan. 27, 1934), 149-51.

Losee, Gordon C. "A History of the Public Utility Holding Company Act of 1935." Master's thesis, University of Illinois, 1935.

Loss, Louis. *Securities Regulation.* 2 vols. 2d ed. Boston: Little, Brown, 1961.

Lubove, Roy. *Community Planning in the 1920's: The Contribution of the Regional Planning Association of America.* Pittsburgh: University of Pittsburgh Press, 1963.

Maass, Arthur. *Muddy Waters: The Army Engineers and the Nation's Rivers.* Cambridge, Mass.: Harvard University Press, 1951.

McCarter, Thomas N. "A Memorial to the President of the United States." *Edison Electric Institute Bulletin,* 3 (Jan. 1935), 3-4.

McCraw, Thomas K. "Morgan v. Lilienthal: The Feud Within TVA." Master's thesis, University of Wisconsin, 1967.

———, *TVA and the Power Fight, 1933-1939.* Philadelphia: J. P. Lippincott Company, 1971.

McDonald, Forrest. *Let There Be Light: The Electric Utility Industry in Wisconsin, 1881-1955.* Madison: American History Research Center, 1957.

McDonald, Forrest. *Insull.* Chicago: University of Chicago Press, 1962.

McKinley, Charles. *Uncle Sam in the Pacific Northwest.* Berkeley: University of California Press, 1952.

Magill, Hugh S. "Investors Win a Great Victory." *Investor America,* 1 (July 1935), 1.

Marpole, Arthur. "Electricity an Aid in Farming." *Farm Engineering,* 3 (June 1916), 281.

Martin, Roscoe C. *TVA: The First Twenty Years; a Staff Report.* Tuscaloosa, Ala.: University of Alabama Press, 1956.

Mavrinac, Albert A. "Congressional Investigations." *Confluence,* 3 (Dec. 1954), 463-79.

May, Henry F. "Shifting Perspectives on the 1920's." *Mississippi Valley Historical Review,* 42 (Dec. 1956), 405-27.

Mehinick, Howard K., and Durisch, Lawrence L. "Tennessee Valley Authority: Planning in Operation." *Town Planning Review,* 24 (July 1953), 116-45.

Middle West Utilities. *Harvests and Highlines.* Chicago: Middle West Utilities, 1930.

Miller, Raymond C. *Kilowatts at Work: A History of the Detroit Edison Company.* Detroit: Wayne State University Press, 1957.

Morgan, Arthur. "Bench-Marks in the Tennessee Valley." *Survey Graphic,* 23 (Jan. 1924), 43-47.

———. "Planning in the Tennessee Valley." *Current History,* 38 (Sept. 1933), 665-66.

Mullaney, Bernard J. "Camouflage and Smokescreens." *The Fifth District Banker,* 2 (July 1930), 13-14.

Murray, Vernon M. "Grand Coulee and Bonneville Power in the National War Effort." *Journal of Land and Public Utility Economics,* 18 (May 1942), 134-40.

Nalle, Albert, "Let the Public In on the Industry's 'Secrets'," *Electrical*

World, 100 (Sept. 24, 1932), 396-97.

Nash, Gerald D. "Experiments in Industrial Mobilization: WIB and NRA." *Mid-America,* 45 (July 1963), 157-74.

"Necks In: Irishman and Jew Keep Quiet Behind Today's Rooseveltian Brain Trust." *Literary Digest,* 123 (May 22, 1937), 7-8.

Neff, Grover C. "Some Problems and Opportunities in Rural Electrification." *Edison Electric Institute Bulletin,* 7 (Apr. 1939), 139-42.

Netschert, Bruce. "Electric Power and Economic Development." In *The Economic Impact of TVA,* edited by John R. Moore, pp. 1-24. Knoxville: University of Tennessee Press, 1967.

Neuberger, Richard L., and Kahn, Stephen B. *Integrity: The Life of George W. Norris.* New York: Vanguard Press, 1937.

"New Deal and the National Power Problem, The." *Congressional Digest,* 13 (Oct. 1934), 233-35.

Noggle, Burl. "The Origins of the Teapot Dome Investigation." *Mississippi Valley Historical Review,* 44 (Sept. 1957), 237-66.

Norris, George W. "The Power Trust in the Public Schools." *The Nation,* 127 (Sept. 18, 1929), 296-97.

———. "The Ultimate Goal of Public Utility Regulation." *Public Utilities Fortnightly,* 5 (Mar. 6, 1930), 266-73.

———. "Boring from Within." *The Nation,* 121 (Sept. 16, 1935), 297-99.

Ogden, Daniel M., Jr. "The Development of Federal Power Policy in the Pacific Northwest." Ph.D. dissertation, University of Chicago, 1949.

Orton, William. "Culture and Laissez-Faire." *Atlantic Monthly,* 155 (June 1935), 46-51.

Padover, Saul K. "Ickes: Memoir of a Man Without Fear." *The Reporter,* 6 (Mar. 4, 1952), 36-38.

Patterson, James T. *Congressional Conservatism and the New Deal.* Lexington: University Press of Kentucky, 1967.

"P. H. Gadsden Takes Advanced Stand On Public Utility Regulation." *Electrical World,* 99 (May 7, 1932), 794.

Phillips, F. R. "Thoughts of an Operating Executive." *Electrical World,* 102 (Oct. 7, 1933), 460-64.

Polenberg, Richard. "The National Committee to Uphold Constitutional Government, 1937-1941." *Journal of American History,* 52 (Dec. 1965), 582-98.

———. *Reorganizing Roosevelt's Government.* Cambridge, Mass.: Harvard University Press, 1966.

"Politics Discovers a Power Trust." *Literary Digest,* 93 (Apr. 2, 1927), 12.

"Power Commission Asks Holding Company Controls." *Electrical World,* 103 (Feb. 3, 1934), 200.

Prendergast, William A. "Has State Regulation Protected the Public's Interest?" *National Electric Light Association Bulletin,* 17 (July 1930), 426-30.

———. "The 'Ordeal by Water' of the Holding Company." *Public Utilities Fortnightly,* 11 (May 11, 1933), 589-95.

Pritchett, Charles H. "Administration of Federal Power Programs." *Journal of Land and Public Utility Economics,* 18 (Nov. 1942), 379-91.

———. *The Tennessee Valley Authority: A Study in Public Administration.* Chapel Hill: University of North Carolina Press, 1943.

Pritchett, Herman. "Why Reject a Government Corporation Into Which All the Agencies Would Be Placed to Form a National Power Policy?" *Journal of Land and Public Utility Economics,* 18 (Nov. 1942), 380-81.

Prothero, James W. *The Dollar Decade.* Baton Rouge: Louisiana State University Press, 1954.

"Purposes and Policies of Public Works Administration." *Monthly Labor Review,* 37 (Oct. 1933), 797-800.

Putnam, George. "Concentrated Power or Divided Risk." *Independent,* 121 (Aug. 11, 1928), 126-27.

———. "Cost of Concentration." *Independent,* 121 (Aug. 18, 1928), 159-60.

Ramsay, Marion. *Pyramids of Power.* Indianapolis, Ind.: Bobbs-Merrill, 1937.

Raushenbush, H. S. "Concentration of Control." *New Republic,* 47 (May 26, 1926), 28-30.

Raushenbush, Stephen. *The Power Fight.* New York: New Republic, 1932.

Reed, Hudson W. "Rural Electrification." *Edison Electric Institute Bulletin,* 3 (June 1935), 182-85.

"Regulation Not Destruction Urged for Holding Companies." *Banker's Magazine,* 130 (Mar. 1935), 355-56.

"Report of the Public Service Securities Committee." *Investment Banking,* 5 (Nov. 14, 1934), 41-47.

"RFC Ready to Lend Utilities $250,000,000 for Program," *Electrical World,* 110 (Nov. 12, 1938), 1380.

Richardson, Lemont K. "The REA Program in Wisconsin, 1935-1955." Ph.D. dissertation, University of Wisconsin, 1956.

Ripley, William Z. "From Main Street to Wall Street." *Atlantic Monthly,* 137 (Jan. 1926), 94-108.

———. "More Light!—And Power Too." *Atlantic Monthly,* 138 (Nov. 1926), 667-87.

———. *Main Street and Wall Street.* Boston: Little, Brown, 1927.

———. "Public Utility Insecurities." *Forum,* 88 (Aug. 1932), 66-72.

Ronayne, John H. "The Development of Farm Electricity." In *Farm Electrification Manual,* edited by Edison Electric Institute, sec. II. New York: Edison Electric Institute, 1947.

"Roosevelt Appoints Carmody REA Head." *Electrical World,* 107 (Feb. 20, 1937), 660.

Roosevelt, Franklin D. "The Real Meaning of the Power Problem." *Forum,* 82 (Dec. 1929), 327-32.

———. "How Will New York's Progressive Proposals Affect the Investor?" *Public Utilities Fortnightly,* 7 (June 25, 1931), 810-12.

———. "Growing Up by Planning." *The Survey,* 68 (Feb. 1, 1932), 483, 506-07.

Rosenman, Samuel I. "Governor Roosevelt's Power Program." *The Nation,* 129 (Sept. 18, 1929), 302-03.

Ross, J. D. "Should All Electric Utilities Be Governmentally Owned and Operated?" *Congressional Digest,* 15 (Oct. 1936), 240-42.

Schlesinger, Arthur M., Jr. *The Coming of the New Deal.* 3 vols. Boston: Houghton Mifflin, 1957-60.

"Sees New Public Attitude." *Electrical World,* 103 (Mar. 10, 1934), 378.

Selznick, Philip. *TVA and the Grassroots: A Study in the Sociology of Formal Organization.* New York: Harper & Row, 1949.

"Senator Norris Answered." *National Electric Light Association Bulletin,* 18 (Feb. 1931), 227.

Sickler, Barclay J. "Bonneville Resale Rates Pay Out." *Journal of Land and Public Utility Economics,* 16 (Nov. 1940), 487-92.

Sloan, Matthew S. "Consolidations in the Electric Utility Industry," *National Electric Light Association Bulletin,* 16 (Oct. 1929), 629-31.

Smallwood, Johnny B. "George W. Norris and the Concept of a Planned Region." Ph.D. dissertation, University of North Carolina, 1963.

"Smith and Vare Barred Out." *Literary Digest,* 95 (Dec. 24, 1927), 10-11.

Smykay, Edward. "The National Association of Railway and Utility Commissioners as the Originators and Promoters of Public Policy for Public Utilities." Ph.D. dissertation, University of Wisconsin, 1956.

Sparks, William O. "J. D. Ross and Seattle City Light, 1917-1932." Master's thesis, University of Washington, 1964.

Stone, James A., ed. "The Norris Program in 1924." *Nebraska History,* 42 (June 1961), 125-41.

Sullivan, Mark. "Political Analysis of the New Congress." *Congressional Digest,* 14 (Jan. 1935), 5.

Thompson, Carl D. *Confessions of the Power Trust.* New York: Dutton, 1932.

Thompson, C. W. "The Contest Over the Right to Regulate the Utility Holding Company." *Public Utilities Fortnightly,* 8 (Sept. 17, 1931), 340-48.

Thorpe, Merle. "As the Business World Wags." *Nation's Business,* 18 (Sept. 1930), 14.

Tompkins, Raymond S. "The Electrified Farmer in the New Deal Dell." *Electrical World,* 105 (Sept. 14, 1935), 42-44.

Trombley, Kenneth. *Life and Times of a Happy Liberal: A Biography of Morris Llewellyn Cooke.* New York: Harper, 1954.

Tugwell, Rexford G. "The Sources of New Deal Reformism." *Ethics,* 64 (July 1954), 249-76.

Twentieth Century Fund. *Electric Power and Government Policy.* New York: Twentieth Century Fund, 1948.

"Twins: New Deal's Legislative Architects." *Newsweek,* 6 (July 13, 1935), 24-25.

Ulm, Adam H. "The Proposal of Federal Aid to States in Holding Company Regulation." *Public Utilities Fortnightly,* 11 (Mar. 2, 1933), 276-82.

Vilett, Everett W. "Investment Merit of the Electric Utility Industry." *National Electric Light Association Bulletin,* 16 (Sept. 1929), 585-89.

Villard, Oswald G. "Presidential Possibilities." *The Nation,* 126 (May 9, 1928), 533-35.

Voeltz, Herman C. "Genesis and Development of a Regional Power Agency in the Pacific Northwest, 1933-1943." *Pacific Northwest Quarterly,* 53 (Apr. 1962), 65-76.

Walsh, Thomas J. "Can a Senator-Elect Be Denied His Seat?" *Congressional Digest,* 6 (Nov. 1927), 303-06.

"Washington Notes." *New Republic,* 46 (Mar. 31, 1926), 169-70.

Waterman, Merwin H. *Financial Policies of Public Utility Holding Companies.* Ann Arbor: University of Michigan Press, 1936.

Welch, Francis X. "Another Year of Grilling for the Public Utility Companies." *Public Utilities Fortnightly,* 8 (Aug. 6, 1931), 169-70.

———. "The Effect of the Insull Collapse on State Regulation." *Public Utilities Fortnightly,* 10 (Nov. 10, 1932), 578-81.

———. "World Wide Electrification." *Public Utilities Fortnightly,* 17 (Mar. 12, 1936), 389-91.

Wells, Philip P. "Our Federal Power Policy." *The Survey,* 51 (Mar. 1924), 569-73, 649.

Wengert, Norman E. "Antecedents of TVA: The Legislative History of Muscle Shoals." *Agricultural History,* 26 (Oct. 1952), 141-47.

West, Harold E. "The Menace of the Couzens Bill." *Public Utilities Fortnightly,* 6 (Nov. 13, 1930), 579-90.

"What the Administrator Says About Bonneville: An Interview with Dr. Paul J. Raver." *Electrical World,* 84 (Jan. 1940), 28.

"What the Progressive Conference Committee Proposes to Do About the Utilities." *Public Utilities Fortnightly,* 8 (Nov. 26, 1931), 676-83.

"What the Senate Says to Pennsylvania." *The Nation,* 123 (July 21, 1926), 50-51.

"What the State Commissioners Are Thinking About." *Public Utilities Fortnightly,* 14 (Nov. 12, 1931), 598-603.

"What the State Commissioners Are Thinking About." *Public Utilities Fortnightly,* 14 (Dec. 6, 1934), 736-43.

Willkie, Wendell L. "The Rayburn Bill Substitute." *Electrical World,* 105 (Apr. 13, 1935), 989.

———. "The Campaign Against the Companies," *Current History,* 42 (May 1935), 118-21.

———. "Why the Rayburn Bill Must Be Stopped." *Forbes,* 35 (May 1, 1935), 11-12.

———. "The New Fear." *Vital Speeches,* 1 (May 20, 1935), 538-41.

———. "The Strength That Comes from Adversity." *Electrical World,* 114 (June 3, 1939), 68-69.

Winger, Sarah E. "The Genesis of TVA." Ph.D. dissertation, University of Wisconsin, 1959.

Winsmore, Robert. "Public Utility Concerns May Become Aggressive in Self-Defense." *Literary Digest,* 118 (Dec. 1, 1934), 36.

———. "Proposals to Curb Power Holding Companies." *Literary Digest,* 118 (Dec. 8, 1934), 36.

———. "Public Utility Firms Plan Court Tests of Power Issue." *Literary Digest,* 118 (Dec. 15, 1934), 45.

———. "The Threat to Utility Holding Companies." *Literary Digest,* 119 (Mar. 23, 1935), 40.

Wolfskill, George. *The Revolt of the Conservatives.* Boston: Houghton Mifflin, 1962.

Zinn, Howard, ed. *New Deal Thought.* Indianapolis, Ind.: Bobbs-Merrill, 1966.

Index